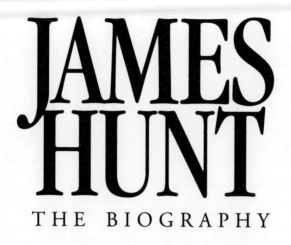

JAMES
HUNT

THE BIOGRAPHY

JAMES HUNT

THE BIOGRAPHY

GERALD DONALDSON

**Foreword by
MURRAY WALKER**

CollinsWillow
An Imprint of HarperCollins*Publishers*

First published in 1994 by
CollinsWillow
an imprint of HarperCollins*Publishers*
London

Reprinted 1994 (twice)

A CIP catalogue record for this book is
available from the British Library

ISBN 0 00 218468 0

Text in Sabon

Printed and bound in Great Britain by
Butler & Tanner Ltd, Frome and London

To Elizabeth and Anny

CONTENTS

ACKNOWLEDGEMENTS

Many of those interviewed during the preparation of this book are mentioned in the text, but I would especially like to thank the following people for their help: Tyler Alexander, Roger Benoit, Jane Birbeck, Mike Branigan, Nick Brittan, Alastair Caldwell, Peter Collins, Jabby Crombac, Nigel Dempster, Mike Dennett, Ron Dennis, Mike Doodson, Tony Dron, Helen Dyson, Bernie Ecclestone, Peter Gaydon, Maurice Hamilton, Alan Henry, Mika Häkkinen, Lord Hesketh, John Hogan, Bubbles Horsley, Sarah Hunt, Sue and Wallis Hunt, Jeff Hutchinson, Chris and Suzie Jones, Niki Lauda, Chris Marshall, Jonathan Martin, Jochen Mass, Teddy Mayer, Brendan McInerney, Mark Milliken-Smith, Max Mosley, Riccardo Patrese, Ian Phillips, John Richardson, Simon Ridge, Taormina Rieck, Nigel Roebuck, Keke Rosberg, Ayrton Senna, Barry Sheene, Jackie Stewart, David Tremayne, Murray Walker, Rob Walker, Professor Sydney Watkins, John Watson, Mark Wilkin, Eoin Young and Helmut Zwikl.

For their help with research and other forms of assistance I am indebted to the following people: Katharine Arnander, Peter Dick, Tony Dodgins, Ann, David, Melissa and Richard Jarrett, Bruce Jones at *Autosport*, Eric Hellman at New Age Word Processing, John Hyland at The Scuderia, Barry Maund, David Morgan-Kirby, Quentin Spurring and Paul Harmer at Q-Editions, Richard Stafferton at Autophile, F. David Stone at Toyota Canada and Bob Wright at Ford of Great Britain.

Special thanks are due to Carolyn Brunton of Vardey & Brunton Associates, and Michael Doggart (Editorial Director) and Tom Whiting (Editor) at HarperCollins*Publishers*.

For permission to quote from their books I am grateful to: Derick Allsop, author of *The British Racing Hero* (Stanley Paul, 1990); Christopher Hilton and John Blunsden, co-authors of *Champions* (Motor Racing Publications, 1993); Eoin Young, co-author with James Hunt (edited by David Hodges) of *Against All Odds* (Hamlyn, 1977); Anna O'Brien, editor of *The Heavily Censored History of Hesketh Racing* (GMB Editorial Associates, 1975); and Niki Lauda and Herbert Volker, co-authors of *To Hell and Back* (Stanley Paul, 1986).

For permission to quote from *Autosport* magazine, published weekly by Haymarket Specialist Motoring Publications Ltd – and which was also the primary source for race reports and results – I wish to thank the publisher, Peter Foubister.

Other reference works consulted include: *Marlboro Grand Prix Guide* by Jacques Descheneux; *British Grand Prix* by Maurice Hamilton (Crowood Press, 1988); *Grand Prix British Winners* by Maurice Hamilton (Guinness Publishing, 1991); *For The Record* by Niki Lauda and Herbert Volker (William Kimber, 1978); *Ronnie Peterson – Superswede* by Alan Henry and Ronnie Peterson (Haynes Publishing, 1978); *Grand Prix Greats* by Nigel Roebuck (Patrick Stephens, 1986); *James Hunt Magazine*, edited by Eoin Young and Maurice Hamilton (1977); and *The Establishment*, edited by Hugh Thomas (Anthony Blond, 1959).

GERALD DONALDSON

FOREWORD

BY MURRAY WALKER

In the ordinary lives that most of us lead we come and go without making any great impact on the world at large. Yet you wouldn't say that about James Hunt. In an all too short existence, he captured the imagination of countless millions by virtue of his achievements, his personal charm, his refusal to conform and his outspoken ability to provoke controversy.

As you read Gerald Donaldson's brilliantly perceptive account of James's life, painstakingly and lovingly assembled after countless hours of discussion with James, his relations, friends and colleagues, you will rapidly appreciate that he was a very unusual and complex person. Like all of us he had his good times and bad times but, being James, his were more extreme than most ordinary folk. I've never made any secret of the fact that, because of our different ages, backgrounds and personalities, we had an uneasy initial relationship as BBC Television's Grand Prix commentators, but over the years our liking and respect for each other grew, enabling us to develop a partnership that communicated well about the thing that mattered so much to both of us – the dramatic, exciting and colourful world of Formula 1.

For thirteen years, sixteen times a year for four days, James and I worked alongside each other and shared one microphone, charged with the responsibility of explaining the pictures to millions of viewers worldwide. There are lots of people who can commentate about a sport and there are many who can participate successfully, but there are precious few who can do both. James had not only driven and won at the highest level to become World Champion, but he was also able to

11

read a race to perfection and then communicate the tactics, the politics and the action, calmly and authoritatively in that marvellous voice of his, like no one else I have ever met. But more than that, he was never afraid to express his always forceful opinion. I didn't always agree with him, but it was communication at its best and the public loved it.

The world is infinitely poorer for James's passing, but at least we have the memories and the videos of his racing exploits and commentaries to remind ourselves of his achievements and presence. What we didn't have until now was a deep insight into the background and factors that made him what he was. He had planned to work on this book with Gerald Donaldson before his death, and I'm confident that it is exactly as James would have wanted it to be – 'warts and all'. No one would have enjoyed reading it more than James himself!

Bless you, James. It may be a cliché to say it, but you really are sadly missed.

1

AN ODD LITTLE
FELLOW

1947–1965

While he was still in the womb he kicked with such force his mother was nearly knocked off her feet. And very soon after his birth, on 29 August 1947, Sue Hunt knew her bouncing baby boy was no ordinary child. Persistently rebellious, given to violent temper tantrums, endlessly restless and physically active to the point of being a danger to himself, it was as if James Simon Wallis Hunt was born with a bee under his bonnet.

'He was an odd little fellow, a rebel right from the moment he was born', sighs Sue Hunt as she recalls having to contend with his contrary personality and trying to harness his boundless energy. Little James fought desperately against any kind of confinement.

As soon as he became aware of the railings around his cot he struggled to climb over them, and at 18 months even the netting laced intricately over the cot failed to contain him. On sunny summer days in Surrey, when Sue put James out on the lawn to sleep, she dared not strap him in his pram for fear he might hang himself when he wakened. 'The little beggar' quickly mastered the escape technique of crawling to one end of the pram, tipping it over, grasping his tiny pillow and toddling back into the Hunt family flat in search of further mischief.

In their flat in Cheam, then when they moved to a house in Sutton when he was 11, and later to a large home in Belmont, Sue and Wallis Hunt wondered about the antics of their first-born son during his formative years, especially when they compared him with his more manageable brothers and sisters.

Sally, who was two years older than James, and Peter, two years younger, then Timothy, David and Georgina, were all active and independently minded children who quickly developed strong personalities. But James's behaviour, especially an individualism which verged on the anti-social, often left his parents bewildered. Sue Hunt: 'He was the most difficult of our children to bring up and he was the only one who ever screamed all night as a baby for no apparent reason'.

Though he was a loner from the beginning, James seemed not particularly to enjoy even his own company and was not a happy child, a fact he realized late in his life, when he also admitted he was 'a very difficult little boy'.

He felt a compulsion to assert himself and was obstinate and extremely persistent in trying to get his own way. His refusal to conform and accept discipline meant there were constant battles against parental authority, battles which Sue and Wallis sometimes lost.

At first it was tearful tantrums. Then, as soon as he learned to talk, James used his burgeoning vocabulary to wear away his parents' resolve. His heart's desire might take the form of something as simple as a toy he'd seen another child playing with. According to Sue he 'was always a completely single-minded little boy' and his relentless quest to get what he wanted was 'like a steady drip, drip, drip which eventually wore you down. If James wanted something, he'd have it. He'd grind away, figure out how to outflank you and seemed to always win out in the end'. But even when he got what he thought he wanted he sometimes changed his mind, and he was very hard to please. James disliked Sugar, a teddy resembling a polar bear, because it was too hard and uncuddly, though he kept it all his life and gave it to his own sons.

As a two-year-old his favourite plaything was a toy mowing machine which James called his 'chine'. When the men arrived to cut the large lawn in front of the block of flats at Cheam, James would trot alongside them, solemnly pushing his little lawn mower. When James had his own home he almost ignored the extensive garden, but was obsessive about the lawn, which he mowed in stripes that had to be absolutely perfect.

Wallis and Sue Hunt, themselves brought up in strict Victorian environments, did not believe in being permissive parents and worked hard at disciplining their 'peculiar' and unruly son. Wallis: 'He was against all authority, but authority felt it had to draw the line somewhere. James was always keen to go that extra mile before one felt he should, before other children his age had done it. Maybe he was justified, because he was an exceptional child, but we thought it was wrong to give him an unlimited amount of rope'.

Sometimes the necessary lessons between right and wrong were learned painfully. When he was four James received a thrashing for thumping his baby brother Pete over the head with a shovel, causing a wound which required several stitches to repair. On another occasion, when they were older, James chose to use his fist to settle an argument with Pete, but the younger Hunt saw the punch coming and ducked. Thus, an unforgiving wall bore the full force of James's wrath. His mother's response to his broken knuckles was to send James to the hospital – on a bus – by himself.

But his rages were always short-lived and he seldom sulked long. As an adult he acknowledged that 'anger dissipates very fast with me. And my mother pointed out to me that I'd never been a vengeful person, which is out of character for somebody who's naturally very competitive. I get angry when people treat me unfairly, or what I perceive to be unfairly, and vow revenge like anybody else. The only thing is that subsequently, as she pointed out, having made the vow, that's it. I then get on with my life. I'm too much of a forward-looker to dwell on past aggravations'.

At home James was naturally closest to the siblings nearest him in age: Sally, known as Sal, and Peter, who was Pete to the Hunts until a newspaper mistakenly referred to the famous James Hunt's brother as Norman, and that became his nickname. There was an age gap of several years between these three and the youngest Hunt children, who were also given nicknames they kept into adulthood. Timothy was Tith, which later became Tim, David was contracted to Dave and Georgina was Jo Jo, then JJ and, finally, Jo. James called himself 'Bubby' (his version of Baby) when he was very small, which the family shortened to Bubs for a while. They also tried Jamie, but very soon he became just James and there he stayed.

* * *

Four decades later, when he was searching for reasons for the troubled man he became, James looked back to his childhood and the way he was brought up. He placed part of the blame on his parents, despite the fact that his brothers and sisters, products of the same environment, became well-adjusted adults and led busy and productive lives. Tim Hunt went through a period of decadence in his youth, though it was much shorter and considerably less intensive than his famous older brother's.

High achievement runs in the Hunt family. As soon as the pressures of mothering six young children eased, Sue busied herself in various community charities. She worked as a nursing assistant in a hospital, chaired a committee to look after unmarried mothers and their children, then became a magistrate in local courts, a school governor. After she and Wallis 'retired themselves at 70', she was scarcely less busy, serving as a church warden and organizing a branch of the meals-on-wheels service for needy senior citizens in the local area.

Sue Hunt's industriousness was matched by her husband, whom she had met on a blind date – he escorted her to a ballet in wartime London – when Wallis, educated at Wellington College, was attending Sandhurst military academy. After a whirlwind courtship of four months they were married in April 1943, but then were often separated by their respective wartime involvements. Sue joined the Wrens and worked as a mechanic on aircraft radios while Wallis served in the armoured corps of the 11th Hussars regiment.

In August 1944, Sue very nearly lost her new husband in a small village in northern France when a German shell hit the armoured car commanded by Lieutenant Wallis Hunt. The car was destroyed and the two other crewmen inside were killed instantly. Wallis was blown completely out of the burning vehicle, suffering from severe shrapnel wounds and the loss of part of his hand.

After the war Wallis joined an international trading company, where his duties required him to spend considerable time abroad, at subsidiary branches in North and South America. His travels during his 20 year tenure with the firm meant that Sue was often left alone with their growing family.

Wallis later became a senior partner in a successful London stockbroking firm. Unfortunately, his appointment as chairman coincided with the very day that an internal fraud, perpetrated by others, was discovered by the Stock Exchange. The company was forced to cease trading and Wallis and all the partners were 'hammered' – held personally responsible for the debt – when a bank bounced a large cheque. The company was forced into liquidation and, though it later emerged solvent, it was one of the worst experiences of Wallis Hunt's life.

But he recovered from the setback and worked in an accounting firm until he reached retirement age. Then he served as governor of Wellington College, chaired the deanery of his church synod and worked for a number of charities.

* * *

As adults, both Hunt girls came to share their parents' social concerns – Sal became a lay pastoral assistant in her church and Jo a social worker with a mental charity – while James's brothers continued the family tradition of business success.

16

Pete, a chartered accountant (he was also James's business manager) is, according to his parents, 'a workaholic'. Tim was head boy at Wellington and a winner of the Queen's Medal as the student who most measured up to the standards of the school's founder, the Duke of Wellington. After graduating from Oxford, Tim did some male modelling, and then worked at Christie's auctioneers, followed by the Andy Warhol Foundation in New York, where he married the American 'Brat Pack' novelist, Tama Janowitz. Dave Hunt, another 'workaholic', though he had limited success in a career as a racing driver (James refused to help him), went on to become a high-ranking marketing executive in a firm selling domestic air and water filters.

The boys, all of whom attended Wellington, also inherited Wallis Hunt's athletic ability. For several years, until he was in his 40s, he captained 'The Hunters', a hockey team in Cheam for promising under-21s. At the age of 60, with one knee locked into position from his war wounds, Wallis ran the first of four marathons, and in his 70s still cycles vigorously for fitness. Pete became a dedicated recreational runner and also ran several marathons to raise money for charity. Tim and Dave were star athletes, distinguishing themselves particularly as rugby players at Wellington.

Tim Hunt also achieved some notoriety as a pioneer bungee jumper with the Oxford Dangerous Sports Society and made a court appearance, in full morning dress, with three daredevil friends to defend their jumping off the Clifton suspension bridge in Bristol. Their April Fool's Day escapade, in 1979, cost Tim and his friends £100 apiece and they were bound over to keep the peace. They treated the verdict as a victory and toasted it with champagne.

If there was one Hunt family failing Sue feels it was 'unshared feelings'. Everyone tended to go their separate ways in the busy household and private emotions were seldom expressed.

James, when thinking about having children of his own, once said 'The only thing that matters is that they should have loving parents who can give them the affection and security they need'.

While there was no lack of love and affection in his own childhood the Hunts were not particularly demonstrative about it. James wondered if this contributed to him withdrawing into himself as a boy and his inability to form close personal relationships as an adult.

In response to his questioning about the way he was brought up Sue wrote James a letter. In it she admitted that she might have treated him differently, perhaps catered more to his special needs, but she didn't recognize them at the time.

She acknowledged that she was young and inexperienced as a parent, especially in dealing with boys, because she had no brothers and there were few males among her close relations. But she assumed what she was doing, the same as her parents had done for her, was best for him. Besides, it wasn't just James: the Hunts were a big and busy family. Moreover, his mother pointed out, his upbringing helped foster the independence, self-reliance and exceptional fighting spirit that brought him success.

Sue said in her letter to James: 'If we hadn't treated you the way we did, if you hadn't had the sort of upbringing you had, which you chose to fight, you might not have been World Champion'.

☆ ☆ ☆

James Hunt's first major fights were over having to go to school, which he loathed. Before his fifth birthday he was enrolled in a nursery class at Ambleside, a pre-preparatory school in Cheam. Sue Hunt had attended the school and daughter Sal was now there, but James despised it above all things in his young life.

Each morning, all dressed up in his school uniform, he would set forth happily, hand-in-hand with Sue. But as soon as they got to the school gates he firmly dug in his heels and shrieked and wailed. His protestations only diminished slightly when Sal was called out of her class to come and comfort him.

James hated the confinement, the rules, the need to conform and perform collectively with other children, and the authority imposed on him by the teachers; the very thought of school enraged him.

In an effort to ease the tumult and shouting he was moved to another preparatory day school, Northlace in Sutton, where his parents thought the greater availability of games would mollify the reluctant pupil.

The physical distractions worked to a degree, but his scholastic despair deepened when, in 1955, aged seven and three quarters, he was sent away to Westerleigh boarding preparatory school at Hastings in Sussex. Sue and Wallis were mystified about why James should regard each beginning of term as a full-fledged catastrophe, when his brothers, all of whom went to Westerleigh, and his sisters were perfectly contented and diligent students.

When he was 11 James finally accepted some instruction gracefully. He learned to drive on a family holiday, at a farm in Pembrokeshire in Wales. His teacher, a farm worker, demonstrated the rudiments of conducting a tractor around the fields. When James found changing gears frustrating, because he lacked the strength to depress the heavy tractor clutch pedal fully, the farmer let James motor up and down the two miles of private farm road in a battered old Rover. He soon graduated to short supervised excursions in the family car and found it all immensely exhilarating.

But his progress remained sedate because James didn't want to abuse the privilege of this new-found joy. 'I knew if I was seen cornering on two wheels that would be the end of it', he said, 'so I raised hell only when out of sight'.

Very soon he decided a driving licence would be just the ticket to give him the freedom he so craved to express his individuality in a pleasurable solitary pursuit.

Much to the amusement of his prep school peers James whiled away some spare time knitting a gift for little brother Tim: a pair of bright green shorts. Sartorially his work was imperfect – there were two right legs, one of which was longer than the other – but a school matron, realizing his heart was in the right place, helped James stitch them together, and Tim wore the shorts proudly for quite a long time.

James remained a loner at school but began to find deeper satisfaction in throwing his prodigious energy into sporting activities. He had considerable athletic ability, but it was his incredible stamina, competitive spirit, determination and tenacity that distinguished him from the other boys.

Though he opened the batting and bowling for the Westerleigh cricket team – and on one occasion took nine wickets – and was for two years the First XI goalkeeper, he was always much better at individual sports, where, for James, winning wasn't everything: it was the only thing.

When he was about 12 he entered a tennis tournament for boys aged 16 and under. James reached the final, but any satisfaction from this considerable achievement turned to despair when he was beaten, by a 16-year-old. James was inconsolable and wept for hours. Sue: 'Only victory would do for James. He always *had* to win. If he didn't, it was the greatest possible calamity as far as he was concerned'.

Despite his preoccupation with athletic pursuits, James began smoking when he was in prep school. His parents suspect he was only 10 when he took up the habit and no amount of persuasion would make him desist.

They were more pleased with his love of animals and birds. James always took a keen interest in the family pets, and one day he returned home on the train from Westerleigh proudly bearing a cage containing a yellow budgerigar. James called the bird, a present from his grandmother, Rita.

Before long Rita had spawned an avian dynasty as James seriously took up the hobby of raising budgies. A battery of breeding cages he built at school was installed in the attic at home and he cobbled up an aviary in the garden.

With typical single-mindedness he thoroughly researched the subject and calculated that the commercial proceeds from developing and selling a strain of well-bred budgies would enable him to retire as a millionaire by the time he was 30. But since he tended to be away at school when the budgie eggs hatched, the rest of the family had to look after the care and feeding of a brood which eventually numbered nearly 30 squawking birds. The first budgie episode in his life ended when the family moved house and the birds had to be disposed of, by which time James had discovered a more enduring passion.

While his schoolmates mostly ignored girls, or perhaps might have developed crushes on each other, from the first stirrings of puberty James was resolutely and vigorously heterosexual.

An early flirtation developed with a comely teenage under-matron at Westerleigh. She didn't discourage the 'puppy love' of the 12-year-old Hunt boy; in fact, she wrote him love letters. An Australian au pair girl, brought into the Hunt household when Jo was born, was also a source of great fascination for James, and they became quite fond of each other.

As Sue puts it 'I think he always had an eye for the girls, and the girls for him. There were always swarms of them around him'.

However, from the age of 13, his involvements with the opposite sex had to remain extra-curricular activities while James spent five years coping with the all-male environment at Wellington College.

★ ★ ★

Wellington, in Berkshire, was built as a public memorial to the Duke of Wellington and the school was originally intended to provide nearby Sandhurst with candidates for military leadership. James briefly considered following his father's example and choosing an army career.

His next choice, a decision to enter the medical profession, owed something to James being highly impressed that the surgeon who removed his appendix drove a Rolls Royce. The idea of becoming Dr Hunt was reinforced when James noted that 'it was the least of the evils in the unimaginative list of careers' presented to him by the Wellington careers master.

His intense dislike of institutional learning, and his refusal to apply himself to studying, meant James Hunt was never going to distinguish himself in matters relating to the Wellington reputation for high academic standards. Nevertheless, the school added finishing touches to his complex character, particularly his strong individuality, which flourished despite the Wellington tradition of strict, military-style regimentation. Of the discipline he said: 'I didn't like it, but it was good for me'.

James was domiciled in Combermere House, where the boys lived in partitioned cubicles lying off a lengthy central corridor. He hated the lack of privacy at the school, but at least his room had a door he could close. Like all the others, his room was about eight feet square with walls of similar height and no ceiling, and was sparsely furnished, with little more than a bed and desk.

From these quarters the new boy Hunt, one of approximately 150 to enter Wellington each year (the total enrolment then was about 750), set about serving his five-year scholastic sentence.

To avoid compulsory evening study sessions he joined the school orchestra, where he played the trumpet with great enthusiasm. In fact, he mastered the difficult instrument with such proficiency that he was singled out as a soloist in the orchestra, playing such complex works as a Mozart horn concerto adapted for the trumpet.

Later, James played at friends' weddings and several times performed in public in front of large audiences. The enjoyment of music ran in the Hunt family, everyone sang around the piano at home, and the other three boys also played wind instruments in the Wellington orchestra: Pete the French horn, Tim the clarinet and Dave the flute.

Nigel Davison, Director of Music at Wellington when James was there, and one of those who spoke at his memorial service in 1993, remembered him as 'one of the most remarkable teenagers I have met in a long career of teaching. He was very single-minded and always seemed to know exactly what he wanted to achieve. He also had a very clear view of how to achieve it, which sometimes conflicted strongly with conventional wisdom'.

Playing the trumpet at Wellington provided James with a rare form of relaxation, because he expended most of his energy in the more vigorous pursuits afforded by the school's sporting tradition. Every afternoon, from Monday to Saturday, the boys were required to disport themselves on the playing fields and in the games rooms. James concentrated on the individual sports: squash, tennis, racquets and cross-country running, and represented Wellington in all of them.

Here too, in his capacity as Master of Running, Nigel Davison had to deal with the often contrary boy Hunt. In the 1965 *Wellington*

Yearbook Davison wrote of the year's cross-country running team: 'With one notable, if successful, exception, the team threw themselves wholeheartedly into the rigorous training program'.

James, the notable exception, studiously avoided training with the team because 'it probably wasn't rigorous enough', said Davison. He devised his own methods of preparing for competition, often ducking out of a training run into the bushes for a quick cigarette, and it worked: 'For he either won or came first equal in every race of that year', Davison recalled, 'including a particularly gruesome and arduous inter-house match, whose finish involved wading through a large lake'.

Another of his Wellington exploits, though it failed to gain mention in the *Yearbook*, is still talked about at the school. The focal point of each dormitory is a high balcony where boys gather to gossip among themselves and shout or throw things at those walking on the gravel path below. One day, according to the legend, the boys on the path were startled to see the boy Hunt land in their midst. James had made the approximately 30 foot leap on a dare.

Until he could permanently escape from behind the ivy-covered walls the medical school candidate had to endure the prescribed physics, chemistry and biology courses. He managed one A level on his own and would need crammer courses in London to get the others. Meanwhile, he went for interviews at prospective teaching hospitals and secured a place at St Bartholomew's Hospital ('Bart's').

But James found it all very tedious ('My heart was never in it'), and for him the most attractive part of being a Wellington boy was the holidays.

*   *   *

Perhaps because he felt so oppressed by the Wellington atmosphere James never formed lasting relationships with any of his school acquaintances. In fact, he only ever had about half a dozen close male friendships in his lifetime and only a couple of them came to begin to understand James Hunt.

But several boyhood friends – Chris Jones, John Richardson and Malcolm Wood, in particular – who also grew up in the Cheam, Sutton and Belmont area, although they went to different schools remained his friends for life. In their company the formerly serious-minded, introverted boy became much more gregarious, his personality blossomed, and he became anything but a shrinking violet.

Later critics of his sometimes childish behaviour and his juvenile antics as an adult interpreted his loyalty to his first friends as a sign of arrested emotional development. But he trusted those he grew up with because he knew them before he became famous. They always regarded him as just James, not James the superstar, and they stayed with him through thick and thin while most of the interlopers who surrounded him at the height of his 'honeypot' era later disappeared. Besides, the carousing teenagers had the time of their lives growing up in Surrey, and, for James, those carefree days were among his happiest memories.

Chris Jones played for the Cheam Hunters, the under-21 hockey team captained by Wallis Hunt, and was often involved in the high jinks perpetrated by Wallis's unconventional son. Jones once organized a large birthday party which involved transporting a number of people by bus on an outing to the country.

'My parents, who were fairly strict, were there', Jones recalls, 'but we had a free bar on the way down and had to stop the coaches for James. Now most people would just unzip and pee facing away from onlookers. But not James. He had to face the three coaches and made us all very giggly.'

There were to be other public bladder-relieving incidents in James's future but Chris Jones doesn't think James was as 'an exhibitionist by nature. He was just unconventional. He always did exactly what he wanted to do. And you could never argue with him. You might suggest something but he'd do it his own way.

'He was always the best sportsman in our group, tremendously competitive. He was a fantastic squash player, though when he first took up golf he wasn't very good because he never had lessons like the rest of us. He used to borrow his grandfather's clubs and come out with us and demand five or six shots handicap. Now, if we made a couple of bad shots we would tend to say "sod it" and move on to another hole and start again. Not James. He would play out every single hole to the bitter end.'

John Richardson, whom James called 'The Kid', remembers that James from the beginning was 'very intransigent. He had his own ideas and he wouldn't be afraid to tell somebody that they were a complete idiot if he felt that they were. He had such self-sufficiency that I don't think anybody was ever able to penetrate it. He was a terribly hard person to get really close to and I don't think many ever did.

'James was also extremely single-minded and so determined he would become obsessive about things. He was obsessive with his regard to women as well. He was extremely attractive to women, starting with Ping, an absolutely wonderful girl who was his teenage love'.

Taormina Rieck is still called Ping by her friends, but James's terms of endearment for her were 'Pink' or, more often, 'Tom Trich', after her maiden name of Rich. They met when they were both about 15, while James was home at Sutton from Wellington.

She was intrigued by him, and James, in addition to his undoubted prurient interest, was attracted by her warm personality and natural charm. They became close friends and that friendship remained after a mutually felt 'magnetism' caused their companionship to take a romantic turn. They became inseparable for several years, and their relationship only ended when Ping could no longer accept his increasing unfaithfulness.

On her first visit to the Hunt house Ping was surprised at his collection of feathered friends. 'I remember thinking, how strange. Being taken by a 15-year-old to see his budgerigars. Still, in many ways he was a conformist in those days. Life in the Hunt family was fairly straight and rigid and he had what you would call run-of-the-mill parents. Sue was very active in local affairs and Wallis commuted to work in London and everyone seemed to go their separate ways'.

Ping often accompanied James to the Sutton Hardcourt tennis and squash club, where she would stand in the balcony watching her boyfriend's relentless pursuit of squash opponents. Ping's spectating sessions tended to be lengthy because 'He was so determined to win. He simply never gave up and ran endlessly around the court. He always went after the ball and the rallies would go on for ever and ever. If he wanted something he went full tilt after it and wouldn't stop until he got it'.

Soon Ping began to follow James to squash matches further afield. He represented the club in tournaments in other towns, then played at county level for Surrey and twice his entry was accepted for the British amateur squash championships. There, in the first year, he was beaten in the first round by an opponent who later became the world professional champion.

The next year James got through a round or two then met a top-seeded Egyptian who needed every move in his repertoire and two hours and twenty minutes to eliminate the precocious lad from Surrey. Many people think if he had concentrated on squash James could have become a top international player.

Like the other women who were most closely involved with him, Ping saw, or perhaps was astute enough to recognize, aspects of his character that were seldom revealed to his male intimates.

Behind the combination of youthful high spirits and intense competitiveness that characterized the James Hunt that most people knew at this time, Ping saw a certain vulnerability. And for Ping, there were signs of his own search for emotional comfort and security in the way he expressed his concern for the youngest members of his family.

'He really enjoyed looking after them, and just seeing the way he behaved with his little brothers and sisters you knew it was instinctive in him. He was always going to be a good father.'

One evening he invited her home where he was babysitting Jo Jo, Dave and Tim. When James had tucked them in he left Ping to read them a bedtime story. When Ping came downstairs James asked her if she had helped them say their prayers. When Ping said no: 'James said to me, "Right. You've missed out hugely there, Tom Trich. Come on, we'd better go and do it". So we did. His attitude was that he was taught to do that by his parents and it simply had to be done'.

But he also practised what he preached, and he believed in the power of prayer. In the troubled years to come James would pray to God for strength and help, and he eventually passed on the bedtime prayer ritual to his own two boys, to whom he became completely devoted.

During his time with Ping he had talked about having children, and she thinks fatherhood earlier in his life would have prevented James from sinking into his period of decadence.

'I felt so sorry for him then because I knew underneath it wasn't the real James doing this. I think he was trying to make life happy, the wrong way. If he had settled down earlier, had a more normal home life with children of his own when he was younger, one could have seen a totally different James.'

* * *

James often said that when he got his driving licence his life really began. However, it might easily have ended, given the motoring mayhem which then ensued. According to his memory of the momentous occasion, a week after his 17th birthday, he passed the test by driving 'immaculately. My hand signals were perfect and I never exceeded 30 miles an hour in a built up area. But as soon as the examiner got out of the car and handed me my pink slip I revved up and roared away like a lunatic!'.

'I'm afraid I was a bit of a terror on the road', James admitted. 'In those days I never drove anything except flat out. I liked to inveigle my friends to swipe their parents' cars to race me, and we'd charge around playing a kind of tag. I had a good feel for the road, but I was very raw and driving with no margin for error. It was incredible luck that I wasn't killed.'

Ping recalls that era as being 'madness, total and utter madness. He was reckless. We all were. But somehow we got away with it and lived through it and didn't kill someone along the way. In those days, when there was no breathalyser threat, everyone went to the pub, had a few drinks and then hit the road. And you'd get people like Chris Jones in his souped-up Mini or his MGB bombing along the road and James trying to beat him and everyone trying to keep up.

'James was always fast, whereas others might be a little more cautious. His attitude, right from the word go, was "Put your foot down and keep it there. I can control this"'.

But control sometimes was lost when his reach for speed exceeded his grasp of the laws of physics. Sue Hunt says his later sobriquet 'Hunt the Shunt', which came after some spectacular accidents during his early racing days, was actually earned in the Hunt family cars.

'He crashed everything we had. He wrote off our Mini van, rolling it across a field near Epsom. He was going too fast around a bend, caught the kerb and flew off. It ended up at least 50 yards from the road in a bed of roses in a market garden, upside down.'

Mercifully, James was only bruised and shaken, but, in the interest of protecting life and limb as well as material goods, the senior Hunts decided the best course of action was not to replace the van and to ban their son from driving their other car. James bought a tiny moped for 10 shillings and puttered around on that, with his Wellington scarf flapping in the breeze. Six months later his parents bought a little Fiat 500 as a second car. Wallis: 'We thought, with its top speed of about 50 and no acceleration, "Well, he can't do much harm in this". So we lifted his suspension but warned him to be very careful. That very night there was a knock on the bedroom door about 2 o'clock in the morning. James stood there, looking rather sheepish, and asked if I could spare a minute to come downstairs. I went down to find a large assembly of his friends, all looking solemn and serious'.

After the pub had closed James and his mates attended a house party where further refreshments were liberally consumed. They then roared off into the night in a procession of speeding cars. James forged ahead in the Fiat, while a friend stood up in the passenger seat and poked his head through the Fiat's sunroof to scream abuse at their pursuers, who were led by Chris Jones in his MGB.

The chase ended abruptly when James encountered a car stopped in the middle of the road. It belonged to another friend who was looking for the party they'd just left. In taking evasive action James managed to miss the car, but planted the new Fiat firmly against a lamp post.

A hasty conference was held and a de-alcoholized version of the truth was concocted for Wallis Hunt's benefit: something to the effect that the Fiat was being toured along gently at about 15 miles per hour when it came upon a car sitting in the middle of the road with no lights on. But James, fearing parental disbelief and wrath, appointed a more senior and, he thought, sober friend to explain the misadventure and brought along several others to corroborate the story.

'So Wallis comes down in his dressing gown', recalls Chris Jones, 'and I thought, "Oh Christ, this isn't going to work at all". It was absolutely hopeless. People were falling asleep and belching. It was quite apparent we'd all had a bit. James refused to talk and the mate who was supposed to make representations to Wallis couldn't quite remember what he was supposed to say and spent the whole time hiccuping.'

For some time the Fiat was deliberately left unrepaired to act as a reminder for James to curb his propensity for daredevilism on the roads. Though there were more fender-bending incidents, it was while he was seeking thrills of another kind that James suffered the worst injury of his teenage years.

His first exposure to skiing, in the Scottish Cairngorms in 1965, whetted his appetite for more, and he immediately made plans to mount a more ambitious expedition to the Swiss Alps the following year during the Easter holidays. In partnership with sister Sal, a decrepit Morris Oxford was acquired for £10, and the two set out for Switzerland. Their venerable vehicle puffed and wheezed them as far as Verbier, where, as James put it: 'the old banger breathed its last'.

The highly efficient Swiss transportation system enabled Sal and James to get to their destination, and their skiing holiday passed without incident. But when they came to make the long journey home, by train, James had one arm in a sling and was in considerable pain.

Though his version of the accident was slightly different from his family's (James said he was posing for a photo while leaning against a balcony railing which broke, while the Hunts think he jumped from the balcony while taking a short cut) the end result was the same: a fall from a considerable height which resulted in a badly broken shoulder.

He was still growing at the time – *en route* to the 6 foot 1 inch and 164 pounds he eventually reached – and Wallis and Sue wonder if the injury might have contributed to his round-shouldered physique. It was probably partly inherited – both parents are tall, with slightly hunched shoulders – and they also speculate that the developing muscles in his upper body might have been elongated and contorted from his constantly wielding tennis and squash racquets.

These activities were necessarily curtailed while his shoulder mended, a state of affairs which left him in a constant dither. Inactivity was anathema to the high metabolic rate which produced in James energy levels that might have classified him as hyperactive. As Ping notes, 'He never stopped and often seemed awfully tense. It was quite difficult to get him to ever switch off and just relax'.

Partly as a means of controlling the extra stress caused by his temporary incapacity, the pace of James's nicotine consumption accelerated. But he disapproved of Ping's smoking habit and managed to cure her of it with a typically forthright expression of his opinion.

'We were at a party one evening and I was standing there with a drink and a cigarette. He came up to me and said, "You look stupid, Tom Trich. You're not enjoying it. Put it out". And I thought, he's absolutely right. So I stopped smoking then and there. I have a lot to thank him for.'

While appearances in this case mattered to James, he was less concerned with the way he looked to others and could never be described as a dedicated follower of the fashions which came from Carnaby Street to suburban Surrey in the Swinging Sixties.

Ping: 'He was never a frightfully smart dresser. It wasn't important to him what he wore. It was usually always the same thing and really rather staid: brown suede Hush Puppy shoes, a pair of ordinary trousers and maybe a V-neck sweater'.

Of course, he dressed in the appropriate blazer and tie while at Wellington, but that was all about to end, as James went off on another tangent that would require him to wear a very different kind of uniform.

*　*　*

If, as James said, his life began when he turned 17 and got his driving licence, his 18th birthday (in fact the day before it) was the major turning point in that life.

His tennis doubles partner, Chris Ridge (they represented Surrey in schoolboy tennis), suggested they attend a motor racing event, so they piled into Sue's van and headed north to the Silverstone circuit in rural Northamptonshire. Chris Ridge's older brother Simon was competing in a club race in a Mini he'd prepared himself, so James's first exposure to the sport that was to take over his life was at the grass roots level and from the inside. He was immediately smitten.

'It was instant commitment', he said later. 'You see, I'd never known there was such a thing as club racing. So far as I knew motor racing was something impossibly remote, a thing carried out by Jim Clark and a lot of continentals with long names. I couldn't identify with them at all. But here was something within reach of a mere mortal. It was the immediate answer to this problem of having my needs satisfied, to compete.

'I thought, this is bloody good! I absolutely adored driving fast anyway, and was always trying to organize races with my friends on the roads around home. Here was my mate's brother, who was about twenty with very little money, but had worked as a garage mechanic and built himself a racing Mini. And all these guys from perfectly ordinary homes had saved up all their money and gone club racing, which is just about within the range of one's pocket if one works at it and one saves up very hard. I thought, well crikey, if they can do it so can I, and I'm jolly well going to have a go'.

But 'having a go' in his mind's eye went far beyond simply participating in what he had witnessed at Silverstone. Thousands of teenagers have similar experiences and make the decision to try motor racing at the local club level. Very few of them pursue it further into the various professional categories of national and international racing.

And only a handful have the requirements – ability, ambition, determination, perseverance, financial wherewithal and plain good luck – ever to make it to the pinnacle of motor sport, World Championship Formula 1 racing, a series of Grand Prix races held in over a dozen different countries.

Each Formula 1 season approximately 30 drivers from around the world compete for the title of World Driving Champion. The odds against James Hunt ever achieving that lofty goal were astronomical, yet that is precisely what, on 28 August 1965, he decided to do.

When he returned home to Sutton that night James announced to his parents: 'All your anxieties about my fecklessness are over. I am going to be a racing driver. And I shall be World Champion'.

His parents thought their boy was mad. Perhaps a surfeit of confusing teenage male hormones had short-circuited his reason, caused him to take leave of his senses.

They had understood the intense pleasure he took in playing with toy racing cars on a Scalextric set, and they had even grudgingly tolerated his proclivity for driving the family cars far too fast. They put it all down to youthful exuberance, and assumed he would grow out of it.

But now he wanted to become a racing driver. And it wasn't to be simply a weekend hobby, but a full-time career, which would come at the expense of his entering the medical profession. Instead of dedicating his life to saving others he would be risking his own, in an endeavour which, Sue suggested, was 'totally useless and unproductive for society'.

James attempted to break down the wall of parental opposition by presenting his father with a business proposition.

'I needed money fast and I offered my old man a deal. It would have cost him about five grand to put me through medical school, but as I wasn't going I'd settle for £2500 cash, now, to get my racing car.'

According to James, his father's short answer was: 'Get stuffed!' Wallis doesn't think he used exactly those words, but he certainly replied in the negative. An approach by James to Sue's mother was similarly rebuffed. She could see absolutely no value in underwriting her grandson's venture into such a dangerous and frivolous endeavour.

Aside from their concerns for his safety Wallis and Sue couldn't afford to invest in his racing. Wallis: 'At the time I was earning a reasonable income, but we had no surplus to throw around. We weren't poor, but we certainly weren't rich. We were just managing to cover everyone's education and take minimal holidays and that sort of thing. And, taking the view that fair is fair, we had six children to help get started in life and we simply couldn't afford to throw it all at one of them'.

Nevertheless, hoping the exercise would get the racing bug out of his system, they paid for James to attend a race driving course. Through a family friend they sought the advice of the retired British driver Stirling Moss, who recommended the school at the Brands Hatch circuit in Kent. Brands would play a major role in his racing future, but James failed to distinguish himself in the driving course. He thought the money was 'wasted' and would have been more usefully applied to purchasing his own racing car.

Stirling Moss, when he embarked on his own racing career, at first had to overcome a certain amount of parental opposition, but soon had their full support. He had the advantage of their being affluent motor sport enthusiasts – his father (a dental surgeon and gentleman farmer) raced cars, and his mother rallied them (she was the 1936 English women's champion) – and at the age of 18 Moss was given his own racing car. He went on to become one of the greatest Grand Prix drivers, though he broke his back in one accident, then had his career terminated prematurely in a nearly fatal crash in 1962.

When Stirling Moss spoke at James Hunt's memorial service in 1993 he included in his remarks references to the kind of character that would prompt an 18-year-old schoolboy to choose a career in a potentially lethal and hugely expensive sport which he knew nothing about.

'James', Moss said, 'was a total non-conformist who was a curious mixture of wit, intelligence and unparalleled stubbornness. Someone who stood firmly behind his actions and beliefs. Right or wrong, he certainly provided food for thought and fuel for debate. Whatever else he may have been, James was not boring. Never.'

⋆   ⋆   ⋆

James wrote a letter to Bart's hospital and said he wouldn't be studying to become a doctor after all. Instead, he was going to get a job to earn money to go racing.

His parents 'gave up' on him, knowing full well that even their most strenuous objections would be unlikely to deter their bull-headed boy from setting out on his intended course of action, though they still harboured hopes that adversity might blunt his resolve. Meanwhile, as he frittered away his time on this preposterous scheme, they would provide him with food and shelter.

'I don't need A levels to be a racing driver', said James after he left Wellington and abandoned all further formal education. Though he later wore the school colours – red, blue and yellow bands – on his black racing helmet, his summation of the Wellington legacy was brief: 'I could speak the Queen's English and I knew how to hold a knife and fork properly, that was all'.

He was being facetious, of course, and his broad vocabulary included salty Anglo Saxon words probably unknown to Her Majesty. But his manner of speaking, his clear and precise diction, especially the authoritative 'public school' accent which commanded so much respect, was in fact acquired at home and in his earlier prep school days. And the deep resonance of his carefully modulated tones owed something to the nicotine addiction which for nearly 30 years saw him puffing his way through up to 40 cigarettes a day.

His skills with a knife and fork are disputed by friends who broke bread with James in later life. John Hogan was one of those who regularly endured James slurping his soup with noisy gusto, even at formal gatherings.

'His table manners were appalling', says Hogey, as James called him. 'Coming from a large family and the public school background you learn to eat quickly and gobble everything up that's put in front of you because, if you don't, someone else will take it away. And gourmet food was completely wasted on him. He loved school food, dreary Shepherd's pie and burnt cabbage.'

But James's pronouncement that 'When I left school I had nothing going for me' gave no credit to the character-building benefits of his private education. What he regarded as 10 years of penal servitude at boarding schools undoubtedly nurtured and developed the tremendous self-confidence which enabled James to slurp his soup, indeed to do anything he felt like in public without embarrassment, and the unfailing self-belief and determination to triumph over adversity.

His more outrageous antics would cause him to be called a spoiled upper class twit, but his friend Chris Jones thinks this was a misnomer. 'It was the press that decided he was upper class, because it made him a better celebrity to sell papers. He went to Wellington because his father went there and he had the right accent. But he came from suburbia like the rest of us and he always preferred to be with his suburban mates.'

Still, James moved easily within the British class structure and was as comfortable with an aristocrat as with a man in the street. Indeed, his best qualities made him attractive to the full social spectrum: a natural dignity, an air of authority and an aristocratic bearing that commanded respect, as well as great personal charm and an endearing common touch.

While the life he led was often directly at odds with The Establishment, a book with that title (*The Establishment, A Symposium*, edited by Hugh Thomas, who later became Baron Thomas of Swynnerton) captures his character with uncanny accuracy. An essay in the book (written by the future Lord Vaizey) describing typical public schoolboys sounds remarkably like James Hunt, both boy and adult...

'Physically they seem to be bigger than the rest of us, with especially long legs... Their faces tend to be long and lean... their voices loud and confident... They are bloody rude unless they make a decision to be charming... They tend to eat like pigs; it is those poised on the social brinks who worry about table manners... They are very confident and emotionally quite uninvolved in what they say: they must never be in a position where it is possible to be snubbed, ridiculed or ruffled.... They must talk deprecatingly about their own, their family's and their friends' achievements, yet they are intensely ambitious and ruthlessly efficient in achieving serious objectives.'

2

BOY RACER

1966–1970

If he was to become the best racing driver in the world James first needed a car to race. Since this would cost money that he didn't have, his first priority was to get a job.

His plan was to emulate Simon Ridge and build himself a Mini for saloon car racing, an ambition which could not be realized overnight, given such basic disadvantages as the fact that his mechanical knowledge was nearly nil. In fact, it would take two years of hard labour, on the car and in various jobs in the workplace, before his Mini turned a wheel.

'I had no money, no knowledge of racing cars or the racing business, and nobody near me to give help and encouragement. Even so, at 18, I reasoned that three or four years of total dedication to a project wasn't going to cost me too much, even if it failed, which – viewed objectively – it might have been expected to do.'

But James wasn't being objective. His first employment, for £14 a week, was as a tea boy bringing back sandwiches from the pub and acting as a messenger and occasional delivery boy for a local printing firm. The delivery boy's vigorous cornering techniques tended to tear the wheels off the printer's Mini van, and his employers were not terribly displeased when he found other work.

A brief foray as an ice cream salesman proved less lucrative than it might have been, since he was too soft-hearted – he sometimes gave the products away free to the children on Epsom Downs – or the ice cream turned to slop when he went out in the summer heat and forgot to turn on the refrigeration in the ice cream cart.

A short stint as a 'can stacker' at Sainsbury's ended when he left over a wage dispute, and an apprenticeship in a local garage working on other people's cars only prolonged the mechanical agonies he suffered cobbling up his own Mini, of which enterprise he said: 'I hated every minute of it.'

'He despaired from time to time', Sue Hunt remembers. 'He was always short of cash, always in debt, mostly to us. But we didn't try to dissuade him from going racing. There was no point. He had made up his mind and he never faltered. He used to fly into tantrums over that Mini, but they were over quickly and all was forgiven. James had a lot of charm, although at this stage he was always more charming when he was out than when he was at home.'

The highlights of his limited social life were trips with the Ridge brothers to various circuits, where watching Simon race reminded James why he was slaving over the preparation of his own Mini. On one occasion they visited a nearby pub prior to camping overnight at the Castle Combe race circuit in Wiltshire. While Simon and Chris Ridge were setting up their tent under the headlights of their car, James, who had a one-man bivouac tent left over from his school days, disappeared.

Simon Ridge: 'Suddenly there was this strange figure rushing in and out of the beam of the headlights, flapping its wings and hooting madly. It was James with his tent over his head pretending to be a ghost.

'He tripped over the guywire of somebody else's tent and fell on the occupant. "Frightfully sorry old man", said James, "I'm afraid your rope has attacked me and I've fallen over." He had everybody laughing within seconds. He had this incredible sense of humour.'

It also seemed he had a highly developed sense of social justice. Once he was with the Ridge brothers in the competitors' grandstand at the Brands Hatch circuit when two drivers who had crashed together in an earlier race began fighting.

'It was a real punch-up', Simon Ridge recalls, 'with fists flying everywhere. We all moved back out of the way to give them room, but James burst straight through between my brother and myself and waded into the fight. Bear in mind he was only 18, though he was tall, and these were two fully grown and very angry men. James grabbed them by the shoulders and said, "Come on, break it up. We're all civilized people here". And he stopped the fight.'

☆ ☆ ☆

With his first savings James acquired the stripped down chassis of a crashed Mini racer and set it up in the garage at home, where he 'stuck bits on it' as he could afford to buy them. Since the parts were mostly obtained from picking through the junk in wreckers' yards his sojourn as a van driver for the Medical Research Council proved to be most beneficial to his scrounging. Whenever there was a lull in the delivery business, to and from the Royal Marsden Hospital in Belmont, James haunted the old car scrap heaps, brought his booty back to the Hunt garage and added it to his growing Mini. Simon Ridge dropped around sometimes to give him advice, but James mostly worked alone, though 'anyone who came up the drive' to the Hunt house was conscripted to pitch in, including the milkman.

Eventually James found and installed an engine and the more the car took shape the harder he worked at earning money.

There was no stopping him during the day – he solved any parking problems with the delivery van by sticking on its windscreen a large sign proclaiming its cargo to be 'Radioactive' (he was, after all working for the radiological service attached to the hospital) – and at night he laboured as a cleaner at the Royal Marsden hospital.

This was as close to the medical profession as James got, and his next enterprise, an attempt to become a bus conductor on the suburban Green Line, was short-lived. He was told he was too tall for a ticket man and that he had 'too much chat'. A suggestion that he become a trainee bus driver came to nothing when it was discovered that he was too young. However, his size, age and gift of the gab were no handicap to another prospective employer, a telephone rental company. He was taken on as a trainee salesman and sent to take a course in London.

In their attempt to turn the gangling, rather unkempt youth into a proper salesman, the telephone rental company required him to get a short back and sides haircut and to wear a suit. Ping, who was also working in London at the time, was most surprised and impressed to see him appear thus coiffed and attired, though she thought he 'never really looked at home' in this uniform. More familiar was the increasingly lived-in look of his everyday wear, which, as he pinched his pennies ever tighter, included holes in the soles of his Hush Puppies.

James said of these impoverished years that he 'lived a life that totally freaked out my friends. They couldn't believe it. They thought I was mad because I gave up everything that was part of normal life for somebody my age. All I ever did was work to earn money and build my car.

'I had no social life, never went to the pub, never spent on anything I didn't have to. I could not accept other people's hospitality because I couldn't reciprocate. My only relaxation was squash. The club had a beer kitty so I was able to get drunk once a week. That was it. The club members simply regarded me as a nutter.'

Ping agrees his friends probably thought James 'was a bit of a nutcase', though they did, in fact, drag him out to the pub on occasion, where they bought the beer. Chris Jones admits they felt James was wasting his time 'fiddling around with a bloomin' Mini and we never thought it would go beyond the Mini racing stage'.

John Richardson found it all 'strangely eccentric. We all laughed at him when he was down to smoking just two cigarettes a day to save money to put into his little blue Mini. But you had to admire his determination, his obsession'.

Eventually, to the chagrin of the Hunts' neighbours, James was able to fire up the raucously rattling engine of the Mini. The distinctly second-hand racing tyres were bald when he got them, so he cut treads in them with a knife. He drove up and down the driveway and then, though the car was unlicensed, he took it out on the street.

It was quite breezy inside, since he couldn't afford windows, and the passenger's seat took the form of a canvas and aluminium deckchair borrowed from the Hunt lawn and bolted to the Mini's floor with brackets from a Meccano set. Nevertheless, the car ran, the proud owner pronounced it raceworthy and made the final preparations to put it to the acid test.

He bought a well-used trailer and, for £15, a 1947 Rover T6 to act as a tow car. The vehicle was as old as its new owner, but not nearly as fit when it was pressed into service to ferry the cobbled-up racing car and the would-be racing driver to the scene of their competition debut: the Snetterton circuit in Norfolk.

Full of anticipation, and with the faithful Ping as his pit crew, James set out on his great adventure very early on a summer morning in 1967. They reached Snetterton without incident, but the Mini never made it on to the track.

The race scrutineers found fault with the nearly bald tyres, being unconvinced by James's insistence that the hand-cut tread pattern was a new secret weapon. The deckchair instead of a proper passenger seat was also against the rules but the main problems were the abbreviated exhaust system, which ended at the engine manifold, and the Mini's natural air conditioning. James had seen no mention in the rulebook of windows being required, but the scrutineers said he couldn't race without them.

'I burst into tears', said James. 'Two years of devotion and all for nothing! I needed windows in my car and I was £50 pounds in debt. My whole world collapsed around me. I was a broken man.'

* * *

As far as his parents were concerned his non-event at Snetterton was a success. As James said: 'My mother was flabbergasted when she saw me come back alive. She was convinced I would be killed first time out'.

But any hopes his parents had of James giving up his racing ambition were quickly dashed. His setback only filled him with greater resolve, and he worked harder than ever to accumulate the necessary funds to bring his Mini into line with the regulations. Though he only ever managed to enter three events, they were enough to convince him the car was uncompetitive and, if anything, it would only impede his racing progress.

A typical result of his Mini racing ventures is contained in an incident and retirement report from a race at Brands Hatch on 8 October 1967: 'Car No. 214 (Dvr: J. S. W. Hunt) retired on lap 5 having been black flagged for dropping oil on the circuit'.

His towing equipment was also seriously deficient. When James and Ping were returning from a Mini race at Silverstone their journey was interrupted by a flat tyre on the trailer. Since his tool-kit did not contain the necessary items to effect immediate repairs, roadside assistance from the AA was required. They set off again only to grind to a halt 10 miles down the road when a wheel bearing on the trailer seized solid.

'The police came along', Ping recalls, 'and told him he would have to leave the trailer there with the Mini on it and come back later to collect it. James told them he couldn't do that because there would be nothing left of it by the time he came back. He had a fairly forceful conversation with the constable who was determined that this was the only course of action open to him. But James said, "No, I'm not leaving it here. It's my livelihood. I need it".

'In the end James persuaded them to turn a blind eye. He produced this frightfully frayed bit of rope and I was put in the Mini and towed all the way down the M1, right across London and back to Surrey. There was no heating in the Mini and I was nearly frozen, but we got the hand signals perfect, to give me the chance to brake when he did, and the rope held, just. When we finally stopped James said, "My God, that was absolutely brilliant!"'

James was less appreciative of Ping on another occasion when, inadvertently, she caused his tow car to give up the ghost. 'He had quite a fiery temper. I remember I was standing outside my parent's house with one of his tennis-playing friends when James came along in the Rover. When he found out we were planning to go off and do something together, without him, he was furious. He put his foot down, the old Rover took off in a cloud of dust and the back end just exploded. It completely disintegrated.

'He wasn't embarrassed, just absolutely livid that now he was going to have to spend money on another tow car, rather than on the racing car. After he did the disaster to the Rover he got an equally used white Austin. All his friends were zooming around in smart little cars and James was always in some great old heap.'

James, who was now earning £20 a week as a trainee manager with the telephone rental company, had obviously benefitted from the salesmanship course. He found a customer for his Mini and persuaded the lucky man that it was a steal at £325.

'I sold it on the spur of the moment', he said. 'All my best decisions have been taken on the spur of the moment.'

Between the expired Rover and the rusty old Austin A90 (which cost him £25) he tootled around on a £5 motor scooter. His bank balance was augmented by a 21st birthday gift of £100 from his parents. He persuaded them to give it to him well in advance of the exact day in August, though they nearly took it back when he told them what he intended to do with it.

All his wheeling and dealing and money saving was in aid of getting him back on track for his next step up the racing ladder: Formula Ford. This category, for spindly little single seaters with open wheels, skinny tyres and 1500 cc Ford engines, was devised in 1967 (at the Brands Hatch circuit in Kent) and quickly became hugely popular. The formula was intended to be an inexpensive introduction to proper racing, but the price per car, then pegged at £1000, and the costs of running it for a season, were well beyond James Hunt's financial resources.

Undeterred, he took a great leap of faith and ordered a new Russell-Alexis Mk14 Formula Ford chassis on 'the never-never' – a hire purchase scheme offered by the car manufacturer and an insurance company. The terms – a £345 down payment and £30 a month – and a similar deal to acquire an engine, made his Mini racing enterprise seem eminently sensible in comparison.

But the deal was done and most weekends during the 1968 season his name appeared on the entry list of Formula Ford races at any of half a dozen circuits around the country. At first he was listed as 'Jim' Hunt, but he strongly disapproved of the contraction and soon set the record straight.

The purpose of the Ford-engined formula was to provide everyone with equal equipment, so that driving ability, rather than mechanical advantage, would come to the fore. Still, inequalities arose when those who could afford it had their engines more finely tuned and replaced their racing tyres frequently.

Even without such luxuries James soon established that he could be competitive in the series. In his first race, at Snetterton, he finished 'about fifth', then found more speed when he discovered an incorrectly set ignition distributor was robbing his engine of 15 horsepower.

However, his efforts to leapfrog quickly to the front of the pack were tempered by his wariness of becoming involved in accidents. His concerns were not so much for his person as his pocketbook, since he couldn't afford costly repair bills. As it was, his money for racing did not extend to such niceties as hotel rooms at distant circuits, and on more than one occasion he economized by overnighting on the floor in the press room at Snetterton.

But his racing prowess improved steadily, and with experience he gained the confidence necessary to battle wheel to wheel with the host of equally determined Formula Fordsters. Soon he became an aggressive frontrunner and, though there were a few minor wheel-banging incidents when he lost disputes with other drivers for the same piece of road, by the end of the summer he had become a winner. His first victory was at the Lydden Hill circuit in Kent, and he also set a Formula Ford lap record, on the short circuit at nearby Brands Hatch.

Armed with this proof of his rapid progress James began trying to sell potential sponsors on the idea that having their name on his car would be good publicity. But not everyone leapt at this splendid opportunity, and the rejections were dispiriting, as he later recalled.

'This was just about the lowest period of my life. I had to go knocking on doors to get sponsorship and the doors were always slammed in my face.'

But he persisted and eventually his powers of persuasion prevailed. He managed to get a minor investment from a car dealer, Hughes of Beaconsfield, then a more substantial offer from another, Gowrings of Reading.

Impressed by his pace in Formula Ford, and by his personal style and flair, Gowrings asked James to prepare a budget for the 1969 season. When his estimate proved to be within their financial range, Gowrings ordered a new Merlyn Mk11A car, with a view to him running it in the last few races of 1968 before embarking on a full Gowrings-sponsored season the next year.

As it developed, the new car became an immediate necessity when the Russell-Alexis was totally destroyed in an enormous accident which James was very lucky to survive.

* * *

Tony Dron, another public schoolboy who had succumbed to the lure of the racing life, was one of James's closest Formula Ford rivals. They became good friends and remained so, even though 'The Dron', as James called him, felt responsible for causing the serious accident that October afternoon at the Oulton Park circuit in Cheshire.

Dron, who went on to become a successful amateur driver and a highly respected automotive journalist, still shudders at the memory of the day when James Hunt's career might so easily have ended.

Dron, in a Titan car, was running in third place with James just a few feet behind as they charged down into the Cascade corner, beside the lake in the centre of the Oulton Park circuit. The accident began when Dron hit trouble and James tried to avoid it, at well over 100 miles an hour.

Dron: 'I regret to say I spun the Titan at the exit from Cascades in a very big way, going off to the right and then to the left. But my car was still raceworthy and I was just engaging first gear to get going again when James passed over my head at undiminished speed with his throttle jammed wide open.

'He hit a bump on the edge of the track and that was enough to launch him. His car flew through a Shell advertising hoarding, breaking off a massive great piece of wood that was holding it up, and I thought "this looks very nasty indeed".

'I've never done it before or since, but I got out of my car and went running after him. I found bits of his car all along the way, from both the front and the back, so he'd obviously been cartwheeling along at fantastic speed. Then I found his rollover bar, which he had modified to clear his head because he was taller, so I feared the worst.

'I got to the edge of the lake and there was nothing to be seen. I looked more closely into the lake and saw his car submerged on the bottom and I thought: "Oh my God!"

'I was standing there with the water around my ankles getting ready to dive under the car to see if I could get him out. In that split second, about twenty yards away, James rose to the surface and stood up, with the water up to his chest.

'He looked as if he'd been made up for a horror movie: blood running down one side of his face and mud the other, oil on his nose, reeds in his mouth, water sloshing around in his goggles. I helped him to the shore and got him to lie down. He obviously wasn't quite all there because he started trying to tell me a dirty joke!'

An ambulance came and took James away for a checkup. His wounds were only superficial and he was given a cup of tea and told to lie down. A very relieved Ping was there to hold his hand. She had been watching in the pits when over the loudspeaker came the news that James Hunt had gone off the circuit.

'And the commentator said "I'm afraid it doesn't look good". Everyone came up to console me and we just had to wait. Eventually he came back from the medical centre and it was obvious he was terribly shaken. He could hardly move because he was so bruised and battered and his face was completely white. I think it was the first time it really hit home what could happen to him in a car.'

James, however, later claimed that the accident 'didn't worry me too much because I was young and stupid'. He seemed more distressed by the loss of his car, which was reduced to scrap metal, but still had to be paid for. It would take two more years of scrimping and saving before the debt was finally paid off.

However, James admitted, it was only good fortune that he hadn't suffered the same fate. 'I was flung clear as the car went over. I remember being on my hands and knees under the water and then suddenly emerging like Neptune. Seat belts were not yet compulsory and I didn't have them because I couldn't afford them. Had I been wearing them I might have drowned.'

⋆ ⋆ ⋆

Tony Dron, who drove James and Ping home that day, was so shaken by what he had seen that 'the experience very nearly put me off racing for good'. But he continued racing and writing about it, and three years later, in an eloquent article in *Motor* magazine, he described the shock he felt at James's accident and included a lengthy list of the assorted trials and tribulations they faced as beginners in Formula Ford. Sections of the article, which was entitled 'So You Want To Go Racing', might easily have discouraged anyone from ever attempting it.

'At best', Dron wrote, 'motor racing becomes a true catharsis of the emotions. At worst, it's sheer bloody misery... The agony of sitting on a grid at a race meeting cannot be fully explained. I always used to decide quite definitely that I would give up racing, sell the car – after all I didn't have to do it.

'But the feeling of fulfilment after a good drive, wherever I finished, filled me with anticipation for the following weekend. Believe me, you have to try really hard and battle with yourself to put up consistently fast lap times. It's quite a struggle to discipline one's self to such an exhausting pastime.

'Every driver must feel the same to some extent – it's the fear of not knowing how hard one will have to try that used to make me twitch in the cockpit right up till a minute before the race started. One driver I knew was physically sick on waking up every race day, yet something compelled him to carry on with great success on the track.'

Tony Dron was also sometimes ill before a race, but the driver he was referring to was James Hunt.

James made no secret of the pre-race ritual of retching and vomiting, which continued throughout his career. Ping, and others close to him, believe it began after the Oulton Park accident, but James insisted it wasn't fear for his life that caused his stomach to turn in those days.

'I was sick with tremendous nerve pressure. But that was basically because I was driving my own car and if I crunched it I was out of money and there was no way I could repair the car. It was when today could be my last-ever race. So it was fear of my future on the financial side and on the job security side. Nothing to do with danger.'

But further down the road the danger factor was uppermost in his mind.

'It's when you arrive in Formula 1 that you realize the death toll, compared to other professions, is very high. I hate this danger aspect. It is the only cloud on my sunny horizon. If you are to survive you realize that the only answer is to get out of racing as soon as possible. But you have to be rational. Once you decide to go for the top, you are committed. You have decided to take the risk. You must live with it.'

That was how he felt in 1976. Meanwhile, there were more risks to survive in Formula Ford.

Tony Dron calculated that in three years of Formula Ford he had 56 spins, half a dozen of them at over 100 miles an hour. James must have had as many and, a few weeks after his Oulton Park crash, he was involved in another incident, again with The Dron. It was on the first lap of a race at Mallory Park (in Leicestershire) with James, now driving the Gowrings Merlyn, in rather too close company with Dron's Titan.

'We came down to the first corner together and James put his back wheel between my front and back wheels and we went around together this way. I'll never forget seeing his back wheel rotating at 90 miles an hour between mine, a few inches from my face!

'But we were okay until someone hit him and he was launched off my front wheel. He flew into the air and for a split second I was right underneath his car. When he came down he chopped the nose off my car, went sideways on the road and I hit him right in the middle.

'We came to rest against the bank, alongside each other, our wrecks neatly parked. We climbed out. He pulled out a pack of cigarettes, offered me one and we sat there smoking and watching the race. The accident wasn't mentioned.'

On several future occasions James would fly into screaming rages at drivers he felt were responsible for causing accidents, even if the facts proved otherwise. But the two involving The Dron he put down to bad racing luck and felt no animosity towards him. That winter they went on a skiing holiday together in Europe, where they compared notes about the frenetic pace of Formula Ford.

What Dron remembers most about James in Formula Ford was his unwavering determination to succeed. 'He was absolutely hell-bent on getting to the top. He told me "If I don't get to the top in motor racing, I'll get to the top in something else". And I believed him. The head of Titan cars asked me who among all the guys I'd raced in Formula Ford would be most likely to make it to the top. Without hesitation I said: "James Hunt".'

Dron was also impressed by his rival's astonishing reserves of energy. It was not unknown for James, after spending the day working on his car and testing at a northern circuit, to drive home and play a county-standard squash match at his club in Sutton. Then he would drive off, sometimes 50 miles away, to a friendly match at a private court and finish off the day with a midnight rendezvous with a girl in London.

Dron: 'He seemed to be able to just drive himself on and on. Maybe he over-revved himself once too often and that lack of subconscious self-control over his body might have damaged his heart'.

Dron estimates they competed in 45 events in the 12-month period from mid-1968 to mid-1969. 'It was pretty stern stuff, really. We used to find that the only time we didn't get a pain in the stomach was on Monday because it started coming back again on Tuesday and Wednesday. By Thursday and Friday you were really tense about the weekend. Then you'd go out and it was worse because we were driving just a little bit over the limit most of the time – going through the barriers of good sense to get faster and faster to get to the front of the grid.'

Getting to the front of the grid in 1969 was harder than ever, as the Ford formula attracted many more drivers. To accommodate the vast entry at most events the organizers scheduled two preliminary heats, from which the top finishers advanced to a final race. James, who managed to avoid most of the inevitable comings-together of the closely matched cars, won his heat on several occasions and more often than not finished in the top half dozen of the final.

The exciting, often hair-raising, Formula Ford competition was very popular with spectators, and in the spring of 1969 the series, under the auspices of Ford, was exported to the continent.

James was quick to capitalize on the opportunity to race abroad in the European Formula Ford Championship, and distinguished himself with a fighting third place at Zandvoort in Holland, followed by an equally well-earned second place at Aspern in Austria, where he also set the fastest lap.

But prior to these worthy efforts, he had also figured prominently – before the race even started – at the Vallelunga circuit in Italy. In fact he sabotaged the start. Tony Dron remembers how James managed, certainly not for the last time, to gain notoriety off the track as well as on it.

'All the drivers were required to have a medical certificate stating their blood group. James claimed this hadn't been mentioned properly in the pre-event regulations and he didn't have the right documentation. But they weren't going to let him start and he proceeded to cause a bit of a stink.

'He'd travelled all the way to Vallelunga and he was buggered if he wasn't going to race. So he drove his car out of the paddock and parked it at 90 degrees across the front of the grid and left it there.

'Up in the grandstand was Stuart Turner of the Ford Motor Company, along with a lot of other dignitaries there to witness the prestigious launch of Formula Ford in Italy. When Turner saw it all being cocked up by an idiot named James Hunt he turned to Nick Brittan and said: "Mark my words, that young man is going nowhere in motor racing!"'

Nick Brittan, one of the founders of the Formula Ford category, was the organizer of the European venture. Though he later became well known for his outrageous sense of humour in his satirical column Private Ear (written for the racing magazine *Autosport* and often featuring the antics of James), Brittan was not amused that day in Vallelunga.

'I took him to task over his silliness and said to him, "Hunt, you'll never make a professional racing driver as long as you've got a hole in your arse!". And the year he won the World Championship he came up to me, grinning wickedly, and said: "I've still got that hole. How am I doing?"'

James's disruptive tactics were seen in some quarters as further proof of the forceful competitive spirit that regularly had his self-prepared car challenging rivals in professionally run teams. When one of those teams, Motor Racing Enterprises, invited him to replace one of their drivers James gratefully set aside his tool-kit and promptly won the next race, at Lydden Hill, in an MRE-entered Merlyn Mk11A.

Other impressive results in their Formula Ford car persuaded MRE to move him up into the Formula 3 category near the end of the 1969 season. Despite his outdated car, a two-year-old Brabham BT21 with a three-year-old engine, James was immediately on the pace. He finished seventh in his Formula 3 debut at Mallory Park and won two Formula Libre events (races for cars of varying types) at Brands Hatch, where he also finished third and fourth in proper Formula 3 races.

'Formula 3 was the right way to go', James said, 'particularly at that time. It was the only place for an up-and-coming driver, the only serious route into Formula 1.'

Indeed, his Formula 3 rivals in 1969 included nearly a dozen drivers who eventually made it to Formula 1, the majority of them well before James. Notable among them were the future World Champion Emerson Fittipaldi from Brazil, Ronnie Peterson from Sweden, who became one of the great Formula 1 heroes (and was destined to die in an accident in which James was involved), the top French drivers Jacques Laffite and Jean-Pierre Jarier, and other drivers from several countries. But the international cast of Formula 3 characters numbered over 70 at major races, and it would take some doing for James Hunt to rise above the rank and file.

While the Formula 3 cars bore a superficial resemblance to the Formula Fords, they were much more purposeful machines, with fat racing tyres on lightweight chassis powered by highly tuned 1000 cc racing engines, called 'screamers' because of their high-pitched wail.

The more sophisticated equipment, the closely matched cars, the internationality of the formula and its tradition (since 1964) of acting as a training ground for potential Formula 1 stars raised the level of competition to a particularly high intensity. While some drivers raced in Formula 3 just for the fun of it, more of them – like James – were deadly serious about using it as a platform from which to launch themselves into Formula 1, the pinnacle of motor sport.

James's cause was aided considerably by a scintillating performance in a classic Formula 3 race at Cadwell Park on 28 September 1969. The beautiful road racing circuit that twists and turns up hill and down dale in the Lincolnshire wolds is considered a real driver's track, and by the end of the day James proved he was a driver to be reckoned with.

Throwing his Brabham around with great gusto he qualified on the front row of the starting grid for his heat, the second of two preliminary races needed to whittle the large entry down to manageable size. Despite clipping another car when he made an impetuous lunge for the lead, James's turn of speed again secured him a front row starting place for the main event.

At the end of the first of the 25 laps he was lying third in a snarling pack of 18 cars which were so closely bunched they could have been covered by the proverbial blanket. His nearest adversary was Ronnie Peterson, the acknowledged star of Formula 3 and now behind the wheel of a newly designed car fielded by his employers, March Engineering. The brave Swede and the audacious Englishman traded places nearly every lap in a stirring battle which raged throughout the remaining laps.

At the finish, the Australian Tim Schenken took the chequered flag first, followed in the blink of an eye by the New Zealander Howden Ganley. A split second later the brand new March and the battered old Brabham crossed the finish line almost as one. The stop watches gave them identical times, but Peterson was a fraction ahead of Hunt.

Besides his eye-opening fourth place in such distinguished company, James, with two other drivers, also established a new joint lap record for the Cadwell Park circuit.

The March team was so impressed by James's effort that they asked him to fill in at the next race for Ronnie Peterson, who had been slightly injured in a race in France. In his substitute role, at Brands Hatch, James had to fight very hard to wring 10th place out of the March, and was not unhappy to revert to his well-used MRE Brabham to finish out the season.

When his 1969 performances, including several wins and high finishes in Formula Ford and Formula 3, were evaluated by a panel from the British Guild of Motoring Writers, James was considered worthy of a Grovewood Award as one of the three most promising drivers in the country. First place went to F5000 driver Mike Walker and third to Formula Ford driver Tony Trimmer. Since his second place award was accompanied by a cheque for £300 James was happy to don a suit and tie to receive it at a function hosted by the Royal Automobile Club at its London headquarters. On an earlier occasion he had been refused entry to the RAC club because he was not wearing a tie.

While the Grovewood Award money was put to good use paying off some of his bills, its prestige also helped open more doors as James made the rounds of potential sponsors for next year. Such sources of revenue were now more vital than ever, since he had forsaken the workaday world for the life of a full-time racing driver.

He found some funding from Molyslip, makers of mechanical lubricants, and an arrangement with Lotus Components produced a

Lotus 59 car with which he proposed to contest as many of the international Formula 3 events as he could manage.

* * *

The 1970 schedule included 60 major races, the majority of them in the countries of western Europe and Scandinavia. From May until November the merry men of the Formula 3 'circus' wandered gypsy-like around the Continent, towing their racing cars as far north as Finland and, if they could afford it, even south into Morocco.

While the 'name' drivers in some affluent teams were well-paid professionals, and several of the wealthy privateers had their racing hobby funded by family money, James Hunt and his ilk relied on the start money doled out by the race organizers, which – they desperately hoped – would be supplemented by a share of the prize money awarded to the top finishers at each race.

The terms of James's Lotus deal included the provision of the racing car, all expenses for engine rebuilds and crash repair and £1000 to help with the running costs and travel. Since these last two items were expected to amount to well over £5000 James was banking on collecting a fair share of the start and prize money.

In fact, at the end of the year his income from these sources of revenue would total about £4500, and the shortfall meant he was several times completely broke. But this was by now a chronic state for James, and he was fully accustomed to racing on blind faith.

To help weather the financial storms while travelling around Europe he lived in a tent, dined frugally at only the cheapest restaurants and restricted his evening socializing to talking shop with his fellow competitors, many of whom were similarly impecunious, in the paddocks of the various race tracks.

Despite his rigid economy measures James ran seriously short of funds in only the fourth race of the European season, at Pau in south-western France. He crashed the Lotus twice in qualifying and was unable to repair it in time for the race, which meant he would not get the starting money from the organizers which he needed to pay for the journey back to England.

Not only was he out of money, but he was also out of petrol. During the night someone had siphoned dry the fuel tank of his tow car. This left James with 'no alternative but to acquire some petrol by the same means, which was easier said than done. I discovered that most French cars had locking petrol caps, which meant creeping around the paddock in the dark on hands and knees, finding one car in ten without a locking cap, and one in ten of the rest with enough petrol to make it worthwhile.

'I finally got to Le Havre after two days on the road with no food – that was bad – and when I got off the ferry I borrowed some money and hitchhiked home.'

A few weeks later he was back in business and scored consecutive fourth place finishes at Silverstone and at Magny-Cours in France. His first attempt at the most glamorous and prestigious of Formula 3 races, held on the narrow, twisting streets of the Principality of Monaco, ended in an accident.

His fortunes improved at the next event, in Austria, but not before he had to endure an arduous journey through deep snow drifts in the Alps and a lengthy argument, over inadequate documentation, with Italian customs officials (who had never before had to deal with a dishevelled, but determined, young Englishman towing a racing car) at a remote border crossing. However, James's persistence was rewarded with an impressive second place result at the Österreichring circuit.

By the end of May the Hunt-driven Molyslip Lotus 59 had scored two more second places, on home ground at Oulton Park, then at Chimay in Belgium, where he was also the fastest qualifier. His Belgian effort was particularly noteworthy, since James spun out of the lead on the penultimate lap and was passed by four other cars.

On the last lap he overtook every one of them, only to lose by six inches when one of the following cars outdragged him to the finish line. The timing devices, which showed the first five cars were covered by 1.9 seconds after 51 minutes of breathtaking racing, revealed just how hard James had driven. In establishing a new race lap record for the Chimay circuit he was almost five seconds quicker than he had been in qualifying in pole position.

Starting from the front of the grid was of less importance at the French circuit at Rouen, where, though the track was dangerously narrow, its long straights created fierce slipstreaming battles which saw places continually being swapped right, left and centre. The necessary tactics placed the cars in perilously close company as they darted in and out of each other's wake, seeking to leapfrog their way to the front, while weaving back and forth trying to break the tow of those following inches behind.

James, who qualified only 18th among the 20 starters – then gave himself more work to do when he half spun on the opening lap – quickly hauled himself up into contention among a furiously fighting pack of 15 cars, any one of which might win.

There were numerous wheel-banging incidents, then a more serious accident on the unlucky 13th lap, when one car crashed heavily into the steel barriers. The driver, the Frenchman Denis Dayan, was whisked away by helicopter to hospital for treatment of severe leg injuries and a broken arm.

The race raged on, with cars screaming flat out three and four abreast down the straights and a different one leading nearly every time they crossed the finish line. The next accident was triggered when someone, without looking in his mirrors, pulled out directly in front of James.

When James took immediate avoiding action the car next to him hit the rear wheel of his Lotus and was launched skywards. It somersaulted over the barriers and disappeared into the trees where the driver, Bob Wollek of France, was removed from the wreckage with chest injuries and a broken arm and taken away to join his countryman Dayan in the Rouen hospital.

Hunt's Lotus, though it suffered a broken exhaust system when hit by Wollek's flying Brabham, continued at unabated speed among the leading pack of dozen cars. With five laps to go James was back in eighth place. Over the next four laps he inched his way forward until he was well-placed to pounce on the crucial final lap.

Coming out of the last corner he suddenly swerved out from the slipstreams of the two cars in front and gradually eased past them as they rocketed down the start/finish straight. James acknowledged the chequered flag by punching his fists in the air, jubilant at winning his first major motor race.

His margin of victory, over the Brazilian Wilson Fittipaldi and Mike Beuttler from England, was a mere tenth of a second, but there was an ominous gap of several seconds to the remaining finishers.

On that last frenetic lap several drivers had made desperate attempts to break free as James had done. One of them, the French Formula 3 star Jean-Luc Salomon, found his way blocked by a solid wall of cars and was launched high into the air. Four other cars were caught up in the altercation and went careening off into the ditch, where Salomon's car landed upside down on top of one of them. None of the other drivers was seriously hurt, but Jean-Luc Salomon died from brain injuries and a broken neck.

James came to grips with the Rouen tragedy in the way most racing drivers do: by blocking it out of his mind as best he could. But he was not as successful at this as some drivers, who, either through poorly developed imaginative powers or too highly developed self-belief, think it could never happen to them.

James was more conscious than ever of danger and, while he prided himself on surviving the 1970 season with an accident repair bill of just £600, his pre-race puking ritual intensified.

He never tried to hide his weakness by ducking into a paddock toilet, where he would undoubtedly have to queue with other drivers intent on relieving agitated bladders and bowels. Instead, James threw up in full view of everyone and was on more than one occasion captured in mid-spew by the cameras of sadistic photographers.

'He wasn't the least bit embarrassed about it', says one of his Formula 3 peers, Brendan McInerney. 'He once told me about throwing up deliberately when he was playing an important squash game. He needed to be sick anyway because he had had a heavy drinking session the night before. Rather than excuse himself and leave the court he did it right there, so he could have time to recover whilst they were cleaning up the mess on the court. Of course, he also psyched out his opponent and James won the match.'

Brendan McInerney, who later became James's Formula 3 team-mate, remembers that his first impression was that 'he was a Hooray Henry type, although I don't think the term had been invented then. I thought he seemed more suited to propping up the bar of a rugby club than being a racing driver. I suppose it was due to his accent and he just looked like a typical public schoolboy at the time'.

Ian Phillips, then a novice motor sport journalist with the magazine *Autosport*, had a similar first opinion of James. Phillips approached him while he was unloading his Formula 3 car from its trailer in the paddock before a race and 'rather naïvely I thought he would be very happy to answer my questions at any time.

'But I quickly got the impression that my timing was inopportune when he gave a very public schoolboy reply to my first query: "What kind of stupid fucking question do you think that is?"'

James then 'stormed off in a huff', but like the majority of people who crossed paths, and sometimes swords, with James, Phillips eventually came to enjoy his company very much. But he remembers the growing pains during his Formula 3 days.

'What distinguished James then was his ability to get involved in incidents both on and off the track. There was occasionally a lot of speed and there were all sorts of excuses when there wasn't a lot of speed. Whether he was crashing a car or just generally falling out with somebody, he wasn't the most popular guy around.

'Part of his problem was that he was at first terribly naïve in the business. He had somehow discovered motor racing and decided it was "a jolly good thing to do, chaps". But most of the people he was up against had a car-trader type of background and they were streetwise, particularly when it came to doing deals.

'So if somebody sold him something James would think he was getting exactly what he was paying for, which wasn't always the case, and James then tended to resent his fellow competitors because they'd got a better deal. One way or another he always seemed half a step away from an argument with somebody over something.'

His most celebrated argument came near the end of the season, at the Crystal Palace circuit in South London. A few weeks earlier James had won his second important Formula 3 victory, in a closely fought race at Zolder in Belgium, and followed that with an impressive third place in the rain at Cadwell Park. Thus, when he arrived at Crystal Palace he was, if not downright cocky, then in a finely tuned state of aggressive fighting trim.

Since the London race was being televised into living rooms around the country, many fans on their first viewing of James Hunt the racing driver might have wondered if he had missed his calling. Perhaps he should have been a prize fighter.

He finished second in his qualifying heat and in the final, while the Australian David Walker was alone in front, James was in the midst of a six car dispute over second place. For the final three laps his chief adversaries were Mike Beuttler and David Morgan, with the latter being especially aggressive in his attempts to outmanoeuvre his rivals. On the last lap, as Walker took the chequered flag and Beuttler edged ahead into second place, Morgan's March made a desperate lunge to claim the last corner and in so doing collected Hunt's Lotus.

The two cars met in an explosion of debris, with Morgan's wrecked March thumping hard into the barriers and Hunt's Lotus, shorn of its right-side wheels, skittering to a halt in the middle of the track. While the closely following pack took desperate evasive action, James extricated himself from his wrecked car, ran over to Morgan and flattened him with a single blow.

Though the incident was witnessed by thousands of people there were varying interpretations as to the guilt or innocence of the combatants. Ian Phillips, who had a grandstand view of the proceedings at Crystal Palace, thought James's behaviour was 'totally unjustified. He simply over-reacted, the way he did when I asked him my first silly question'.

When the *Autosport* journalist Justin Haler wrote in his race report that 'a justifiably enraged Hunt felled Morgan in the heat of the moment' it prompted a letter to the magazine from an indignant

Mrs H. B. Morgan, mother of David. Mrs Morgan was 'quite incensed' at her son's treatment by the magazine. 'At what stage', she queried, 'does pressing on, harrying and holding off turn from a virtue into a vice?'

The flurry of letters which then appeared in the *Autosport* correspondence columns even included one from Mike Beuttler's mother, who wrote that she was 'quite horrified' by it all, 'the boy Hunt being extremely beastly to my son, who, as always, drove beautifully, although his father and I do rather wish at times he had chosen a more sedate occupation. As for Mr Morgan, mere words fail me. A pity they didn't fail his mum.'

Other letters, from readers unrelated to the drivers, included opinions that Hunt's 'disgraceful behaviour can only bring our sport into disrepute' and 'any talent-spotting team manager would have been singularly unimpressed by the driving tactics of one driver and the lack of self-control of the other'.

The Royal Automobile Club was also unimpressed by the Hunt versus Morgan contretemps, and the two were summoned to appear before an RAC Tribunal.

The governing body of British motor sport heard evidence from both drivers and a spectator witness brought along by Morgan. But James gathered together a large number of witnesses who testified on his behalf and produced a copy of the BBC TV film which showed that his car had not hit Morgan's first. When three other drivers gave their opinions that Morgan had overtaken in a dangerous manner the Tribunal ruled that Hunt was innocent. But everyone was shocked at Morgan's unusually severe sentence: a 12 month suspension of his racing licence.

One of those attending the Tribunal on James's behalf was John Hogan, then working as an account executive with an advertising agency. They had met a couple of months before the Crystal Palace incident, when James approached Hogan asking for advice about how to get sponsorship.

'The first thing I remember him saying to me was that he was going to be World Champion in 1974. So he missed it by two years, but I've never been confronted with somebody who was so convincingly ultra-confident.'

Hogan, in his future role as head of the Marlboro cigarette company's Formula 1 involvement, would get 'phone calls every week from somebody who said they're going to be World Champion and "can't you sponsor me?". But this was the one and only time I actually believed what I was hearing'.

After that meeting Hogan arranged for James (and the Scottish driver Gerry Birrell, who was later killed in a race at the Rouen circuit) to get a small amount of sponsorship from Coca Cola, one of his advertising clients. They became firm friends and James asked 'Hogey' to help organize his defence for the Tribunal hearing. But Hogan's protégé performed exceedingly well on his own behalf.

'It was one of the few occasions where I saw James actually use the old school tie to full effect. He used his public school background to influence the old fuddy-duddies on the RAC. Dave Morgan was just a regular guy, but James impressed them with his presence, his accent and his articulation. But he conceded that the sentence to Dave was a total injustice.'

Many people felt David Morgan was made a scapegoat to discourage the increasingly wild driving in Formula 3. Early in 1971, when he appealed against his 12-month ban from racing, the RAC gave him his licence back and Morgan got into no further trouble. But the man who punched him certainly did.

3

HUNT THE SHUNT

1971–1972

While many of the leading Formula 3 drivers moved further up the ladder in 1971, either into Formula 2 or, in certain cases, directly into Formula 1, James 'hoped that by staying in Formula 3 I would be able to get good sponsorship, really get into the racing and clean up, then jump straight into Formula 1'. Instead, though he did win four major races that year, his season was punctuated by a series of mechanical problems and numerous spectacular accidents which led him to be burdened with the infamous soubriquet: 'Hunt the Shunt'.

A change to 1600 cc engines eliminated the thrilling exhaust notes produced by the 1000 cc 'screamers', but Formula 3 racing was more frenetic than ever, as a host of ambitious and aggressive young men tried to barge their way to stardom.

At first, James seemed well-equipped to do battle, when March Engineering, having been impressed by his earlier drive for them at Cadwell Park, invited him to contest the season in their works car with sponsorship from Rose Bearings, manufacturers of joints used in the construction of racing cars.

James also had some sponsorship from Coca Cola again and his standard of living improved to the point that he could stay in cheap hotels instead of a tent. Though the team was well presented, money was always tight, and at several races James and his March crew were reduced to selling cans of Coca Cola to improve the cash flow. By scrimping and saving he finally paid off the debt for the wrecked Formula Ford and his new racing equipment cost him nothing. But soon James was calling the March 713 'disastrous' and its engine 'useless'.

Still, at the first continental race of the year, at Montlhery in France, his equipment was good enough for James to defeat the top international field, and he repeated this achievement two weeks later, at the mighty Nürburgring Circuit in Germany.

A few days later, in Barcelona, Spain, James was leading by a minute and a half when he touched the barriers after a sudden cloudburst soaked the track. Damage to the March's radiators caused the engine to overheat and he had to stop. He continued to figure prominently in several of the next races, not for winning them, but for exiting them spectacularly.

At Pau in France his March flew out of the race on the first lap when he was caught up in someone else's accident. He lasted longer in front of the home crowd at Silverstone, but on the last lap James was one of seven drivers arguing over the same piece of road when his March rammed the back of the Brabham driven by the Brazilian Jose Ferreira.

James's car was pitched high into the air and smashed heavily into the barriers. When Ferreira emerged from his car, which had tyre marks from the March on its bodywork, he was favouring an arm which proved to be fractured in three places. James was unhurt, but a week later he was injured in one of the most spectacular accidents of his career.

James arrived at Zandvoort with his March rebuilt after the Silverstone crash, but his weekend at the circuit in the sand dunes on the Dutch coast got off to a bad start when a seized engine limited his practice to just two laps.

Unaccustomed to starting from the last row of the grid he threw himself into the fray with even greater resolve than usual, though his March, perhaps not fully recovered from its previous accident, was not, he thought, handling up to par. James, however, had manhandled it up into the middle of pack by the end of the first of the two 20 lap preliminary heats and was optimistic about a strong finish in the final.

He was running in a group of half a dozen cars on the 11th lap when disaster struck at the notorious Tarzan corner, a 180 degree right-hand bend just beyond the Zandvoort pits where many drivers have come to grief.

The Hunt March made contact with another car and flipped upside down, its roll-bar protecting the driver's head snapped off and the inverted car skated along for a hundred yards, showering sparks on the tarmac, then throwing up a cloud of dust as it ploughed into the fencing on the outside of the corner.

Fearing the worst, the track marshals ran up to the car and struggled to right it. They were astonished when from inside the wreckage a voice began to curse vehemently.

James had saved his neck by pushing his head down between his knees inside the cockpit but during the wild ride, while hanging onto the steering wheel for dear life, his knuckles were scraped to the bone. He also suffered damaged vertebrae, torn back muscles and severe bruising, but these were relatively minor injuries from such a potentially lethal accident.

His biggest worry (in fact he later said it was his most fearful moment in racing) was being 'trapped upside down in the car which could have burst into flames at any moment'.

Brendan McInerney, who finished fourth in the race, witnessed the terrifying inversion from a ringside seat. 'I couldn't believe my eyes when I came around on the next lap. There he was sitting up beside his car. I just couldn't believe he was all right. But the accident happened when James was being naïve, trying to take a proper racing line through the corner with about six other Formula 3 guys slipstreaming all around him.

'There were plenty of laps to go. It wouldn't have mattered if he'd dropped to the back of the pack because within a lap he'd have been right back near the front again. But he was trying to drive as though there was no time left and nobody else there.'

McInerney noted that the crash was in fact the second physical trauma suffered by James that weekend in Holland. The previous evening they had gone out together for dinner, then retired to their adjoining hotel rooms. McInerney was just dosing off when he heard an almighty scream from next door.

'It turned out that James had an attack of crabs and was treating himself. The bottle of lotion had leaked and, rather than diluting it, he mopped it up with a towel and dabbed himself liberally with that. But it was a bit stronger than he anticipated when he applied it to the affected parts.'

A few weeks earlier, before the parts had become affected, they were put on exhibit before a shocked audience of patrons in a restaurant at Pau where some members of the Formula 3 circus gathered to dine, and wine, after the race. One of the journalists in the entourage bet James 100 francs that he wouldn't relieve himself on the restaurant floor. The challenge, according to Brendan McInerney, produced two inevitable results. 'One was that James pissed on the floor as he was leaving the restaurant – reversing out the door and laughing uproariously as he went about his business – and the other was the guy who bet him wouldn't pay up. James was extremely upset that he didn't get paid.'

James's carousing began to intensify dramatically, partly because he simply enjoyed a good time, partly because he was making up for lost time after his earlier financial deprivations, and partly because he thought his time might suddenly come up.

The fatalistic belief that there might be no tomorrow gained strength when he compared notes with another driver, after a particularly wild race in Sweden. The driver was Niki Lauda, who would go on to become James's adversary in an epic duel for the 1976 World Drivers' Championship. But in Sweden, where they were struggling Formula 3 drivers, the young Austrian and his British rival talked seriously about the dangers they faced.

'Racing drivers never talk among themselves about death', James said, 'but that night in Sweden I did discuss it with Niki. We came to a practical rather than some philosophical conclusion. We both realized that, because of the game we had chosen, there was really no point in leaving the celebrations till later.

'It was quite a simple rationalization. The chances were pretty high that we'd both get killed. So we decided, then and there, that we'd celebrate as we went along.'

☆ ☆ ☆

James's vow to live it up while he could, coupled with his naturally keen interest in other women, meant his fidelity to Ping, his long-suffering girlfriend, was seriously diluted. She had accompanied him to most of the races in England and occasionally travelled with him abroad. But she felt his solo continental forays, especially a couple of licentious sojourns among the liberated blonde ladies of Sweden, had led James too far astray ever to be recovered.

He dutifully sent her letters while he was away, but they tended to be race reports, not love letters, and there was never any mention of what he did at nights. Her distrust deepened when she discovered that his sudden cancellations of several of their prearranged rendezvous for supposed 'business meetings' in London were really assignations with other women.

'I suppose it happened over a year, and it was very difficult and painful for both of us. We were such good friends, had been through so much together and knew each other really well. When we were quite young, there was never anyone else. Just the two of us.

'We grew up together and the good times were unbelievably good, even when he was really down and out. And I suppose that's why I stayed with him for so long. Because I loved him a lot. And he said he did me too.

'But he changed. Maybe it was as if his life was like motor racing: the new challenge and the new conquest he felt he had to make, then move on to another. He'd always come back but he was never honest and open about what he had done, I suppose because he wanted to spare my feelings.

'He was a very loving, thoughtful person in his way but I knew in my heart of hearts he was never going to change. I might have tagged along a bit more, but got hurt a lot more. And I wasn't really prepared to spend my life sitting at home thinking, "Oh God, what's he up to tonight?"'

As Ping moved out of his life (they finally parted in May 1971, though they later became friends again) his family and friends in Surrey saw less of him too. James spent more and more time in London, where he stayed in a succession of flats. One of them, near the World's End in Chelsea, consisted of a single room containing little more than a large mattress, furnishings which his acquaintances saw as being particularly appropriate, given his priorities.

For a time James also shared a flat with Niki Lauda, who called him an 'open, honest-to-God pal'. On one occasion, when Lauda was living on his own, James remembered it was his friend's birthday and treated him to a night out on the town. Lauda thought James was 'game for anything and taking life as it came. With him around things were always pretty hectic, and there were always a couple of pretty girls about. James was always good at that'.

His casual dalliances with many girls twice blossomed into longer relationships. He was involved for several months with Michelle, a French girl who had been married previously, then had a more permanent arrangement with Chantal Lacluse, a waitress he met at a favourite hangout, Thierry's Restaurant on the King's Road in Chelsea.

Chantal, a Belgian national of Polish Jewish extraction, had married a champion boxer at the age of 16, then left him shortly after their baby died of meningitis. She was a tiny, slim girl with long black hair and a vivacious outgoing personality that complemented her racing driver boyfriend. James acquired a larger flat in Earl's Court Square and they moved in together, though the man-about-the-house was often not at home.

James threw himself with considerable gusto into the nightlife around the Earl's Court/King's Road/Fulham Road area, drinking in the neighbourhood pubs, chatting up the waitresses in the restaurants, often becoming the temporary object of their affections, and generally living his version of the good life as a young man about town in the London of the early 1970s.

James called this his 'hippy phase' and it went on long after most of the other 'flower children' had wilted. (Twenty years later he said he was still a hippy at heart, but 'too old to be practising'.) The contemporary fashion of casual attire and unkempt appearance suited him particularly well since it meant he didn't have to cut his shaggy fair hair, wash his grubby T-shirt, change his tattered jeans, or even wear shoes.

Also tailor-made for his personality was the trend to look at life from a 'laid back' perspective, to affect a worldly-wise state of weary nonchalance. Some achieved this by becoming 'spaced out' with drugs and alcohol, but James at this stage was not party to excessive substance abuse. He drank beer, but had a strict personal regimen of never imbibing after the Wednesday before a race. He tended to make up for the abstinence from Sunday night on, but didn't yet use alcohol, or drugs, to forget his troubles.

Though intense racing situations could cause his passions to boil over, James was able to roll with the punches in his private affairs more easily, and accepted most of the vagaries of his life with easy equanimity and, preferably, with humour. Brendan McInerney: 'James, I think, thought that life was a huge joke. He was constantly amused by things other people would do, as well as by the silly things he would do himself. He found everything very funny'.

When he was enjoying himself he did so with great enthusiasm and radiated an attractive bonhomie. 'James was always at the front end of the bar in the evening and he was the guy who likely had a girl on each arm', Nick Brittan recalls. 'He was larger than life, boisterous and excessive in nearly everything he did and he had a rather delightful arrogance. There's a fine line between supreme confidence and arrogance and James teetered on the brink. But I think people who are going places need that.'

Though James was still a long way from getting where he was eventually to go, he stood out in a crowd, not just because of his height, but through a natural 'presence', a pop star aura that commanded attention. He was even accorded a kind of celebrity status when he visited the pubs back home in Surrey.

In many ways he was still the same old James, but his conservative mates were impressed by his increasingly exotic lifestyle, and they listened with rapt attention as he regaled them with tales of his racing and after dark adventures. In London, Ian Phillips often met him socially. 'Even then James had star quality. Swanning around the hot spots of Chelsea he was a star, though all he had ever done of note at that stage was punch a fellow competitor on TV!'

While James never shied away from the attention, he didn't seek it out, nor did it swell his head. Brendan McInerney remembers James 'hated snobbery. He couldn't abide a bunch of people standing on ceremony and being pompous'.

But he could still muster up the necessary social graces when required. On one occasion James showed up without proper attire at the stately Berkeley Hotel, where McInerney's mother, on a visit from Dublin to see her son, had invited them to dinner. The hotel supplied James with a coat and tie and the evening was a great success. Mrs McInerney found him to be wonderfully charming and was especially impressed when James later sent her a thoughtful letter of thanks.

★ ★ ★

After his Zandvoort accident James missed several races while his hands healed, and when he returned to action Brendan McInerney, who had been running his own Brabham car without much success, became his team-mate.

The March Engineering team was reorganized and re-named Team Rose Bearings/Baty Group, the latter part of the appellation referring to new sponsorship from a manufacturer of precision engineering equipment. The revised team was set up by the experienced Formula 3 entrant Chris Marshall and based at his Sloane Marshall Garages in Barnes, from which premises McInerney and Hunt, outfitted with brand new March 713M cars and a transporter purchased by McInerney, tackled the rest of the season.

The new arrangement looked promising when James won their first race, at Crystal Palace, but this was followed by him retiring in disgust after a few laps at Brands Hatch, where he and McInerney were penalized one minute for jumping the start.

James's limited patience was further tested throughout the summer by a series of mechanical malfunctions, though he persevered to score several top three finishes, then managed an excellent victory at Brands Hatch, where he duelled mightily with the rapidly rising Formula 3 star, Roger Williamson, and beat him to the finish line by inches.

In late summer James made his Formula 2 debut when he was entered by March Engineering in an international event at Brands Hatch. For this one race James was given a well-used March 712M chassis, motivated by a down-on-power engine, with which to make his way in the 26 car entry.

His competition included the twice World Champion Graham Hill on a busman's holiday from the Formula 1 series, as well as Ronnie Peterson and Emerson Fittipaldi, who were beginning to establish their Formula 1 careers while continuing to race in Formula 2. Peterson won the race from Hill, while Hunt, though he finished in 12th place, acquitted himself well before being slowed by a misfiring engine.

James's mixed fortunes in Formula 3 continued for the rest of the season. He led another race at Crystal Palace, on a damp track, but spun and then was hit by another car. At Mallory Park he was relegated to the role of spectator after a practice crash wiped two wheels off his March. In practice at Snetterton he crashed heavily when a shock absorber broke and threw his car into an earth bank, where it was badly damaged.

Injuries to his shoulder and arm in this incident were diagnosed as torn ligaments, but he finished a plucky second at Thruxton, despite having trouble changing gears. James raced hard and well in the final events of the year, though the pain from his Snetterton crash persisted. It was only later that a second x-ray revealed a broken bone in his right forearm and a broken shoulder.

In his year-end review of the 1971 Formula 3 season the *Autosport* journalist Ian Phillips ranked David Walker, Jody Scheckter and Roger Williamson as the top three drivers. James Hunt was fifth and, Phillips wrote that he had been 'one of the disappointments of the year. The season started well enough but suddenly a run of accidents and mechanical problems struck.

'It seemed he was a victim of his own enthusiasm but he really suffered at the hands of those less experienced than himself who by the nature of Formula 3 were able to mix it with the quicker drivers. When he was able to get clear he proved that he was capable of showing everyone the way round and hopefully things will turn out better next season.'

'I actually believed in the guy', Phillips says, 'but it was bloody difficult to justify sometimes. Unfortunately his hot-headedness sometimes betrayed his sense of responsibility, which was highly developed.

'The thing that impressed you most when you got to know him was that he was an extremely intelligent person – probably one of the most intelligent racing drivers I've ever known. But for two or three years the things he was most famous for were thumping Morgan, having accidents and being called "Hunt the Shunt".'

Speaking of his 'Hunt the Shunt' label James said: 'It didn't bother me because, to the ease the pain, I told myself it was a natural rhyme and not necessarily an aspersion'.

Besides, he insisted, most of his shunts were triggered by other drivers who lost control of their cars and hit his. He admitted that he might have avoided some of them but for his 'over-eagerness and inexperience'. His self-instigated crashes were 'brought on by not really having a competitive car. I had to stick my neck out more than most, trying to make up for the deficiencies of my car'.

Brendan McInerney, who finished in the top six half a dozen times in 1971, agrees that they suffered from inferior equipment, particularly down-on-power engines. The same engine builders supplied several different teams and could only afford to give 'tender loving care' to two or three motors, which they then rationed out to certain 'favoured drivers, of which James certainly wasn't one.

'Guys like Dave Walker and Roger Williamson were, but I think it's also fair to say that Roger crashed as much as James, if not more, and nobody made any bones about it. In truth, if you didn't have two or three big crashes a year you just weren't trying.'

McInerney also remembers that while 'we all thought we were the bees' knees as drivers, in the back of our minds was the suspicion that one person might just be a bit better than the rest of us, and that was James.

'He wasn't a spectacular driver, like Jody Scheckter, just very quick and very smooth in a forceful sort of way. But the journalists were impressed by spectacular drivers and they would use words like "natural talent" and "car control" for people like Scheckter. I think it was just a lack of technique, which hadn't developed at that stage. Scheckter became a much smoother driver in Formula 1 but in Formula 3 his confidence was able to take him beyond his technique. So Scheckter got good press and James didn't.

'I was glad to see that James, even when he became a media person himself, was always looking for ways to deflate the egos of some of those media people.'

His Formula 3 team manager Chris Marshall also thought 'Hunt the Shunt' was a misnomer.

'You could have called anybody else 'The Shunt', because if you were in with a chance, fighting it out in the slipstreaming, and you dived out at the last minute and anything went wrong: Bang! – you were up in the air. So, it wasn't usually his fault. We thought James had enormous potential and he showed us tremendous determination.'

James's determination on one occasion saw Marshall negotiating with

Wallis and Sue Hunt on his driver's behalf. When James learned from his grandmother that he would inherit some money in her will he immediately wondered if the process could be speeded up and the funds applied to the worthy cause of furthering his racing career. Rather than waiting a few years, an injection of capital now, perhaps to buy better engines, would help him make his mark faster.

His sense of propriety prevented him from making such a proposition to his grandmother, but he was determined to explore the possibility. It would have to be done through his parents, who might advance him the funds and, James decided, Chris Marshall was just the man to persuade them to do it. After thoroughly briefing his – rather reluctant – advocate James arranged a meeting with Sue and Wallis.

'So James and I turned up on the appointed day', Marshall winces at the memory, 'at this lovely big house in Belmont. We went into the sitting room where proper tea was served by his mother, a very ladylike person. His parents were both very charming. We got the pleasantries over with and I explained that we were short of money to run James. If he could benefit from his inheritance now, at this crucial stage of his career, it could have enormous influence on his future.

'So his parents thought about this for a while. Then his father said "I have a simple philosophy. I believe that education is very important and we've given our six children the best education we possibly can. Then we leave them to it. James still has a room here. We have food in the kitchen. There will always be a meal. He'll always be welcome. But there is no money for racing. Would you like some more tea?"'

* * *

James, who was now 25, viewed the 1972 season with a growing sense of urgency. While he seemed to be going nowhere fast, his friend and rival Niki Lauda, who was nearly two years younger and had an even less impressive Formula 3 record and at least as many frightening accidents, had signed to drive with the March team in both the Formula 2 and Formula 1 series.

Never mind that Niki, from a prominent Viennese family, had bought his ride, paying March £35,000 borrowed from an Austrian bank and covered by a life insurance policy. James, instead of climbing further up the motor racing ladder, was still clinging rather precariously to a bottom rung.

When his strenuous efforts – letters, phone calls and personal visits – failed to produce anyone interested in sponsoring him in Formula 2 James reluctantly agreed to spend another year in Formula 3. He accepted an offer to join the STP March team, again with Brendan McInerney as his team-mate.

The STP March 723 cars looked impressive in their flame red livery (the colours of the petroleum product sponsor) but were plagued by inconsistent handling characteristics and a shortage of straight line speed. The mechanical shortcomings, political manoeuvring, dissent and strife within the team caused *Autosport* to describe the 1972 works STP March effort as 'shambolic'.

In the first race of the season, at Mallory Park, James finished third, but was told he could exclude himself from the results when his engine was found to contravene the rules. His car passed scrutineering at the next two races at Brands Hatch, but James's best efforts there could only produce distant fourth and fifth places. At Snetterton his March wandered alarmingly all over the circuit and James finished a despondent eighth.

He tangled with two other cars and crashed at Oulton Park, but bounced back to finish third at Mallory Park, where his duel with Roger Williamson was a highlight of the day. Two consecutive races at Silverstone resulted, respectively, in a depressing seventh place and another accident, this one caused when a spinning car punted his March off the track and hard into an earth bank. Before he could drive it again James was fired by the March team.

In early May the March cars failed to appear for a race at Zandvoort, ostensibly because new bodywork was being designed to improve straight line speed, but James, who was at the Dutch circuit as a reluctant spectator, sensed there was something more in the wind than aerodynamic changes.

There were rumours that March, chronically short of funds, had been approached by Ford of Germany with an attractive offer to find a place for their protege, Jochen Mass. If this was true, James's position would be vulnerable, since he was being paid by March while Brendan McInerney was paying his own way.

When James tried to contact his employers at the March factory in Bicester he found them mysteriously uncommunicative. He hoped they were applying all their energies to readying his equipment for the next event, the prestigious race supporting the Monaco Grand Prix, which was vitally important for drivers hoping to catch the eye of Formula 1 teams. But when he arrived in Monaco for the practice session there was no sign of his car.

James watched the first practice session in a state of considerable agitation. Eventually, very late at night, a March transporter drove into the Formula 3 paddock, but the car it bore was far from being ready to race.

The March, with its wheels pointing in all directions, had obviously been screwed together in haste and would require several hours of work to set it up for the final qualifying session, which was scheduled for very early the next morning. But the lone March mechanic told James he was exhausted from the long overland journey from England and was going to go to sleep.

James was furious and rushed off to consult his former team manager Chris Marshall, who was now running his own team using the March equipment from the 1971 season and money from French sponsors. Marshall explained to James that, since one of his French drivers had his licence temporarily suspended, he had a spare car. They decided that if James's regular machine was not ready at daylight, if the engine would not fire up when he pushed the starter button, James would drive Marshall's car.

When the STP March engine did not start on cue James duly qualified Marshall's Equipe La Vie Claire car for the Monaco Formula 3 Grand Prix.

James, emotionally and physically drained from what he described as 'the Monte Carlo fiasco', was dozing in the cockpit of his car while waiting to go out for his heat in the race when he was shaken awake by a messenger sent by March director Max Mosley.

The content of Mosley's message said, in effect, that James either drove the STP March or he left the team.

James, who by now was convinced that March was deliberately trying to freeze him out and that he was going to get fired anyway, pulled on his helmet and threw himself into the race, or rather into a guard rail, where the La Vie Claire car collapsed with suspension damage.

A few days after the Monaco race March formally announced that James Hunt had been dismissed and was being replaced by Jochen Mass, and that Brendan McInerney (who thought the car was 'horrendous' and the team 'terrible') had also left to pursue other avenues.

Speaking on behalf of March, Max Mosley admitted that the fault at Monaco, the delay in preparing the car and the failure to communicate with Hunt, lay with the factory, but the March directors felt it was wrong for their sponsors that Hunt should race for another team. This and the recent lack of results had brought about the firing. Besides, Mosley offered, Hunt would probably go much better without the pressures of being in a works team.

While James said privately that March had 'sabotaged' him at

Monaco, he modified his feelings for public consumption in a statement released to the press. 'It was only the climax of a situation which had existed all year, and it stemmed from a variety of problems caused basically by a lack of interest and enthusiasm. I made every effort to inject either interest or enthusiasm but without success. Thus I now feel that the interest of my career would be better served by racing on my own.'

He later summed up the reasons for his March dismissal with characteristic forthrightness: 'Ford Germany approached them with a bag of gold to put Mass in the car, so they fired me and snatched it'.

Max Mosley, one of the four founders of March Engineering (he was the 'M' in the name), continued to cross paths with James for the rest of his life. Mosley, educated trilingually in England, France and Germany, gained an honours degree in physics at Oxford (where he was secretary of the Union), was called to the Bar in 1964, and specialized as a barrister in Patent and Trade Mark law for three years. He then concentrated on his real interest, motor racing, where he reached the Formula 2 level in 1968, then retired from driving to set up the March organization at Bicester in Oxfordshire.

Mosley later played a key role (with his good friend Bernie Ecclestone) in creating the structure of modern Formula 1 racing and eventually became president of the governing body, the Fédération Internationale de l'Automobile, and thus the most powerful man in international motor sport.

James always called Max Mosley 'The Great Chicken of Bicester' or, when he was feeling more Continental, 'Le Grand Poulet de Bicester'. The nickname originated after James left March and joined Hesketh Racing, which was short of engines. Mosley was amused when he heard that James and the whole Hesketh team had been seen at one race congregated in a circle on their knees behind their transporter praying to the Great Chicken in the Sky to bring them another engine. He sent a message to James that March had a spare engine, and thus Mosley, the saviour, became the Great Chicken of Bicester.

According to Mosley this was just James's way of getting revenge for his own wordplay with Hunt's name when James first drove for March, at Cadwell Park in 1969, where he deputized for the injured Ronnie Peterson. At the time Mosley joked that his only choice for a replacement driver was between two accident-prone characters, Ian Ashley and James Hunt. 'I'm afraid I couldn't resist saying it would be either Crashley or Shunt.'

But Hunt the Shunt impressed Mosley at Brands Hatch and his later persuasive plea, in a letter which Mosley still has, got him the March ride. 'He made me a proposal which basically said, "I'll win". He was always very sure of himself. He was a very quick driver, though certainly not an obvious candidate for World Champion when he was driving for us in Formula 3. Of course that all ended up with us firing him, but our Monaco row was only a short affair and it was soon all amicable and friendly and we actually helped him get on his way again.

'One tends to forget all the hard work that went into getting up into Formula 1, the years of terrible effort, trying to find a sponsor here, scrape a drive there, the hardship of it all. It's only the most persistent people who succeed. And James was nothing if not persistent.'

The humiliation of being sacked by March only served to heighten James's determination. By now he was so accustomed to setbacks he used them as inspiration. Indeed, he thrived on adversarial situations to the point that if they didn't exist it sometimes seemed he went out of his way to create them, then employed the Hunt theory of reverse psychology to turn negatives into positives.

'I'm a great fatalist. Whenever I think I'm going to achieve something, it turns out that I don't. I always have to "negative think" to get the best out of myself.'

There was no need to manufacture adversity now, and following the Monaco debacle he met Chris Marshall to contemplate his uncertain future. Marshall told him he would be pleased to let James have one more race in his car, in Belgium, but after that his regular driver would get his licence back and James would be out of work. Since he had used up all his sponsorship money, Marshall suggested James should forget about racing for now, concentrate on seeking sponsorship for next year and get a job.

'We were sitting in my office', Marshall remembers, 'and he jumped up and thumped the desk so hard I thought for sure he was going to break his hand. "*No way! No way!* I'm not getting a job!" He really yelled at me. So I said, "Okay, fine, right. We'll have to find a Plan B".'

'Plan B' materialized in a toilet located in the middle of a manure-strewn Belgian cow pasture.

★   ★   ★

When he appeared in Marshall's La Vie Claire car at the Chimay circuit in rural Belgian James, in a thinly-veiled reference to his previous employers, pronounced himself 'delighted to be driving for a team with so much enthusiasm' and responded to his new circumstances by setting the second-fastest qualifying time, his best grid position of the year. That it was done in a year-old March 713M was particularly satisfying, since it added weight to his argument that the 1972 works Marches were uncompetitive.

On the first lap of the race James avoided an accident which sent two cars cartwheeling off the track, and he was lying seventh on the fifth lap when two other nearby cars crashed. Two laps later yet another collision put two more cars into the ditch, where one aggrieved driver began to pummel the other.

But James kept his head and was up into second place with three laps remaining when a tyre began to deflate, probably after he ran over some of the accident debris. He lost more ground in the slipstreaming dash to the finish line, but still finished a noteworthy fifth.

Among those who noticed him was one Anthony Horsley, who was driving a Dastle for a new team entered by Lord Alexander Hesketh. Hesketh Racing was looking for a second driver and Horsley had, through a third party, earlier investigated the possibility of running Hunt before James had signed with March.

Now, at Chimay, Horsley set out across the farm field that served as a paddock to find the former March driver. Meanwhile, James, in search of his Plan B, began looking for Horsley and 'we met in the middle of a field full of cowpats. For once I kept quiet and let Bubbles talk, which was great because it established our relationship from then on'.

'We sort of found each other', says Horsley. 'We sort of needed each other. It was a marriage of convenience. No other driver was exactly knocking on our door, we were frankly a huge bloody joke as a Formula 3 team. Nobody was about to give him a drive either.

'He was a naturally attractive character and one instantly became friendly with him. And he looked right. You looked at him and you said to yourself, "Now that bloke ought to be quick". You couldn't put your finger on it, it was just a feeling.'

James was quick to accept Horsley's invitation to meet the owner of the Hesketh team and the formal introduction took place in the Chimay loo, a fetid and tattered old army tent that had survived two world wars. Thus Anthony 'Bubbles' Horsley and Alexander 'The Good Lord' Hesketh entered James's life – but their partnership got off to a distinctly inauspicious start.

Lord Hesketh's first impression of his new recruit – 'this gangling, blond, long-haired, knock-kneed youth, smiling very nicely and obviously rather pleased with himself' – was tempered by the reputation which preceded him.

'Bubbles was of the opinion that James was quick, but I also knew he had this tremendous reputation for crashing cars. The first race I saw him drive for me was at Silverstone in the wet. He actually took the lead, which we'd never done before, indeed we'd never even been near the front of the grid. But when he was leading it was backwards – because he'd spun, he must have travelled about 40 yards in this way – then he crashed into the pit wall right in front of me, which I wasn't very impressed by.'

After laying a destroyed car at the feet of his patron, James's next misadventure was more serious. In fact, it finished Hesketh Racing's Formula 3 team.

In mid-July two Dastle Mk9s for Hunt and Horsley to drive were entered in the Brands Hatch Formula 3 race, a supporting event for the British Grand Prix. The weekend began badly for Hesketh when Bubbles' car was sidelined in a collision with another competitor during qualifying. Then his team-mate suffered a similar, but much more spectacular fate which caused James to admit that 'James thought James was going to die'.

He was following another car closely when a suddenly deflating tyre caused it to spin wildly. James threw his car into an avoidance spin but it wasn't successful, contact was made and the Dastle was launched skyward, where it performed terrifyingly complex aerial manoeuvres then crash-landed – upside down – astride the barrier on one side of the circuit. After teetering there for a moment, what was left of the Dastle righted itself and sagged slowly to the ground in a smoking heap.

Chris Marshall, who was watching how his own cars were performing at this particular corner, ran across to the former Dastle, with his heart in his mouth. 'But James was sitting there in the driver's seat with his finger on the start button screaming to himself "Fucking thing won't start! Fucking thing won't start!".

'He was so pumped up he didn't know what day it was and the adrenaline had to go somewhere. It took me some time to calm him down and persuade him to look over his shoulder. Then he saw why his car wouldn't start. The engine was on the other side of the track.'

James was uninjured in this accident, but more shunting was in store for him that weekend. In company with his girlfriend Chantal and Brendan McInerney (who qualified well in a new Ensign, but retired from the Formula 3 race with accident damage), James decided to watch the first part of the British Grand Prix at Brands Hatch. Then, to avoid the post-race traffic, they would dash across country to see the end of the race on television at his parent's home in Surrey. They set out on the journey in a Mini borrowed from another of James's close female acquaintances, Chris Marshall's secretary.

With James at the wheel the Mini was speeding around a corner when it encountered a Volvo on the wrong side of the road because its driver thought it was a one-way street. James was caught by surprise, there was a heavy impact as the two cars met head on, and another one as the Mini struck a tree.

McInerney, who was in the back seat and had room to manoeuvre, ducked his head down but was propelled with such force into the back of Chantal's seat that four of her ribs were broken. McInerney suffered shock and torn chest muscles and James was in considerable pain from injuries inflicted on his large frame in the cramped driver's seat.

Bloodied but unbowed, James, who treated himself with emergency first aid in the form of a pint of beer obtained from a nearby pub, was carted off to hospital. He was told his injuries, severe cuts and lacerations caused by a window winder gouging into his thigh and an eight track tape embedding itself in his knee, would require him to be hospitalized for up to a week. But he was released prematurely.

In an effort to cheer him up some of his Formula 3 mates procured a female 'specialist' to administer to the needs of the wounded driver in his hospital bed. When a shocked matron entered the room and discovered James, again with a pint of beer in his hand, and the lady engaged in a private therapy session he was sent packing for flagrant misuse of visiting hour privileges.

* * *

While his wounds healed James desperately sought ways to salvage something from his wreckage-strewn career. By now the 'Hunt the Shunt' reputation and his accident-about-to-happen image had frightened away all but a few loyal believers in his future.

Even his tenuous link with Hesketh seemed close to being severed, since the Lord himself had witnessed the destruction of his racing team at Brands Hatch and was put into further bad temper after becoming embroiled in a 'tedious' argument with some 'ghastly' circuit authorities over where his helicopter should be parked. Lord Hesketh was fed up. 'We were obviously going nowhere in Formula 3 and I thought it was all very boring.'

James, now a battle-scarred veteran of four largely unsuccessful years in the Formula 3 wars, had also had enough of the category, but certainly not of racing. Thus, using the skewed logic that had seen him overcome, or at least sidestep, so many obstacles in the past, he decided to abandon Formula 3 and enter Formula 2 racing. To accomplish this feat would require him finding such basic necessities as a car, an engine, four racing tyres and money to pay for them.

Together with Chris Marshall he devised a plot to prise a car away from March Engineering. They composed a letter to Max Mosley, threatening to sue March for unfairly dismissing James from his Formula 3 contract, although, the letter implied, they might perhaps be persuaded to forget the legal proceedings if a Formula 2 chassis was made available.

Mosley responded with a good-humoured telephone call ('Marshall, I'm the lawyer, you can't go around suing me!') but admitted they had a case. Mosley agreed to loan them an old March 712 chassis in which was installed an 1850 cc F2 engine, purchased by Lord Hesketh in lieu of the salary he had agreed to pay James in Formula 3.

An estate agent friend of Marshall's was persuaded to use the funding of the running costs of the car as a tax write-off, another friend was inveigled into contributing £1000 for tyres, 'Hesketh Racing' was painted on the side of the car, and the hastily cobbled up team appeared at Brands Hatch in late August 1972.

The event, the Rothmans 50,000, was for a combined field of Formula 1, Formula 5000, Formula 2 and sports cars. As expected, Emerson Fittipaldi, the current leader of the World Championship standings, ran away with the race in his Formula 1 Lotus, but James fared much better than might have been forecast.

Though handicapped by a smaller engine (most of the Formula 2 opposition had engines closer to the two litre displacement limit permitted in the formula), he was the second fastest Formula 2 qualifier. In the race he took on all comers and after 118 laps of smooth, well-judged and crash-free driving he finished an impressive fifth, behind three Formula 1 machines and a proper Formula 2 car. Equally rewarding for James and his makeshift team was the £2500 prize money, which would go toward contesting as many of the remaining Formula 2 races as possible.

A week later the Hesketh Racing entry gained more credibility when James qualified on the front row of the grid for a round of the European Formula 2 Championship at the Salzburgring in Austria. He ran with the leaders for many laps, but was forced to retire with a blown engine.

The continental trip was more successful at Albi in France, where James finished fifth, despite being hampered by a lack of engine power on the circuit's long straights and having to drive much of the race with no clutch.

Also at Albi James's battered body began to play up on him. Nerve damage to his leg caused him such discomfort that the start of a preliminary heat was delayed while he was helped from his car and taken for a walk to restore circulation.

In the next race, at Hockenheim in Germany, the leg was less troublesome, but an engine misfire cost him several places and he dropped back to eighth at the finish. But the real turning point of 1972 came closer to home, at Oulton Park, where a top field of international drivers gathered to contest the final round of the British Formula 2 series.

Leading the entry list were John Surtees and Graham Hill, both former World Champions, as well as people like Ronnie Peterson, Jody Scheckter, Tim Schenken, Roger Williamson and Niki Lauda, all of whom had gone on to make names for themselves while James had languished in Formula 3.

At Oulton Park this formidable opposition also had the benefit of better equipment and more professional organizations backing them up, but James immediately qualified his elderly March a sensational second, right behind Peterson in the state-of-the-art works March car. While the rest of the field continued to pound around the circuit, James parked his car to save his one and only engine, because there was no money to buy another.

At the end of the first racing lap Hunt was fourth, behind Scheckter, Peterson and Schenken, and ahead of Lauda, who was driving the second factory-entered March. When Scheckter dropped out with clutch failure, Schenken led briefly, then stopped with a broken fuel pump. Their retirements left Hunt in second, sandwiched between the March team-mates Peterson and Lauda.

Half way through the 40 lap race the rear wing on Hunt's car began to sag, causing his car to oversteer dramatically, but the Hesketh Racing machine stayed glued to Peterson's gearbox and continued to fend off Lauda's best efforts. Hunt's wing looked progressively more fragile, yet his persistent pursuit of Peterson became even more aggressive.

With four laps to go Hunt drew alongside Peterson on the main straight, out-braked him into the next corner and forced the Swede to give way. Hunt's car snaked viciously as it crossed the line in first place, with Peterson and Lauda snapping at his heels, rather embarrassed at being led by a newcomer in an old March and trying everything they knew to restore the balance of power.

With a couple of laps to go the determined Peterson barged down the inside of a tight corner, forcing Hunt onto the spent rubber and dirt on the outside of the track. The reduced adhesion caused Hunt's car to twitch wildly, then plough off into the undergrowth.

The Hesketh Racing March was undamaged, but the 17 seconds it took Hunt to extricate himself from the weeds put him back into third place, where he finished, behind Peterson and Lauda. But he got a hero's reception from the enthralled crowd at Oulton Park and among the first to congratulate James were the works March team-mates Ronnie Peterson and Niki Lauda. They weren't surprised at the gritty performance of their former Formula 3 rival and both were genuinely happy to see James finally get a share of the success they felt he deserved.

James was particularly pleased at causing March 'embarrassment by blowing their cars into the weeds at Oulton Park'. His showing there also served to rekindle Lord Hesketh's interest in his driver's potential. He had missed the race (he was on a shooting holiday in Scotland), but the idea of a more serious effort by his team appealed to Hesketh's competitive instincts. Hesketh was impressed that James, in inferior equipment, could challenge the likes of Peterson and Lauda in better cars. Hesketh also liked backing an underdog and defying the nay-sayers.

'The critics were very rude about him: "Hunt the Shunt", bit of a wild boy, and all that. Well, I thought, if these guys think they're so brilliant, this is a challenge to take on the establishment.'

At a meeting in the 'Good Lord's' London office, Hesketh House in Mayfair, it was decided that Hesketh Racing would be reorganized, with Bubbles Horsley as team manager, to back James for a full assault on the European Formula 2 Championship in 1973. Meanwhile, they would gain experience by finishing off 1972 in South America, in the Brazilian Torneo Formula 2 series of three races at the Interlagos circuit in São Paulo.

The Torneo organizers flew 20 F2 cars out from England to South America for some of the top international drivers, including the local hero and Formula 1 star Emerson Fittipaldi, who had just become the first Brazilian World Drivers' Champion, and the newly crowned European Formula 2 Champion Mike Hailwood. In terms of his racing achievements James ranked well down the entry list and his car was still not on a par with most of the competition.

Despite handling problems at the first race he qualified seventh on the grid and finished fifth overall in the two-heat event. The next weekend James qualified near the front but crashed heavily in the pre-race warm-up. He missed the first heat while rudimentary repairs were made so that his car could complete the first lap of the second heat and thus qualify for the start money. In the final Brazilian race the rebuilt

Hesketh Racing March stayed on the road and went well enough for James to be classified fourth overall, and he was ranked sixth in the series.

His Lordship had not made the trip to Brazil but the telex in his London office kept him up to date with news of the mixed fortunes of his team and the hectic social activities of his driver.

According to the journalist Ian Phillips, James was the 'tour leader of the British contingent. It was all overgrown schoolboy stuff, which irritated the authorities immensely, but somehow James always got away with it. He ended up getting an invitation to play in the Brazilian Open golf tournament, while I ended up spending 48 hours in jail!'.

Alan Henry, another journalist on the trip, was impressed by the strength of James's magnetism. 'The first time I shook hands with him it was like putting your hand in a vice. I remember thinking, "Well, he's not your average wimp by any stretch of the imagination". He was very powerful, both from a physique point of view and through his presence.

'He was an attractive character with quite a thrusting personality so that you were always aware of James, whatever he was doing. And the bloke's energy was extraordinary. It wasn't just a question of all the booze and birds, it was his lack of sleep. He must have got by on two or three hours sleep a night when he was hell-raising in Brazil.'

Ian Phillips remembers that one of James's late night pranks (of a libidinal and potentially libellous nature) so grossly offended an influential female member of the British entourage that she was moved to scream at James, according to Phillips: '"My husband and I will ensure that you never, ever get into Formula 1!". That pompous outburst remains etched in my mind. For James it was another notch in the tightening belt of his resolve to buck the establishment'.

As a racing venture his month in Brazil was not particularly impressive, but as a dress rehearsal for the high jinks James and Hesketh Racing were to become famous for it was a roaring success.

4

SUPERSTAR

1973

Thomas Alexander, third Baron Hesketh of Hesketh, went on to become Government Chief Whip in the House of Lords and a respected pillar of the establishment. But as the proprietor of Hesketh Racing the portly (245 lb) and flamboyant 22-year-old was called 'a Falstaffian figure' and 'an eccentric British peer'.

At the age of five he succeeded his father to the peerage and in 1971 he inherited part of the family fortune and the estate, Easton Neston, near Towcester in Northamptonshire. The Hesketh holdings (which all became his in 1980) include 9000 acres of farmland and the Towcester racecourse and, though Easton Neston is within earshot of the Silverstone circuit, Alexander was brought up to appreciate horseflesh more than horsepower.

His first motor sport experience, competing in a local car rally, ended 'when I had a slight misunderstanding with one of my tenant farmer's combine harvesters and wrote off the car. Most embarrassing'.

When he was 15 the rebellious Alexander ran away from Ampleforth College in Yorkshire, though his education was eventually salvaged at a crammer where he got three O-levels. His experiments in the workaday world included stints selling used cars in Leicestershire and ship-broking in Hong Kong. To acquaint himself with the intricacies of financial management, Alexander also spent some time working in an investment bank in California, where, presumably, he also absorbed aspects of conspicuous consumerism.

The youthful Lord Hesketh kept track of time with a diamond-encrusted gold Rolex watch and wore monogrammed and coroneted shirts, augmented on more formal occasions by a white suit with a red carnation in the lapel. His personal transport included a Jet Ranger helicopter, a Porsche Carrera RS, an SSK Mercedes and a chauffeur-driven, telephone-equipped Rolls Royce Silver Shadow, each panel of which was outlined in a yellow pinstripe. He smoked expensive cigars, quaffed the finest champagne, enjoyed the company of beautiful young women and 'had quite a low boredom threshold'.

So had Bubbles Horsley, whom Alexander met at a mutual friend's wedding in 1967 when Horsley was going through his motor trading phase. 'Alexander was pointed out to me as a young man who had rather a lot of money. I had in stock a Rolls Royce so I thought I could sell him that. By the end of the day, both slightly the worse for wear, I ended up buying his Mercedes. He was only about 17 at the time and it turned out it was his mother's Mercedes. So I had to give it back, and chase him for the money. But we became friends and stayed in contact.'

Anthony Horsley, born in Newmarket in 1943, was educated at Dover College in Kent and studied estate management at Cirencester only long enough to realize it was not for him. In 1962 he went to London to seek his fortune, but instead found work first as a restaurant waiter and subsequently as a van driver and sales manager for a motor racing team based in Shepherd's Bush, an area of London which also harboured such racing personalities as Piers Courage (the brewing family heir who was killed in the 1970 Dutch Grand Prix) and Frank Williams (who went on to found one of the most successful Formula 1 teams). When Horsley promoted himself to racing driver by acquiring a racing car from a well-known lady racer, Bluebell Gibbs, her name became his nickname, which was then contracted by Piers Courage to Bubbles.

Bubbles spent the mid-1960s wandering around Europe as a Formula 3 nomad, sleeping 'among the bits' in the back of a van and scraping a living from the prize and appearance money, much as James did a few years later. His continental racing adventures ended when he crashed into Frank Williams' car at the Nurburgring in Germany. 'I was so busy watching this prune, who later turned out to be Frank, bouncing through the trees that I followed him in sympathy. The net result was a great big binge in Hamburg to celebrate and back to England with a few quid's worth of broken car in the back of my van.'

The carless Horsley was twiddling his thumbs one day when another former driver asked him '"What are you doing?". I said "Nothing". So he said "Let's go to Bhutan then". And we did, in an old Land Rover'.

During his year long tour of the Far East, mainly in India and Nepal,

Bubbles sought spiritual enlightenment, fished, hunted and spent all his savings. On his return he resumed dabbling in the car trade as the proprietor of Horsley's Horseless Carriages, though Frank Williams suggested a more accurate name for the enterprise might be 'Horseless, Gearless and Brakeless carriages'.

Bubbles purveyed secondhand vans and became something of a guru to ambitious hippies who wanted to emulate his travels to the exotic East. He also supplemented his income by becoming an actor, mainly in television commercials extolling the virtues of beer and sausages. In 1971, when Alexander Hesketh returned from his year in America, they 'partly out of boredom, as a sort of weekend hobby, decided to go racing'.

As a racing driver Bubbles Horsley's suspicions that he was a better actor or car dealer were confirmed shortly after he met James Hunt among the cowpats in Belgium and hired him to drive for Hesketh Racing. When he saw how quickly James went, Bubbles, who was then running the team as well as driving, happily relinquished his seat in the cockpit and by 'self-appointment' assumed the role of team manager.

'When we started it was a very laissez faire arrangement because we never really had any future strategy mapped out as to what we were trying to do or where we were going to go with the project. But when James started doing well in our cars his future career gave us a focus and we said, "Okay, let's go for it".'

⋆   ⋆   ⋆

Early in 1973 Hesketh Racing announced that not only would James Hunt contest the Formula 2 series in a new Surtees TS15, he would also some time during the year make his Formula 1 debut, in a Surtees T59B, as part of an exploratory program prior to embarking on a full Formula 1 season in 1974.

This startling news was greeted with considerable scepticism by the motor racing establishment. There was amazement at the arrogance and presumption of Hesketh Racing, owned by a zany, playboy peer and managed by a failed Formula 3 driver named Bubbles, whose ignorance of the finer points of the sport was confirmed by his choice of driver.

While Hesketh's plans represented an amazing change of fortune for James, his critics felt he would always be 'Hunt the Shunt'. Playing into their hands was the broken arm James suffered a few weeks before the start of the season. 'I was down in the country having lunch', said James, 'then started playing silly games on the lawn afterwards, like they do in the country, and just fell over.'

For disbelievers this laconic public schoolboy explanation only reinforced their conviction that the incorrigible Hunt lacked the necessary seriousness of intent ever to become a proper racing driver. Further ridicule was heaped on his absurdly ambitious upstart team when it was learned that the Hesketh personnel would defy the tradition of dull, drab (and usually dirty) uniforms by being kitted out in garish outfits 'like American footballers'.

For his team colours Lord Hesketh chose stripes of red, white and blue on a white background, not because they were the racing colours of the Hesketh stables, but for reasons of patriotism. In the past motor racing entries from various countries were assigned colours: silver for Germany, red for Italy, green for Britain, and so on. Lord Hesketh thought 'British racing green was magnificent, though rather too subtle. But I'm a great believer in this country. So we ran with the colours of the Union Jack'.

In the tradition of American footballers the Hesketh Racing team members had their names stencilled on their shirts and anoraks. Alexander thought it 'would look rather ridiculous' to give such prominence to 'Lord Hesketh' but wanted something to show he was the proprietor. He chose 'Le Patron' which was originally used by the famous French car constructor and racing team entrant Ettore Bugatti.

The team mechanics rejoiced in such labels as 'Ball Of String', 'Ferret', 'Rabbit' and 'Thomas The Tank Engine'. Bubbles was, of course, 'Bubbles' (and still signs cheques and legal documents that way). Le Patron, still referred to by James as 'The Good Lord', called his driver '"Superstar", because I thought it was very important to endorse the product early on so there was no misunderstanding'.

To 'bait the pompous' motor racing establishment was a prime motivator for Lord Hesketh, who still derives considerable satisfaction from having done that. 'At the top of every undertaking, in sport, in politics, you name it, the establishment always like to preserve the impression that they have a number of great skills and arts which are not easily acquired or, even more to the point, impossible to acquire. And one of the great advantages of being young is that you can take that on. You don't mind driving into brick walls and picking yourself up and carrying on. With perseverance and a bit of luck you can make huge strides. And that's what we did.'

When Hesketh Racing arrived at Mallory Park for the 1973 season-opener the team workers in matching outfits of T-shirts, jackets and trousers set up the racing car while a steady procession of helicopters and limousines ferried in Lord Hesketh's entourage. With their needs attended to by a liveried butler who dispensed champagne and caviar the Hesketh 'hangers-on' proceeded to enjoy themselves boisterously – as if they were at the kind of country house weekend where people fall over and break their arms.

James, whose arm was healing nicely, was quick to take advantage of this atmosphere, though equally quick to point out that it masked a strong sense of purpose. 'Alexander would bring his mates and they'd have a huge party. But behind the smokescreen – because it was very difficult to see through – the team were very serious and professional. The combination of fun and seriousness suited me. When I was concentrating on the race it didn't interfere or bother me having all the fun around. They were a jolly nice crowd, and after the race, when it was time to stop work, I was able to join the party.'

Some observers at Mallory Park found Hesketh Racing's extrovert behaviour refreshingly entertaining, but many thought it had no place in motor sport. 'More money than sense', said the nay-sayers, and they were unsympathetic when 'Superstar', who qualified well, retired from the race after the right front wheel fell off his car.

Undeterred, Hesketh's merry band of racing rebels appeared a week later at Brands Hatch, where James made his Formula 1 debut in the Race of Champions. He qualified his Surtees T59B a respectable 13th in the field of 29 cars, which included several F5000 machines, but admitted the transformation to the extra power and grip of a Formula 1 car was not going to be easy.

'The car is driving me', James said, and his baptism was further complicated by a blown engine and a sticking throttle during practice and qualifying. However, everything came together in the race, and in the final few laps, urged on by 'Go' signs on the signalling board wielded by Le Patron in the Hesketh pit, and 45,000 wildly cheering fans around the circuit, James sped to a splendid third place at the chequered flag.

As soon as their Brands Hatch celebrations were over Hesketh Racing set about trying to improve their Formula 2 effort. To increase the straight line speed of the Surtees TS15, Bubbles and his crew removed its wings and brought it to the Goodwood circuit for a test session.

Their aerodynamic theories proved to be correct, to a point, and James flew around Goodwood at an impressive rate for a few laps. But the wings had also served to keep the car on the ground, a fact that was made breathtakingly obvious when the car became airborne and James soared high over an embankment. While the experiment may have set the Formula 2 altitude record it also suggested Hesketh needed engineering help.

The rebuilt car, with wings firmly in place, was brought to Germany for the first race of the European Formula 2 season. Three chauffeur-driven Mercedes limousines, linked by radio, transported the Hesketh army into the Hockenheim paddock, but the team's racing car again proved troublesome. A fuel pump belt fell off in practice, stranding James out in the forest at the far end of the circuit. His race also ended there, before it started, when a diaphragm in the metering unit fractured on the pace lap.

Bubbles' explanation of the problem mystified the German journalists who were unaccustomed to his British sense of humour. 'A bloody great buzzard flew out of the trees and landed on the rollover bar, whereupon it proceeded to peck through a fuel line before attacking James's helmet. It got so bad he just had to stop.'

According to Bubbles the same buzzard followed the team back to England, to the Thruxton circuit, where it attacked him while he was unloading the Formula 2 car from the transporter. In his agony Bubbles dropped the car and a wheel crushed Lord Hesketh's foot, breaking a bone. Perhaps the offending buzzard also pecked a hole in a tyre because a puncture put James out of contention in the Thruxton race and he finished a deflated tenth.

Lord Hesketh missed the next avian attack, not because of his broken foot, but because as patron of the Northampton Scout Troop his presence was required at the trooping of the colour ceremony at Buckingham Palace. His racing colours did not fly well at the Nürburgring in Germany, where James's Surtees was plagued by boiling brake fluid in qualifying, and he retired from the race with more tyre trouble.

The team's woes worsened at Pau in France, where a mechanic broke his arm in a paddock mishap and James wiped off the front of the car in a practice crash. The car was withdrawn from the race.

However, all was not lost for James, who befriended Miss Pau and spent the rest of the weekend, which turned out to be his last in Formula 2, with the beauty queen.

Bubbles and James were becoming fearful that Le Patron might become bored with his racing enterprise and move on to something else.

In explaining his reason for funding Hesketh racing Lord Hesketh said: 'A lot of people want to make a lot of money to store it away. I want to make a lot of money to be able to spend it. I like spending to create something which is entirely my own and this is why I have the racing team'.

But the road to riches for a private entrant in motor racing is rocky, and Le Patron soon learned the truth of the old adage that it's easy to become a millionaire in the sport as long as you're prepared to spend two million to get it.

All the other Formula 1 teams were funded by sponsors, some of them to the tune of several million pounds. John Player Team Lotus, Elf Team Tyrrell, Yardley Team McLaren, Marlboro BRM and the others measured their success in terms of public exposure for the brand names and consumer product messages that adorned the bodywork of their cars.

But the defiantly pure livery of the Hesketh March, white with the Union Jack stripes, meant the team was racing for the glory of Britain and Le Patron's personal satisfaction. Thus, his return from his investment would have to come from seeing his team produce positive results and he admits that he 'used to be hysterical with fury if we weren't on the first three rows of the grid'.

Since Formula 2 was causing him hysterics it took little persuasion for Bubbles and James to convince Le Patron to accelerate their Formula 1 program. James noted that 'Alexander was very encouraged and excited when we came third in the Race of Champions, our first Formula 1 race. His attitude was that we were doing pretty badly in Formula 2 and for very little additional cost we could do badly in Formula 1!

'He felt that there would be a hell of a lot more fun doing proper Grand Prix racing, so he said, "Let's go and mess about at the back of Formula 1". Monaco happened to be the first race that we were ready for. But that suited his Lordship very well. He could arrive with a bit of flash!'

★ ★ ★

Hesketh Racing's headquarters at the Monaco Grand Prix was aboard the 162 foot *Southern Breeze*, one of the biggest yachts in the harbour, but not big enough for Le Patron, who was disappointed to find another team had commandeered a craft 20 feet longer than his. He took some solace in having the most exotic tender in the harbour, his Bell Jet Ranger helicopter, with which he whisked his guests back and forth from the Nice airport.

For ground transportation there was the pinstriped Rolls Royce Corniche, an exotic new Porsche Carrera and an expensive Suzuki motorcycle. The galley in the *Southern Breeze* was presided over by a master chef, but the crew seemed composed mostly of scantily clad nubile young ladies.

In the Hesketh pit, under the umbrella pines beside the harbour, sat a brand new March 731, which had been bought from Max 'The Great Chicken of Bicester' Mosley, to replace the hired Surtees Formula 1 car. Watching over the March was the team's new recruit, Dr Harvey Postlethwaite PhD, who had been lured away from March Engineering, where he was the chief development engineer.

'The Doc', as he became known at Hesketh, was highly respected in the rather black art of designing racing cars, though his detached, professorial demeanour meant that he was considered to be something of an eccentric in racing circles. Confirmation of this, for many at Monaco, was his decision to associate himself with Le Patron's band of dashing dilettantes. The Doc's explanation of his move to Hesketh was that 'They got me drunk'.

Pete Lyons, the veteran *Autosport* Grand Prix journalist, was amused by Hesketh Racing's gaudy trappings and colourful antics and welcomed the team as a breath of fresh air in the staid and rigidly conformist 'F1 circus'. He was particularly intrigued by 'Superstar', the Hesketh driver.

'He looked to be comfortable on the Monte Carlo quais', Lyons wrote. 'Tall, lean, good looking in a hard-lined sort of way, he favoured shirts that showed the fine suntan and the strings of beads on his chest, and his splendid Nordic hair was left dashingly long.

'He made a good photographer's fashion model; or perhaps he was a rising film actor; or maybe he was only a rich playboy. But anyway he fitted in well on the Riviera. He had the kind of appearance that attracts the eye; once seen, he was remembered.'

James was anything but comfortable and composed as he sat strapped into the cockpit of the March on the Monaco starting grid. After qualifying 18th in the field of 25 cars, here he was buried among all the famous names in racing.

On the front row were Jackie Stewart in his Tyrrell and Ronnie Peterson in a Lotus. Next up were Denny Hulme in a McLaren and Stewart's team mate François Cevert, followed by Emerson Fittipaldi in the other Lotus and Niki Lauda in a BRM. There were several other drivers James had raced against before, but any comforting familiarity he felt was dwarfed by his fears about what lay ahead in his first Grand Prix.

The Monaco circuit had mercifully not claimed many lives, but in this race six years earlier Lorenzo Bandini had been burned to death in his Ferrari. Sitting there, surrounded by 40 gallons of volatile petrol in the fat-tyred March's fuel tanks, and with power the equivalent of 500 runaway horses reverberating against his backside, James was petrified.

'I was nervous, very nervous. Before any race I became nervous, particularly if it was important to me. And that race was very important. Monaco is a pretty tough place to start a Grand Prix career. The track is so narrow, you're shifting gears all the time and there is absolutely no room for error. Five hundred horsepower is a lot to tame in that confined space. Before I got into the car I was puking all over the place and on the grid I was just a shaking wreck.'

He also had a severe headache. 'I had gone home and stayed with my parents in order that I could become really fit before my first Grand Prix. I was fit as a fiddle from the neck down but I had been having blinding headaches four or five days a week. I was frightened to go and get anything done because I thought there might be something seriously wrong.

'Later I had it attended to and found it was a legacy of some of my shunts. I'd gone on my head so many times my neck muscles had sort of seized up from the abuse and the blood supply was restricted. I was right as rain after treatment, but I was very worried about my fitness at Monaco.'

Alone in the cockpit James blinked rapidly, trying to concentrate on the task at hand. Steeling himself for the start, he was oblivious to the mass of humanity packed into the tiny Principality to witness the most glamorous of all motor races.

James's forward view was confined to the wide rear wings and tyres of the cars immediately in front of his March. He glanced at his instrument panel where the needle of the rev counter flicked up and down in response to his agitated right foot tramping on the accelerator pedal. Were his heart being monitored it would register levels three times its normal rate.

As he popped the clutch James's helmet jerked backward and banged on the rollbar. Immediately the discomforts of his churning stomach and splitting headache were obliterated in billowing clouds of tyre and oil smoke and the blast of noise from 12,500 collective horsepower.

As the pack erupted forward in a melee of shaking metal and spinning rubber that spanned the full width of the road, James's gloved right hand flicked the tiny gear lever from first into second, then third, while his left hand remained firmly clenched on the small, thickly padded steering wheel. His large racing shoes, with the toes cut away so that he could operate the pedals in the narrow footwell, tapped out a frantic tattoo on the clutch and accelerator.

The March slingshotted forward with tremendous velocity, then slowed abruptly as James's right foot stomped hard on the brake to negotiate Monaco's first corner, the Ste Devote hairpin. There were 78 laps to go, but already his driving suit was soaked with perspiration and the sweat was pouring off his forehead beneath his fireproof balaclava.

While Jackie Stewart went on to an untroubled win at Monaco, his 25th World Championship victory in 90 Grand Prix appearances, James Hunt was classified ninth at the finish of his first Grand Prix, though his car did not take the chequered flag. When the engine in his March blew up on the 73rd lap, James, who had been running as high as sixth, was not unhappy to end what had become an ordeal that left him white-faced and trembling with exhaustion.

'I was going well for the first third of the race, then suddenly it hit me. I couldn't drive at that pace any more. I was simply going to drive off the road. The heat plus the physical effort of driving the car had me completely knackered.'

But he recovered quickly and was able to participate fully in the post-race celebrations, which lasted until dawn. The mood was especially festive for James, who just one year ago had been unceremoniously fired by the March Formula 3 team at this same event.

Aboard the *Southern Breeze* Hesketh Racing's happy-go-lucky band of amateurs toasted what for them amounted to a thrashing of the Formula 1 professionals who had greeted their arrival with hoots of derision.

There was even more embarrassment for the Formula 1 establishment at the Paul Ricard circuit in France. The scoring system, which awarded points to the first six finishers, meant Ronnie Peterson got nine points for winning the French Grand Prix, six points went to François Cevert for finishing second, followed by Carlos Reutemann (four points), Jackie Stewart (three) and Jacky Ickx (two points).

The best of the remaining 19 drivers in the field was James Hunt who, by finishing sixth, scored one point in the World Drivers' Championship. Thus, James got his name into the record book in only his second Grand Prix.

In the race James showed great presence of mind when the air scoop on the engine cover of his March came loose, and he veered the car from side to side to dislodge it. He did this to avoid being black-flagged by the authorities to come into the pits for repairs. But the sight of the vigorously weaving Hesketh March might also have been interpreted as a cheeky gesture of defiance at the Formula 1 regulars, some of whom glowered resentfully at the audacious newcomer.

While James took great satisfaction in so quickly distancing himself from his 'Hunt the Shunt' image, he was under no illusions about deserving his Superstar nickname.

'I don't consider myself as somebody who's got enormous natural talent. I'd put myself in the second rank, behind people like Peterson. I can drive a car about as quickly as, say, the Fittipaldis and the Reutemanns and the Scheckters. Maybe I can't do one-off banzai laps in practice like Ronnie, but I reckon I can get the job done over 80 laps or so. Even Ronnie has got to drive a race distance like the rest of us mortals, and a Grand Prix is quite a strain, both mentally and physically.'

This latter aspect of Formula 1 racing was one where James felt he could gain an advantage, and with typical resolve he threw himself into a rigorous fitness regimen. He began working out with Chelsea Football Club. From the players he learned a method of strengthening his weak neck muscles – he spent lengthy periods lying on his back and heading a ball against a wall – and to build up his endurance he began running, everywhere.

'I carry my running kit with me wherever I go. In London, for instance, at seven in the evening, or whenever, you'll see me padding out for my daily run, rain or shine. Even if I've just done two good hard hours of tennis or squash I always try to follow it up with a run. Maybe I don't really need it physically by then, but I look at is as being good for mental discipline. It can't hurt to do something that hurts.'

But James, unlike his uncle Father Boniface Hunt, a Benedictine monk in Lancashire, was not about to adopt a completely monastic lifestyle. 'It was good that I chose racing: that way I still have a bit more room for social frills. Now I can be chatting up a bird and were I a serious professional athlete I'd have to go off to bed at ten. But as a racing driver I can perhaps stay with her another hour, and that might make all the difference!'

★ ★ ★

As confirmation of his increasing respectability as a driver, James was invited to enter the 1000 mile Tour of Britain, a mixture of racing and rallying held over three days on public and private roads, as well as several race tracks, in southern England. James, with *Autosport* magazine's deputy editor Robert Fearnall as his co-driver, spun his unfamiliar Chevrolet Camaro early on, in order, he said 'to get it out of my system'.

According to Fearnall, 'James intended to blow up the Camaro's engine at the special stage around Silverstone, since this was just down the road from Lord Hesketh's pile, to which we would adjourn for a bit of a party'.

But when he was fastest on the Silverstone stage and the engine held together, James became serious about the competition and, against everyone's expectations, including his own, he went on to win the event.

Shortly after this James was able to enjoy a party at Hesketh's Easton Neston estate; in fact, he was the guest of honour. The occasion was following the British Grand Prix at nearby Silverstone, where the patriotic Hesketh Racing team was particularly keen to show well. It was also their 'home' circuit: they knew it well and their confidence level was much higher than might be expected of a team in only its third world championship race.

The red, white and blue Hesketh helicopter beat a steady path between Easton Neston and the circuit and the usual limousine transfer service operated at peak capacity all weekend. At the Hesketh hospitality pavilion in the Silverstone paddock lobster was one of the four main courses on the menu. Le Patron bustled about entertaining his guests, most of whom knew very little about the sport which now consumed their colourful host. 'Formula 1 racing', he explained, 'is like a very flat bottle of champagne. We intend to give it a vigorous shake.'

James, who moved easily between the social and practical sides of the team, described how the two divisions differed. 'There were the workers who came along and stuck their noses to the grindstone and worked extremely hard. Then there were Alexander's friends, a set of extremely keen and committed partiers. For them, it was the same as a weekend in the country. They would certainly be on the vodka by ten in the morning had they been up at Easton Neston, so they just moved the party along with the racing team.'

During practice and qualifying at Silverstone it seemed Hesketh's social division was destined for more success than the workers. James was quick enough when he was on the track, but a balky gearbox limited him to just a few laps. When it was repaired he only managed nine fast laps before a front wishbone snapped as he braked heavily for a fast corner. It was 'a very nasty experience', though fortunately he was able to keep control of the car.

After the suspension problem was rectified the engine began to lose power and James had to stop. Nevertheless, he had recorded a time good enough to place the Hesketh March 11th on the starting grid.

James was 'highly suspicious of our situation as regards reliability'. However, 'I was enormously encouraged by my qualifying time after so few laps. I had known that I could be very competitive at Silverstone.

You do know these things, you see, although you don't tell people about it in case it doesn't come off and you look a bit of a twit.'

On the first lap of the race James did not look like a bit of a twit; indeed, he did not look at all. 'I crouched down, put my head under the dashboard and closed my eyes.'

His defensive posture was in response to the enormous accident which caused the race to be stopped. The incident, which involved nine of the 28 starters, was triggered when the South African Jody Scheckter lost control of his McLaren on the exit of Woodcote, Silverstone's fastest corner, and spun into the path of oncoming traffic.

The first few following cars swerved safely around the wrecked McLaren but the detours attempted by others caused a chain reaction of frightening spins and crashes. The start/finish line was immediately transformed into a scene resembling a massive motorway pile-up and the red flag was shown to stop the race. Mercifully, the only driver injury was a broken ankle suffered by the Italian Andrea de Adamich, but there had been many near misses.

As James prepared for the restart, which would be taken by the 19 still raceworthy cars, he reflected on the moment when the detached rear wing from Scheckter's car sliced through the March's airbox inches behind his head. 'I had a very lucky escape. I'd suffered badly from nerves all morning. I'd really been in a terrible state. So I was very surprised to find that while we were waiting I wasn't at all nervous. I suppose in a sense the event as such had started, so I was no longer jumpy.'

James's recollection of part two of the British Grand Prix was hazy. 'I have to confess I don't remember a lot about it, but after being passed by a hell of a lot of people at the start I made up a lot of places. Perhaps I shut my eyes again and just kept my foot in it.'

Indeed, as he applied pressure to the frontrunners his heavy right foot secured him the fastest lap of the race (an average of 134.06 miles an hour). At one stage he was running third, behind the eventual winner, the American Peter Revson, and at the thrilling finish he was a scant four tenths of a second behind the New Zealander Denny Hulme (the 1967 World Champion), who was in turn just two tenths of a second behind the second place man, Sweden's Ronnie Peterson.

As the leading quartet roared across the finish line separated by less than three seconds the Silverstone crowd erupted in ecstatic cheering, most of it for the local hero in fourth place. The next best British driver was Jackie Stewart, who finished tenth after uncharacteristically spinning out of second place.

'The Wee Scot' was a guest of Lord Hesketh at Easton Neston where he had given valuable advice to James. In the race the now out of contention Stewart 'slowed down for me to pass – very nice of him', said James of the three-time World Champion.

For James, who was hampered by a tyre vibration in the final laps, to finish just a few feet away from a place on the victory podium was a huge step forward in his career. His splendid effort was also recognized by a panel of journalists who presented him with the Prix Rouge et Blanc, an award (in memory of the Swiss driver Jo Siffert who was killed at Brands Hatch in 1971) given to the driver who made the biggest impression at each Grand Prix.

Beyond his personal satisfaction at Silverstone James was especially thankful to be able to reward Hesketh Racing. 'I must say I'm very pleased with the result because it enormously encouraged the team and it was good for the happy atmosphere which we have. I've never been as happy in a racing team before.'

Following the British Grand Prix James made a brief appearance in an ill-fated 24 hour saloon car race at Spa in Belgium. His car (co-driven by Richard Lloyd), a Chevrolet Camaro similar to the one he used to win the Tour of Britain, did not last the distance and James was not unhappy to depart early from the fast and dangerous circuit, where accidents in the race claimed the lives of two drivers and seriously injured several others.

There was to be more tragedy in James's next race, the Dutch Grand Prix. At Zandvoort James qualified the Hesketh March seventh on the grid and was running fifth on the eighth lap when he passed another car, upside down and engulfed in flames. As the race went on the accident scene became obscured in thick black smoke from the burning car and finally, much later it seemed, white smoke from fire extinguishers.

Lap after lap the cars roared by, and when the smoke eventually cleared, James and the other drivers noticed a tarpaulin had been thrown over the burnt out car. They didn't know it also covered the body of Roger Williamson.

Jackie Stewart's victory at the Dutch Grand Prix was the 26th win of his career, one better than the previous record holder, the late Jim Clark. Stewart's Tyrrell team mate François Cevert crossed the finish line in second place, six seconds ahead of the third place man, James Hunt. But there was little joy for the threesome on the victory rostrum on that dark day in Holland. They soon learned that Williamson's car had suffered some kind of mechanical failure and crashed into a steel guard rail which threw it back onto the track where it caught fire. The track marshals were slow to react and despite heroic rescue attempts by Williamson's team mate David Purley, the only driver to stop, the young British driver perished in the flames.

For James the Williamson tragedy hit close to home. He knew Roger well from their days as Formula 3 rivals and now he had been killed in a works March 731, a car identical to his Hesketh Racing machine. James vividly remembered his own big accident on this same circuit two years earlier, when his Formula 3 March flipped over and he was trapped for some time with petrol leaking around him.

That night James watched Williamson's terrible accident on television news with John Richardson, who had come to Zandvoort to watch his friend compete. 'I think it was the first time he really realized his profession could have such awful consequences', Richardson recalls. 'As we watched it he was absolutely appalled. It was horrifying to see a man burned to death and the irony of it was that James had had such a brilliant race.'

All the drivers were angry at the inefficiency which contributed to Williamson's death. Jackie Stewart remembered that his friend Piers Courage had died in a similar fiery crash at this same circuit three years earlier.

Denny Hulme, president of the Grand Prix Drivers Association and one of the few drivers in the race who saw what was happening to Williamson, had tried to get the race stopped by slowing down and shaking his fist at the organizers. He also said that unless fire fighting was improved at circuits 'I don't want anything more to do with motor racing'.

The veteran New Zealander was one year away from retiring after a 10 year F1 career in which he had seen far too many drivers killed. But James was just beginning, and, though there would come a time when fear for his life became uppermost in his mind, for now he was able to keep his misgivings at bay.

On his return to England the next day James went straight to his former Formula 3 team-mate Brendan McInerney who was now racing in Formula 2. 'He knew that Roger Williamson was a very big mate of mine. So James came around to see me. He had Chantal with him and he said, "Come on, we're going to take you to Chessington Park to cheer you up". I really thought that was very special.'

James returned to Zandvoort a couple of weeks later, for another saloon car race, and was again successful at the Dutch circuit. Driving a BMW (shared with Brian Muir) he finished the four hour marathon in second place. This result was repeated a few weeks later in the same car (with Jacky Ickx also driving) at a six hour race on the Paul Ricard circuit in France.

Near the end of the season James went further afield, to Kyalami in South Africa, for a sports car endurance race. The long journey proved worthwhile, when James (co-driving with Derek Bell) finished second overall after nine hours of racing.

For variation James also went on an excursion to America, where he was invited to contest a round of the CanAm sportscar series at Elkhart Lake in Wisconsin. But his car, a UOP Shadow, developed engine problems and he was unable to race, so he went swimming instead.

☆　☆　☆

His next Formula 1 race, the Austrian Grand Prix in mid-August, began badly when a tyre suddenly deflated during a quick practice lap on the Österreichring circuit and the Hesketh March spun wildly. James managed to scrub off enough speed so that the encounter with a barrier resulted only in a damaged wing. But an engine blew up in qualifying and in the race a motor malfunction caused his retirement on the fourth lap.

There were more woes for Hesketh Racing at the Italian Grand Prix. The weekend began on an optimistic note for James when he acquitted himself well in a foot race around the Monza circuit. The competition, for drivers and team personnel, was organized by Frank Williams, who now had his own Formula 1 team. Williams was a keen fitness runner and won his own race, but James finished a worthy second and collected £300.

While in this case James never put a foot wrong, he did in his racing car and never made it to the starting line for the Italian Grand Prix. In practice on Friday he crashed heavily because, he said, he failed to make allowance for fading brakes and tried to take a corner too fast. The car was too badly damaged to repair and the team packed up and went home. But not before James and Bubbles Horsley had a flaming row.

After he wrecked the car James found Max Mosley in the Monza paddock and learned that the Great Chicken of Bicester had another March chassis at the factory. James wanted Bubbles to fly the replacement chassis out to Italy, but Bubbles said no, there wasn't enough time to do the job properly, and he insisted the team should go back to England and get ready for the final two races of the season, in North America.

'James was furious at that', says Bubbles. 'He would get quite fired up while driving, onto another plane. After he made the mistake and went off the road his short fuse was well and truly lit and we had a tremendous row.

'He was always quite emotional and in the early days he didn't really have control of his emotions. When that happens and you're driving you're going to lose concentration and have accidents. I think that was part of the problem in his "Hunt the Shunt" days. So we had to work on keeping his temper under control.

'We were all on a learning curve and when I made mistakes on the management side he was very hard on me, accusing me of costing him races and so on. It would get quite heated, but after I learned my trade I would give him a hard time. I'd say, "Look, you're not going to make it if you carry on like this. You're wasting our time. A lot of money is going into this and you're letting the side down".'

This kind of criticism proved very persuasive and gradually Bubbles was able to curb James's fiercely independent tendencies and mould him into more of a team player. James was accustomed to having to fight for everything he got and his me-against-the-world attitude further fuelled his competitive fires. But this approach could be disruptive in a team environment, and Bubbles, who understood James's mentality, was able to channel most of his contrary driver's volatile emotions in more productive directions.

James, fully aware that he needed guidance, was grateful for the focus Bubbles gave him, and he respected him more than any team manager he ever had. Eventually they became best friends, bound together, among other things, by their shared sense of humour. James delighted in telling funny anecdotes about Bubbles and one of them, involving the Horsley method of applied driver psychology, particularly appealed to James's priorities of racing and the opposite sex.

Some time after James left Hesketh Racing, Bubbles had a driver who fancied himself as a champion, both in the cockpit and in bed. One of those who disagreed with his self-assessment was an attractive woman who continually refused his advances. Finally, in a desperate bid to lure her into his hotel bedroom, the driver said to her: 'But I might be killed in the race'. The seduction attempt failed, the lady refused to comply, and promptly told Bubbles all about it.

The next day, prior to the final qualifying session, Bubbles, who was fed up with the driver's feeble attempts to qualify his car, was strapping the 'world's greatest lover' into the cockpit.

Bubbles leaned closer and said: 'Going to die in the race, are we? We'll have to go a lot quicker in qualifying then, won't we?'. According to James, who invariably fell about laughing when he told the tale, the very embarrassed and angry driver went faster than he'd ever gone before and managed to qualify the car. But, for James, the punchline was that the driver never did achieve his goal with the girl.

While mirth and merriment were very much a part of James's make-up his fiery temperament was never far away when he was racing. Among those who had to contend with his mood swings was Harvey Postlethwaite. The Doc's assessment of James was that 'He was never cool, calm and collected. He raced on his nerves. He'd always be losing his temper and complaining and whingeing and moaning before a race'.

Even when he was winning races James could fly into tantrums, and some of his most celebrated rows were with Teddy Mayer, leader of the McLaren team when James became World Champion. When James moved to the Wolf team near the end of his career his temper was even more frayed. Peter Warr, the Wolf team manager, was shocked by his red-faced rages.

'He was the most nervous driver I ever worked with. His eye movements would be rapid. He'd be snappy and almost quivering. When his car broke down, he'd jump out shouting "This car's a fucking heap of shit!". You'd just reel under the shock of his onslaught.'

★ ★ ★

'We have not been in the limelight for nearly three weeks', said Lord Hesketh after his team's failures in Austria and Italy, 'and this seems like a good opportunity to announce our plans for 1974.' Le Patron revealed that next year Hesketh Racing would contest the full Formula 1 season and field its own car, designed by Doc Postlethwaite and built by the team at their headquarters, the converted stables off the courtyard at the Easton Neston estate.

(The Good Lord also announced his intentions to build a Hesketh V12 engine, but it never materialized. 'I'm quite prepared for it to become a museum piece from the start', said the Lord of the motor.)

'The object', Le Patron continued, 'is to be fully competitive. James has shown that he's capable of winning Grands Prix and to win I feel that you've got to build your own cars. There's no point in playing amateur heroics at the back of the grid. Our intention is to create an exciting new car and race to win. But we're in this game to entertain just as much as we are to race.

'I am convinced that one of the essential ingredients that makes this team work is that it is decidedly British. I am a completely unashamed jingoist. I am proud to be British, to have a British passport and to paint my car red, white and blue. Our ambition is to win a World

Championship for Britain – with a British driver.'

Lord Hesketh also said his team would have a strict budget in 1974, probably about £200,000: 'If we didn't, then no doubt we'd be up in front of the Official Receiver by early next year'.

His expenditure for eight Grands Prix in 1973 eventually amounted to £68,000, a fraction of what most teams spent. Le Patron also pointed out that £38,000 of this cost was recouped in prize money from James's excellent results, and Hesketh Racing still had the residual value of the racing equipment.

James's share of the booty for 1973 was a £2,500 retainer and 45 per cent of the prize money. He could now pay the back rent owing on his basement flat in Earl's Court and was finally able to buy himself a decent road car, a Ford Capri, which cost him most of his retainer.

The new vehicle afforded him the opportunity to improve on the primitive automotive sound system to which he was accustomed: a battered old record player playing at full blast in the back seat of his succession of rolling wrecks.

The sophisticated stereo tape system he had installed in the Capri meant he no longer had to worry about a needle jumping off a record whenever he hit a bump, and he treated himself to high-speed full volume concerts of everything from the Beatles to Beethoven.

* * *

'Just drive to finish. No heroics', were the instructions Bubbles gave to James for the Canadian Grand Prix at Mosport Park. After the long transatlantic flight Le Patron also thought James needed to take special measures to fight off jet lag, so he 'took away his girls promptly at 10 p.m.'.

James responded to the team orders by qualifying a safe 15th on the grid and he finished a steady seventh in the race. Hesketh Racing then set off on the overland journey to the Watkins Glen circuit in New York state. At the United States Grand Prix, the final race of the season, they intended to pull out all the stops.

James, who had never seen the picturesque and challenging American circuit before, played himself in slowly. He also needed to regain his composure. 'After I had made an error and cocked the whole thing up at Monza, in Canada the brief was just to finish and restore confidence by having a good steady run. It was really good fun, with no pressure and just racing for racing's sake. But we hope to go for it here.'

On Friday James was 17th fastest in the 28 car field. On Saturday morning he was fifth, just half a second behind the Tyrrell driver François Cevert. But shortly after their times were recorded Cevert had a terrible accident when his Tyrrell brushed a guard rail on one side of the track, then shot across to the opposite steel barrier which parted and sliced the car in two. The handsome and popular Frenchman died instantly and horribly.

Jody Scheckter, the first driver to arrive at the scene of Cevert's accident, was so devastated by what he saw that it affected the rest of his racing life. From then on, the formerly rambunctious South African became among the most safety-conscious of drivers and, he said: 'My preoccupation was keeping myself alive'.

For Cevert's team-mate Jackie Stewart, it was the last straw and he retired from racing then and there, forgoing what would have been his 100th Grand Prix. Stewart had already clinched his third World Championship and won 27 Grands Prix, more than any other driver, but he had also seen such close friends as Jim Clark, Piers Courage, Jochen Rindt and now François Cevert lose their lives in 'the cruel sport', as he now called it.

James, like many racing drivers, employed a rather ruthless philosophy for emotional survival in his potentially lethal occupation. 'I had a fairly well-balanced approach to the dangers. I'd already worked it out in my mind and was as comfortable as one can be with the fact you can get killed. I don't think I ever really got a sudden jolt through one accident, though you certainly felt the sense of loss when someone died.

'But amongst racing drivers when somebody gets killed there is an attitude of "there but for the grace of God go I". The law of averages says "that's one out of the way", as it were. It's cruel, but it's a way to make it easier for yourself.'

His fourth-fastest qualifying time put James on the second row of the grid, alongside Emerson Fittipaldi's Lotus. In front of them were Ronnie Peterson, on pole in the other Lotus, and Carlos Reutemann in a Brabham.

At the start James beat Fittipaldi into the first corner and three laps later he overtook Reutemann. James later claimed Reutemann thought he 'was barking mad, an impression I never tried to discourage', and the Argentinian always moved over whenever he saw Hunt looming in his mirrors.

For the next hour and a half James sat on Peterson's tail as the two streaked around Watkins Glen in a class by themselves. In the last few minutes James applied even more pressure, setting the fastest lap of the race and pushing the nose of the Hesketh March right under the rear wing of the Lotus.

As they crossed the finish line, separated by 0.688 of a second, the jubilation of their respective teams was equally close, though Bubbles, Le Patron and their joyous crew beat the Lotus bunch in vaulting over the pit wall to embrace their Superstar.

For his sterling performance in the United States Grand Prix James was again presented with the Prix Rouge et Blanc as the Man-of-the-Meeting.

On his return to England he was awarded the Campbell Trophy by the RAC, the august body that once considered banning him from Formula 3 racing, to mark the best performance in motor sport by a British driver in a British car. The citation accompanying the Campbell Trophy read: 'In his first season of Formula 1 racing James Hunt in the Hesketh March consistently showed outstanding ability against established racing stars'.

In the final standings for the 1973 season Jackie Stewart was World Driving Champion with 71 points, followed by Emerson Fittipaldi, Ronnie Peterson, the late François Cevert, Peter Revson, Denny Hulme and Carlos Reutemann. Next, though he only competed in eight of the 15 races, was James Hunt, whose 14 points signified he was the eighth best driver in the world.

As for his future with Hesketh Racing James said: 'You know I have a theory about rich people – and Alexander in particular – that when they touch something it turns to gold. After all, nobody was prepared to give any sort of chance to a new Formula 1 team managed by someone called Bubbles Horsley and with a driver named James Hunt'.

5

THE GOOD LORD'S BOY WONDER

1974–1975

Lord Hesketh was laid up with a cold when his pride and joy emerged from the former stables at Easton Neston on a cold and wet January morning in 1974. His 12 man crew loaded the brand new Hesketh 308 onto a transporter and set off on the short journey to Silverstone, where they would see if it worked. Le Patron's sniffles meant he would have to miss the historic occasion, but he was full of optimism and spoke proudly of his team, on which he would this year invest over £200,000.

'I decided to build the car at home in the middle of the country which I think is a much nicer place to work than on a trading estate. Then I converted a farmhouse into flats for the mechanics and the result is that we have a tremendous rapport.

'Hesketh Racing is a team made up of rulebreakers. We've managed to break many of the unwritten rules: that you can never come into Formula 1 unless you have a completely professional team, you can't come in with no sponsors and only a rich young man who knows nothing about it, with a driver who has a reputation for crashing cars, and with a team manager who's an ex-used car dealer.

'For me, Bubbles is the man who has made Hesketh Racing what it is. He is the guy who revs James up, he's the guy who stops the Doctor from falling asleep as he is prone to do, thinking about wings and ride heights and things.

'We have a tremendous *esprit de corps* that doesn't exist in any other teams. If you look at it like a football team, all the other teams have played so many games that they have a certain amount of staleness,

Above The 'odd little fellow' (about three years old) with his favourite toy: a mowing 'chine. *Right* Wallis and Sue Hunt with James (age four and looking perplexed, perhaps at having to wear a tie), Peter (two) and Sally (six), the bridesmaid at a family wedding.

Above left The caring 10-year-old brother: holding baby Tim, with Sal (twelve) and Pete (eight). *Above right* The reluctant schoolboy, happily home from Wellington College and eagerly seeking ways to avoid medical school.

Above *Listening to advice from Bubbles Horsley, his team manager at Hesketh Racing and his lifelong friend.* **Right** *Fighting at the front of the Formula 3 pack at Crystal Palace in 1970, shortly before crashing and then punching a rival.*

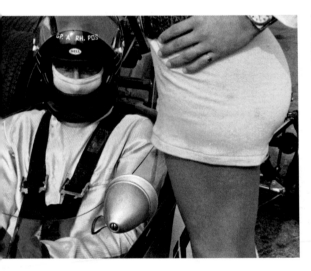

Above *Torn between his two passions, racing and girls, prior to a Brands Hatch Formula 3 race in 1969.* **Right** *On the starting grid – after his pre-race ritual of throwing up – trying to steady his nerves for a Formula Ford event.*

Above left Stirling Moss congratulates James (a reluctant bridegroom and rather the worse for wear) on his 1974 marriage to Suzy (who later married Richard Burton). Wallis Hunt looks on. *Above right* The 'Superstar' in Lord Hesketh's patriotic Formula 1 car – 'Racing for Britain, Racing For You' – at Brands Hatch in 1974.

Left 'Hunt the Shunt' having one of his worst Formula 3 accidents – at Zandvoort in Holland in 1971. **Above** Alexander 'The Good Lord' Hesketh.

A tax exile in Spain with Oscar, his beloved Alsatian.

The Formula 1 team at a 1974 charity cricket match. Back row: Ken Tyrrell, John Watson, Guy Edwards, Mike Hailwood, James Hunt, Graham Hill, Patrick Depailler, Peter Gethin, David Purley, Clay Regazzoni. Front row: Jody Scheckter, Derek Bell, Niki Lauda, Jackie Stewart, Ronnie Peterson, Jochen Mass, Denny Hulme.

His first Grand Prix win – in the Hesketh at Zandvoort in Holland in 1975.

Far left The elegant Suzy supporting James in practice: note his distinctive footwear. **Left** A fierce competitor at a charity tennis match at the NEC, Birmingham.

With the World Championship hanging in the balance, James rages in the cockpit during the frantic McLaren pit stop in the 1976 Japanese Grand Prix.

Teddy Mayer, at the end of the Japanese race, soothes his irate driver by convincing him that by finishing third he is indeed the new World Champion.

James in the McLaren contests the lead with Niki Lauda's Ferrari at the first corner in the 1977 South African Grand Prix.

Above left *James was greatly affected by his involvement in the accident during the 1978 Italian Grand Prix which claimed the life of his friend Ronnie Peterson.* **Above right** *His last race – in the Wolf at Monaco in 1979 – after which he retired from the sport 'for reasons of self-preservation'.*

A skiing injury shortly after he retired made life difficult for James and his girlfriend Jane Birbeck.

whereas we're still filled with a childish enthusiasm. And I think one of the essential ingredients of our team is that we have to keep it funny.'

For his racing insignia Le Patron adopted a cuddly yellow teddy bear. He had seen the teddy on a postcard in an airport and drew on it a helmet with a Union Jack flag on the front. With apologies to Superman he called it Super Bear, from the planet Bear Krypton, and embarked on 'a crazy "Back British Bears" advertising campaign' which included procuring a large outdoor sign at a prominent location in London. The sign featured Super Bear and proclaimed 'Hesketh Racing, the biggest little racing team in the world. Racing For Britain And Racing For You"

'We're just trying to sell Britain', said Le Patron in explaining his plan to sell Super Bear T-shirts to loyal British fans at the races. 'We want to give the public – to whom the Hesketh Team seems very important – the opportunity to participate and identify their support both at home and abroad.'

And, he promised, while other Formula 1 cars, festooned with corporate logos and commercial messages, acted as high-speed billboards for a myriad of consumer goods and services, the Hesketh 308 would remain virginal white, with only the red, white and blue stripes.

The team produced a glossy booklet, entitled *The Heavily Censored History of Hesketh Racing* which contained the following foreword.

Dear All,
When I first entered motor sport most people thought me a buffoon with a lot of money and astonishingly little sense.

However, this theory is now totally demolished, not so much through the heroic efforts of a man with a long history of attempted suicide by means of thumping into Armco (steel guardrails) called Hunt, not by a figure sought by Interpol in every country where loons do speed, known as Bubbles, nor by the invention of the Madman Postlethwaite, but by the fact that I have persuaded you to unload... for this nonsensical publication.

Nothing has given me greater faith in the future of Hesketh Racing than this selfless act of extravagance on your part which indicates that Bears are destined to breed at a rate hitherto unknown in British history.
    I remain yours faithfully,
(signed)
Le Patron

When James first saw Doc Postlethwaite's creation he pronounced it 'beautiful'. The Hesketh 308 – 3 for 3 litres and 08 for the 8 cylinder

Ford F1 engine – was stylish, sleek and small, except for the cockpit, which was tailored specifically for James's relatively large form.

For driving it in 1974 his retainer was increased to £15,000 and to earn it he would have to do a lot more testing, an often tedious activity that was at odds with his restless mentality. 'Testing is a necessary evil', said James, 'and I would never shirk it because it is the means to the end. I want to win races, and in order to win races I have to test, so I go to test sessions with enthusiasm. But I have to work at the enthusiasm all the time because I don't enjoy it. When I test I drive as if I'm racing, as fast as I can all the time.'

His first tests of the new Hesketh were limited to only a dozen laps on the wet Silverstone circuit. James found it to be more stable than the March 731 he raced in 1973, but it was agreed the new car needed more work before it was race-ready. The team decided it would also be prudent to also bring the March to the first two events, in South America.

On their return from Argentina and Brazil James was again strapped into the now perfected Hesketh 308 for a test at Silverstone.

'Watching him then', says Bubbles, 'when the Woodcote Corner at Silverstone was one of the most exciting spectacles in Formula 1, was something I'll never forget. He took the corner absolutely flat, never a hint of a confidence lift on the accelerator, and when he hit the bump on the exit I could see the whole underside of the chassis.

'James reported back to the pits, white in the face and talked of the state of his underwear. After a conflab with Doc Postlethwaite he went straight back out and was flat out around Woodcote again, without even a crowd to play to, as it was a test day.'

Bubbles has less happy recollections of his brave but foolhardy driver's exploits in the opening race of the 1974 season.

★　★　★

On the Buenos Aires circuit in Argentina it at first seemed that their new car might be superfluous to Hesketh Racing's needs. James, in the elderly March 731, recorded the fastest lap in the opening qualifying session and a subsequent time on the second day was good enough for fifth on the grid. He was in a very confident mood.

The eighth fastest qualifier was his old friend Niki Lauda, in his debut with the illustrious Ferrari team. As James climbed from his March he dashed off to the Ferrari pit 'to be rude to Niki about beating him'.

At the start of the race Ronnie Peterson's pole-sitting Lotus surged into the lead, followed immediately by James, who had shot into second place from the third row of the grid. Behind them several other cars were involved in an accident, but James kept his foot to the floor and passed Peterson half way round the first lap. But Superstar's first ever lead in a Grand Prix was of short duration. When Peterson came around to complete the opening lap he was alone in front.

Peterson, who later admitted he fully expected James to fly off the road on his own, had assisted this manoeuvre by moving alongside the March on the entry to a corner, feinting as if to overtake, then braking at the last minute. In reaction to Peterson's ploy James forgot his own braking and skidded off the circuit in a cloud of dust and flying foliage.

He kept the car going and crawled back into the pits, where some debris was removed from the radiators, though not enough of it to prevent the engine from overheating after a few more laps in the race.

Bubbles was livid that James 'lost his head' while leading a Grand Prix he might have won had he shown more patience. He should have been content with second place for a few laps while trying to pressure Peterson into making a mistake. Instead, he threw it all away on the very first of 53 laps. Bubbles delivered a stern lecture to his chastened driver and James took heed of what he heard.

James later said that the Horsley technique, which would vary from person to person, 'was to keep me in fear. Particularly in those early days he kept me under constant threat of the sack. And I knew if I got sacked from Hesketh Racing at that stage, there weren't going to be too many other offers'.

While Bubbles showed him little mercy James felt his driving errors were understandable, if not forgivable. 'You have to remember that to this point my career had been so chequered and so dogged with financial problems I had relatively little practice at leading races, let alone winning them. Eventually I won more Grands Prix than all my other international wins put together. The few Formula 3 races I'd won had been slipstreamers, where you only had to be in the right place on the last lap to win.

'So the main mistakes I made early in Formula 1 were when I was in front. And to find myself in the lead of a Grand Prix provoked some very silly things by me, through just abject panic.'

After his abbreviated Argentinian GP James flew up to Rio de Janeiro with Peter Gaydon, a former racing driver who now had Hesketh Racing as a client in his race management business. Gaydon had made the team's South American travel arrangements, which included a stay in Rio's luxurious Copacabana Palace hotel, during the interval to the Brazilian Grand Prix in Sao Paulo.

'We arrived in Rio about midnight', Gaydon remembers, 'and we came into the very grand lobby of the hotel where James, who never looked the smartest of creatures, was a source of considerable curiosity in his frayed jeans, tatty T-shirt and with his hair all over the place.

'I produced a thick roll that Bubbles had given me that had ten 100 dollar bills on top, though the rest were all ones. We were immediately assigned the presidential suite and surrounded by flunkies who fought over carrying our luggage, which consisted of my few cases and James's helmet bag, which was bigger than the scruffy old sack which contained the rest of his clothes.

'In the suite James changed into something even more revolting, like his orange swimming trousers, and we opened a bottle of wine and sat looking out at the Rio beach in the wonderful starlit night. James was grinning from ear to ear and turned to me and summed it up with exquisite brevity, "Gaydoon", he said, "this is the life".'

The good life got even better when Le Patron arrived and informed his troops that he had £7,000 to spend on recreation. Everyone got their money's worth over the next few days and tall tales are still told of Hesketh Racing's raucous time in Rio. One of them concerns Le Patron and Superstar returning to the hotel very late after a boisterous night on the town. With them was an attractive young woman who, the doorman of the hotel informed them, was not welcome in the hotel at such a late hour.

'How dare you insult this lady?', said Le Patron of his dark-complexioned companion. 'She happens to be my sister.'

When Lord Hesketh arrived at the entrance to the Interlagos circuit in suburban Sao Paulo his patriotic eye immediately noticed that the Union Jack was flying upside down. He insisted that the organizers must right this disrespectful wrong forthwith, and as it was being done the Hesketh Racing team ceremoniously stood to attention and saluted the raising of the flag.

In the Brazilian Grand Prix, aboard the Hesketh March, James flew the flag with more circumspection than in Argentina and finished an uneventful ninth, though he complained his ill-handling March had made it all very hard work.

After the race several teams stayed on at the Interlagos circuit to test. As James prepared to put the new Hesketh 308 through its paces the rival teams, stopwatches in hand, looked on with interest. Being unexpectedly competitive in a proven car like a March – even much quicker than the factory versions run by March Engineering – was one thing. But, said the Formula 1 regulars, wait until Hesketh tries building their own car. Then they'll find out just how difficult this business is.

Following a few exploratory laps James came back into the pits for some adjustments then announced to Bubbles that he was ready 'to do a lap in anger'. That lap proved to be a second quicker than Emerson Fittipaldi's McLaren had managed in securing pole position for the Grand Prix and was a full four seconds better than James's qualifying time in the March.

For Bubbles this immediate display of speed, in front of many of their disbelieving rivals, was one of the Hesketh Racing's most satisfying highlights. 'At first we came from obscurity to being something of a joke in the paddock. We were greeted with a certain amount of wry amusement by some, but a lot of the regulars disapproved. We weren't typical of the kind of people in the professionally run teams. We did some fairly extraordinary things, like standing around in a circle and clucking, praying to the Great Chicken in the Sky for a good weekend and reliability in the race, and so on.

'Then, when we started becoming serious threats, there was some resentment, especially from those who'd been at Formula 1 for a long time and had found success hard to get. We'd come along with this carefree attitude and suddenly – Bang! – we were up there on the pace and also, of course, attracting what some may have considered an unfair slice of the publicity cake. So it was very special when our new car was so quick right out of the box and everybody went "Ye gods!".'

The next weekend Hesketh Racing was one of several teams to appear at a new circuit in the Brazilian capital of Brasilia for a non-championship race. There, the new Hesketh developed a leak in a fuel tank which couldn't be repaired, and James had to revert to the March. Clutch problems in qualifying relegated him to the last row of the grid, and then a malfunctioning gearbox ended his race after only four laps. 'Never fear', quoth Le Patron as the team packed up to return to Europe, 'We'll be back in fighting form at the next race'.

★ ★ ★

Their mixed fortunes at the next event, a very wet Race of Champions (though it was not a race for the Formula 1 Championship) at Brands Hatch, proved to be a forecast of what was to come in Hesketh Racing's 1974 season. James put the 308 on pole position by being quickest in qualifying, when it was dry, but the teeming rain in the race, together with the loss of some front bodywork when the Hesketh touched another car, magnified handling problems and James retired after just a few laps.

In South Africa, the first proper Grand Prix for the new car, James was running easily in fifth place when he was sidelined by a broken driveshaft. In fact, Bubbles said, the car ate driveshafts, there was obviously a lot of hard development work to do and 'reality had set in'.

For James this meant more of the dreaded testing (which he hated even more following the death of the American driver Peter Revson in a private test prior to the South African Grand Prix) on the team's return to their home circuit of Silverstone, where they would prepare for the *Daily Express* International Trophy race in early April.

Though it was a non-championship event, many of the Formula 1 leading lights came to Silverstone for the International Trophy race. Also included in the field of 30 cars were several of the top runners from the F5000 series, but after qualifying it seemed there was a third, uncatchable, category which had only one representative.

James was simply in a class by himself in setting a pole position time in the Hesketh that was an astonishing 1.7 seconds quicker than the next car, the Lotus, driven by the fastest man in Formula 1 racing, Ronnie Peterson.

Prior to the start, James emptied the contents of his stomach in a corner of the Hesketh garage and climbed into his car, his whole body trembling and his mind reeling with instructions from Bubbles (which included 'do not wheelie' – accelerate so quickly at the start as to cause too much wheel-spin).

As he sat on the starting grid with his left foot on the clutch pedal and his right hand on the gear lever he experienced a sudden surge of panic as both controls failed him. The clutch was slipping, the gear lever knob came off in his hand and the stationary Hesketh was immediately engulfed in a flood of racing cars.

James fumbled around desperately in the cockpit and by the time he was able to coax his machine off the start line 14 cars had passed him. Then, without using the clutch and by effecting gear changes with only the sharp stub of the gear lever, he began to make up for lost time. By the fifth lap he had carved his way up to fifth place and by the 13th lap he was in second place, seven and half seconds behind Ronnie Peterson.

Observant race watchers among the 33,000 in attendance at Silverstone noted in the Hesketh cockpit that James's helmet began to incline further forward, acting as an indicator of the steely determination which saw him relentlessly reel in Peterson's Lotus.

By the 20th lap, the halfway point in the race, the two cars were nose to tail and James began to look for a likely place to pass. No one expected him to try it at Woodcote Corner, a long sweeping right-hand turn and one of the fastest and most daunting landmarks in the racing world.

As the cars roared around to complete the 28th lap they came streaking into Woodcote at 160 miles an hour. In shocked disbelief the entranced spectators crowded into Woodcote's grandstands saw the Hesketh pull alongside the Lotus and, in unison, the two cars proceeded to perform a breathtaking ballet of high-speed car control.

Dancing on the very edge of adhesion the cars entered Woodcote sliding sideways, with the Hesketh on the inside, their spectacular power slides maintained by the two drivers applying full opposite lock on their steering wheels to combat the centrifugal force which contrived to throw them off the track. For a moment the Hesketh slewed viciously as its two right tyres ventured onto the grass but its screaming engine note never faltered. As the cars powered out of the corner and onto the start/finish straight the Hesketh inched ahead of the Lotus and a mighty roar of approval erupted from the grandstands.

A couple of laps later, his tyres worn out from the struggle, Peterson prepared to enter the pits, only to have his overworked engine expire in a cloud of smoke. James continued at unabated speed, setting a fastest lap that was the equivalent of 137.38 mph around Silverstone's 2.93 miles. He punched his fists (the right one blistered and bloodied from repeatedly slamming his hand into the knobless gear lever) triumphantly skyward as he crossed the finish line.

For Lord Hesketh the moment was 'paramount' among his racing memories. 'When he took Ronnie with two wheels on the grass at Woodcote it was, I think, the only time that manoeuvre had ever been accomplished there.

'Returning to our pit James leapt from the unmarked red, white and blue car, on that beautiful April day, walked towards Bubbles and Harvey, Mickey and Chicken and Tom and all the rest of the team – we were hysterical with laughter and tears – and then suddenly flung away his helmet and belted out a rendition of the Dambusters' March in which we all dementedly joined.'

In the Silverstone press room Ian Phillips, in his *Autosport* editorial, noted that James Hunt's average race speed of 133.58 mph made this the fastest post-war race held in Britain. Beyond that, Phillips wrote: 'to see James bring the car up from a poor start and catch and overtake Ronnie Peterson in a historical moment at Woodcote was overwhelming. It gave a breath of fresh air to Formula 1 and a shot in the arm for patriotism'.

Autosport's Grand Prix correspondent, Pete Lyons (an American), elaborated on the flag-waving theme: 'The way James threw his Hesketh in beneath the Peterson car and powered on through to take the lead and win the race became etched on that imaginary but very real bronze tablet that every British enthusiast keeps near his heart. It was a magnificent moment'.

* * *

Led by the motoring press the Hesketh Racing effort captured the imagination of more and more racing fans around the country. James was hailed as the new British racing hero, the man most likely to succeed Jackie Stewart as the next British World Champion. His difficult rise from obscurity, his former 'Hunt the Shunt' reputation, his anti-establishment characteristics and his underdog status served to increase his stature in the eyes of the fans.

But his fame spread beyond the racing enthusiasts as the popular press took note of this new 'Golden Boy' of British sports. James's pop star good looks made young girls swoon and his girl-chasing reputation impressed red-blooded young males. His defiance of convention and party-loving ways were good copy, as were the colourful antics of Hesketh Racing, which sometimes seemed reminiscent of a bizarre *Monty Python* sketch.

The raffish young ex-public schoolboys – known as Superstar, Bubbles and Le Patron – were engagingly eccentric, and reports of their shenanigans spread from the sports pages of the newspapers into the gossip columns. It was noted that the principals of Hesketh Racing traditionally spent their Sunday night post-race debriefings in Trader Vic's bar at the bottom of the London Hilton hotel where they drank Mai Tais until daylight.

At the races the team's entourage had grown larger and the corresponding increase in the social factor required the appointment of an official team photographer, Christopher Simon Sykes (who went on to produce elaborate coffee table books of English gardens and the countryside) to document the proceedings.

The team catering was now being handled by Tom Benson, the chef/owner of a fashionable restaurant in Beauchamp Place, and the official 'van driver' was Charles Lucas, another public schoolboy whose credentials included a successful career as an amateur racing driver and a wealthy background (his grandfather built St Pancras station and the Royal Albert Hall) which made him the second richest man on the team, after Le Patron.

Also of keen interest was the Good Lord's impressive list of toys, which this year would include the stately *Nefertiti*, whose size among the exotic craft bobbing in the Monaco harbour was exceeded only by the super-yachts of the Greek shipping magnates Onassis and Niarchos.

Nearby was moored the *Henry Morgan*, another, slightly smaller yacht for the Hesketh 'workers' (namely James, Bubbles and Doc). Then there was the Hesketh helicopter, the pinstriped Roller, the Mercedes limo and the rest, though the Porsche Carrera RS had now disappeared. 'James took it one day', said Le Patron, 'and said he'd get it serviced. I haven't seen it since'.

The team patron was always good for entertaining quotes, as was his often outspoken driver, the one with the long hair, tattered jeans and custom made golden teddy bear pendant (fashioned from one of the melted down Prix Rouge et Blanc trophies he'd won) around his neck.

Of course James took a liking to 'nice ladies screaming and shouting after me, who wouldn't? They're attracted by fast cars, which have always been considered sexy. But most of all I think it's because racing drivers are nasty. Women always prefer nasty men. You have to be nasty to be competitive. Of course, I actively try not to be a bastard. But I probably am'.

James enjoyed role-playing with the popular press but there was never any guile in his equally pungent comments about his sport and its players. He always called a spade a spade, or a slow driver a 'wanker'.

He freely gave his opinions of his main racing rivals in the 1974 season. His assessment of Ronnie Peterson, was that 'Superswede is without doubt faster than anyone else in Grand Prix racing'. Emerson Fittipaldi, he thought, was not particularly fast, but clever and needed to be respected. James (momentarily forgetting his own histrionic outbursts of 'Latin temperament') said the Brazilian can 'become hysterical at times when things are going wrong, but he does get over it quickly.... I guess we all throw wobblies at times'.

James also had great respect for Niki Lauda: 'He is a real thinker, a master tactician and he doesn't make mistakes under pressure'. But Carlos Reutemann had 'a tendency to give up and not fight'. Of the Swiss Italian driver Clay Regazzoni, James said: 'Frankly, I think he is over the hill', and Hans Stuck from Germany 'flies off the road too much'.

But James was compassionate toward the Frenchman Jean Pierre Beltoise, who raced with an arm crippled in a motorcycle accident: 'a tough little blighter with a lot of courage', and of the perennially unlucky New Zealander Chris Amon, who never won a race despite leading many of them, James said: 'I really feel sorry for Chris'.

Hesketh Racing responded to the Grand Prix starting flag 14 times in 1974 but was never able to duplicate their Silverstone success in the Grand Prix races, though James put in some notable drives. In Sweden he finished third after a lengthy scrap with Niki Lauda, which was resolved when the Hesketh scrabbled past the Austrian's Ferrari in the dirt. That manoeuvre, and James's all-out effort thereafter, saw him again being rewarded with the Prix Rouge et Blanc for outstanding fighting spirit. In Austria, another hard charge, after stopping for a tyre change, netted third place again, and in Canada James was fourth.

Perhaps his best Grand Prix of the year was in America, at Watkins Glen, where James overcame engine and brake problems to finish an excellent third. But once again his visit to the victory podium was overshadowed by the death of a fellow driver. Last year it had been François Cevert, now it was the young Austrian Helmuth Koinigg. Competing in only his second Grand Prix Koinigg was killed when his Surtees car inexplicably plunged head on into the steel guard rails and he was decapitated.

The dark side of his profession continued to haunt James, especially when he was involved in accidents, three of them in consecutive races. At the Dutch Grand Prix he collided with the Shadow driven by the hard-trying young Welshman Tom Pryce. Two weeks later, when the two came together again in the French Grand Prix James was enraged, though not at Pryce. Their accident, James felt, had been triggered by dangerous driving on the part of Emerson Fittipaldi.

When James climbed from his wrecked Hesketh he proceeded to make his feelings known to Fittipaldi (who was *en route* to his second World Championship), shaking his fist vigorously at the Brazilian each time his McLaren came by.

Two weeks later, at Brands Hatch in mid-July, when leaving the pits prior to the start of the race, the Hesketh hit a mechanic from the Tyrrell team, breaking the unfortunate man's legs. Two laps into the British Grand Prix the Hesketh's rear suspension broke in the middle of a corner, sending the car into a spin, then a steel barrier.

James unbuckled his safety harness, extricated himself from the cockpit, wrenched off his helmet and strode away purposefully. He had to catch a flight to his new home – in Spain – and a rendezvous with the woman he planned to marry.

*　*　*

In the spring of 1974, James, following the advice of the International Management Group, which was managing his business affairs (though shortly after this he asked his accountant brother Peter to assume these duties) had taken up residence in Spain.

For James the move from his beloved Britain, far away from his friends and favourite haunts, would be a considerable wrench, but the prospect of saving up to 80 per cent on British taxes was appealing. He said his goodbyes, cancelled the lease on the new flat he had just taken in London, packed his few possessions into Le Patron's Porsche and set off – alone – for the Spanish Costa del Sol.

When he arrived he was 'absolutely homeless' and at first stayed in a succession of hotel rooms while he searched for more permanent accommodation. But finding a place to call home was only part of the void James had to fill, and he began to experience feelings of loneliness, similar to those that bedevilled him when he was sent away to private schools as a boy. Here, there was no one he could call even a nodding acquaintance and none of the locals had ever heard of James 'Superstar' Hunt.

Even the sunny Spanish weather failed to dispel his deepening gloom, until one day, 'sitting in a strange hotel bedroom in Torremolinos, I suddenly realized that I was totally alone. I knew nobody. I could barely speak the language. Thus, stricken by loneliness in a strange country, and with no home, no chance of even trying to make new friends because of my constant coming and going to races throughout the world, instead of following my heart and instincts, I began to think'.

Despite his gregariousness in his own milieu James was essentially a shy person in unfamiliar social circumstances and found it difficult to make new friends. Now, his feelings of isolation made him begin to realize that the strong sense of independence and self-confidence which had so far served him so well had always been reinforced by the knowledge that his family and close friends, and especially his girlfriends, were close by. Perhaps he was not naturally a loner after all.

Previously he had thought it a 'stupid myth' that it was necessary for Grand Prix drivers to have a stable home life in order to cope with the stresses and strains of their profession. Still, nearly all his racing rivals had one main woman in their lives, and James decided he, too, should find someone to 'help my career and ease my life in exile'.

His search for a companion was short – they met a few weeks after he arrived on the Costa del Sol, at Lew Hoad's tennis club in Fuengirola. Suzy Miller came into his life and a few months later she became Mrs James Hunt.

Susan Miller, a year younger than James, spent her childhood in Rhodesia and later became a successful fashion model in London. She was blonde and beautiful, of course, and her warm and pleasant personality and quiet, thoughtful manner appealed to James, though he at first treated their affair as one of convenience.

She, too, had just moved to Spain and had not yet found many friends, and besides offering the companionship he now craved she provided him with a place to stay, at her flat on the Spanish coast.

But Suzy was not content just to be a casual girlfriend of a racing driver, a sport about which she knew nothing and cared less. What she did care for was a more serious relationship, and when James seemed reluctant to agree to this she sent him packing back to his hotel room existence. The isolation proved too much for James and he 'talked himself back in' to her affections, then 'relapsed into my former semi-interested habits, only for her to repeat the booting out process'.

Their relationship see-sawed back and forth this way for some time until James made a final offer. 'Knowing that the prospect of marriage would swing Suzy around I went back to her and proposed'.

His proposal was immediately accepted, their engagement was formally announced in mid-July and the wedding date set for October, immediately after the last race of the 1974 season.

Suzy had wanted to get married right away, but James wanted time to think it over because, unlike in a racing car where he constantly made split-second decisions on which his life depended, he was unsure of himself in matters of the heart. Though he was widely experienced in dealing with the opposite sex on a physical level, the emotional component of a relationship for James was still virgin territory.

'Despite a constant and widespread search', as he put it, he didn't think he had ever really been in love. In fact, he was unclear as to what it actually was, or even if it was a necessary ingredient in a marriage. Eventually, he decided the warm feelings he felt for his bride-to-be would suffice, but the prospect of making a commitment to spending the rest of his life with her, with anyone, was daunting.

His former girlfriend Ping was now married – James had been a wedding guest and his brother Peter had played the trumpet at the ceremony – but she found it surprising that James was taking a bride. She accepted an invitation to his engagement party at Peter Hunt's flat in London. There, James admitted his misgivings, saying to Ping: 'I don't know why I'm doing this'.

'When I asked him: "Well why the hell are you, you silly clot?", he said, "I can't get out of it". So I said, "Come on James, you're stronger than that". But he wasn't and I could see he was very confused.'

All the wedding arrangements had been made, and paid for, by Lord

Hesketh, who was to be the best man at a grand ceremony (Roman Catholic in deference to the bride's religion – James was Anglican) in the historic Brompton Oratory in central London.

A full symphony orchestra would play the music, everyone would be dressed in their finery and, besides friends and family, the invited guests would include prominent members of the media and the racing fraternity would be represented by such famous drivers as Graham Hill, Stirling Moss and Ronnie Peterson.

The closer his wedding day came the colder James's feet became. 'Absolutely legless' was how he described the condition in which he walked down the aisle, because he could not face up to the mistake he was now convinced he was making. He wanted desperately 'to cut and run and get out of the whole dreadful situation but was too chicken to do it. I just couldn't handle the whole scene so I went out and got blind, roaring drunk. For four days I went on the most stupendous bender of my life'.

Some of his friends thought he was simply indulging in prenuptial celebrations on a grand scale. When he confessed his terror they assured him everyone was nervous before they got married. Those who knew the truth about the reluctant bridegroom presented such arguments as his obligation to perform as expected and not let down his fans now that he was a public figure, to do the decent thing and marry the girl as he had promised, it would all work out in the end, and so on.

James, who sat up drinking until 6 a.m. on the morning of the appointed day, then had two quick Bloody Marys to prepare himself for a liquid lunch, was married in an alcoholic haze.

Other than the beautiful music, which he had chosen, he remembered little of the event, and at the wedding reception he needed the full support of Le Patron and Bubbles, each with a firm grip on his sagging frame, while he accepted congratulations and mumbled incoherent greetings to his guests.

Following the wedding, James and Bubbles, who was married a few weeks earlier, took their brides on a honeymoon to the Caribbean island of Antigua. There, according to Bubbles, 'James and I went and played pirates and ignored our new wives'.

*　*　*

'We recognize that if we are to survive we must turn completely professional', said Bubbles of Hesketh Racing's future.

Their 1974 results, based on only four points-scoring finishes, netted James just 15 points, only one more than in the previous season. James was again classified eighth in the world championship, which was won by the McLaren driver Emerson Fittipaldi, but the team's upward mobility had been seriously arrested.

But improving their fortunes was not going to be easy, since Le Patron would be spending less of his on Hesketh Racing. His prized status as an unsponsored amateur entrant had come at a price he was no longer prepared to pay.

Perhaps, his Lordship hinted, he might now even entertain the idea of having a commercial sponsor for his team. In any case, he declared, because of the economic downturn, which had adversely affected his other business enterprises, Hesketh Racing must become self-supporting.

He noted that Doc Postlethwaite would probably use up £80,000 in creating the new Hesketh 308C in the Easton Neston stables, his driver's retainer would be approximately the same amount (James eventually received only about half the £75,000 owed to him, from his retainer and his share of the prize money, though he was allowed to keep Le Patron's Porsche) and the total budget requirement for the 1975 season was estimated at £360,000.

'I want to build the best car in the world and I am personally committed to seeing that James Hunt becomes the next British World Champion, and not just to have fun and games. We did very badly last year and I can't afford a repeat of that performance.

'Winning a Grand Prix means £14,000 to us. We have got to win some races and money, or else. We'll still have fun, though perhaps fun is now related to success. Entertainment is being cut to a minimum. Yachts are out and all the money available is being spent on the racing car.'

To begin his austerity measures the helicopter was sold, as were some of his cars, and his regular personal transport became a Vauxhall Chevette. At Monaco the team's sleeping quarters was a hired motorhome, driven there by Le Patron. There, too, he could be found vigorously hawking the famous Super Bear T-shirts, the sales of which were needed to buy a new Ford racing engine. Le Patron eventually did get his £14,000 win, in Holland, but the money was immediately dispersed to pay the mechanics' wages for the next week.

By midsummer the purse strings were so tight there was a danger the team would be unable to attend the French Grand Prix, until Bubbles found the necessary funds by summoning up his old skills as a car salesman. When Le Patron discovered his Rolls Royce had been sold Bubbles said he 'wasn't very pleased, though he forgave me when we came second'.

★ ★ ★

James and Suzy were living in a rented villa in the tiny mountain village of Mijas, a short distance inland from the Spanish beaches. James pitched himself into preparing physically for the new racing season, running up and down the hilly roads in the early morning and playing strenuous games of tennis every afternoon at Lew Hoad's club.

By the time he arrived in Argentina for the first race his hair was bleached blond by the sun and his tanned muscular physique, which tended to be displayed prominently because of his custom of wearing the minimum of clothing in warm climates, marked him as probably the fittest of the drivers.

The combination of his finely tuned body and Doc Postlethwaite's updated Hesketh 308 (lack of funds was delaying the new car) was good enough to secure sixth place on the starting grid at the Buenos Aires circuit.

Remembering how he threw away his short-lived lead in this same race the year before James was this time more circumspect, though no less quick. He was fourth for the first seven laps, then third for the next seven. When the car in front of him spun off James was promoted to second and there he sat behind the Brabham driven by the local hero Carlos Reutemann and ahead of Emerson Fittipaldi's McLaren.

On the 26th lap Reutemann made a slight mistake and James slipped through into the lead of the Grand Prix of Argentina. This time James held his ground and reeled off a succession of impressive laps which increased his lead over Fittipaldi who had also found a way past Reutemann.

But again the responsibility of leadership proved more than James could handle, and on lap 35 he spun off the road at the final hairpin. By the time he regained the circuit Fittipaldi was well on his way to winning the race. For James, who was seething at his mistake, second place behind the reigning World Champion and his best ever Formula 1 result was little consolation after a race he should have won.

'If he really wanted to win he wouldn't keep falling off the road while leading motor races!', fumed Bubbles, whose resolve to make Hesketh Racing more professional had received a major setback.

'James Hunt is basically interested in James Hunt, so he has a large ego. He has a boyish charm, so one finds it difficult to say no to him. He's very intelligent, which is possibly a mixed blessing. The road he has climbed to get here has been hard, he's come a long way in a short time and he now enjoys all the trappings of a Grand Prix driver.

111

'Perhaps the trappings of his style of life don't necessarily interfere with his job of being a racing driver, but possibly they do with winning races. Yes, sure, he has the raw talent, but so does everybody else in this game. Other qualities must be added beyond talent. If he doesn't work out we can always find another driver.'

James, fully aware of his shortcomings and embarrassed at having let the side down, took the criticism meekly and in the Brazilian Grand Prix he brought the Hesketh safely home in sixth place. In so doing he fought off a strong challenge from Mario Andretti, an exercise which James treated as a practice session. 'I was pretending I was in the lead like in Argentina, and trying not to fall off the road this time.'

In South Africa James kept his cool but his engine didn't, and blew up. The same problem denied him a chance of winning the non-championship International Trophy race at Silverstone. There, in a fiercely determined effort, he put the Hesketh on pole and led the first 25 laps convincingly, only to coast to a halt in a cloud of steam. He was still judged to have been the star of the day, but his problems continued in races which counted for the World Championship.

James led the first six laps of the Spanish Grand Prix, then crashed into a barrier. There were many other accidents in this ill-fated race, where the circuit inadequacies also led to the death of four bystanders when the car of the German driver Rolf Stommelen vaulted a railing and landed among them.

At Monaco, where James also crunched into a barrier (though not while leading), he stood beside the wrecked Hesketh for many laps, shaking his fist at the McLaren driver Jochen Mass, whom he blamed for shoving him off the road. Mechanical problems put James out of both the Belgian and Swedish races, and now, with over half the 1974 season gone, it seemed Hesketh Racing's fortunes had never been lower.

* * *

While James's private life had become more subdued since his marriage there were only so many hours a day he could spend sweating under the Spanish sun to keep fit. At the numerous parties in the 'gringo' community on the Costa de Sol, where he now enjoyed celebrity status, James practised his philosophy of enjoying himself as he went along. For many of his racing rivals their sport was the only thing in their life, but James was more interested in making life a sport.

'To a certain extent I'm obliged to enjoy some of what's going on now, because if I just sit there and wait until I retire I may not be around to enjoy it. Of course I'd prefer a sport where there was no risk involved because I don't want to die.

'But a racing driver is in quite a difficult position. He makes quite a lot of money and it's certainly the only way I know of to make a lot of money. I do work immensely hard at it, but really it's a pretty easy life, all things considered. So you're slightly captivated by it, and that can be a debit.

'Some drivers carry on when perhaps their will to win is gone, their enjoyment is gone – when their fear of being hurt exceeds their reason to do it. The trick is to make your pile as fast as you can and get out alive.'

To accumulate that pile, let alone contribute to the survival of his increasingly impoverished team, he would have to start winning races. To begin to do that his team manager decided James, like the rest of Hesketh Racing, would have to focus more on his profession. 'We never stopped him carousing', says Bubbles. 'If he wanted to be on the piss all night that was his business, as long as it didn't affect his driving. What we tried to do was focus where discipline was needed, and we did have to discipline him in both his racing and in his private life.

'Maybe discipline isn't really the right word. Anyone outside your life can see you much clearer than you can perhaps see yourself. On that basis we were able to see, on occasions, that he was leading the kind of lifestyle that would not help his driving, so we tried to keep him on the straight and narrow.'

In this case the prescribed path was straight back to Easton Neston. Bubbles called a team meeting where weaknesses were examined and views frankly exchanged. All 20 members of Hesketh Racing would have to bear down harder and the driver was told he had to become more closely involved.

'It was necessary to change our ways a little', James explained. 'There was a feeling that perhaps my living out of the country has caused a schism in the team. So now I'm going to be coming back between races on a regular basis to just go up and visit the shop. I'm not sure anything really valuable will come of it, but there's got to be an intangible benefit, seeing the lads, keeping closer together.'

* * *

It was with a new spirit of togetherness that Hesketh Racing arrived at Zandvoort, the circuit among the sand dunes beside the North Sea, for the Dutch Grand Prix.

After qualifying an excellent third on the grid, behind the pace-setting

Ferraris of Niki Lauda and Clay Regazzoni, James felt he was 'in pretty good shape'. But his hopes did not extend much beyond second place. Lauda had won the previous three races in a row and Zandvoort was considered to be a circuit where the Ferrari power advantage would be even more significant.

Before the start rain began to fall intermittently, and most teams decided to set their cars up for wet weather racing, softening the suspension settings and increasing the angles of the wings to create better adhesion.

But as Bubbles stood talking to James on the damp starting grid they looked out beyond the dunes and saw a tiny patch of clear sky. They took it as an omen that the weather would clear, so they left the Hesketh settings as they were – for dry conditions. They would start with rain tyres, like everyone else, but James decided the moment the track began to dry he would come into the pits to change to slick racing tyres.

As the field sailed away the cars were immediately obscured in a cloud of spray. James, running in fourth place, kept a watchful eye on the brightening sky overhead and the dwindling rooster tails of spray thrown up by the cars in front of him.

Very soon two narrow strips, worn dry by the traffic, appeared on the tarmac and on the seventh lap James suddenly veered into the pits, where the Hesketh crew methodically, to avoid making mistakes, poured over the car to effect the wheel changes.

James was 19th when he rejoined the race, but in the next few laps all the cars in front of him also called into the pits to change to dry tyres. By lap 15 James was in the lead. But there were still 60 laps to go.

In the many laps it took for the track to dry completely, James was absorbed in the task of toeing the dry, racing line – his dry tyres would give him only limited adhesion on a wet surface –. while still maintaining the necessary pace to keep ahead of the scarlet machine looming in his mirrors. For Niki Lauda's Ferrari was snarling threateningly behind the Hesketh, and most people expected the Italian car's inherently superior speed, if not the Hesketh driver's propensity for falling off the road while leading, would eventually tell the tale in Holland.

As the track dried Lauda poured the power and the pressure on James who, besides fending off the Austrian's high-speed challenges, also had to concentrate on making safe progress through the traffic they were lapping at a terrific rate. It was now strictly a two-car race.

Round and round they roared in tandem, the nose of the red car glued to the tail of the white car, the large British contingent in the crowd screaming itself hoarse, Le Patron standing spellbound in the Hesketh pit with his fingers, arms and legs crossed and Bubbles and the crew clucking madly to the Great Chicken In The Sky and every other know deity.

James, every fibre of his being wrapped in concentration so intense it would leave him emotionally and physically exhausted, pressed on with relentless precision and determination. Instead of being intimidated by Lauda's intense pressure he actually began to use the Ferrari's proximity to deepen his resolve. There was absolutely no way Niki was going to get by.

In the final five laps James was so confident he stepped up his pace even more and the interval between the Hesketh and the Ferrari could actually be measured on the clock. As he streaked across the finish line – after 1 hour, 46 minutes and 57.40 seconds of the most furious racing of his life – James was 1.06 seconds ahead of Niki.

The Hesketh pit erupted in unprecedented scenes of rapturous delirium. Eventually the pandemonium subsided and the heroes of the day – the first English driver to win a Grand Prix since 1971 and the first private entrant to win since 1968 – were sent off on a victory lap.

Pete Lyons recorded the historic moment in *Autosport*: 'His Lordship, virtue triumphant incarnate, almost floated onto the back of the flower garlanded lorry and, his face shining with effervescent ecstasy, rode backwards along the entire front row of the pits saluting his rival teams with a peculiarly English digital gesture.

'In front, facing the right way and waving in a more sober manner, but his face similarly incandescent, James Hunt set off on the first victory lap of his Grand Prix career. It had been a long, long time coming. But every line in his face proclaimed what a worthwhile wait it had been.'

Lord Hesketh thinks his hand signal was probably a combination of both a rude gesture and a 'V' for victory sign. It was immensely satisfying to beat the Grand Prix establishment at its own game, and he probably got as much pleasure from winning as James did. But Le Patron's most abiding memory of 22 June 1975 did come during the lorry ride around the circuit.

'Zandvoort is a pretty gloomy place. It's just a lot of sand dunes. And on top of every dune were just waves, waves and waves of Union Jacks. It was a wonderful feeling to know that those people, who had travelled with us all the way around Europe and had seen frustration after frustration, finally saw the result they wanted. And even today, so many years later, that memory still gives me goose pimples.'

James called it the most important race of his career. It was significant for being his first Grand Prix win and Hesketh's only win. 'This alone made it very special because Hesketh Racing gave me, and taught me, everything in Formula 1 and it was where my soul was. I have always felt they deserved more than one Grand Prix win.

'But that race rounded off my education. I hadn't the experience of leading races and suddenly finding myself leading a Grand Prix with somebody snapping at my heels was too much for me. It unnerved me and I made mistakes.

'At Zandvoort I laid that ghost to rest completely because I couldn't have had greater pressure than I had in that race. I had commanded a race from the front. When the others are sitting behind you can jolly well dictate your way of doing things. And Zandvoort was the completion of my training as a driver.

'My education in racing owed a lot to Bubbles Horsley. He took a close interest in me and my approach, and certainly helped me mature. He taught me how to deliver of my best all the time, instead of some of the time.

'His criticism of my driving and my mental approach was always constructive. He taught me how to prepare mentally, to spot when I wasn't properly motivated. He taught me how to persevere and how to pull out of bad situations. Above all, he taught me how to know myself better.'

★　★　★

After James left the team, following the financial crisis in 1975, Bubbles was able to resurrect Hesketh Racing and, in fact, he kept it in Formula 1 for another two seasons. But there was little success.

'We were at the back of the grid, running rent-a-drivers, going downhill rather fast. But making money, thank God, because that was the object of the exercise. I found the way I could cope was just to keep my head down and work. But I found it quite hard and James was always very good about it. He would come and chat with me at the races, trying to cheer me up and he would say "Bubbles, I never would have done it without you, you know".'

James respected Bubbles' balanced and reasoned perspective and came to rely on him for counsel and support for the rest of his life, and in every aspect of his life. They became, besides business partners in various investments, the closest friends and confidantes (and godfathers to each other's children) and there was no area too intimate for discussion, including James's already deteriorating relationship with Suzy.

Suzy, who stayed home in Spain, missed her husband's momentous triumph in Holland and the raucous party that raged late into the night among the sand dunes, where an entourage of James's old friends were among the celebrants.

'He was an unrelenting partier', John Richardson recalls, 'in the same way he was an unrelenting driver. He came back to our camp site and we had a monumental party, which soon included all the Brits at the circuit. James was very approachable and developed a wonderful rapport with the English fans.'

When the partiers ran out of beer Chris Jones remembers that 'Superstar' used his influence to replenish the supply.

'He'd go off into the night to the tents and caravans and talk to the fans who couldn't believe the actual winner of the race was right there among them. He'd sit with them for 10 minutes or so, signing autographs, laughing and joking and answering all their questions – which he genuinely loved to do – then he'd mention we were out of beer and he'd come back to the party with more pints and more people.'

His mates were well accustomed to James's exuberant and irreverent ways, but it did seem rather unusual for a newly married man to be sporting a badge sewn on his racing suit which proclaimed that 'SEX IS A HIGH PERFORMANCE THING'. Of course, the statement was his idea of a joke. But it might also have been construed as an advertisement.

★ ★ ★

The essential incompatibility of James and Suzy was apparent as early as their honeymoon in Antigua. James wanted to 'play at pirates' and talk shop with Bubbles, or read books and relax. Suzy wanted to talk, and not about racing. At the few races she did attend Suzy was bored stiff and, she said: 'I literally felt like a spare part. Was I just there for the show?'.

They made a beautiful couple, but Suzy soon found out that being a racing driver's wife, at least James Hunt's wife, was not to be a glamorous bed of roses – indeed, her husband was often not in it.

When Sue and Wallis Hunt went on holiday to the newlyweds' place in Spain, James was hardly ever there, and even her mother-in-law sympathized with Suzy's plight. 'She is absolutely gorgeous', Sue Hunt said. 'Just a super girl, most of his girls are. But I can see that for James to be married is impossible. His lifestyle doesn't suit it. I'm bound to say I love him dearly, but I'd hate to have him for a husband.'

James had, of course, suspected that his marriage was a mistake from the beginning, but he never blamed Suzy for its disintegration. It was a matter of clashing lifestyles and personalities. 'I am very much into racing and doing my own thing', he said, 'and I move very fast. Suzy wanted the reverse: a slow pace, a good solid base and a solid relationship. Ironically, the very things I married her for in the first place.

'If she stayed at home while I rushed around the world it was boring for her. If she came with me it was no fun for her. I was always looking over my shoulder to see if she was there and she was always struggling to keep up with me. It was a heavy deal for both of us.'

He began to look for a way out of his marriage, but consideration for Suzy's feelings was going to make it difficult. Her sympathetic understanding of his problem with the marriage and her concern for his happiness heightened his sense of responsibility for her welfare. 'I was very, very anxious not to hurt her. There are nice ways and nasty ways to do things and I hope I can never be a hurtful person.'

He offered to set her up in a flat in London and support her, but she was reluctant to make the break. They continued to live under the same roof but by midsummer of 1975 they began to go their separate ways socially, though they kept up appearances and their estrangement wasn't made public for some time.

James filled the matrimonial void with a succession of temporary replacements and got on with his racing life, which was now on footing as unfirm as his marriage.

Hesketh Racing's financial crisis deepened. Costs for the still not ready new car had escalated to £100,000 and the team was forced to take on a succession of drivers (four different ones) who paid for their rides with their own or sponsors' money.

Le Patron, much against his will, began actively to pursue sponsors for his team, promising that 'they'll get a hell of an advertising campaign for a very reasonable investment'.

James was less sure of Le Patron's commitment to accepting outside money. Several deals came close to being signed, but Le Patron seemed to 'torpedo it just as it was about to happen. He'd get cold feet. He didn't really want to give it away. We raced off our earnings on the track and a bit of ducking and weaving by Bubbles'.

James's contributions to the team's coffers included the prize money for second place in a thrilling French Grand Prix, where he finished a mere 1.6 seconds behind Lauda's Ferrari, having fought off the best efforts of the third place man, Jochen Mass in a McLaren.

At Silverstone James led the 'shambolic' British GP for eight laps, one of seven different drivers to do so, but then became one of the 10 who crashed when a sudden cloudburst inundated the circuit and caused the race to be stopped.

In practice for the Austrian Grand Prix James stopped at the scene of an accident involving Mark Donohue. The American driver's car had flown over a barrier and the track was strewn with debris. As another car sped by it sent a fencepost flying which nearly hit James on the helmet. In his accident Donohue had already suffered the same fate and, though he was conscious when taken to hospital, he later died from his head injuries.

Again, heavy rain in the race caused it to be stopped prematurely and James was in second place when the red flag was shown. The Italian driver Vittorio Brambilla was so surprised at winning, his one and only Grand Prix victory, that he crashed spectacularly just beyond the finish line, having removed his hands from the steering wheel to wave at the crowd.

The new Hesketh 308C made its debut in Italy, where James drove an excellent race, recovering from a spin caused by handling problems to finish fifth. He placed one better than that at Watkins Glen in America – the final event of the year and what proved to be James's last race for Hesketh.

It had been a splendid season. James was fourth overall in the 1975 driver standings, behind the World Champion, Lauda, and Fittipaldi and Reutemann, all of whom had considerably more Formula 1 experience and resources behind them. James had scored points in every race he finished and his results enabled Hesketh Racing to finish fourth in the Constructors' Championship, refreshingly close to the big budget teams of Ferrari, Brabham and McLaren.

But Hesketh Racing's short-lived celebrations ended at midnight on 14 November 1975, the deadline set by Le Patron for obtaining £300,000 in sponsorship necessary for the team to continue the next season.

The following day Superstar, Bubbles, Doc, Le Patron and the rest of the team appeared at a Hesketh Racing 'Farewell' at the Thruxton circuit. James did several demonstration laps in the Zandvoort-winning car. The event was televised live to millions of viewers on the BBC Grandstand program.

For his contribution to British motor sport the British Automobile Racing Club presented Lord Hesketh with a gold medal. He then announced that Hesketh Racing was no more.

'I owe an enormous debt to Alexander Hesketh and his team', James said. 'First and foremost they gave me the break which I needed at a crucial point in my career. All of us were plucked out of nowhere, particularly me.

'They showed great confidence in me which, considering my performance in Formula 3, was not strictly deserved. Yet they stuck by me and took me all the way. More particularly they gave me a very happy period in my life.

'The encouragement they gave me extended to enjoying life and having fun. Parties played a big part in things, but for the people in the racing team the attitude was always work first, play afterwards. We've been a team of very close friends. That is something I feel will be difficult to replace.'

Le Patron paid tribute to his driver's loyalty. 'I'm a very lucky man in having enjoyed a friendship and a relationship with James Hunt to the extent that he knew several months ago the problems that we had to face in racing next year. I am deeply grateful to James for having stayed when the going got tough. The fact that he has not secured his future drive for next year is because he believed in a dream that we all believed in.'

Lord Hesketh's feelings about his involvement with 'Superstar' have not changed to this day. 'It was my honour and privilege – and still the greatest thing I ever took part in – to have been able to give James his chance.'

6

GOLDEN BOY

1976

'I firmly believed that a fairy godmother with a large chequebook was just around the corner to save Hesketh Racing and I had only vaguely talked to other teams when everyone was rushing around signing new contracts.' But his loyalty left James now unemployed at the worst possible time: with less than two months before the 1976 season.

Among the few vacancies remaining was one at Team Lotus, but that came to nothing after an ill-fated meeting which 'comprehensively wasted three hours of my life. I had difficulty talking any sense to them at all. They seemed to be of the opinion that their drivers shouldn't be paid. They didn't even buy me lunch. That left me out looking for lunch in London at four o'clock on a Sunday afternoon.'

The clock kept ticking towards 25 January, the first race of the 1976 season, and James's immediate Formula 1 future became increasingly dim. He spent many hours on the telephone, hoping somehow to find an opening, but all the doors seemed closed. For several days he explored the possibility of driving a third car for the Brabham team, but that, too, fizzled out and it seemed all hope was lost.

But late in November two telephone calls saved his racing life. The first one was to James, from the manager of Emerson Fittipaldi, with the confidential news that the Brazilian would not be renewing his contract with the McLaren team. 'This fine gesture by Emerson, from a business point of view, gave me warning – time to get myself ready – because at that point it was obvious that McLaren would need me.'

There were no other top drivers still on the market and, as McLaren was about to find out, they were suddenly in desperate need of the services of James Hunt.

Teddy Mayer, the McLaren team director, received a telephone call at seven o'clock on a Thursday evening, two hours after James had already heard the news. While James had been ecstatic, Teddy Mayer's conversation with Emerson Fittipaldi had turned his complexion a pale shade of grey. His Brazilian driver explained that he was not going to sign the McLaren contract he'd been carrying around in his briefcase for three months. Instead, Emerson and his brother Wilson were going to form their own team, an all-Brazilian effort with sponsorship from the state-owned Copersucar sugar marketing organization.

Mayer was in shock. In his two seasons with McLaren Emerson Fittipaldi had finished first and second in the World Drivers' Championship (he was also World Champion with Lotus in 1972) and his departure left a huge void. Mayer still had Jochen Mass on the payroll, but the German driver had so far not shown signs of being a world-beater.

The list of potential team-mates for Mass was depressingly short. At the top of it was a man with a dubious reputation, both on and off the track, but Mayer wasted little time in contacting him. 'I barely stopped to say goodbye to Emerson before I got onto James and asked if he would drive for us. Within 36 hours we had concluded a deal.'

James, forewarned and therefore forearmed, was already in deep discussion with his good friend John Hogan, who was now head of racing activities for Marlboro cigarettes, McLaren's main sponsor. 'Hogey', after helping James with sponsorship (Coca Cola) and public relations during his Formula 3 days, had risen to a position of considerable power, since Marlboro (owned by Philip Morris) had one of the biggest Formula 1 budgets, and he was largely responsible for deciding how it should be spent, and on whom. With Hogan on his side it seemed James couldn't lose the McLaren seat, but he nearly did.

James, with his brother/manager Peter and a lawyer, met Hogan and other Philip Morris executives to sign the deal. The financial terms of the contract – which included a basic £45,000 retainer for James – were quickly agreed. But James balked at a clause in the contract which stipulated that Marlboro-sponsored drivers should always be dressed in a presentable way, especially at public functions, where a blazer, shirt and tie and tailored flannel trousers were regulation wear.

'He was sitting there at the table', John Hogan remembers, 'with no drive, without a pot to piss in and with everything to lose. And he said, "No way! I'm not wearing a blazer. You guys are wrong trying to make people conform like that. It's not what appeals to the younger generation. They don't want to see people all dressed up like Jackie Stewart!".

'And he wouldn't bloody well budge. Everybody reacted with shock and horror. This was a key part of the contract, that our drivers must present a clean-cut image. So I took him out of the room and said, "Look, take my word that I won't make you wear a shirt and tie. But I've got to have it in the contract to protect the company". So he agreed to sign it.'

For James, who was still smoking 40 cigarettes a day, his refusal to dress up like 'a Marlboro cigarette carton' was a matter of principle: 'to do what I want to do whenever I can. Life is too short to be bound by regulations when it isn't absolutely essential.

'I told them I wasn't going to get into those silly blazers and ties. I'd work hard for them but it would have to be my way and they would get a hell of a lot more out of me if they would just let me be myself. Of course, I'm not going to turn up in a T-shirt at Buckingham Palace, and when I attend more formal functions I'll dress accordingly.'

But he didn't and his refusal to be 'packaged' caused John Hogan 'basically, three and a half years of headache in this company. He would turn up at social events, management functions, banquets, cocktail parties and the like, wearing jeans and a tattered sweatshirt and sometimes in his bare feet, shaking hands with VIPs – and charming them all'.

Having James Hunt's signature on the contract was only the first hurdle for Marlboro and McLaren. It was still unclear that he was capable of performing up to the standards of an organization accustomed to success.

The team was founded by Bruce McLaren, a New Zealander who raced for the British Cooper team for several years, then fielded his own Formula 1 cars, beginning in 1966. McLaren was killed while testing one of his sports cars at the Goodwood circuit in 1970, but the team carried on, operating from their factory at Colnbrook, near Heathrow airport. The McLaren cars were perennial frontrunners, and by the end of 1975 the team had won 15 Grands Prix, most of them under the leadership of E. E. 'Teddy' Mayer, an American lawyer.

Teddy Mayer's connection with McLaren began in 1964, when his brother Timmy raced with Bruce McLaren in the Tasman series in New Zealand and Tasmania. Teddy, a law graduate from Cornell University in New York state, decided to pass up the bar to look after the management of his brother's career, which looked promising. But when

Timmy Mayer died in a practice accident at Longford in Tasmania, Teddy was devastated and returned home. A few months later Bruce McLaren persuaded him to move to England to invest in the team and help run it, and when McLaren was killed Mayer took control of the enterprise.

Over the years Mayer had successfully handled a succession of drivers with strong personalities, but he had never before encountered such a complex character as James Hunt. At the time he signed him Mayer said: 'I am particularly pleased we got James. From what I know of him he should be easy to work with as he is a driver dedicated to winning, and that's what counts at McLaren'.

But Mayer soon found out James was often not easy to work with and there were to be tempestuous times in their relationship. 'In terms of pure physical ability James was really outstanding. And what people choose to call talent these days, he had plenty of. But from time to time he let his emotions get in the way of the discipline a modern racing driver needs.

'It was a strange combination really, because he was quite analytical. He would be aware of situations and able to think about them in quite a detached manner, but at the same time apparently not able to control his instantaneous emotional reactions. His outbursts led to some embarrassment from time to time. And it led to raised eyebrows as well.'

Mayer's eyebrows were first raised in a row with James came at the opening race of the 1976 season, at the Brazilian Grand Prix.

Before arriving at the Interlagos circuit James had only two test sessions at Silverstone, both of them abbreviated and inconclusive because of wet weather. While the Hesketh car had been tailor-made to suit James's large size, the cockpit of the McLaren M23, now entering its third year of development, was built to smaller dimensions, and James found it 'undriveable'. The footwell was too crowded for his big feet, his knees were up around his chin, his elbows banged against the sides of the cockpit, the steering was too heavy and furthermore, fumed James, the whole McLaren team was 'a rudderless ship and didn't have any direction'.

While Hesketh Racing revolved around just James, McLaren was a two-car team: a much larger operation, with more personnel, but at least half of them (perhaps more) were devoted to fulfilling the needs of his team-mate Jochen Mass. No doubt James already felt a certain resentment to 'Herman the German' (as he called Mass) because James had been fired by the March Formula 3 team to make room for Mass.

Now, after a season and a half with McLaren, Mass was the senior driver and therefore James's rival. Their cars were supposed to be exactly equal in performance, but James knew that the team would naturally concentrate on the veteran, not the newcomer.

James, accustomed to being a one-man show, took this perceived fragmentation of effort as a personal slight and immediately embarked on a course of action to tip the balance of power in his favour. 'With relatively little experience I had to establish myself in McLaren as the senior Championship contender, and luckily that happened emphatically at the first race of the season. It might have destroyed any relationship I could have had with the Wiener (Mayer's nickname), but it would put the team 100 per cent behind me.'

In the first of the three qualifying sessions at Interlagos James floundered around among the midfield runners. He came into the McLaren pit waving a blistered thumb as tangible proof of the McLaren's heavy steering. Changes, coming far too slowly to suit James, were made to make the steering lighter and an enlarged cockpit surround was installed on the car to give him more room to work. James responded by setting the seventh fastest time, while his team-mate Jochen Mass was fourth quickest, behind the provisional polesitter Niki Lauda, in his Ferrari. Then James felt a sudden rattle from the Ford engine behind his back and dived into the McLaren pit for a replacement.

As the lengthy engine installation ate into the final hour of qualifying James became increasingly agitated. He was also fussing around the car demanding different suspension settings, something which Teddy Mayer felt should be left to the engineers. James, accustomed to speaking his mind to anyone he felt stood in his way, proceeded to do so in no uncertain terms to his new team leader.

'I had to have a shouting match with the Wiener about how the car was set up because I was going out with twenty minutes left on a five mile track. You don't get many laps in that time. I was guessing the settings and he said "You can't do that".

'But I said I was driving the bloody thing. I wasn't going to be pushed around when I knew what I wanted. I insisted, and this was in the garage in front of all the mechanics. I went out and on my first flying lap I got the first pole of my career. I was rather pleased about that and, of course, it impressed the boys. They like to see chargers and they'd seen me stand up to the Wiener. After that I was very much number one.'

At the start of the Brazilian Grand Prix James was unable to maintain his leadership status, when, fearful of burning out the clutch, he set off somewhat gingerly. He recovered well and for most of the race ran a strong second to Lauda's Ferrari.

Then the McLaren's Ford engine began to fire on only seven of its eight cylinders when an injection trumpet fell off. This handicap at first caused him to fall back, then lose control when the offending trumpet fell onto the throttle slide, jamming it open in the middle of a high-speed corner. The McLaren slid backwards into the catch-fencing with enough force to crumple the oil coolers and he was out of the race.

Niki Lauda went on to win easily, solidifying his position as favourite to repeat the World Championship he had won the previous year. (Emerson Fittipaldi's uncompetitive Copersucar could only manage a lowly 13th in front of the disappointed Brazilian fans.) Jochen Mass went on to salvage some honour for McLaren, by finishing a steady sixth, but it was clear the new boy Hunt was going to be no pushover in 1976.

For James, his first performance in a McLaren was a personal victory because, despite his outward air of bravado and self-confidence, he had nagging doubts about whether he was really up to the task – as did others. His employment had not been unanimously endorsed by everyone in the upper management of Philip Morris. Hogan had persuaded them James could do the job, but James had not been reassured by the hesitancy to hire him.

He had only ever driven the Hesketh in Formula 1. How much of his success in that car was due to his own ability and how much credit should go to the designer Harvey Postlethwaite? Could he do justice to the work of the McLaren designer Gordon Cuppock, whose M23 car was a proven race winner? How would he fare on his own, away from the helping hand of Bubbles Horsley, the man who had made him a winner? Would he be able to earn the McLaren team's respect after their succession of top-line drivers?

'Fortunately we got it all together in Brazil', said James, 'and I think everyone, particularly Teddy Mayer, John Hogan – and me! – heaved a big sigh of relief.

'Actually, the permanent silly grin on Teddy Mayer's face was even bigger than normal when we got pole position. He hadn't been very pleased when Emerson left the team, and for me to get pole in front of a Brazilian crowd was almost more than he could take!

'It was important psychologically because we immediately had each other's respect and I was able to establish my normal way of behaviour, which was not what McLaren had been used to with Emerson. If you behave 'badly' in terms of what is traditionally good behaviour, nobody minds it when you are doing well. But as soon as you are not doing well they point the finger and say "that's the reason".'

✩ ✩ ✩

'I thought he was very noisy, outgoing, good fun. Not boring. A bit of a yahoo with this playboy image, and egotistical like most racing drivers. And I was glad he didn't drive for me.' Alastair Caldwell's first impressions of James Hunt, formed when James was at Hesketh Racing, didn't change much during their time together at McLaren. But Caldwell, the McLaren team manager, very quickly came to appreciate having Hunt on his side.

Born in England and raised in New Zealand, Caldwell described himself as a 'prickly bastard' when he came to England in 1967 to work for the Kiwi team: McLaren. One of the reasons he left New Zealand was to get away from the memory of seeing his brother Bill killed in a crash at Teretonga, in the car which Alastair had worked on.

Though he shared the loss of a brother with Teddy Mayer, Caldwell at first found him a 'little bastard' to work for. But Mayer 'became more amenable' after Bruce McLaren's death and promoted the hard-working Caldwell up through the ranks until he was appointed team manager in 1974, the year Emerson Fittipaldi won the driving title with McLaren.

Caldwell, a rock-jawed, no-nonsense taskmaster who was known in the team as 'The Guv', supervised the efforts of the mechanics (many of them from New Zealand or Australia) who worked on James's car: Lance Gibbs, Mark Scott, Steven Bunn, Dave Ryan, Ray 'Kojak' Grant and Howard 'Hampton' Moore. They called Teddy Mayer 'Wiener', because, Caldwell says of the small, gnomish director, 'he looked like a baby pig'.

James, they decided, was 'Quasimodo', because 'with his long legs, relatively short upper body and rounded shoulders and with his hands touching his knees he looked like the Hunchback of Notre Dame'.

Caldwell remembers how Quasimodo won the team over in Brazil. 'Poor old Jochen was terribly worried because he was number one and basically this unknown bloke came in and blew him away. But it doesn't matter if the guy has got number one written on his forehead or tattooed over his whole body. If he's second fastest, he's number two, period. It's always been that way, even in the best run teams.

'These guys are all racers at heart and the focus automatically shifts to the quickest man. James, of course, had lucked into a beautifully developed car. It was in very competitive order when Emerson left. But

127

James was instantly very quick and we were all as happy as pigs in shit from then on.

'And the mechanics enjoyed working for an eccentric. I think James worked at being an eccentric, prancing around wearing unconventional clothes, doing crazy things and getting his name into the papers and so on. But it drew attention to the whole team and everybody enjoys working for somebody who's important.

'A lot of the journalists called him a spoiled brat, but I don't believe anyone at McLaren would have called him that. I was never one to suffer fools gladly, and James was no fool. But in my opinion most journalists were and they knew what I thought of them. They were frightened of me. Teddy was the one that normally dealt with the press, the bullshit side of the business, and there was a terrific amount of that with James around.

'We had a fair amount of exposure when Emerson won the championship, but with James on board the whole bloody press world suddenly descended on us. It started when we were in South Africa, with that business of his wife running off with Burton.'

*   *   *

Though they were still estranged, James and Suzy had been invited to spend Christmas and New Year with friends in Gstaad. James, worried about getting an injury that might interfere with his racing, no longer skied but happily accepted the offer to visit the Swiss ski resort, because he wanted to put Suzy into a situation where she might meet some new people.

James left her there while he went off to Brazil, and when he returned home to Spain Suzy called him to say she wanted to stay on in Gstaad because she was having a such good time. James happily gave her his blessing and flew out to South Africa for the second race of the season. There, of course, he proceeded to have his own good time.

In the week leading up to the race at Kyalami, near Johannesburg, his constant companion was Paddy Norval, an attractive South African actress. She was soon replaced by Carmen Jardin, an exotic Portuguese beauty, described by James as 'a super looker'. They met at the Kyalami Ranch hotel, where most of the drivers stayed and where James quickly charmed her away from a host of other admirers. When Miss Jardin, who had once been a lieutenant in the Portuguese army while on national service in Mozambique, gave James a lingering kiss prior to the pre-race test session at Kyalami he responded by breaking the lap record for the circuit.

Their romance was brief, however, and when James turned his full attention to the Grand Prix Carmen Jardin said, 'I don't think any girl on earth could win James away from his car. When he is free, he is great fun to be with. But try pinning him down! That's impossible'.

James spoke in his defence: 'I prefer to be on my own at the races because really there's enough to do looking after myself. It's more than I can handle to keep myself under control at a race meeting without trying to look after someone else as well and have more responsibilities and worries. I find that if I want an early night before a race or if I want a couple of hours to cool off and relax before dinner, I can do better to read a book or listen to music, and therefore it's better to be on my own.'

But away from the races his need for female companionship remained paramount. 'Life is too short not to get out and enjoy yourself when you can. I have the best time I can when it fits into my schedule and when it isn't going to interfere with my driving. They call me a playboy and there's nothing I can do about it. I admit that I love having beautiful women around me. But I can't make it a full time occupation, not when it threatens my racing.

'I don't usually have sex before a race because I am very definitely concentrating. I find that it is the communication between two people that makes it worthwhile, and before a race I am pretty uncommunicative. However, if, say, I have an hour or so to spare before dinner on the night before a race then I can enjoy the physical release. But I will only do it with someone who is fully understanding.'

He could be disarmingly frank about his private life, which is one of the reasons why the popular press pursued him in South Africa. The Kyalami hotel was staked out by a throng of jostling journalists and photographers – none of them interested in the race – and there were phone calls from around the world at all hours of the day and night. Everyone wanted to know how James Hunt felt about his wife keeping company with Richard Burton.

Suzy Hunt and Elizabeth Taylor's estranged husband met one snowy January evening on a street in Gstaad. Their age difference (he was 50 and she was 26) was no obstacle for Richard Burton, who described his first sight of her: 'There was this gorgeous creature – about nine feet tall'.

The Welsh film actor, beset by Celtic demons and depressions that drove him to drink to excess, later credited her with saving his life. 'For the first time I am mentally content with my private life. Susan is largely responsible for that. She is wise far beyond her years.'

After their first days together in Gstaad Suzy and Burton went their separate ways for a week, she to Lausanne as a guest of the wealthy German industrialist Gunther Sachs, while Burton flew off to New York. Then, ostensibly as a guest of her friend, Brook Williams (son of the actor and playwright Emlyn Williams), who also happened to be Burton's personal assistant, Suzy arrived in New York to stay at the same hotel as Burton.

In short order the New York and London papers discovered that the glamorous blonde 'mystery woman' on the arm of Richard Burton – who was the toast of Broadway as the star of the newly opened play *Equus* – was the wife of the racing driver James Hunt. Suzy Hunt, the gossip columnists predicted, was going to break up the Elizabeth Taylor–Richard Burton remarriage (they were first married in 1964, when they met filming the movie *Cleopatra*), which had taken place the previous October.

None of this was news to James because Suzy had kept him informed by telephone. (When she told him Burton had invited her to go to America, he said 'Fine, on your bike and off you go. Or words to that effect. And off she went'.) But both of them were cautious about what they said to the press. Suzy claimed she was not in New York with anyone in particular. She did admit that her marriage was in a precarious state. And yes, she and James had discussed divorce, but they were still very close and they would meet again after the South African race.

To pacify the journalists in South Africa, James said, 'Naturally I am perturbed about all the publicity about my wife in Europe and America but I must concentrate 100 per cent on the Grand Prix. If there is a problem it is just going to have to wait until after the race. Meanwhile I'm far too busy sorting out the car and keeping myself fit'. Then, under the hot African sun, he trotted off on another six mile training run.

In fact, James ran more freely than he had in the 16 months since his wedding day at the Brompton Oratory. The Suzy Hunt and Richard Burton alliance was a huge weight off his shoulders. He and Suzy had effectively gone their separate ways in July of 1975, so the press was not probing a painful area, but the difficulty of getting her life restructured and reorganized weighed heavily on James. He felt responsible for her and it was interfering with his first love: racing.

'So her running off with Burton is a great relief to me', he said privately. 'It actually reduces the number of problems I have to face outside my racing. I am mainly concerned that everyone comes out of it happy and settled. Meanwhile, it is probably a good thing that I am still technically married. I have that as a safety valve. It will stop me from doing anything silly again!'

James celebrated his new sense of freedom in fine style in the South African Grand Prix. In qualifying he put his best foot forward and again beat Niki Lauda for pole position. In the race he never put a foot wrong, finishing a fighting 1.3 seconds behind Lauda's Ferrari with its superior V12 engine power.

After they took the chequered flag James pulled alongside his friend Niki and the two exchanged a jaunty salute of mutual congratulations. And when James took off his helmet his wide grin of satisfaction was only exceeded by those on the faces of the McLaren team, who greeted their new charger with hearty slaps on the back and generous words of praise. In their minds James looked entirely capable of being a worthy successor to their departed World Champion Emerson Fittipaldi.

In mid-March, when Niki Lauda arrived at the non-championship race at Brands Hatch, he was on his honeymoon. The secretive Austrian's marriage to his girlfriend Marlene Knaus caught everyone by surprise but it paled in comparison to the continuing saga of the increasingly fragile marital state of British motor racing's 'Golden Boy'.

The tabloids were full of the latest developments. James Hunt's excellent victory in the Brands Hatch Race of Champions, where Lauda's Ferrari had a mechanical failure, was virtually ignored. Instead, it was noted that Vanessa Hecklunk, a Swedish model, embraced him warmly in the pits and the majority of the journalists clustered around James at the post-race celebrations wanted to know about him and Suzy.

James was in a hurry – a helicopter was waiting to whisk him away to Heathrow for a connecting flight to New York – but he gave them what they wanted to hear. 'It was great to win but I had to mentally switch off about all my marriage problems. I had to just think about driving, otherwise I would have gone off into a bank and I wouldn't be here now. I'm only going to be in New York for 24 hours before flying to Long Beach in California for my next race. I have a very tight business schedule but I've spoken to Suzy and we're hoping to meet briefly to discuss our future.'

James had stayed with his parents during the Brands Hatch weekend and before his departing plane was over the Atlantic the aggressive press tracked down his mother for her comments about her 'errant daughter-in-law'.

Sue Hunt admitted she had reservations about Suzy being linked with a man of Burton's dubious reputation and she also had misgivings about their age difference. But she refused to blame Suzy, whom she thought was 'a delight. I am very fond of her and I am terribly sad for her. I believe in the stability of the family. Things like a settled marriage still mean something, even today. But I realize these marriage breakdowns happen and I can understand it, in James's case particularly. He is totally dedicated to motor racing. He's always been an odd fellow'.

At Kennedy airport in New York the throng of journalists and photographers gathered to meet Mr Suzy Hunt was estimated at 200. But James was now fed up with all the attention and refused to contribute further material to the stories of him being the distraught, cuckolded husband. 'I will talk about racing all day long but I have no intention of discussing my marital affairs.'

Left to their own devices the newspapermen reported that James and Suzy spent an hour together at James's hotel. After their brief encounter James gave her a lift back to the hotel where she and Burton were staying. There was even speculation that Hunt and Burton met briefly. Before they parted James and Suzy embraced and kissed fondly, a gesture which was gleefully interpreted by the press as a further thickening of the plot.

* * *

When James arrived in Long Beach complaining of a stomach pains some people wondered if it was because all the gossip-mongering was gnawing away at him. But he would only admit to feeling increasing pressure to produce better results. He felt he had Niki Lauda's number at Brands Hatch and James only wished the Ferrari hadn't broken down.

'Or I wish it would break down in a race that counted! Now I have to deliver for my team. I need the points to stay in the championship. I need a victory to make Niki sweat and I need one to know I can do it.'

James, though he enjoyed the freedom of American society and was amused by its elements of crassness and vulgarity, found little comfort in the bizarre arena in which his forthcoming drama would have to be played.

It was hoped by the organizers of the United States Grand Prix West that some of the glamour of the jet-setting Formula 1 circus would rub off on the decaying city near Los Angeles. Exercising the most extreme poetic licence the race through the streets of Long Beach was billed as an American version of the Monaco Grand Prix. In truth, the two locations shared only a proximity to water, and the muddy Pacific harbour filled with oil derricks (their grime only partly hidden by brightly painted hoardings and fake palm trees) was a far cry from the glories of the Mediterranean.

Certainly the Long Beach ambience rivalled Monaco in curiosity value. The Principality had nothing like the liner *Queen Mary* anchored in the harbour as a permanent hotel, nor did it have a piece of bizarre statuary as big as the Spruce Goose, the enormous wooden aeronautical folly of the eccentric billionaire Howard Hughes, which was on display near the temporary Formula 1 paddock.

Downtown Long Beach consisted of decrepit hotels, run-down apartment buildings, abandoned places of business and sleazy theatres showing pornographic movies, past which the Formula 1 cars were to race on bumpy, worn out streets bordered by concrete walls topped by chain link fencing.

James (whose street racing experiences at Monaco and Barcelona were events 'in which I didn't exactly cover myself with glory') thought this race would be 'bloody difficult. There's no margin for error at all. And I agree with Niki that on this course either you keep your mind on your business every inch of the way or you've had it'.

James had it on only the third lap. After qualifying third he was holding that position behind the Tyrrell driven by Patrick Depailler, who was in turn on the tail of Clay Regazzoni's Ferrari.

James, who had already slipped past Depailler on one occasion but was forced to drop back when his engine skipped a beat (because of a momentary vapour lock in the fuel system), saw the Frenchman clip a barrier, then begin to slide wide on a fast corner. James seized what he thought was an open door invitation only to have it slammed in his face. The Tyrrell moved over on the McLaren and shoved it into the wall, whereupon the driver was immediately seen to leap out of the car. But he wasn't heading for safety behind the concrete barrier.

On the next lap Depailler's team-mate Jody Scheckter came roaring around the bend past the parked McLaren and: 'I couldn't believe my eyes. There was James standing in the middle of the bloody track, just off my racing line. It was very foolish'.

James, his face the colour of his scarlet fireproof racing suit, stayed there for several laps shaking his fist and screaming obscenities at Depailler each time he came around. Eventually he left his dangerous position (and later claimed he could easily have dodged any wayward cars), but his rage had not abated in the two hours it took for the race to finish and the top three drivers – Regazzoni, Lauda and Depailler – to appear at the post-race press conference.

In the large press room, before an assembly of amazed journalists –

many of them Americans bored by the race for 'funny little furrin cars' who brightened visibly at the possibility of a punch-up – James launched himself into an extravagant verbal attack on a bewildered Depailler who, though he had no trouble hearing it, needed the services of an interpreter to translate the finer points of the Anglo-Saxon tirade into French.

'It was just flagrant stupidity!', James bellowed. 'I came alongside you and you saw me but you just moved over and squeezed me out. You made a complete cockup of that corner and the first thing you should do when you make a cockup is to look where all the others are. The first thing you must do is to bloody well learn to drive!'

Depailler protested that he hadn't seen James because he was distracted by a brake problem with his Tyrrell. He was very upset and apologized: 'James I am desolate at what has happened. I am so sorry'.

James said he was 'bloody well sorry too', warned the diminutive Frenchman to 'Watch it!' and strode out of the room, muttering about crazy Frog drivers and that the whole episode 'was a helluva setback. I had a sure second place'.

While James was venting his spleen one of his mechanics had driven his abandoned car back to the pit. The only damage appeared to be a crumpled nose section and there were suspicions that James could have continued to race had his anger not overpowered his reason, that he had exaggerated the incident out of all proportion and perhaps he had indeed cracked under the strain of his crumbling marriage.

James felt his tantrum in Long Beach was fully justified, though he later modified his stance to an error in judgement on his part. He kept a mental file on each driver and in his book Patrick Depailler (who was killed in an accident in Germany in 1980) was not to be trusted at close quarters.

'You behave differently with different people and I made an error in trying to pass him where I did. With anybody else it would have been quite all right. But I don't see how that vindicates him in any way. And I don't think I was too hard on Depailler.'

The incident did help James to understand better the explosive nature of his own character on a race weekend. He felt it was necessary to build himself up to an emotional peak of tension in order to get the best performance. The process began on the Wednesday before the race, and by Sunday morning he knew he had worked himself up into the desired state of readiness when he became physically ill.

'I'm very nervous and you have to be nervous to the right amount. I've got to the point now where I can control it. I can make myself more nervous by thinking about the race and if I'm too nervous I deliberately stop thinking about it. Now all that requires a lot of mental effort, a lot of concentration, a lot of introversion. When you're driving you have to be in total control of your emotions. It must be purely practical work. Otherwise you're playing with a dangerous thing.'

Alastair Caldwell had never seen a driver as nervous as James. 'Before a race a lot of my drivers pretended to be sleeping. Either they would be overcome by adrenaline or in an attempt to control it they would go into a passive mode and try to lower their metabolism by dozing. But James couldn't keep still. He would pace around the garage chain-smoking cigarettes, put his helmet on, then take it off again and he nearly always threw up in the pits.

'It would get worse when we brought the car out onto the grid. Just before the start he would get so uptight that the car was actually shaking on the grid. If you sat on the sidepod with him in the cockpit his legs would be going up and down like jackhammers and you would think the engine was running.'

Formula 1 team managers can be fairly ruthless when it comes to motivating their drivers. While James was with Hesketh, to inspire him to speed up during practise and qualifying, Bubbles Horsley would take advantage of his very low tolerance for indolence by having the mechanics deliberately work slowly on his car. If Bubbles thought James was capable of going faster on the track he would alter the lap times on the pit signalling board, showing him a slower time than he had actually recorded, and James would speed up accordingly.

Alastair Caldwell soon discovered how his driver's mind worked and sometimes practised his own form of psychology to harness James's supercharged emotions before the start of a race. 'James needed distraction to keep him from getting too excited. Sometimes I used to get Teddy to have an argument on the grid about money because that was James's favourite subject. They would have this huge row about hotel accommodation or first-class airline tickets and that took his mind off worrying.

'But he put more into driving than anyone I knew. He had so much adrenaline that if his car suddenly stopped he must have had several pints of adrenaline left over and it had to go somewhere.'

James admitted that his adrenaline overload often took the form of excess ire. 'When the race suddenly stops – whatever happens, an accident or a mechanical problem – I'm always in a highly emotional, discharging state. To open that emotional door at the end of four or five days is obviously a great relief. I think it's a normal and human way to behave, and if it upsets anyone that's unfortunate. But it can put me a bit out of control.'

Though Teddy Mayer would sometimes get scalded when James's emotional kettle boiled over, he was prepared to forgive him. 'I suppose it's not a bad way for a driver to be. They've got to have some fire and determination and at least if he blows off steam, it's gone. If he carried it around bottled up it could do all sorts of harm. So I don't see that as a particularly bad characteristic. It might be unpleasant for a few moments but you can learn to live with that.'

* * *

His histrionics in America and his wife's dalliance with the movie star continued to make headlines, but James's performance in the next event, the Graham Hill International Trophy at Silverstone, focused more media attention on his ability as a driver. Though it was a non-championship race (and the Ferraris were not entered) it had special significance for British fans because it was held in memory of Graham Hill, the two-time World Champion who was killed in a plane crash the previous November. Hill's second driving title, in 1968, was the last time an Englishman had won the World Championship.

James, in a smooth and unflustered display of driving perfection, completely dominated the race in front of an adoring crowd of partisan fans. At the finish, when he was handed the Graham Hill Trophy by Hill's widow Bette, James said to her, 'If I can achieve only a small percentage of what Graham achieved in his life I will be happy'.

In his report of the event in *Autosport* Ian Phillips noted how apt it was that James should win and how well suited he was to succeed Graham Hill as a Britain's top representative at the pinnacle of motor sport.

'James is a natural to fill the gap left by the sport's much loved ambassador and everything he did over the weekend was as the master would have done it himself. His style was impeccable, both on and off the track, which should shut up the childish newspaper critics for good and all.

'The message was loud and clear: James Hunt has no problems and will carry Britain to the fore in this year's World Championship. Let's hope the ignorant members of the popular press get off his back and let him carry out the job he does so well.'

But Graham Hill, though he was a colourful character with a quick wit and an entertaining sense of humour, was the product of an earlier, more innocent era. During his career, which flourished from the late 1950s to the early 1970s, motor sport coverage was provided by only a few journalists, whose work appeared mainly in the specialist racing magazines. They concentrated on what a driver did on the track and seldom ventured into print any mention of his personal characteristics.

Times had changed, and the cult of personality, led by the non-racing press, was beginning to prevail. And James Hunt – the swashbuckling, outspoken, hot-tempered, fanatically dedicated, ruthlessly ambitious, ex-public school glamour boy – perfectly fitted the newly defined role of sporting hero.

His rise to prominence, aided and abetted by the 'popular' press, brought a whole new audience to Formula 1 racing and made the sport more popular than ever before. The tabloid newspapers created, and catered to, the appetites of modern fans and quite likely a large percentage of the 75,000 spectators at the Graham Hill International Trophy Race were attracted as much by James's colourful image and his increasingly public private life as by his undoubted driving prowess.

No one knew this better than the man himself, and, though constantly being in the limelight would eventually drive him to distraction, James was always fully cognizant of the part his personal notoriety played in elevating him to the 'Superstar' status that Le Patron had jokingly conferred on him when he first came into Formula 1.

Now, he thought a lot of what was printed about him and Suzy was 'absolute rubbish', but it was also 'bloody good publicity for me, which turned out to be a good boost for my career'.

After the Silverstone race James returned to Spain for a final rendezvous with Suzy. They met over morning coffee at a restaurant in Malaga and soon decided a reconciliation would not be possible.

In a frank but amicable discussion James told her that his marriage, with the misery and feelings of being captured and imprisoned that he'd inflicted on himself, had given him time to think. It made him realize that he'd made a big mistake, though none of it was her fault. She had married him in good faith and he had betrayed it. He accepted full responsibility for leading her astray and was very sorry about it.

When they were married James thought Suzy was ideal in every way and his opinion of her had not changed. But their conflicting lifestyles were simply not compatible. His penchant for consuming life in a rush, and her preference for a more leisurely pace left Suzy struggling to keep up and James in a state of anxiety about her welfare. The fact that he failed to fulfil his responsibilities as a good husband weighed heavily on his conscience until it became a source of serious irritation to him.

He was delighted she had a new man in her life; he approved of him and thought they would be good for each other. Following their brief meeting in New York (which had indeed taken place, as the press suspected), he had several telephone conversations with Richard Burton and James thought he was 'a very nice guy, not at all the "monster" the media made him out to be. He called himself my father-in-law and he's been a very nice father-in-law ever since'.

Suzy was very relieved and told James that she and Richard wanted to get married and were investigating ways to get divorced. James said he would not stand in her way. He only wanted her to be happy and, he added, if she was ever unhappy there would always be a place for her with him. They parted on friendly terms and remained that way for the rest of James's life.

In June, Mrs Susan Hunt and Mr Richard Burton obtained quickie divorces (in Haiti) from their respective spouses and they were married on 21 August, in a quiet ceremony in Arlington, Virginia. They lived as man and wife for several years, but eventually the strain of nursing Burton through his bouts of drinking and depression, then his serious illnesses, became more than Suzy could bear. When her own health began to suffer she left him and Burton married Sally Hay who stayed with him until he died.

Had Suzy stayed with her racing driver she might easily have had to endure difficulties similar to those that she had with the troubled movie star.

* * *

After he made his peace with Suzy and she flew back to New York, James went out on the town in Marbella, throwing himself headlong into a riotous evening at a discotheque. Becoming overheated by his exertions he went outside and jumped fully clothed into a swimming pool. His attempt to rejoin the party was barred by a large doorman who objected to his soaking form and leaking shoes. The two engaged in a shouting match and James sloshed off to reorganize his domestic affairs, which were now in charge of his new 'Girl Friday', a 24-year-old blonde from Holland.

Anita Todd was recently separated from her British husband Ian Todd, a former Olympic skier. In response to James's request to help find him a new home she came up with a luxurious villa just outside Marbella, overlooking the Costa del Sol. It belonged to Jackie Lane, a former film star, and had five bedrooms, three baths and a swimming pool. James was so pleased with Anita Todd's house-hunting efforts that he asked her to move in with him and become his housekeeper and personal secretary.

'We know what people will say', said James, 'but there is no romance in it. She is strictly a housekeeper. It doesn't pay to fraternize with the staff. It would only lead to aggravation which would become a big pain in the arse. If you're going to sleep with your housekeeper you may as well make her your wife and I've already been through that. I have no steady girlfriend now, though there are several girls among my close friends'.

Indeed there were, including the British film actress Joanna Petit, whom James met at a celebrity tennis tournament in Gstaad. After a cosy sojourn with her he continued to play the field, and there was a steady procession of attractive female guests at his Spanish villa. But they seldom stayed long.

'It's nice to look at pretty girls but you can't just look at them forever. You've got to talk to them sometime and for me it's important for a girl to be able to communicate. I like women with open minds and nice personalities and I like fun people. But it takes me a long time to get to know someone, to establish trust. Only then can I relax.'

To most people his vigorous fitness regimen looked anything but relaxing. Much of the time his Porsche (formerly Le Patron's) sat idle in the garage while James ran down the roads to and from his daily squash, tennis and golf games. To the locals he encountered on training runs he was still Señor Hunt, the mad, nearly naked runner, attired in nothing but flimsy shorts and battered plimsolls with his shaggy blond hair flapping in the wind.

As he ran, James thought not of the bikini-clad women lounging around his swimming pool. He confined his thoughts to racing in the belief that 'the more you think about it, the better you do. Disciplined exercise is good because racing is a disciplined business'.

When it came to personal discipline his new team was leaving him entirely to his own devices, a state of affairs which James had not been accustomed to. With Hesketh Racing he was kept in line by 'terrible rollockings from Bubbles Horsley, a very heavy disciplinarian who didn't hesitate to haul me back to England from Spain to tell me to pull my socks up.

'When I left Hesketh I rather doubted whether I would be considered serious-minded enough for McLaren. I was not sure I could wear the poker face I feared they might expect. But in fact I have been pleasantly surprised, and the discipline imposed on me has been much lighter than under Bubbles.

'At McLaren they have paid me the compliment of treating me as though I were Fittipaldi – a professional capable of making my own decisions about my lifestyle. Besides, I've discovered the people at McLaren and Marlboro all quite like a joke and a few drinkies!'

But John Hogan remembers that James, when not in his racing mode, liked more than a few drinkies, as well as other substances.

'He was quite good at being the pot calling the kettle black. He always used to accuse other people of having a low tolerance for alcohol but his own was very low. He was a great mixer of drinks, which is the quickest way to get yourself out of shape.

'He'd go to a cocktail party and grab two or three of whatever was on the passing trays: those coloured drinks with cherries on top and the little umbrellas sticking out of them. Then he'd sit down to dinner and start with white wine, move on to the red and finish it off with port. That's guaranteed to knock anybody over.

'We used to have vociferous debates over his drinking and about drugs, especially marijuana, which he was smoking from about 1975 onwards. He used to argue that it was no worse than alcohol and spent years trying to convince me the law should be changed and pot should be made legal.

'But my position was that it was still illegal. The law is the law and I told him if he got caught his contract would go straight into the shredder. Of course my own very indignant position meant that I could never afford to smoke a joint. Not because I didn't want to sometimes, but because if he ever found out I would have absolutely no credibility with him whatsoever!'

Yet Hogan admired his friend's tremendous willpower. James certainly loved his 'drinkies' but rigidly avoided them on the days leading up to a race. 'From Wednesday night any form of alcohol is absolutely taboo for me. It's purely personal discipline because there is no harm at all in having a glass of wine with dinner or even two glasses of wine. Or a beer. It's just a matter of principle and if you make a rule for yourself, you've got to stick to it.

'I know plenty of drivers who have a drink with their dinner. Nothing wrong with that at all, it can't possibly do any harm. But I have my rule that I don't touch it. After all, who wants one glass of wine anyway? If I'm going to have some wine, I want ten glasses!'

*　*　*

The fourth round of the 1976 season was the Spanish Grand Prix, at the Jarama circuit in the countryside outside Madrid.

Niki Lauda was well ahead in the drivers' standings but the McLaren team had its share of points, Jochen Mass having collected enough of them to be in fourth place overall. James was fifth, and while he had been closer to a win than his team-mate the usual situation within a team was that the leading points scorer had the seniority and the lower scoring driver would have to back him up. For Mass, who had won the 1975 Spanish Grand Prix (at Barcelona) in a McLaren, a strong showing now would strengthen his position.

Born in Munich, he was a year older than James but had less racing experience, having only become interested in the sport at the age of 21, after a career in the German merchant navy. A quiet, introspective man, he spent most of his spare time on his sailing yacht which he kept on the French Riviera. Mass was well-liked by everyone in the McLaren team and thought his new team-mate was 'a real extroverted character'.

Occasionally, Mass admits, James's antics made him angry, especially his way of mocking him (and calling him Herman the German) and 'going too far with his foolishness'. It may have been partly a cultural clash, and a failure to understand James's personal version of a British sense of humour, but Mass also felt James 'was chasing his own image sometimes, and I found it a bit unfortunate that he needed to do that.

'We would say to him, and I wasn't the only one on the team to say it, "James, for God's sake you must be crazy!". But he just shrugged it off and laughed about it. We had a lot of laughs, actually. He could be great fun, and though we had the normal twists and turns as team-mates, basically, we got along fine. It was a very happy team.'

However, it was not a happy team by the time the Spanish race was over. It all began well when the two McLarens split Lauda's Ferrari at the front of the starting grid, with James again on pole and Mass in the third spot. The race looked especially promising for the McLaren drivers, since the Austrian was handicapped by a painful injury.

Two weeks earlier, while working on a new swimming pool at his chalet near Salzburg, Niki's tractor had overturned and two of his ribs were broken. He was given a pain-killing injection for the race, but admitted he could feel the ribs grinding against each other in the cockpit and he wasn't sure about his stamina, or his speed.

The start had been delayed while King Juan Carlos I arrived by helicopter and, when James also was slow to get away from the start line, Lauda accelerated into the lead and held it for the first 31 laps. Then James, who had been hounding the Ferrari all the way, began to sense Niki was tiring and eased past him. As Hunt pulled away Mass also overtook Lauda and the stage looked set for a McLaren one-two triumph. But a few laps from the finish the engine in Mass's car blew up and James was left alone to collect the win, his first Grand Prix victory for McLaren.

On his way to receive the victor's laurels James grabbed an orange drink and when it was accidentally knocked out of his hand he lashed out at the unfortunate perpetrator. 'I had just won the race, I was tired and thirsty and this drink was the only thing I had in the world. This guy knocked it out of my hand and I punched him. It was a terrible thing to do because the poor guy hadn't meant to do it but I didn't have time to think about it. I felt awful about it afterwards and tried to find him and apologize, but I couldn't find him. I'm not a punchy person normally, but I'm always punchy when I get out of the car.'

As James was being crowned race king of the day by Juan Carlos I his car was wheeled away for the customary post-race scrutineering. It was a popular victory and, everyone agreed, well-deserved, if devalued somewhat by the Ferrari driver's handicap. Lauda finished a gritty second and on the victory podium James shook his hand and paid tribute to his courage. Then the very happy winner went off to accept the congratulations of his team and, he fully expected, some serious celebrating.

The revelry in the McLaren motorhome in the paddock was short-lived. The scrutineers delivered the bad news that Hunt's car was illegal. The offence – the rear tyres protruding 1.8 centimetres (five eighths of an inch) wider than the maximum width allowed by the regulations – would have to be punished by disqualification.

Teddy Mayer was outraged and said that this was like being given the death sentence for a parking violation. He argued that such a minuscule discrepancy couldn't possibly give his driver any advantage and the ruling by the Formula 1 governing body was 'unbelievably harsh and unjustified.'

Most people agreed, but the irony of it all was that the McLaren cars, the widest of all, had been used as the template to establish the maximum width dimension in the new rules which had been devised at the request of all the teams. The rulemakers, the Sporting Commission of the Federation Internationale de l'Automobile (FIA), had been asked by the teams to come to Spain and check the dimensions of every car.

That the scrutineers had twice measured the McLarens before the race particularly incensed Teddy Mayer, who pointed out that no mention was made of any irregularity then, and his driver had gone on to risk his life in the race. Mayer intimated that there must have been some collusion in certain quarters, perhaps even a conspiracy instigated by Ferrari to take away the points McLaren earned in Spain.

Mayer, bringing his legal training into play, resolved to take the matter up with the highest authorities. He would formally protest the severity of the sentence and, if any penalty was warranted, he would suggest that the team be fined for its oversight and that the nine points for the win should be given back to James. The appeal would take some time. Meanwhile, Mayer said, 'The entire McLaren team extends its sympathy to James Hunt'.

James's reaction to this setback was mixed. On the one hand he found it all 'a bit of a bore and there was no point in getting uptight about it'. But he also thought McLaren's failure to check the width of the car was a 'fantastically sloppy performance'. Alastair Caldwell accepted the blame for the oversight. He knew the car's bodywork was exactly the right width, but had failed to allow for the new Goodyear tyres, which bulged slightly beyond the bodywork. Caldwell's car preparation and his innovations, including the development of a six-speed gearbox (most teams had only five gears), were responsible for keeping the rather elderly McLaren M23 competitive in 1976, but after the Spanish disqualification he decided to take no chances with his other recent modifications.

Worried that the now zealous CSI rule enforcers would take issue with the repositioned oil coolers at the back of the car, Caldwell and the McLaren designer Gordon Cuppock decided to move them back to their original position. They also slightly lowered the rear wing and moved it forward and, of course, narrowed the wheelbase the required 1.8 centimetres.

The combined effect of the relocated items was to affect the car's aerodynamics adversely by interrupting the air flow around the rear wing. This caused a loss of the downforce which helped keep the rear wheels glued to the road and the resulting lack of adhesion, according to James, made his car 'utterly hopeless'.

★   ★   ★

At the Belgian Grand Prix his McLaren lurched and yawed alarmingly around the Zolder circuit as James tried with all his might to overcome the handling deficiencies. He managed to establish the third fastest time in qualifying (behind the Ferraris of Lauda and Regazzoni), though he also crashed in one session.

Out of the car the driver seemed equally twitchy. He tried to keep up appearances, cracking jokes and larking about, but it all seemed as forced as his driving, and in *Autosport* Pete Lyons described him as being 'as jumpy as a stud horse with a bad tooth'.

In the race James drove like a cowboy on a bucking bronco, in the process incurring the wrath of some of his peers. While Lauda galloped away to win easily, Hunt's contrary, and slow, McLaren proved dangerous to pass. Several times Jody Scheckter's Tyrrell was nearly shoved off the road before he managed to scrape by, and when Jacques Laffite tried it his Matra was given a poke in the side by the McLaren's front wheel.

Finally, the McLaren coasted to a halt with gearbox failure at the halfway point in the race – not a moment too soon for Patrick Depailler, who was still smarting from James's condemnation of his driving in Long Beach. 'Hunt was driving very wild, holding everybody back', said Patrick. 'You ask Jacques Laffite who put a wheel into his car. You know, if Hunt says all these things about crazy French drivers like Patrick Depailler, he for sure should not drive in the same way himself!'

In the streets of Monte Carlo (where Niki Lauda won, again) James qualified an unlucky 13th on the grid and in the race his misfortunes continued, because: 'I have to say that I spun the car through my lack of interest – sheer bloody frustration'. He got going again but was soon put out of his misery when his engine blew itself into smithereens.

At Anderstorp in Sweden James spun a total of six times in practice and qualifying. But he managed to stay on the track during the race and was fifth at the finish, though 'miles behind in a very undriveable car'.

Still, he thought his wrestling match with the ill-handling McLaren – when cornering it was 'oversteering' madly, with the rear of the car continually trying to overtake the front – was one of his best drives of the year, and by season's end his hard-earned two points would be especially important.

The Swedish Grand Prix was dominated by Jody Scheckter and his team-mate Patrick Depailler, who finished one-two in their bizarre-looking but briefly efficient six-wheeled Tyrrells. As it developed, this was a freak result and a Tyrrell would not win again that season, but it was a refreshing change from the dominance of the Ferraris.

While Niki Lauda was third, his worst result of the year to date, the chances of him not winning his second consecutive World Championship with the famous Italian team seemed most remote. Even more of a long shot was any possibility of James Hunt, with the season nearly half over, overcoming Lauda's massive 47 point lead in the standings.

7

UNDERDOG

1976

Lauda and Hunt were both slightly ill at the next race, the French Grand Prix, though when it was over the Englishman was in much better shape than the Austrian.

Niki's ribs were now healed, but he came to Le Circuit Paul Ricard in the South of France suffering from a bout of flu. James, after wolfing down mounds of pâté de foie gras at dinner on Friday night, was nauseous for the rest of the weekend. His puking ritual before the start failed to purge him of his plight, and near the end of the race he had to fight back the urge to vomit in his helmet. But the knowledge that he was about to win his second race of the year helped quell his queasiness.

The McLaren cars, restored to the specifications with which they began the season and with the aerodynamics improved by a tidying up of the rear wing and bodywork configuration, were now back in fighting trim.

James had again secured pole position, but at the start of the race, to his chagrin, further proof that the status quo had been restored came when Niki Lauda once more beat James into the first corner. However, a wisp of vapour from the back of the Ferrari boded ill for the Austrian, and after only eight laps he coasted to a halt with a blown engine. Lauda's first mechanical failure of the season left the way clear for James to win again, and the pâté rising in his gorge was soon forgotten.

Within 24 hours of the win in France it became necessary to celebrate another Grand Prix victory, though James didn't have to drive again to win it. Instead: 'It was handed to me on a plate'.

On Monday morning he flew to Paris to appear before a jury

convened by the FIA to hear the McLaren appeal against the severity of his sentence at the Spanish Grand Prix. Besides James, presenting the McLaren case that the punishment didn't fit the crime were Teddy Mayer, Colin Chapman (the founder and owner of Team Lotus and an acknowledged expert in Formula 1 technology) and Dean Delamont (head of the Royal Automobile Club).

After several hours of deliberation the five-man FIA jury rendered its decision on the Spanish disqualification: 'The exclusion incurred by the McLaren car driven by James Hunt, who had won the event, was annulled, with all the consequences that this measure entails'.

What it entailed, besides a $3,000 fine which McLaren had to pay, was a dramatic change in James's fortunes in the points standings for the 1976 World Drivers' Championship.

James regained the nine points he had earned for winning in Spain while Niki Lauda, who had been bumped down into second place by the FIA decision, lost three points.

Thus, with the season half over, James suddenly found himself in second place (tied with Patrick Depailler) in the Championship. Still, the leading Lauda had 52 points, twice as many as James, and with eight races to go the odds certainly favoured the Ferrari driver.

This fact did not appease an aggrieved Enzo Ferrari, the imposing founder and dictator of the best known team in racing. At the age of 78 he was still such a formidable force that in Italy, where Ferrari-worshipping flourishes to the point of being a religion, it was said that Enzo Ferrari's stature rivalled the Pope's.

Now, Ferrari decreed, the FIA decision which adversely affected his car (his affection for his machinery tended to overshadow his feelings for his drivers) was 'a wicked verdict'. He always suspected the Formula 1 fraternity, especially the English-based teams, of conspiring against him, and this Spanish affair seemed further proof of that.

The perfect revenge for Enzo Ferrari would be for his cars to trounce the offending McLaren team on their home turf, at the next race, the British Grand Prix at Brands Hatch.

* * *

When James came over to England to prepare himself for his home Grand Prix the full extent of his popularity with the British public became evident.

In the build-up to the race the concept of James Hunt as Superstar was played for all it was worth. Sponsors traded on his celebrity by parading him around at a variety of functions: he attended an arduous round of charity engagements, met Members of Parliament, made an appearance at the Kent County Show, presented prizes at a children's safety competition, and so on.

As a fan of the Rolling Stones, James attended the rock group's concert at Earl's Court where the attention he received seemed to rival that accorded the prancing Mick Jagger. Later, at the Royal Albert Hall, James took to the stage himself – in his trademark jeans and T-shirt – treating the capacity audience to an enthusiastic trumpet solo during a televised 'Grand Prix Night of the Stars'.

Everyone thought James played admirably well, though there was an admitted curiosity value to his performance. According to the journalist Eoin Young (who would later collaborate with him on a book about his championship season), James's trumpet virtuosity 'might be compared to the dancing bear – applauded not so much for the quality of the dance as the fact that he could do it at all'.

Racing fans were delighted at their hero's extra dimensions but were more concerned with the possibility of him becoming the first English driver to win the British Grand Prix since Peter Collins (in a Ferrari) in 1958. But the tabloid press, now that Suzy was gone from the scene, wanted more inflammatory material, and got it in the Tour of Britain.

For the event, which was sponsored by Texaco (the oil company supplied fuel to the McLaren team and also had a personal contract with James), James was entered in a Magnum provided by Vauxhall (with whom he also had a publicity contract and a personal vehicle provided for his use in the UK).

His co-driver in the Tour (held on public roads and at several race tracks) was the popular BBC radio disc jockey Noel Edmonds, who was also an enthusiastic saloon car racer. But the partnership between the two personalities produced fireworks, according to the headline writers.'Race Ace Has DJ In Spin!'..., 'Hunt Hits Tree And Starts Row!'..., 'Noel's Shunt With Hunt!', proclaimed the papers.

There were reports of a dice down country lanes with Lord Hesketh's Rolls Royce, rude gestures being made at other motorists and at least one of them being shoved off the road, a crash into a tree with the famous racing driver at the wheel, complaints about excessive speeds on public roads, a police chase of the offending Vauxhall and the arrogant racing driver being apprehended to help the authorities with their inquiries, and, finally, a fierce argument between the prima donna racing driver, who wanted to withdraw from the Tour because they were so far behind, and the record spinner who thought they should continue because they had a moral obligation to the thousands of fans who were following their adventures.

The Hunt/Edmonds duo did pull out of the Tour, but they got more publicity than if they'd won.

James, who was condemned by the traditional motor racing press, though the popular papers loved it, thought he had 'behaved in a very reasonably and restrained way, considering all the aggravation. Every time I opened my mouth, made any sort of comment at all, I got a big load of earache from the press and everybody else.

'A lot of the problem was simply sensationalist reporting. They said that Noel and I had a row, which is complete and utter rubbish. We never had a cross word. We discussed the pros and cons and I thought we should stop, he thought we should go on. It was blown up out of all proportion. It was one of those days when it would have been much better if I'd stayed in bed.'

With that he withdrew to the tranquillity of his parents' home in Surrey to compose himself for the Grand Prix. He restricted his activities to reading a book and going for his daily run through the nearby lanes and vowed to distance himself from any further distracting hoopla.

'You have to or else you simply get swamped and crack up. A lot of it is unnecessary bullshit. I realized I had been living my life up to the red line and I had drained myself completely. The peace and quiet is like a cocoon to me. I need my solitude days to help me get through the crazy ones.

'Now I need to wind down totally before cranking myself up to the intense pitch which is vital to a good result in the race. I want to be World Champion, although the chances this year are now very slim.'

                                          ★   ★   ★

Brands Hatch on race day was jammed with 77,000 spectators, the vast majority of them there to witness the next instalment in the continuing adventures of James Hunt.

The demands on his time were heavy but James managed to extricate himself from the throngs of well-wishers and autograph hunters to find an old friend, Tony Dron, who was competing in the Formula 3 race which was a supporting event at the British Grand Prix. James might be the star of the show but he hadn't forgotten his mate from his Formula Ford days. As 'The Dron' sat in his car waiting for the start he was surprised and delighted when James came along to wish him luck.

James was second on the Formula 1 starting grid, after qualifying a mere six hundredths of a second slower than Niki Lauda's pole-setting time. But the entire 26 car field was covered by just over three seconds and, as James told the fans, it promised to be 'a super race'.

It certainly looked that way at the tumultuous and unruly start, but all the excitement came to a spectacular halt after only five seconds of racing when, as James put it, 'The Ferraris attacked each other. Clay Regazzoni had a serious bout of brain fade in the first corner and assaulted his own team mate'.

In James's estimation the mustachioed Swiss (who was permanently paralysed in an accident at Long Beach in 1980) was: 'pretty fierce and you've got to keep clear of him in the opening laps. When he's doing his little charge after the start he tends to get a bit erratic'.

When the starting lights flashed green Lauda led 'Regga' by a wheel length, with James in close attendance as they prepared to negotiate Paddock Bend, the first corner at Brands Hatch. Suddenly the two leading Ferraris touched and the instantly ensuing bedlam was obscured in billowing clouds of tyre smoke and dust.

There were glimpses of two red cars spinning viciously, then, from the midst of the melee, a red and white car soared aloft into the bright blue Kentish sky.

James Hunt's airborne McLaren floated almost lazily, then thumped down hard, though mercifully it remained upright. Somehow the following pack had manoeuvred safely around the accident scene, but the track was littered with debris, dust and stones and the red flag was shown. The race would have to be restarted.

James, who had been launched skyward when his McLaren, aided by a thump in the back from another car, had ridden up over Regazzoni's rear wheels, but kept the engine running throughout his flight. His only injury was strained ligaments in his right thumb, a legacy of being clipped by the flailing steering wheel when his McLaren crash landed. As he set off again it was gingerly, because it immediately became apparent that the car's steering was deranged: the left front wheel was pointing at an odd angle.

'I didn't have time to be frightened or to realize that I could have been on my head. I was just heartbroken that I'd done only 150 yards of the Grand Prix I wanted to win. The car was still just driveable, though it was leaping about, and as I was motoring slowly around and saw the red flags I gave a whoop of delight. I thought all my birthdays had come at once! One second I was despairing of my luck and now it was all on again.'

James took a short cut into the paddock, parked his disabled machine and the McLaren mechanics began to get the spare car ready.

Regazzoni's Ferrari and Jacques Laffite's Ligier were also not raceworthy, so their teams prepared spare cars for them and all three new cars were wheeled onto the starting grid.

Meanwhile, the race officials, under the supervision of the Royal Automobile Club, consulted the FIA rulebook to confirm the procedure for getting the British Grand Prix back on track.

There was an option of either beginning an entirely new event, in which case spare cars would be allowed, or restarting the aborted race, which would mean the exclusion of spare cars. The latter course of action was chosen, and therefore any driver who did not complete the red flag lap was finished for the day.

An announcement was made over the loudspeakers that the race would begin again shortly, but with only 23 cars. The field would not include Clay Regazzoni, Jacques Laffite and James Hunt. The mention of that last name on the list sparked an immediate uproar, the likes of which had never been seen or heard in three-quarters of a century of British motor racing history.

Much of the Brands Hatch circuit, including the control tower, paddock and starting grid, is contained in a natural amphitheatre, and the bulk of the impatient and now very angry crowd was congregated there in the grandstands and on the terraces. The news that James Hunt would be excluded was greeted with a frightening outburst of disapproval.

The boos and catcalls from thousands of outraged voices echoed around the Kentish hills. A torrent of crumpled crisp packets and flattened soft drink and beer cans was hurled over the fences in the direction of the control tower, aimed at the dastardly officials who dared to deny the incensed fans the right to see their hero in action. The mood grew uglier and there were fears of a riot.

In the control tower the worried officials hurriedly thumbed through the rulebook again. On the starting grid – now thronged with mechanics, officials, journalists and assorted hangers-on – there were angry exchanges, particularly between the personnel of rival teams, their arguments for or against the decision not to allow spare cars to restart varying according to what they stood to gain.

The din of the crowd became deafening, the rain of debris intensified and it was patently obvious that the only way to salvage the British Grand Prix was to have James Hunt in it.

By now nearly an hour had elapsed since the original race-stopping incident, and the McLaren team had used the interval to good advantage by repairing the damage to James's original car. In fact,

Alastair Caldwell and Teddy Mayer deliberately prolonged the debate in the control tower to gain valuable time for their mechanics to fit a replacement steering arm and suspension link.

First, though they knew it was wrong, the McLaren leaders argued with the officials that spare cars should be allowed to start. Then, as James's repaired car was being wheeled onto the starting grid to replace the spare, they took the position that, since it had still been mobile during the red flag lap it should be allowed to start. The exasperated race officials finally agreed. Everyone would be allowed to take the new start and any irregularities would have to be sorted out later. The grid was quickly cleared of bystanders and the event was on again.

The start of the second version of the race was more orderly, with Lauda leading Hunt and a more circumspect Regazzoni. When the latter driver and Laffite dropped out with mechanical problems the question of their right to be in the race became irrelevant and there was an official sigh of relief in the control tower.

And as Hunt began to seek ways around Lauda, the British fans began cheering as loudly as they had booed earlier. So vociferous was the clamour of the crowd that James could hear it above the sound of the engine screaming behind his back.

He found the fan support tremendously inspirational, and on the 45th lap – 'I just shut my eyes and went!' – the McLaren overtook the Ferrari – 'and when I went into the lead the place just went mad'.

James took control of his race, Lauda fell back somewhat, though he maintained second place, and the remaining 30 laps passed without incident. His cruise to the chequered flag was accompanied by a tumult of shouting fans and waving Union Jacks, and after he crossed the finish line James raised both arms aloft to acknowledge the salutes of the ecstatic crowd.

A photograph of that triumphant moment was one of the few he kept of his racing career and he remembered this as 'certainly my most emotional race. Brands is such an intimate circuit anyway, and you feel the crowd more than you do anywhere else. You can sense the emotion and the movement all the time, even though you are not necessarily looking at the crowd. It's there and you respond to it.

'From the crowd's point of view I had the perfect race. Being British and having all that support and emotion was terrific. There was no way I was going to miss that race. The crowd went completely hooligan. I'd never known anything like it.

'It was a fantastic feeling for me – as I sat in my car to know I had all this support – really quite incredible. They'd got fed up with the rules and they didn't want any more rubbish. They wanted to see a motor race. The organizers knew that they had to start me, even if I might later be disqualified.'

That prospect loomed as soon as the race was over. While James was delightedly spraying champagne from the top of the victory podium, the Ferrari, Tyrrell and Copersucar teams (each with a car which would gain valuable points from James's exclusion) lodged official protests. They claimed that the winning McLaren should not have been allowed to race, as had been originally announced by the officials. After a lengthy debate in the control tower Tyrrell and Copersucar withdrew their protests, but Ferrari refused to budge and declared they would take the matter to the FIA in Paris.

Meanwhile, James had another nine points to bring his total to 35, against Lauda's 58, and that achievement was toasted liberally in the Brands Hatch car park, where many of his friends were camped for the weekend in tents and motorhomes. The raucous celebrations went on until midnight, by which time James no longer felt any pain in his injured thumb.

★ ★ ★

James was now at the height of his powers as a driver, and he was particularly pleased when his very demanding employers at McLaren publicly acknowledged it. Alastair Caldwell went so far as to say: 'I think Britain now has another Jimmy Clark situation with James Hunt. A super driver'.

James was flattered at comparisons with the late, great Scottish driver (though he always insisted on calling him 'Jim', as if the informal 'Jimmy' was not suitable for his stature), and even Teddy Mayer, a man not noted for being overly generous in praising drivers, had become a Hunt fan.

Mayer said: 'Of all the drivers we've had, James has the greatest talent – by far, in fact. Possibly he makes more mistakes than, say, Emerson Fittipaldi, but he certainly is quicker than Emerson ever was when he drove for us and I think James is as consistently fast a driver as anyone I've ever seen.

'I would begin to compare his talent with Jackie Stewart's in his ability to win races driving a car that, in my opinion, is about the same as many others. Drivers like Jimmy Clark generally won races because they had superior cars. I think James's car is good, but I don't think it's any better than several other cars. Possibly it's more reliable, but it's quick because James is quick.'

James: 'When McLaren made particular mention that they were happy with me it made me very happy and to keep the car pointing in the right direction at a point-scoring speed was very gratifying.

'You've got to remember I had a pretty funny career up to Formula 1 and I didn't have any real practice at leading races – and you need practice. At first I was cracking under the pressure. I was so worried about leading that I was busy telling myself to be careful – that when I got to the next corner I was still talking to myself and not concentrating and I would do something silly and throw it all away.

'I finally worked out that you had to just sit and relax and get on with it, just drive in the normal way you do when you're not leading. I've had a bit of practice now at getting into the mood for it, and once you get into the lead and realize you're really the guy in charge, you get confidence and you're in much better shape.

'The mood thing is very important, because once you get in the mood and get confident things get easy. There was a point at the beginning of this season that I broke down, but I was behind Niki and we were very closely matched. He just had the edge, but it was only a tiny edge. And I always said half of that edge was the fact that he was on a winning streak and I was not. It only needed a tip of the scales and now it seems the scales have tipped in my direction.'

In the seven remaining races of the 1976 season the precariously balanced scales of fate would fluctuate wildly, for both the Austrian and the Englishman, to produce the heaviest championship drama Formula 1 racing has ever known.

* * *

In early August the Formula 1 circus arrived for the German Grand Prix at the mighty Nürburgring, the mother and father of all road racing circuits. Carved out of rugged terrain in the heavily forested Eiffel mountains west of Koblenz, its tortuous, tree-lined 14.19 mile length punctuated by 177 distinct corners and many lesser curves and kinks, represented the ultimate challenge for the bravest men in the fastest racing machines.

But the daunting test of courage and skill around the madly writhing roller coaster ride of a track – where speeding cars slewed sideways through the eccentric swoops and swerves, hurtled inches from the trees over a surface made damp by the nearly always present mist and fog, flew six feet into the air over the blind brows – was also a great leap of faith for the drivers. And over its 50 year history, the treacherous Nürburgring had become notorious for creating as many martyrs as heroes.

Fatalities had claimed an estimated 130 lives since the circuit opened in 1920. Deaths and injuries had been reduced in recent years by safety measures – mainly more catch fencing and steel guard rails to keep cars from flying into the trees – but the circuit remained the most dangerous in the world.

Average speeds had increased from 66.49 miles per hour, recorded during the first German Grand Prix there, in 1927, to the 119.79 mph clocked by Clay Regazzoni in a Ferrari in 1975.

The accident potential had increased many-fold, the circuit was simply too long to police effectively, there were too many places where crash scenes could not be reached quickly by safety crews, and many drivers thought the Nürburgring should be put out to pasture before it claimed another life.

Jackie Stewart was one of the most vociferous critics, though he won the German race three times and his victory in the pouring rain here in 1968 was probably the most impressive of his illustrious career. 'Nothing gave me more satisfaction than to win at the Nürburgring and yet I was always afraid. When I left home to race in the German Grand Prix I always used to pause at the end of the driveway and take a long look back. I was never sure that I would come home again.'

In qualifying for the 1975 version of the race Niki Lauda had put his Ferrari on pole with the first ever lap under seven minutes at the track. But this year, at a drivers' meeting, he had proposed that they boycott the dangerous Ring. He was voted down and reluctantly accepted the decision of the majority of his peers.

'Some of them wanted to seem brave', Niki said, 'others were simply too stupid to know what they were doing. I steeled myself to drive that fast lap in 1975, although my brain kept telling me it was sheer stupidity. The antithesis between the modern-day racing car and the Stone Age circuit was such that I knew every driver was taking his life in his hands to the most ludicrous degree.'

Speaking before practice began, Niki was particularly worried about the proximity of guard rails to the tarmac and the lack of run-off areas to slow down an out-of-control car.

'My personal opinion is that the Nürburgring is just too dangerous to drive on nowadays. On any of the modern circuits if something breaks on my car I have a 70/30 chance that I will be all right or I will be dead.

'Here, if you have any failure on the car, one hundred per cent death! We're not discussing if I make a mistake, but if I have failure on the car. If I make a mistake and kill myself, then tough shit.'

Still, the circuit was tremendously exhilarating. The Swedish driver

Gunnar Nilsson (who died of cancer two years later), after his first exploratory trip around the Nürburgring in his Lotus, was moved to exclaim: 'It's so exciting, each corner is like a blue movie!'.

'I'm frightened, I don't mind telling you', said James after qualifying. 'I'm glad to see the finish line every lap. But whether they're frightened of the Ring or not, everybody wants to win here. When it comes right down to it, you either don't come, or you get on with the job of racing. So I've got on with the job and I've wound up on pole position again.'

Niki, who had clocked a time just under a second slower than James, was alongside him on the front row as they sat waiting for the commencement of their 14 lap journey into the great unknown.

Both men had set their fears aside in qualifying – they were over a second quicker than the next fastest drivers – and looming over the prospect of another instalment of the Hunt versus Lauda battle in their see-saw struggle for supremacy was the irony that neither man liked the circuit.

As usual, the uncertainties were heightened by the unpredictable skies overhead, which now began to deposit drops of rain on the track, at least at the starting line, and showers were reported on other parts of the circuit. Every driver, except one, chose to start on treaded, wet weather tyres to provide better grip on a slippery surface. The exception was James's team-mate Jochen Mass who, familiar with the vagaries of the meteorological conditions at his home circuit, gambled on starting with his McLaren shod on treadless racing slicks. His hopes that the rain would dissipate and the stiff breeze would quickly dry the track were soon realized.

At the start both the McLaren and the Ferrari bogged down on the front row, their furiously spinning rear tyres shooting up clouds of spray in futility while several other vehicles, benefitting from more delicate applications to the throttle, surged past. Further along on the opening lap the track was drier and Jochen Mass, despite starting from the fifth row of the grid, was up among the frontrunners.

Near the end of the first lap Mass was in the lead, followed by James and Ronnie Peterson who, along with the rest of the pack, now knew that Mass had the appropriate tyres for the conditions and everyone would have to stop to effect a changeover.

Just before the approach to the pit lane James played a trick on Peterson, surreptitiously slowing down just enough to let the speeding Swede by, then suddenly diving into the pits. Too late, Peterson realized he had been duped and was committed to another full lap on now useless wet tyres.

James rejoined the race in second place, 45 seconds behind Mass, but the possibility of a McLaren one-two finish ended abruptly.

At the end of the second lap only 14 cars came past the pits and in the ensuing ominously eerie silence it became obvious that there was trouble somewhere out on the treacherous Nürburgring. The red flags were shown and an announcement was made that a serious accident had blocked the track at Bergwerk, the most northerly corner of the circuit.

Niki Lauda, who was 20th when he came into the pits for his tyre change, had been quickly making up for lost time when his Ferrari left the road due to a suspected mechanical failure. Travelling at an estimated 120 miles per hour the car flew through the catch fences on the outside of the corner, scattering wooden posts and wire, slammed heavily into an earth bank which ruptured the fuel cells, then rebounded back out onto the track, slithered to a halt and erupted in flames.

The first following car, a Hesketh driven by Guy Edwards, managed to avoid the burning Ferrari by zig-zagging through the ribbon of fire that surrounded it. But Brett Lunger's Surtees slammed head on into the flaming wreckage and the carnage intensified when Harald Ertl's Hesketh skidded into both the stationary cars.

As Lunger and Ertl clambered unhurt from their wrecked machines through the flames they could see the Ferrari driver waving his arms as if to ward off the fire from his face. Somehow his helmet had been knocked askew and Niki Lauda was trapped in the blazing cockpit.

All the remaining cars stopped safely short of the accident scene and several drivers ran to Lauda's aid. The heroic rescue efforts were led by the American Lunger (a Vietnam veteran and a member of the wealthy Dupont family – he had just learned of his father's death the day before), the Englishman Edwards, the German Ertl (a journalist/driver who, like Edwards, was driving for Bubbles Horsley's resurrected Hesketh team) and the diminutive Italian Arturo Merzario (driving a Williams).

Fearlessly, the four in their fireproof driving suits and helmets charged into the searing flames and worked frantically over Lauda, trying to lift him out. But their best efforts at first met with failure because he was being held in place by his safety harness.

The rescuers became increasingly desperate and after a few moments, as Ertl ran off to get a fire extinguisher, Lunger straddled the cockpit and pulled on Lauda's shoulders while Merzario reached in to search for the release mechanism on the seat belts. In the fearsome struggle Lauda's helmet fell off and the flames licked around his fireproof balaclava. Ertl quelled the fire somewhat by emptying an extinguisher over the rescue operation but the conflagration soon flared up worse than ever.

Finally, after what seemed an eternity, Merzario was able to unfasten the belts and Lunger and Lauda tumbled out of the horrific inferno and onto the ground. Amazingly, Lauda was still conscious and with the help of Lunger, John Watson, Emerson Fittipaldi and Hans Stück, he was able to stagger to the other side of the track, where he was made to lie down.

As they stripped off his scorched driving suit Niki began babbling in Italian to Merzario, but his face was badly burned, and when they removed his charred balaclava both Merzario and Lunger got blood on their hands.

Only those drivers who had witnessed the terrifying holocaust at Bergwerk understood the implications of Niki's crash: having sat for so long in the fire, he must be seriously hurt. The accident had happened a mile or more behind the frontrunners and for them the news that he was able to walk and talk was reassuring. To James it seemed that Niki had got off remarkably lightly.

'He was taken off to hospital and obviously wouldn't be racing again that day, but we thought he'd have his burns patched up and we'd see him at the next race in Austria. That was what we felt then; there were no alarm stories so one was able to get into the car and go racing again with no qualms.'

While James and the others readied themselves for the restart of the German Grand Prix, Chris Amon had had enough. The veteran New Zealander had already suffered several serious accidents in his Ensign this season and after crashing badly at the race in Sweden he sat in his shattered cockpit for a while 'sort of taking in the fact that I was still alive.' He was one of those most reluctant to race at the Nürburgring, and now, after seeing how slowly and inadequately the circuit's emergency services had responded to Lauda's accident, he withdrew.

As the 14 lap race began all over again James cleared his mind of everything but the task at hand and streaked into a lead that was never threatened. He called that first lap: 'probably the most aggressive piece of driving I did all year. I was absolutely determined to get as big a lead as possible and everything turned out right'.

Round and round he roared, taming the desperate challenges of the notorious Nürburgring with great skill and daring, his pace scarcely slackening over the full 198.66 mile race distance.

By the time he had finished, half a minute ahead of the second and third place men, Jody Scheckter and Jochen Mass, James had accomplished what he always considered to be one of his most satisfying drives. But his abiding memory of the day was Teddy Mayer's reaction.

'It was the Wiener's face. McLarens had never won at the Ring and had always gone home with written-off cars in the truck. So when I stood on the winner's rostrum there was the Wiener in his Goodyear cap, which doesn't fit him anyway – it's far too big for him – with that ridiculous grin on his face that he wears and can't wipe off. If you tell him to behave himself it just makes it worse, just splits him from ear to ear and he looks like a monkey standing there grinning.

'But it was tremendously gratifying to me to see him so happy. He's really an enthusiast, the Wiener, pure and simple. He could do plenty of other things with his life and make a lot more money but he goes racing because he loves it. To see that result was so gratifying for him. He was absolutely thrilled, beside himself with joy after the race. I got more pleasure out of that than I did from winning the race!'

As for the absence of any competition from Niki Lauda, James, whose victory had brought him to within 14 points of his rival, pointed out that he was well ahead of the Ferrari when the accident happened and felt that this was always going to be his race to win.

But he wished his friend a full and speedy recovery. 'The thing I want most of all is for Niki to be fit and well and back on the track again. The last thing I would want would be to win a World Championship with him watching me on a television set from his hospital bed.'

Sadly, Niki was then in no condition to watch anything. In fact he was nearly dead, and on Monday morning when James heard the bad news he felt 'so utterly hopeless and helpless.

'I couldn't visit him so I went home and sent him a telegram. I can't remember exactly what I said but it was something provocative to annoy him and then I told him to fight, because I knew if he was annoyed and fighting, he would pull through. If he relaxed and gave in, he would probably die. You've got to stay conscious and physically fight it yourself, and I knew Niki would be aware of that.

'I got on very well with Niki and always had done since we first met in Formula 3 and gypsied around Europe together. We raced against each other but we also teamed up as mates, not just casual acquaintances.

'It was suddenly very important for me that Niki should live, in a way I hadn't realized, and I felt awful because there was nothing I could do about it. There I was sitting at home enjoying life even when I didn't particularly want to, when I wanted to go and help or do something and I couldn't. It was a strange time for me.'

From the Nürburgring Niki Lauda was flown to a special burns hospital in Mannheim where a team of six doctors and 34 nurses tended him round the clock. His injuries were diagnosed as first to third degree burns on his head and wrists, several broken ribs and a broken collarbone and cheekbone.

Much more serious were the poisonous fumes and toxic gases inhaled from the Ferrari's burning plastic bodywork, from the burning fuel and from the fire extinguisher powder. His windpipe and lungs were scorched and the build-up of fluid in his lungs was life-threatening. The medical people told his wife Marlene, who never left his side, there was nothing more they could do for him.

To Hell And Back was the apt title Niki chose for one volume of his memoirs. In it he says his 'last recollection before the race is of changing from wets to slicks and driving away from the pits. Next, the chatter of a helicopter. I'm lying in bed. I'm tired. I want to sleep. I don't want to know any more. It will all be over soon'.

On the third day a priest was brought into his room to give him the last rites. Niki wavered in and out of consciousness but he understood what was going on as the man of God laid his hands on him and prayed over his body. They were giving up on him.

'He speaks in Latin. It sounds like a judgement. You can die from extreme unction like that just as you can die from shock. The priest says nothing kind, never mentions the possibility that I might recover. This is very bad. They should give you some encouragement. I was so cross I wanted to shout: "Hey, stop this, this is the worst fuckup you make in your life! I am not going to die!"'

His 'lungs had turned to shit' but Niki kept himself alive, according to the doctors, by sheer force of will. By the fourth day he was declared out of danger and began an astonishing recovery that made the medical profession marvel.

Mercifully, it was some time before he was able to read the headline in a German tabloid newspaper which asked the question: 'My God, Where Is His Face?... it is no more than raw flesh with eyes oozing out of it... how can he face life without a face?'.

After many skin grafts his face was made reasonably presentable, his eyelids were rebuilt with plastic surgery, but angry scars remained and no attempt was made to replace the missing half of his right ear. Niki said it made it easier for him to talk on the telephone.

* * *

Two weeks after his accident Niki Lauda was well enough to watch the next Grand Prix, his home race in Austria on television, but the race was held without his team.

Enzo Ferrari, smarting from being 'cheated' by McLaren at the Spanish and British races, announced that his cars would not be competing in Austria. Furthermore, he threatened to boycott the sport until such time as the rules were enforced and 'justice' prevailed.

There were also suggestions from Italy that the event at the Õsterreichring should be cancelled, out of respect for the country's national hero who was fighting for his life in the hospital. This compassionate plea was greeted with cynicism by those accustomed to Ferrari's reputation for manipulating situations to suit his team's needs.

However, Lauda's absence greatly reduced the number of spectators and without the Ferraris there were only 25 cars at the circuit. But it was an exciting race and when John Watson won it, his first Grand Prix victory, he gladly shaved off his beard, that being the condition of a bet he made with his American team owner, Roger Penske. For the Penske team it was an emotional triumph, because their driver Mark Donohue had died after an accident in the 1975 Austrian Grand Prix.

Watson, from Belfast, shared the front row of the grid with James, who once more was on pole position. As in Germany the race began on a wet track which proceeded to dry out, but again the early dampness caused accidents. In the biggest of them Jody Scheckter's Tyrrell comprehensively destroyed itself, fortunately without injury to the driver, but the track was littered with debris from the wrecked car and pieces of the surrounding landscape.

James, whose McLaren was already hampered by a handling problem, ran over a large rock, knocking the front wing askew and further hampering his efforts to keep pace with the charging Watson. But James, absolutely determined to salvage as many points as possible, put his head down and proceeded to wring the maximum performance out of his crippled machine. In the end he finished fourth, but setting the fastest lap of the race was testimony to how hard he had tried.

John Watson, who never wore a beard again, would have more racing battles with James (and like him would later become an astute Grand Prix television commentator) and had the highest regard for him as a driver.

'Part of his make-up was a belief that he was never wrong and it was this, I think, that gave him the strength of character to pursue what in many people's minds was an almost impossible task: to win the 1976 Championship.

'It was a terrific long shot but James recognized that he still had a mathematical chance of doing it. So he adapted and he committed himself, even above the very high levels to which he was already committed. He had a very good team and a very good car but it was his own determination that served him so well. He was also a very intelligent man and he applied that intelligence in the race car to very good effect.'

The respect was mutual. James thought John was 'one of the good drivers to race against. Fast, tough, always a competitor, a man to beat on his day', and they went head-to-head at the next event, where James celebrated his 29th birthday after the most thrilling race of the year.

★   ★   ★

The Dutch Grand Prix at Zandvoort on 29 August was significant to James for more than being his birthday, for this was also the site of his ground-breaking first Grand Prix victory, a year ago in the Hesketh. That day he had learned how to win and the lesson had served him well ever since. But now, especially since his chief adversary of 1976 was no longer racing, he was expected to win, and James was not yet well-schooled in responding to that extra pressure.

Further complicating the chances of him providing his own birthday present was the improving form of John Watson, now with a confidence-boosting win under his belt, and several other drivers. In Holland James would also have to contend with a Ferrari, driven by Clay Regazzoni.

James wondered if Enzo Ferrari's decision to go racing again was simply to place an obstacle in his path to the Championship. But there was another, more troubling, matter on his mind, brought on by the accident to his friend in the Ferrari. James had several times spoken to Niki on the telephone. In their conversations, some of which lasted nearly an hour, Niki joked about how his missing ear made talking on the telephone easier and James kidded him about how the now even uglier face of the brave racing driver would make him even more attractive to the girls.

But behind the masquerade of his macho posturing, the dangers of their profession began to weigh more heavily on James. He felt a closer bond with Niki: they had been through so much together in their careers, their shared experience had included tempting fate on too many occasions, and James was filled with thoughts that his own luck might run out as easily as had Niki's.

James would later claim that Niki came out of his accident 'a stronger, happier and better person. He would be the first to tell you that. It changed his life absolutely for the better'. But that was in retrospect and, now, in the immediate aftermath of the Lauda accident James had another point of view.

'The thought of being killed is a shadow that follows you always. It's a cloud that hangs over your head, even though you don't always look up at it. Racing is a terribly horrible gamble. I realize the risk I take every time I race. I don't want to be killed driving.

'The thought of dying frightens the hell out of me. I think about what it's like being dead and if there's a life after death. I want to retire when the time comes. Voluntarily. To do that I have to survive and to survive in motor racing means not exposing yourself to the risks for too long. Motor racing makes me come alive. But it also scares me to death.'

As usual, the positive part of the racing driver's desperate dichotomy predominated as James got ready for the Dutch Grand Prix.

James complained of 'terrible' handling problems in qualifying – a lack of traction and severe understeer, which he blamed on his car's tyres. But he still managed to make the front row, alongside Ronnie Peterson's pole-sitting March and just ahead of Tom Pryce's Shadow and John Watson's Penske. But with the front half of the 26 car grid blanketed by a scant second the 95 minute chase around the demanding Zandvoort circuit promised to be very closely contested.

Peterson rocketed into the lead at the start and as the rear tyres on Hunt's McLaren churned up smoking clouds of wasted effort Watson surged into second place, giving James a ringside seat for the ensuing struggle between the March and the Penske.

James, his car's handling problems now exacerbated by a loose brake cooling duct on a front wheel which interfered with the air flow around the front wing, had no choice but to play a waiting game behind the torrid Peterson/Watson dispute for the lead.

Eventually his involuntary patience paid off and he was able to capitalize on mistakes made by the two frontrunners.

When Peterson bobbled momentarily, Watson barged into the lead and James scrambled into second. Watson's term in front proved to be short-lived when he, too, went wide on a corner and James usurped the lead.

But there were still over 60 laps to go, and Watson, in fighting form, was not about to give up. The aggressively driven Penske closed right up on the McLaren and, as they sped down Zandvoort's long straight,

Watson suddenly veered out of James's slipstream, intent on being first into Tarzan Corner.

But James sternly defended his position, holding the inside line around the steeply banked turn and forcing Watson up onto the outside where spent rubber and accumulate sand and dirt afforded poor grip.

The Penske skittered alarmingly but Watson refused to back off and the two cars negotiated the corner in a thrilling wheel-to-wheel clash of wills. At the exit of Tarzan James emerged slightly ahead and stamped hard on the accelerator, sending the McLaren briefly sideways and giving Watson a face full of fat rear tyres. To avoid them Watson swerved briefly off course, over the curb and into the grass and sand. In the cloud of dust his car could be seen to oscillate viciously as he fought for control, but the Irishman regained the circuit and gathered his wits and bravery together for another attack.

When it came, a few laps later, there was exactly the same result: a side-by-side duel around Tarzan, a cloud of dust at the exit, and the McLaren still ahead of the Penske. After several more attempts were similarly rebuffed Watson then prudently fell back, holding station just astern of the McLaren, and applying constant pressure in the hope of forcing James into an error. None, however, was forthcoming, and their conflict was eventually resolved when Watson's car suffered a gearbox failure and he had to park the Penske.

The chase was now taken up by Clay Regazzoni who, in the lone Ferrari, relentlessly began to carve great chunks of time out of the McLaren's advantage. With five laps to go the gap was under three seconds. Another lap and Regga had lopped off another second and James – mindful of the spoiling role the Ferrari could play in the points standings – was 'in an absolute panic!' He hung on grimly, focusing intently on the finish line and trying to ignore the Ferrari looming ever closer in his mirrors.

As they commenced the last lap Regga was only 1.25 seconds behind and over the remaining 2.626 miles the time separating them shrank progressively. But enough of it – 0.80 seconds – remained for the McLaren to flash past the chequered flag a car's length ahead of the Ferrari and James threw both arms aloft in his familiar gesture of triumph, whereupon the McLaren immediately swerved alarmingly toward the barriers and he quickly dropped one hand to the steering wheel to regain control. His subsequent one-armed victory salute was apt testimony to an exhausting and fiercely fought Dutch Grand Prix.

James also had his hands full at the extensive post-race festivities, which were made all the merrier for him by the new driver standings which showed him now a mere two points behind Niki Lauda. There was also the need to celebrate his 29th birthday, as well as the first anniversary of his Dutch Grand Prix win.

To these double ends the race organizers provided a giant birthday cake, in the shape of the Zandvoort circuit, and among the sand dunes that night there were many well-wishers wanting a slice of the cake. James's mother Sue and his youngest brother David were there, along with many of his mates from England, and around a roaring campfire everyone raised their voices in an exuberant songfest conducted by the delighted race winner and birthday boy.

* * *

Before the next Grand Prix, in Italy, James flew over to Canada, to the town of Trois Rivières in the province of Quebec, where he was one of several guest stars invited (and paid $10,000) to contest a round of the Formula Atlantic series.

Ostensibly, the cars (approximately equivalent to Formula 2 machinery) were identical in performance and the presence of the European imports was guaranteed to raise the competition factor even higher in a category already noted for its no-holds-barred racing. In the hope of furthering their own careers the Formula Atlantic regulars would try their utmost to distinguish themselves against such Formula 1 opposition as James Hunt, Patrick Depailler, Vittorio Brambilla and Alan Jones.

One of the favourites at Trois Rivières, and the points leader in the Atlantic series, was Gilles Villeneuve, a charismatic and daring young man from nearby Berthierville. From an impoverished background Villeneuve had overcome financial hardship (even selling his home to buy a racing car), and many accidents, to become one of the best road racers in North America.

Word of Villeneuve's colourful exploits – his fabulous car control and penchant for spectacular sideways driving – had spread far and wide, but there was a suspicion abroad that the best driving talent North America had to offer was still most likely below the standards necessary to perform well at the pinnacle of motor sport. Villeneuve, especially since his team-mate in this race was James Hunt, a candidate for the world driving title, was desperately keen to make his mark and proceeded to do so in dramatic fashion. The French Canadian qualified on pole, five places ahead of James who, though he was in an Ecurie Canada March identical to Villeneuve's, had trouble coming to grips with its unfamiliar handling characteristics.

In the race James gained confidence with every lap and fought his way up to a fine third place at the finish, right behind a hard-charging Jones, and just ahead of an obstinate Brambilla.

But the Formula 1 stars had been left struggling in a class of their own – miles behind the flying Villeneuve, whose breathtaking pace was exceeded only by the wonderfully wild, yet obviously well-controlled abandon with which he threw his car around the difficult circuit.

Understandably, the large crowd greeted the local hero's exceptional showing with unrestrained delight, and those drivers he had so soundly trounced were also quick to extend their congratulations. But James, in an act of admirable generosity – and, as it developed, considerable foresight – went further than that. He might have been accused of having a vested interest in preserving his own reputation, after having been blown away by an 'unknown', but James was genuinely impressed by Gilles Villeneuve, both as a driver and as a man.

They had got along well in their brief stint as team-mates, Villeneuve's very obvious driving ability warranted a promotion and James decided to do something about it. He called Teddy Mayer back in England and said: 'Look, I've just been beaten by this guy Villeneuve and he's really magic. You ought to get hold of him'.

Mayer eventually signed Villeneuve to a contract and he made a brilliant Formula 1 debut, as James's McLaren team-mate, in the 1977 British Grand Prix. When McLaren failed to pick up Villeneuve's option he was snapped up by Enzo Ferrari and went on to become one of the fastest and most popular drivers in Formula 1 history. After he was killed in his Ferrari, in a dreadful accident during qualifying for the 1982 Belgian Grand Prix, the legend of Gilles Villeneuve grew stronger than ever, and he remains one of the best-loved drivers the sport has ever known.

In a postscript to his eventful Canadian visit James went south across the border to the Michigan International Speedway for an event called the International Race of Champions (IROC).

There, in a Chevrolet Camaro identical to those driven by his rivals – including several top American drivers who were specialists on the high-speed banked oval track – James managed to qualify on pole at an average speed of nearly 150 miles per hour. He was travelling at approximately that velocity when he crashed into a cement wall.

He escaped with only minor bruises to his shoulder and arm and was much more concerned about the jagged piece of metal guard rail that had pierced a door of his Camaro. As he climbed out of the heavily damaged car he made his displeasure at the circuit's suspect safety precautions known to the officials in the control tower by shaking his fist at them.

Later, James was also quite frank in expressing his feelings about this form of competition. 'I was immensely pleased with myself when, in the same car as all those other top aces, I put the thing on the front row. But I got in the race and I didn't have a clue! Didn't know whether it was Monday or Tuesday. Because of all the high-speed drafting and this sort of thing I was right out of my depth. To tell you the truth I was scared shitless!'

* * *

Nicholas Andreas Lauda, six weeks after he was given the last rites of the Catholic church, appeared at the Autodromo di Monza, near Milan, not to spectate but to race his Ferrari in the Italian Grand Prix.

His arrival was greeted at first with amazement, then with misgivings. On the one hand this heroic return from his death bed was an act of outstanding courage never before seen in racing. But he was obviously still very frail and weak, his badly disfigured face was difficult to look at, his head was heavily bandaged, and there were doubts about his physical – and mental – fitness. This latter attitude was reflected in the move by his employer, Enzo Ferrari, to enter a third car, for Carlos Reutemann (who had left the Brabham team) in case the brave Austrian should falter.

James was full of admiration for Niki and understood his need to race again. 'You have a lot of time to think in hospital and once he had decided to come back he had to get on with it. He had a terrific amount of motivation too, because he was still leading in the Championship and he really wanted to win it. It was a massive stimulus to get back and get stuck in.

'Here was a challenge; he accepted it and it would help speed up his recovery. We were all set for a grandstand finish and then the Italians attacked'.

The 'attack' began at the Italian border where the McLaren trucks carrying the racing equipment were detained unnecessarily by zealous customs officials. The team was prepared for trouble since the chauvinistic Italian press had been full of stories about how Hunt was taking advantage of the nearly dead Ferrari hero Lauda and that McLaren was even cheating in the races.

Besides the continuing charges of Hunt's 'unlawful' car in Spain and his 'stolen' victory at Brands Hatch there were accusations that McLaren was using 'illegal' fuel, doctoring the regulation pump petrol with banned additives to raise the octane level and improve engine performance. When McLaren arrived at Monza they were met with banners proclaiming 'Basta con la Mafia Inglese': 'Away with the English Mafia'.

In the wet qualifying sessions on Friday James set a relatively slow time before spinning off and damaging the nose of his car, much to the delight of the *tifosi*, the rabid Ferrari fans. Some of them had actually spat at him when he first went out on the track and on Saturday their lusty boos at the hated Hunt turned to cheers when his understeering McLaren could only manage the ninth fastest time. On Sunday morning the announcement that the McLaren qualifying times recorded on Saturday would be disallowed was greeted with whoops of joy from the *tifosi*.

On Saturday the Monza race organizers took samples of fuel from several cars, paying special attention to the Texaco variety in the McLarens, but the team was not worried since tests in the Texaco laboratories had shown that their fuel was within the allowable octane limit. Teddy Mayer, strongly suspecting that Italy's national racing team had instigated the investigation, said: 'I think Ferrari believes that if James can beat them, we must be cheating and they are trying to find excuses'.

'They cheated on cheating', was the way James described the fuel testers at Monza, after they declared that the samples taken from both McLaren cars and John Watson's Penske, were illegal and only their Friday qualifying times would count.

It was later proven that the fuel readings had been wrongly (purposely, James felt) interpreted, but the damage was done and James would have to start the Italian Grand Prix from the second last row of the grid and he was effectively 'stuffed out of the race'.

The actual 'stuffing' was partly his own fault. James was so angry at the fuel fiasco he was tempted not even to start the race. But he needed the points and by the 11th lap had worked his way up to 12th place when he skated off the road and into a sand trap, where the McLaren became irretrievably bogged down.

As was his wont in such circumstances, when his race was rudely interrupted, James was enraged and the full brunt of his ire was inflicted on the person of Tom Pryce, whom James believed was responsible for the contretemps. According to the Welshman, when he pulled his Shadow alongside the McLaren on the entry to a corner James became distracted and simply braked too late. From James's point of view Pryce had unnecessarily blocked him, a manoeuvre which he found 'absolutely brainless!'.

On reflection, James amended his assessment of the incident to a terse: 'I just made a mistake', a more reasonable attitude which owed something to his more reflective frame of mind after the race. On the long walk back to the pits the throngs of Italian *tifosi* had spat, whistled, booed, hissed and jeered at him with a vehemence he found disturbing.

'I'd be walking along and they'd be spitting, hissing and making fun of me. But if I swung round suddenly, looked one of them hard in the eye and said "Boo!" – he'd immediately smile, go all weak at the knees and thrust out a piece of paper for my autograph. It was pathetic, really.

'But I must admit I was quite pleased to get out of there unscathed. The propaganda campaign against me in the Italian press was really quite incredible. A very heavy deal for me. They really hated me in Italy, to an extent that was quite unbelievable. Anybody would think it was I who had caused Niki's accident.'

When Niki, who had outqualified both his Ferrari team mates, took off his helmet after the race his balaclava was soaked in blood. The wounds from his still healing burns had opened up during a courageous comeback that had exceeded all expectations.

'His race speaks for itself', said James. 'To virtually step out of the grave and six weeks later to come fourth in a Grand Prix is a truly amazing achievement. He just got in the car and had a go, drove a typical Niki race: well-contained within himself and within the limitations of his fitness. He knew I was out of the race so there was no pressure on him from that point of view. He was just putting a few more points in the bag before he went into battle in earnest in the next races. He did a super, super job.'

Niki's three points for finishing fourth in Italy (the race was won by Ronnie Peterson) gave him a 61–56 point lead over James. But, before they raced again, the gap between them would spread even wider.

8

WORLD CHAMPION

1976

The first two of the remaining three races in the 1976 season were in North America and James arrived early to prepare for the Canadian Grand Prix at the Mosport Park circuit near Toronto. He was playing squash in a Toronto club when he was given bad news that completely threw him off his game. His Brands Hatch victory had been taken away from him.

An FIA Court of Appeal in Paris had disqualified the Hunt McLaren from the results of the British Grand Prix. In an 11 hour session the six-member jury, composed of FIA delegates from France, Germany, Spain, Brazil, Switzerland and the USA, listened to the evidence presented by Ferrari and McLaren and ruled in favour of the Italian team.

Ferrari's argument, presented by the team manager Daniele Audetto and two lawyers, stated that after the accident at the start of the British race Hunt's car had been abandoned by the driver and was being pushed by the McLaren mechanics while the race was still in progress and was thus incapable of completing the first lap.

McLaren's defence, given by Teddy Mayer and a lawyer representing the RAC, stated that Hunt stopped only when he saw the red flag being displayed, that the car was only pushed after the race had been officially halted and that Hunt could have completed the lap had he felt it necessary.

Teddy Mayer, who had shown the court a BBC video of the race which he thought substantiated McLaren's claim, said of the FIA decision: 'The worst part of it was that James won the race fair and square, there was no question about that, or of the car being illegal.

Ferrari were just trying to use the rules to get out of competing with James and to me that is very sad'.

Alastair Caldwell claimed that the FIA jury had been swayed by the appearance of a surprise witness for Ferrari. 'To get the court's sympathy they brought Niki to Paris with a bloody bandage on his head, long after his wounds had healed. The little prick was as bouncy and fit as a jack rabbit. He didn't need any bandages. But it worked. They introduced him to the members of the jury: "Here's the victim, poor Niki Lauda, the man who nearly died, the living saint". And the silly old sods who did the deciding decided that it was unfair on poor Niki.'

James was incensed that his hard-earned win, that wonderfully satisfying performance in front of his home crowd, now counted for nothing. His nine points had been taken away and given to Niki. The score now stood at Lauda 64 and Hunt 47, a 17 point difference with only three races to go. For James it seemed his boyhood dream had surely been shattered.

'Ever since I saw my first race as a kid winning the World Championship was all I ever wanted. I thought I'd got my hands nearly on it. Instead, here I am screwed. And you don't think I'm bitter?

'As far as I'm concerned you can forget about the sport, the sport's gone out of it. I happened to be the guy who was beating the great Ferrari machine. They didn't like it and they've done a lot of work to make sure I didn't succeed, starting with the fuel business at Monza, and now this.

'Niki and I were level pegging for a possible grandstand finish to the season but the Championship has been totally devalued. It's worthless. The whole thing has been completely rigged. I'm out now for the winning and for the money. What else is left?'

Well, there was something left, still some value in being a famous racing driver whom women found wonderfully attractive. Plenty of them were more than willing to help a handsome hero drown his sorrows.

'Star fuckers', Alastair Caldwell calls them, 'they flocked around him like bees at a flower. And James was definitely a happy flower child. He went with whatever would lie down. And when he drank he drank to get pissed and would drink any substance he could find. Usually, he would behave himself at the races but when he got the message from Paris, which was monumentally unfair, James was both enraged and depressed.

'He didn't snap really, he just became more outgoing, if that was possible. He proceeded to drink whatever was at hand and poke anything that would stand still or lie down long enough. In Canada he went quite lunatic.'

In the first instance of lunacy, at Mosport, Caldwell and the McLaren mechanics found themselves having to shield their driver's daring daylight sexual escapades from prying eyes.

The team had arranged a private test session at the circuit and there was a small crew of course marshals and safety officials in attendance. Several of them had brought female companions, one of whom soon caught James's wayward eye. In short order he lured her into an ambulance parked behind the McLaren pit, where the regular man in her life was watching Caldwell and the crew preparing the racing car. Horrified at James's audacity the McLaren men quickly engaged the unknowing bystander in deep conversation, while in the background the ambulance rocked vigorously.

The distraction tactic worked like a charm, as did the vibrator James once asked his mechanics to repair. He had incorporated electronic aids into his love-making repertoire and impressed the team with his extensive knowledge of the various vibrating devices available, and the techniques of using them. To some of the team it seemed he was better informed about, and certainly more interested in, this subject than he was with the boring business of setting up and testing a racing car.

James was keen to share his information, indeed the whole business of the delights of the opposite sex, with a young and inexperienced McLaren mechanic. On the birthday of the virginal crew member in question James decided he should be given a present and arranged for a prostitute to stay with him for the night. They had adjoining hotel rooms and in the morning James met the beaming mechanic at breakfast and delivered an apology. 'I'm awfully sorry', James confessed, 'but after you went to sleep I'm afraid I played with your present.'

On the Saturday night before the Canadian Grand Prix James found further distraction in the person of the attractive lead singer who was performing with a band in the McLaren team's motel. James, liberally consuming quantities of strong Canadian beer, watched appreciatively as the songstress in her form-fitting dress gyrated seductively through the band's first set. He approached her and she accepted his invitation to join him at the table, where Caldwell and a couple of others from McLaren were sitting. James, on learning she had a half-hour break between sets, suggested that they retire to a more relaxing atmosphere and together they disappeared up to his room.

The singer returned to the stage on cue, James again took up his beer-drinking vantage point in the audience, and once again they spent the interval between performances in James's room. This procedure was repeated until the band packed up and left, at two o'clock in the morning, by which time, Alastair Caldwell says: 'James was paralytic. I mean, he was a playboy type Grand Prix driver, if you like, but even he didn't do this kind of thing on race night.

'Normally I would have told him "James, come off it!. Go to bed. By yourself!". But because of the situation, because the Championship looked gone, I let him go to it, and I must say he responded magnificently!'

The Ferrari personnel were staying at the same motel and when the team manager Audetto tried to convey his regrets to James about the British Grand Prix disqualification he was told to get lost. Audetto said he was only doing his job, but in James's opinion: 'It will take Ferrari a long time to live this down – if they care, which I very much doubt'.

Indeed, it seemed that Niki Lauda didn't care much about James's plight, since the Austrian, well known for expressing his views in a forthright manner, had responded to the FIA Court of Appeal ruling with: 'I'm madly delighted!'.

Some members of the Formula 1 press, eager to make the most of a potentially inflammatory situation, showed James a copy of the Paris appeal and a newspaper article quoting Niki's reaction. James responded with predictable anger and the journalists revelled in the possibility of a grudge match between Hunt and Lauda in Canada. Such a prospect looked even more likely when the two had a row even before the cars took to the Mosport track for qualifying.

Several drivers were critical of the circuit's safety facilities, and the Grand Prix Drivers' Association's Safety Committee, which included James and Niki, decided to hold a meeting to discuss the matter. When Niki asked James to attend the meeting James said, 'To hell with safety. All I want to do is race'.

Niki realized that James was peeved about the Brands Hatch disqualification but had no sympathy for him. 'We have been friends but James broke the rules in England. If you break the rules you are out. No argument. Now he shouts at me. This is not right. He should respect me as a driver. We have a job to do. Bad feeling only makes it more difficult.'

James claimed his outburst – which the press viewed as a tactless slight against the badly scarred survivor of the Nürburgring accident – was only a ruse. 'I was deliberately trying to make Niki think that I was freaked out by what was happening so he would steer clear of me on the track. It was purely a professional piece of gamesmanship. If you can psych another driver out and make him frightened of you then he's much easier to pass. I certainly wasn't about to shove him off the track, but I wanted him to think I was in that frame of mind.

'By this time I was fired up and really wanted to drive, and the only place I could be on my own and get on with the job was in the car. So I enjoyed my driving more than ever because it was such a super relief. The rest of it I hated.'

James forgot his troubles in fine style, driving one of his best races of the year. He started from pole position and then, despite a comprehensive hangover and seriously depleted energy reserves, the legacy of his dalliance with the singer the previous night, James took complete control of the Canadian Grand Prix.

The only real opposition came from Patrick Depailler, who kept his six-wheeled Tyrrell close enough to the speeding McLaren to pounce should it falter in the heavy traffic around Mosport. But James scythed serenely through the back-markers – 'They all gave way to me beautifully' – who were perhaps mindful of his supposedly 'barking mad' mood.

The stirring pursuit by Depailler ended mysteriously with a few laps remaining and James, who complimented the driving of the man who had provoked his fist-waving outburst at Long Beach, wondered what had become of the Frenchman. Depailler did manage to wobble across the finish line in second place but was on the verge of unconsciousness and fell down when he was dragged out of the car. A tube connecting the cockpit fuel gauge to the Tyrrell's tank had ruptured, spraying him in the face with fuel.

'I became quite drunk', said Patrick, 'and in the last laps I am driving by automatic pilot. Also for the last eight laps I have only one eye to see. The left eye, she is completely closed. The only thing that is good for me in the car is the pain, like a fire, of the petrol in the seat. Fortunately, it keep me awake.' A problem with his Ferrari's rear suspension had relegated Niki Lauda to an eighth place finish. James paid tribute to his rival's persevering drive with an ill-handling car, but he wasn't displeased at Niki's failure to score points because, coupled with his own nine point reward for winning, the situation had considerably improved for James.

Before the race he had estimated the odds against him winning the Championship were stacked on the order of 20 to 1. At that stage he was 17 points behind Niki and to beat him he would have to collect 18 points – more than 90 percent of the drivers score in a whole season, let alone three races.

Now, after the Mosport result, the point spread between them had been reduced to eight, but, with two races to go, Niki would surely score again.

James: 'It was really too much to do and I wasn't too bothered about the Championship. But I hadn't given up completely because where there's life there's hope. I could only knuckle down and go after each race as it came and try to win it. If I couldn't win I had to finish as high as I could'.

But he wanted a fair fight in an atmosphere of good sportsmanship, and after the Mosport race he spent some time with Niki discussing the reasons for their strained relationship. Niki said his 'absolutely delighted' remark was a flagrant misquote by some vicious journalist and James was also adamant his anti-Lauda comments were unfounded. They shook hands and their brief feud was over.

'The press was winding us both up badly and we got a bit irritated', said James. 'For a few hours we hated each other, but after we got it sorted out our good relationship continued. For example, after Mosport we went to Watkins Glen, where we had adjoining hotel rooms, and in the evenings we had our door open and we socialized together. I'll never forget Niki's attempt to psych me out on race day.

'I always got up at eight o'clock on race days to be at the circuit at nine. Knowing full well what time I had my call booked for Niki barged into my room at seven o'clock. He was fully bedecked in his overalls and stood to attention over my bed as he said: "Today I vin ze Championship!". With that he marched out again. I thought it was hilarious.'

* * *

Another driver whose company James enjoyed was Jody Scheckter, with whom he would have a fierce battle in the United States Grand Prix at Watkins Glen.

James felt a special kinship with the South African and nicknamed him 'Fletcher', after the crash-prone bird in the book *Jonathan Livingstone Seagull* because Scheckter, like Hunt the Shunt, first gained notoriety for having numerous accidents. Scheckter also lived as a tax exile in Spain for a while and it was there that James became better acquainted with the driver who had a reputation for being an angry young man.

'I like Fletcher because he has an exceptional intelligence and wit. He's very funny. It used to take a long time to get it out because he's not an educated guy and because of his intelligence he was aware that he lacked education. He felt he was at a disadvantage, and therefore he was very defensive, but he's got over that now. He's got his confidence. I like people with good minds: I find it stimulating, and Fletcher has an exceptionally sharp brain.'

Scheckter was also very quick (and would be World Champion in 1979) and at Watkins Glen his Tyrrell shared the front row of the starting grid with James, who, for the eighth time in the season, was on pole position. At the start James got away smartly but Scheckter was even more prompt and stormed off into the lead. Holding station behind the pace-setting Tyrrell for lap after lap James began to look for reasons for his lack of progress.

Pit signals from the McLaren crew on every lap showed James that the gap to Scheckter was a steady three seconds, while the interval between James and the third place man, Niki Lauda, was an equally constant five seconds. But James couldn't afford to accept the status quo; he needed to win, and to do that he would need to get into another mental gear.

He came to realize that instead of focusing his mind on gaining ground he was driving on 'auto-pilot', concentrating not on the physical act of driving the car but on the idea of just finishing the race. Instead of driving 'like an old grandmother' he resolved to 'get his act together'.

His McLaren was oversteering, its rear wheels stepping alarmingly out of line around Watkins Glen's many corners, and James was also making potentially dangerous mistakes through lack of concentration. He became angry with himself for driving badly and spent 20 laps concentrating on ironing out the kinks and polishing the technique necessary to go faster. His self-administered driving lesson later gave him great personal satisfaction. 'I got myself together. This is very important in all walks of life, to be able to catch yourself when you're doing something badly and to make sure you improve.'

He gritted his teeth, grasped the McLaren's steering wheel more firmly, and zeroed his mind in on the Tyrrell that stood between him and the victory he was now determined to get. As James bore down on Scheckter, leaving Niki further and further behind, he planned ahead, looking for likely passing places and opportunities to outmanoeuvre the leader.

On the 36th lap, when Scheckter was delayed by another car slowing for a tight corner, the McLaren tucked in behind the Tyrrell's rear wing. As they accelerated down the following straight section James veered out from Scheckter's slipstream and took over the lead.

But another of Fletcher's notable characteristics was determination, and he was not about to give up without a fight. Four laps later, at exactly the same place on the circuit and in the same circumstances – James was held up by a slower driver and in his frustration missed a gear change – Scheckter was in front again.

James fought to keep his fury – at himself and the tardy back-marker – under control. His adrenaline level was dangerously high, but emotions could not be allowed to overrule the rational thought needed to improve his situation in the remaining 19 laps. James would have to drive on the ragged edge to get close to the Tyrrell again, and then he would somehow have to muscle his way past the obstinate Scheckter.

He pressed on, and within another lap was again within striking range. For several laps the McLaren hovered opportunistically in the Tyrrell's wake, with James feinting left and right and filling Scheckter's mirrors with distraction. But Fletcher refused to be out-foxed and the pace and ferocity of their duel was breathtaking.

Finally, with a dozen laps to go, James gathered up all his courage and skill and forced his way alongside the Tyrrell on the entry to a slower corner. The two cars rounded the bend in perilously close company and on the following straight the McLaren gradually assumed command and James was gone.

As if carried away by the exuberance of his own velocity James then reeled off a succession of ever-quicker laps. Right near the end of the race – in a time which was nearly a second faster than his pole position – he established a new lap record for the Watkins Glen circuit.

James shot across the finish line eight seconds ahead of Fletcher, while Niki, plagued with severe oversteer, was nearly a minute behind them in third place.

When James climbed from his car, exhausted and shaking and soaked with perspiration from his all-out effort, he hadn't the reserves of mental energy left to mull over the full implications of his victory. He had closed to within three points of Niki, but the various mathematical permutations of the points situation, what he would need to do to in the one remaining race, were far too complicated for James to consider now. For the moment he only wanted to celebrate winning the United Grand Prix. A six-pack of cold American beer, not the traditional champagne offered to the victor, seemed a good way to begin.

Later that night he really let his hair down, or rather covered it up. On the way back to his motel he confiscated from a construction site a road-worker's yellow hard-hat, adorned with a flashing orange light. In the bar he cavorted and danced around, with the flashing hat perched at a jaunty angle on his happy head. A cigarette and a drink dangled from one hand while the other fondled his female companion for the night.

★ ★ ★

With his clean sweep of the two North American races James had set the stage for a thrilling World Championship showdown with Niki in Japan. After such a tumultuous season it seemed only fitting that the final act of their intense drama for supremacy at the pinnacle of motor sport should be played out at the Mount Fuji circuit, under the shadow of the sacred snow-capped volcano. No dramatist could have created a more riveting scenario, or two such heroic characters.

There could be no real loser in Japan. From either the human interest or racing points of view there was little to choose between the two competitors who between them had won 11 of the 15 Grands Prix to date.

The wonderfully brave Austrian had fought for both his life and his professional career with tremendous courage and resolve, and the colourful Englishman had defied expectations and overcome staggering adversity with sheer bloody-minded determination and no small amount of skill. Their respective achievements and attributes had by now attracted an audience much wider than just the traditional fans of motor sport. And as the exploits of the gruesomely scarred Ferrari driver and the golden-haired charger in the McLaren were reported and embellished by the media around the world both men had become international celebrities. But, at least in the matter of making headlines, it seemed James had the edge over the more reclusive Niki.

After bursting into the limelight with Lord Hesketh's rich and racy version of a Formula 1 team the brashly confident and badly dressed public schoolboy/playboy was transported into stardom in the jet-set world when his wife ran away with a famous movie star. The 'jilted husband', in the eyes of the media, on his own proved to be entirely worthy of perpetuating his notoriety. He was seen variously as arrogant, intelligent, truculent, articulate, rude, charismatic, boorish and charming – especially to women. James Hunt might well soon become the best racing driver in the world, but already he had more fame, and infamy, than all the previous World Champions put together.

Being a Formula 1 superstar was what James had always wanted, but the fact that he had also become a pop star, even a cult figure, did not rest easily on his shoulders, which seemed to have become even more hunched under the mounting pressure.

For James the glare of the spotlight highlighted the sharp edges of success and it made him uncomfortable. He worried that the price of fame might include costly changes to his character; in fact, he was already concerned that 'all the things that have happened to me have hardened me up. That bothers me because one day, when I retire, my ambition is to go back to being a normal person – one who likes other people, whom other people like.

'When you are doing well people spend a lot of time telling you how clever you are and it's very easy to believe. I've seen too many people become victims of such flattery and start taking themselves too seriously. That's when they destroy themselves and their personalities. And those same people who push you to the top want to knock you down when you get there. When they jump you the only way not to be hurt is to become hard.

'I try to be myself but I worry that I've lost the ability to enjoy life. I'm a tax exile, but England is where my heart is and where my friends are. But everywhere the demands on my time are so great that already my private life is shot to hell and I feel the loss of close friends. The main problem in this business is that you lose your individuality. Whatever you do or say is watched. You are used as evidence against yourself.'

There was more evidence, for both the prosecution and the defence, in Japan.

⋆ ⋆ ⋆

The week before the race at Mount Fuji several key members of the McLaren crew stayed at a luxurious hotel in Tokyo where James made extensive use of the fitness facilities, running, swimming and working out with the exercise equipment. He played squash every day, beating the hotel professional and several other partners brought in to give him competition. Using the same technique of relentlessly wearing down his opponents he also won at backgammon, another game that had become a passion.

He played backgammon for money, the stakes varying according to the skill of his opponent: up to $70 a point for someone he knew he was going to beat and for considerably less if he expected to lose. That way, so his theory went, he got his lessons cheap. He estimated that so far he was ahead $3,000 for the year.

When he brought his backgammon board into the lavishly appointed hotel dining room the head waiter frowned on James's bare feet, jeans and T-shirt and told him this was not a playhouse. 'But', James protested, 'the whole world is a playhouse!', and if the dining room was out of bounds he would go and play in his room with his new playmates.

To his great delight he had discovered that the hotel was used for overnight stays by British Airways flight crews. Each morning James greeted the arriving stewardesses in the lobby and advised them it would be open house that evening in his room. His open door policy attracted a surprising number of visitors and James had to devise a complex rotation system to accommodate his harem.

Another guest at the hotel was Barry Sheene, the British motorcycle World Champion who had become friends with James. Since Sheene had to visit Japan on business anyway, he decided to come early to 'hang out' with his mate and give him immoral support.

'I got on really well with James because we had the same daft kind of mentality then, before I was married. We were both sportsmen and we drank and smoked and chased women, went to places you shouldn't go and did things you shouldn't do. We had a lot of laughs.

'It was hilarious in Tokyo when James would make the Japanese embarrassed at all his press conferences by showing up in his jeans and T-shirt. I hated wearing formal clothes too but I loved going somewhere with James because he always made me look well dressed!'

★ ★ ★

James was wearing his driving suit, but on race day at the Mount Fuji circuit rain gear would have been more appropriate. The sacred volcano was obscured by low clouds, the surrounding countryside was shrouded in gloomy mist and fog, and the 2.708 mile track where the cars were supposed to race at speeds up to 180 miles an hour was awash in rivers of water.

The Japanese belief that to be able to see Mount Fuji meant you were in for a lucky day boded ill for the drivers and for the 80,000 spectators gathered at the circuit to witness the first ever Grand Prix of Japan.

After several cars had crashed in the morning warm-up session, one of them even aquaplaning off the main straight, many of the drivers wanted the race to be cancelled, or at least postponed. A debate concerning that possibility was now in progress in the control tower.

The organizers had invested over $1 million in staging the event, and the spectators had paid high admission prices to see the Formula 1 heroes in action. Also waiting expectantly were millions of television viewers around the world.

Before this season Formula 1 racing had been shown only

intermittently in a few countries. But now, with the extraordinary fight between Hunt and Lauda about to reach its climax, a host of international TV networks with precise schedules had booked expensive satellite time and the Japanese Grand Prix simply had to begin.

The vast grandstands running the length of the straight opposite the pits was packed with fans sitting silently beneath a sea of umbrellas. There was little for them to see. The Formula 1 cars were covered in tarpaulins and the team personnel huddled in groups in the garages. Occasionally, when a driver would venture out from his shelter and look up at the sodden sky, the crowd would respond with polite applause.

Then, from the McLaren garage, the very tall driver with the long blonde hair, immediately recognizable as the famous Englishman James Hunt, came over toward the pit wall. The crowd, many of them with binoculars, watched in fascination as he peeled down the top half of his driving suit and commenced, as James put it 'to have a tinkle'. His audience was flabbergasted at this strange pre-race ritual, but rewarded it with vigorous cheering and hand-clapping.

But relieving his bladder before the multitude had not eliminated the matter weighing heavily on James's mind, and in the increasingly tense atmosphere in the McLaren garage he retched and coughed more than ever. Even the steady stream of witty banter from Barry Sheene failed to distract him.

The pressure was on James as never before in his life. He was second on the starting grid, one place ahead of Niki. In qualifying they were separated by a mere 0.28 seconds but Niki's three point advantage in the Championship towered over James's head like Fuji, the mountain which he couldn't even see.

Mario Andretti, in pole position in his Lotus, didn't relish playing the role of spoiler in the race, nor did he want to take sides between the World Championship contenders. But the American pointed out that the Ferrari driver had much less to do than the man in the McLaren. 'Hunt's got everything to lose. You don't have to be a mathematician to work it out. Lauda just has to beat Hunt, but Hunt's got to beat him – and all the rest of us. He's got to win.'

James, however, didn't even want to race: 'I would rather give Niki the title than race in these conditions.' They held a private discussion and James told Niki he would have to drive if everybody else did, but they should try to get the race postponed. Niki agreed, and as the senior members of the Safety Committee they presented their case to the other drivers and to the race officials. The flooded track was dangerous enough in itself, visibility in the already foggy atmosphere would become impossible in the spray thrown up by speeding cars and the Japanese Grand Prix should not be held in these appalling conditions.

However, their position didn't receive unanimous support from their peers. Ronnie Peterson, Vittorio Brambilla, Clay Regazzoni, Alan Jones and Hans Stück, all of whom fancied their chances on a wet track, thought they should get on with it. Tom Pryce, agreed, saying they were supposed to be the best racing drivers in the world and should be able to handle a few puddles.

When James heard this he knew he was fighting a lost cause. Once a few drivers lined up on the grid others would surely follow. The team managers, who always wanted to race come hell or high water, would resort to pressure tactics on any reluctant junior drivers, threatening them with the sack if they didn't race. It was like the system used for breaking labour strikes, and once a few went back to work the barriers would go down and the job would get done.

In the McLaren pit Alastair Caldwell began his own strike-breaking tactics, by encouraging the mechanic Lance Gibbs, the team's unofficial 'Entertainment Officer', to work up the crowd in the grandstands. Besides his wrenches, Gibbs carried in his tool box an Acme Thunderer whistle, the type used by football referees. Caldwell suggested that Lance should try it on the bored fans, many of whom, it developed, had whistles in their race-watching kit.

A dialogue was soon struck up and the piercing sounds of thousands of whistles chorused alarmingly around the Fuji circuit. Gibbs then proceeded to conduct his orchestra in an exercise of slow hand-clapping. The bored fans joined in enthusiastically, the din became deafening and, for the race organizers, the environment seemed menacing. It was reminiscent of the situation at Brands Hatch, where the hostile crowd helped frighten the organizers into letting James re-start the delayed British Grand Prix.

Caldwell dashed up to the control tower, where he played up the potential riot factor. The organizers, stunned by the uncharacteristic display of emotion from the normally inscrutable Japanese fans, listened intently.

Caldwell received strong support from Bernie Ecclestone, owner of the Brabham team and the man who had arranged for the international television coverage, which would put large sums of money into the coffers of the teams. So far the cameras had shown only umbrellas and puddles of water. Networks around the world were waiting impatiently and Japanese honour was at stake.

The race should have started an hour and a half ago, and in another two or three hours the Mount Fuji circuit would be in darkness. Finally, a decision was made and announced over the loudspeakers: the Japanese Grand Prix would begin in five minutes.

* * *

In the gathering gloom the cars were pushed out onto the water-laden starting grid. A mechanic drilled ventilation holes in the visor of James's helmet in the hope of keeping it from becoming too fogged up. Another McLaren man placed a plank over the small lake surrounding his car, and James walked it.

Sitting in the cockpit James felt dampness rising up from the seat to meet his own perspiration. He wiped the moisture off the steering wheel with his gloved hands and wearily, it seemed, laid his helmet back against the headrest beneath the rollover bar.

A dozen photographers poked their clicking cameras at him as he sat there with his eyes closed. Journalists, intent on capturing the intensity of the final moments of James's personal drama, crowded closer. One of them, Pete Lyons of *Autosport*, wrote: 'Either side of his hips was a bath of 40 gallons of fuel. Behind his shoulders was 485 horsepower. Ahead of him was a road covered in many places by water inches deep. Above him the air was heavy with mist. Steady rain fell out of it.... "I'm not going to race", he said in a very small, slow voice, "I can't. I'm just going to drive around".'

James made one of the best starts of his life, his McLaren's fat rain tyres sending up plumes of thick spray that completely obliterated all in his wake. Only the leader could see where he was going; the other 24 brave men were navigating on blind faith, and James sought to maximize his advantage.

He slammed the accelerator to the floor, banged the gear lever through five quick changes and in a few seconds was travelling at 140 miles an hour down Fuji's sodden straight. His seemingly suicidal pace hardly slackened when he forded the first stream running across his path. James clung to the steering wheel for dear life as the McLaren wobbled wildly and buckets of water shot skyward.

Somehow, he slithered out of the shower still in control, then safely waded through several more rivers, successfully navigated the circuit's six substantial corners, and in a breathtakingly short time a giant rooster tail of spray preceded by a red and white McLaren sailed across the finish line to end the first lap.

James seemed nearly a nautical mile ahead of the dense wall of water that contained the rest of the pack. Buried near the back of it was a red Ferrari, in which the drenched driver struggled with his emotions. In his comeback drive at the Italian Grand Prix, 33 days after he had nearly been burned alive at the Nürburgring, Niki Lauda claimed he had conquered his fear quickly and cleanly. In his book, *To Hell and Back*, Niki admitted this was a lie, that he had to play the hero to avoid showing any signs of weakness to James. 'At Monza I was rigid with fear. Terrified. Diarrhoea. Heart pounding. Throwing up.'

Now, in the teaming rain at Mount Fuji, the fear was back and Niki didn't try to fight it – or hide it. 'I drive slowly, keep away from the other cars so that none of them shall run into me. I think how stupid this race is. You can't see. On these streams you are as helpless as a paper boat. Even going slowly you could be washed away. After the second lap I go into the pits. I am not going to drive, because it is madness.'

'It's just like murder out there', said Niki as he climbed out of his Ferrari. 'I'm not going to do it. Sometimes I could not tell which direction the car was going. For me it was the limit. For me there is something more important than the World Championship.'

For the first time in his career Niki had given up. His problems with visibility were exacerbated by the legacy of his Nürburgring burns, which prevented him from blinking his eyes. But he didn't need any excuses to save face and he also rejected the Ferrari team's suggestion that they should announce that he stopped because of engine trouble.

Three other drivers – Emerson Fittipaldi, Carlos Pace and Larry Perkins – felt as strongly as Niki and they also pulled out of the race. But the Japanese Grand Prix went on and on.

☆ ☆ ☆

As James sped past the finish line for the third time he glimpsed the message on the McLaren signalling board: 'NIKI OUT'.

'Poor Niki!', said James afterwards. 'In a perfect world we would have shared the Championship, but that is impossible. Let's hope that no fool blames him for packing it in. He's come through a terrible accident and his comeback has been marvellous. But I think he made the right decision and I feel awfully sorry for him. I feel sorry for anyone who's got to race in such ridiculous circumstances.'

James pressed on, regardless of the ridiculous circumstances. Niki might be gone, but the three-point deficit remained, as did 70 more laps around the treacherous Mount Fuji track. Slipping and sliding around the corners, twitching treacherously down the straights, James maintained the lead over his pursuers, who were now led by the charging Vittorio Brambilla.

'The Monza Gorilla' was waging his own private war, hurling his skittering March inexorably onward in a mad-looking manner which seemed not to be taking into consideration the perilous lack of adhesion on the wet track. On lap 22 Brambilla splashed alongside James, then abruptly lost control, his March missing the McLaren by inches as it slewed wildly off the circuit in a shower of water and mud.

Following Brambilla's exit James, who later claimed he had given him 'the old elbow', was comforted by the sight of his team-mate's McLaren in his mirrors. In second place, Jochen Mass would provide an effective barrier to any other drivers with ambitions of overtaking the leader.

However, the insurance factor and the prospect of a McLaren one-two finish was short-lived. Mass had driven very hard to arrive in second place and when he got there, and slowed down to hold station behind James, he failed to maintain the intense concentration necessary to stay on the tricky track. On the 35th lap, in the midst of one of Fuji's temporary streams, his McLaren got away from him and slithered off into the steel barriers.

But now, half way through the race, James had much more than the departure of his loyal team mate to worry about. In his peripheral vision, each time he roared past the grandstands James noticed fewer and fewer umbrellas in the crowd, and in the background there were occasional glimpses of the snow-capped mountain. The cloud cover was lifting, taking with it the rain, and a strong breeze was beginning to dry out the track. Speeds picked up accordingly, the gaps between cars shrank appreciably, and in fact the Japanese Grand Prix was about to begin in earnest, though in circumstances equally as unstable as before.

The track conditions were not yet dry enough to warrant stopping for slick racing tyres but tyre conservation had become of prime importance. The treaded wet weather tyres were designed to bite through water and grip the road. But the drying surface was provoking the opposite condition: the road was consuming the rubber. Heat build-up in the soft rubber compounds caused them to shred and chunk and the tyres would wear away rapidly unless they were cooled with water.

To cool their tyres the more alert drivers began to seek out wet sections of the track, off the beaten path, and drive through them. But

James didn't seem to be paying much attention to this new development and stubbornly stuck to the rapidly drying racing line.

'COOL TYRES' was the message posted on the McLaren signalling board, but James appeared to ignore it. Few drivers had more intense powers of concentration, but to effect them James required absolutely no distractions. When driving quickly on public roads he would sometimes ask his passengers to stop talking so that he could give his undivided attention to the task at hand.

Now, even though Niki's departure meant a third-place finish would give him the four points necessary to win the drivers' title, James seemed so preoccupied with winning the Japanese Grand Prix that he failed to give proper consideration to the increasingly parlous state of his tyres.

His attention was further diverted by the sudden appearance of Patrick Depailler who, with just 11 laps to go, barged his Tyrrell past the McLaren and into the lead. Moments later Mario Andretti's Lotus also overtook the McLaren and from the perspective of third place James was able to absorb the tyre wear lesson to be learned from the two cars in front of him.

Andretti had been conserving his rubber by driving through puddles of standing water, but Depailler hadn't and his tyres were nearly bald. Within two laps the wildly sliding Tyrrell was forced into making a pit stop for fresh tyres, and Andretti assumed the lead.

For James, with his own tyres worn down to their last shreds of tread, second place – indeed any points-finishing position in the race – was becoming more and more tenuous. In his anxiety he looked to the McLaren pit for inspiration and what he saw there made him more and more angry.

The McLaren signalling board showed an arrow which meant the team was waiting with new tyres and it was up to James to make the decision to come into the pits. The other signal used in such circumstances was a message consisting of the single word 'IN', which was an order, not an option, to come into the pits. This had been the McLaren arrangement 'since Christ was a cowboy', according to Alastair Caldwell, but with so much at stake in this race Caldwell and Teddy Mayer felt James should decide if, and when, to stop. Only he knew how much life was left in his tyres and whether he could afford to risk losing the time it would take to change them.

James thought exactly the opposite and began gesticulating furiously each time he passed the McLaren pit. 'The tyres, the tyres, that was the only bloody thing I could think about! And I didn't want to make the fucking decision! The team had all the information about the rate of tyre wear, they'd seen what happened to other cars and they should have told me what to do. Instead, in response to my frantic requests for information they hung out the arrow, like a huge bloody question mark!'

The question was answered by the left front tyre which, on the 68th lap, disintegrated on the corner before the pit straight. The sagging McLaren, shredding bits of flapping rubber and spraying up sparks from the dragging chassis, swerved into the pits.

As the disabled car trundled down the pit lane the Ferrari personnel began waving their arms and cheering with undisguised pleasure. Their driver, Clay Regazzoni, was now in second place and, more importantly, Niki Lauda, though he was now a spectator, was still the World Drivers' Champion.

The McLaren scrabbled sideways into its pit where the crew fell upon it. As the severely agitated driver blipped the throttle with his impatient right foot the engine note screamed higher and higher, providing a demented mechanical musical accompaniment to the desperate ballet performed by the wheel changers in their race against time.

The car sat too low for the jack to slip under it. Caldwell and one of the mechanics lifted it bodily. Caldwell suspected that the furious vibrations emanating from the car probably owed as much to his driver's state of mind as to the highly revving engine which seemed in danger of exploding.

Working with purposeful fury, the other crewmen threw themselves at the four corners of the car. Precious seconds ticked by as wheelnuts were attacked and removed – old wheels tossed aside – new ones slammed on – wheelnuts tightened.

In 27 seconds the men at the wheels jumped upright, those holding the car up dropped it to the pavement and everyone ran for cover. Leaving behind twin ribbons of black rubber the refettled McLaren screamed out of the pits to rejoin the race.

The extraordinary Japanese Grand Prix might yet have a fairy tale ending for James but the eerie setting seemed more appropriate for some bizarre, surrealistic fantasy.

The Japanese emblem of the rising sun was sinking below the horizon, bathing the remaining clouds overhead in a golden afterglow and casting purple and orange shadows over the snow fields on Mount Fuji's conical peak. The mighty mountain towered ominously over the circuit, where a kind of volcanic eruption was under way.

For James, his whole driving career – all those years of hardship, sacrifice and disappointment – had boiled down to just five more racing laps.

He didn't know how much time he had lost in the pits. He didn't know where he stood in the race. He didn't even know if there was still a chance of salvaging enough points to attain his lifelong ambition. He only knew how he had come this far: by racing as hard as he knew how, and that was how he would finish the 1976 season: 'All I could do was just shut my eyes and pass as many cars as I could'.

The metaphorical act of shutting his eyes was made easier by the proverbial red mist which covered them. He was enraged at what he perceived as his team's incompetence over the pit stop question, indeed he held the bloody Wiener and Caldwell personally responsible for the burst tyre which had blown his race lead – and surely his World Championship – into oblivion.

In the cockpit his fury mounted as James cursed his team, his tyres, his luck, the weather. His vituperation extended to any cars which dared to clutter up the path he intended to wipe clean during the remaining 13 miles of the Japanese Grand Prix.

Throwing out the window his self-imposed rule of not letting his emotions interfere with his driving James jerked his McLaren recklessly around the corners, slammed it down the straights and, in one teetering-on-the-brink manoeuvre on the outside of a still slippery curve, he overtook both the Ferrari of Clay Regazzoni and the Surtees of Alan Jones.

As he blasted past the McLaren pit in those final laps James thought he saw 'P5' on the signalling board – meaning he was in fifth position – or was it 'P6'? By the time 'P4' – and, possibly 'P3' – appeared on the board James was confused. Either he was making some kind of progress or the pit signals were inconsistent – yet more evidence of 'McLaren screwing up again. With their abysmal track record in responding to panic and crisis I wasn't about to believe their lap chart!'.

Straining against his seatbelts he hunched further forward in the cockpit and set his sights on the next car in front of him, the blue and white Tyrrell of Patrick Depailler, which, James could see, was immediately preceded by the black and gold Lotus of Mario Andretti.

As the trio roared across the start/finish line – one/two/three in the blink of an eye – James was startled to see the chequered flag being waved vigorously. The Japanese Grand Prix was obviously over. He was unsure of his finishing position. But he was convinced that his team had let him down.

The cooling down lap failed to have that effect on James. He ignored the applause and cheers directed toward him by the fans around the circuit. As he trundled down the crowded pit lane, blipping the throttle belligerently, he might have wondered about the curiously congratulatory gesticulations directed towards him by the other teams – except for Ferrari – and the strange behaviour of certain members of his own crew who leapt on the McLaren's sidepods even before it had stopped.

James was oblivious to all the attention. He still had a job to do, and that was to 'strangle' Teddy Mayer.

In a rage James fought his way out of his safety harness, struggled out of the cockpit and towered over his tiny team leader, shaking his fist and screaming a torrent of profane abuse that his thickly padded helmet failed to muffle. When the helmet came off the furious beration intensified and the crowd around the McLaren car warily moved back out of harm's way.

But instead of wavering under the onslaught it seemed the beaming Wiener wanted to embrace his demented driver. He made a peace offering to James in the form of three fingers on his right hand and waved them slowly in the front of James's red face.

Other team members, journalists, photographers and well-wishers gave him the three finger salute. A mechanic stripped the number 11 from the side of his car and ripped it in two and triumphantly waved the number '1'. This was a signal that James could understand and gradually the message was absorbed by his befuddled brain.

He had finished third in the race. He had scored four points, one more than the pre-race gap between him and Niki Lauda. He was now number one. He must be the new World Drivers' Champion.

Standing on the victory podium, beside the winner Andretti (who was in fact a lap ahead of the field), and the second place finisher Depailler, James still refused to abandon himself to comprehending the full implications of this day, 24 October 1976.

'I was absolutely determined not to think I was World Champion and then get disappointed, because there were 300 good reasons why something should have gone wrong. After all the protests, disqualifications and bullshit that had gone on during the season anything might still happen.

'I didn't feel that confident when they put me up on third place on the rostrum because I wasn't sure that I wouldn't be dragged off there at the last minute. It was only really when I checked the lap charts and the organizers said I was definitely third and there were no protests in the wind that I started half believing it.

'It was nearly dark by the time the podium presentations were over and I went into the press room for a bit of a chat with the journalists. When I came out it was pitch black and everyone had gone. The place was deserted.

'I reckoned that even if anyone had wanted to do anything about taking the title from me they couldn't be bothered. Nobody was interested. They'd had enough. I decided to accept it. I must be World Champion.'

* * *

The post-race celebrations began in the dining room at the Mount Fuji circuit, where the members of the Formula 1 circus were in a festive mood after the long and gruelling season.

The McLaren table was especially jubilant, and relieved, that all their efforts had finally paid off and partook freely of the liberal quantities of champagne on offer. Their new Champion drank Japanese beer and offered further thoughts on the race and the season.

James still thought it had been 'madness' to start the race in the dreadful conditions, though he allowed that he was now 'kind of glad that they did.' He also completely agreed with Niki's decision to stop and still wished they could share the driving title.

Looking back over the year James said he had learned several things. First, he thought Niki Lauda was the bravest man he had ever met. Second, just because a driver crosses the finish line first does not mean he has won the race. Third, the authorities in charge of Formula 1 racing are not really capable of running today's motor racing at the top level. Fourth, said James, McLaren is the best team in Grand Prix racing.

Furthermore, he said, they also enjoy their racing as much, if not more, than anybody else, and before the drunken evening was over James had made peace with the McLaren leadership.

Alastair Caldwell blamed James for not 'reacting' to the pit board message to cool his tyres. Mario Andretti had done it and went on to win the race on the same set of tyres. He also argued that the pit messages relating to James's position in the race were always exactly correct.

Caldwell revealed that at one stage, when the Lotus driver Gunnar Nilsson was ahead of James, he had offered the Lotus boss Colin Chapman $50,000 to bring Nilsson in for a pit stop to get him out of James's way. The offer was refused and, anyway, it was all academic now. James had great respect for Caldwell and later went so far as to give him much of the credit for winning the Championship.

Teddy Mayer now recalls the scene in the pits with wry amusement. 'It was all a bit confusing and at the end he was furious. It was quite apparent from all the fist-shaking that he had wanted us to make the decision about coming in to change tyres but we wanted him to decide because we didn't know as much as we thought he knew about their state of wear.

'When it was over we knew that he'd just squeaked by to win the Championship and we were all delighted for him. But he came in jumping up and down in a rage and berating me. When he made up his mind that he wanted to behave in a particular way it was pretty hard to turn James around. But eventually he took it all in and started to look a bit sheepish and it all became fairly hilarious.'

Mayer thought James was fully deserving of the drivers' title. 'In a straight fight I think James was more than Niki's equal. Our car was fairly ordinary and James just gave it a hell of a drive. He had an enormous amount of talent and ability to drive a car quickly.

'I will always remember what Tyler Alexander said when he came to the Canadian race at Mosport. Tyler was running our IndyCar team in America and hadn't seen much Formula 1 for a while. After he watched James at Mosport he said to me: "Teddy, don't worry about the car as long as you've got James in it. He just drives it harder".'

* * *

Niki might have ultimately thrown away his chances of winning when he pulled out of the Japanese Grand Prix but James had done everything he had to do, especially over the course of the last half of the season – overcoming a seemingly impossible points deficit in brilliant fashion.

Niki's point of view was that James was 'one helluva driver. I have to say that I had the best car but he drove incredibly well towards the end'.

John Hogan: 'In the sequence of events leading up to the last race James was simply unbeatable. He was uncatchable. All right, he lucked out in a way when Niki didn't race in Japan, but in Canada and at Watkins Glen those were two of the most extraordinary pieces of Formula 1 driving you've ever seen.

'The unfortunate thing was, because they weren't on television, people didn't see what happened. Then, because of James's amazing comeback every television company in the world piled into the Japanese Grand Prix. In fact, the fight between James and Niki is what put the sport of Formula 1 on television to stay.'

However, there were accusations from some quarters that James only became Champion because his rival was unable to defend himself properly after the Nürburgring accident. James took the trouble to go back over the detailed results of the season's races and decided that when Niki's misfortune was weighed against his own trials and tribulations they balanced each other out and James had no qualms in saying: 'I had to drive flat out all year – absolutely balls to the wall all the way. I think I'm the Champion fair and square.

'The World Championship is only a paper thing, I know, but it's the most measurable thing in racing. And to be at the top of your chosen field is immensely satisfying. Now I can look back on life and say 'I'm a winner' because I did what I set out to do.

'Still, I worry about whether the Championship will live up to what I always imagined it to be, or whether it will be only a temporary sort of elation.

'Most people think I have a lot of fun and that I'm a pretty good driver but they don't take my driving all that seriously. And I don't help that, in a lot of people's view, by the way I behave and my lifestyle.

'I intend to rub it in for them on the track until they say I'm good – but I don't intend to change the way I behave for their benefit.'

☆ ☆ ☆

Proof of his intentions to continue conducting himself in the manner to which he was accustomed was apparent to those who flew with James on the Japan Air Lines flight back to London. Among the happiest passengers were his boyhood friend Chris Jones, who had come out to Japan to bring his mate good luck, and John Hogan, the man from Marlboro who was delighted that his belief in James had paid off so spectacularly and so soon.

James drank nearly all the way and when the JAL crew offered to seat the honourable new World Champion in the First Class section he refused, saying he wanted to stay down at the back where all his mates were. However, when the bar in the Economy section of the 747 ran dry James did stagger up to First Class, and returned with an armful of drinks – several times.

Somewhere over the North Pole the plane ran out of alcohol and nearly everyone fell asleep. But James, still in full flight, grabbed the intercom microphone and announced, in Japanese which he had learned from a stewardess, that the best racing driver in the world was commanding that all the party-poopers should bloody well wake up!

On the descent into Heathrow airport James admitted that he was absolutely shattered and had a wicked hangover. But any lingering effects of his over-indulgence were soon forgotten in the incredible scene that awaited him when he came out of Customs.

The crowd greeting the conquering British hero – brandishing a toy monkey named 'Smilie' given to him by the McLaren mechanics – was estimated at 2,000, among them Sue and Wallis Hunt and his brothers and sisters.

'I hadn't expected my family to be there and it was the most unnerving thing to have to say hello to them in front of all those people. The press conference was an ordeal. It was all quite overwhelming.

'In most situations I feel in control but when I get out of control I'm not sure whether I'm doing or saying the right thing. Not because of what people want to hear, so much as the difficulty of what I want to say to them. That's what makes me feel uncomfortable. It was a bit of a heavy deal, with mother freaking out and everything – that's what really threw me.'

The proud mother hugged and kissed her embarrassed son and wept tears of joy. 'He's done it! He's done it!', Sue Hunt exclaimed. 'I'm elated. Absolutely elated. It's magnificent. He may be the World Champion but he hasn't changed. He's still my naughty James!'

Sue and Wallis had watched the Japanese race live in the ITN television studios in London. With them were James's mate John Richardson and his wife Mary, who worked for ITN, and it was in the Richardson's car that James travelled from Heathrow to a champagne breakfast in a friend's flat in London. The trip turned out to be a high-speed procession as zealous journalists and photographers, some of them on motorcycles, pursued Richardson's car.

'James was completely knackered', Richardson recalls, 'but still on an adrenaline high and very happy. We barged through all the reporters and got inside the flat and opened the champagne. The enormity of what he achieved still hadn't hit him, I think.

'He'd gone out and proven he was the best in the world in his chosen sport, but yet he comes back and all he wants to do was sit down and have a drink and a bit of a smoke with his mates.'

Back at the Hunt home in Belmont, the front door was covered with photos of James and his victorious McLaren and a large Union Jack and even the family Labrador had a British flag tied around his collar. But James saw none of this as he was spirited away on an exhausting round of duties that took him far away from family and friends.

☆　☆　☆

He was mobbed by fans at the Earl's Court motor show, then flew to

His helmet bore allegiance to Wellington College (red, blue and yellow bands) and some of the sponsors who made him a wealthy man.

Above Britain's 'Golden Boy' was uncomfortable in the role of hero. Here he ponders the adulation of his fans at the 'Tribute to James', 7 December 1976, at Brands Hatch. *Right* James, here at work in his McLaren in Spain in 1976, only really began to enjoy racing as a sport after he stopped driving and became a BBC television commentator.

Above left James had an uneasy, but fruitful, relationship with Teddy Mayer, the McLaren team director. *Above right* Celebrating his penultimate Grand Prix win, with Niki Lauda on the podium after the US Grand Prix at Watkins Glen in 1977.

Above left Jane Birbeck, the girlfriend who stayed with him longer than most.
Above right The exhausted World Champion flies home, with his boyhood friend Chris Jones
and, in the back, John Hogan of Marlboro (left) and Alastair Caldwell of McLaren (right).

He smoked up to 40 cigarettes a day for over 20 years.

Accidents like this one at Long Beach in 1977 made him increasingly worried about the danger factor. James finally decided to quit racing midway through the 1979 season.

His battle-scarred rival, Niki Lauda, who was nearly killed in a fiery accident at the Nurburgring in 1976, was James's closest friend among the drivers.

While the Wolf team tried to make him more competitive, James was looking for a way out.

Many hours in the aviary with his prized budgerigars failed to distract James from his troubles. His menagerie included Humbert, a foul-mouthed parrot.

Above left *He was late for the ceremony and had to borrow a tie, but James and Sarah Lomax were married on 17 December 1983.* **Above right** *James had great difficulty adjusting to the non-racing life. Even their children couldn't keep him and Sarah together.*

Above Happier times – on a skiing holiday in Switzerland with Helen Dyson and the boys. *Right* Contentment at last, with Helen – the love of his life. *Far right* Sarah and the boys at the memorial service: A Celebration of the Life of James Hunt.

James lavished affection on his two 'little men' – Tom and Freddie. Here they are in 1993 with their grandfather Wallis, on Wimbledon Common shortly before James's sudden death.

James Hunt, 1947–1993.

Cologne for a personal appearance, then returned to Brands Hatch for a 'Tribute to James' day, an event attended by 12,000 patriotic fans and by Niki Lauda, who graciously saluted the British Champion. That evening James hosted a party for the McLaren mechanics. The next day he went to the Vauxhall factory at Luton to reinforce his sponsor's slogan: 'Take my advice. Test drive a Vauxhall'.

At an earlier ceremony he was made a 'Freeman of the City of London' and at the fifth anniversary of the Ladbroke Club in Mayfair James had a family reunion of sorts. Among the 150 guests were Mr and Mrs Richard Burton. The three of them chatted and gossiped like old friends and Burton joked with James that people seemed more interested in getting Suzy's autograph than either of theirs.

James flew to Linz in Austria to open the Jochen Rindt racing car show, then went to Geneva for press interviews arranged by Marlboro. Two days later he was in Munich at another racing car show, then returned to London to judge the Miss World contest. There were two days of personal appearances in Dublin, then a trip back to Europe for the opening of a car show in Essen. Next came the opening of a discotheque in Vienna and there too he helped his Austrian friend open the Niki Lauda racing car show, before rushing off to accept a magazine award in Zurich and appear at a banquet in Marseilles.

Back in London there was a Royal Automobile Club prize-giving lunch and the British Racing Drivers' Club dinner dance at the Dorchester Hotel. James, whose escort was a beautiful French model, Valentine Monnier, was the guest of honour at the prestigious BRDC event where, by his own admission he became 'legless'. It was traditionally a formal occasion but James was dressed in jeans and an open-necked shirt and wore sandals with no socks. The Hon. Gerald Lascelles, president of the BRDC and a cousin of the Queen, suggested to James that his attire was not befitting a World Champion and there was much clucking of tongues and mutterings of disapproval when the World Champion, in his disrespectful garb, was presented with an award by the Duke of Kent.

Before the BRDC evening was over James staggered into a bystander, a saloon car racer, who was in the act of sipping a gin and tonic. The man's eyebrow was cut and in the ensuing scramble a pair of spectacles were trampled under James's sandals. The spectacles, it turned out, had been on the face of the solicitor of the man who was cut by the flying gin and tonic. For a few moments there was talk of possible legal action for assault but James apologized profusely, and joked the incident had been nothing more than 'a racing accident!'. With that he departed into the night, with Miss Monnier on his arm, and the next day he had recovered sufficiently to appear on a live BBC television show.

Soon he was off to Italy for a magazine presentation and a motorcycle show in Bologna, followed by a press reception in Milan. At these events James was startled to find the rabid Italian fans – who seemed ready to lynch him at the Italian Grand Prix – mobbed him for autographs and he had to be escorted everywhere by a flying squad of policemen.

Also in Milan, while he was attending an official Marlboro lunch, John Hogan's car was broken into and among the souvenirs carried off were James's passport, diary and the visa for his next trip, to Warsaw.

When he had sorted out his itinerary again James found himself in Geneva for a press conference, followed by an appearance in London at the BBC Sports Personality awards, a press conference in Paris, and a dinner in London where the Sports Writers' Association named him the Sportsman of the Year.

Finally, on December 17, he flew to Paris, where he was presented with the trophy which proclaimed him to be the 1976 World Drivers' Champion.

★　★　★

'I feel like a bloody ping-pong ball being bounced all over the place', James said. 'Everybody is tugging at me from all sides and I seem to be moving in a world that's gone completely mad!

'I had guessed that I would be busy but I never really thought it would be possible to squeeze so much into a short time. These have been the most hectic two months of my life.

'I am still very new to this. Everybody is gunning for you if you are on top and the massive invasion of privacy is worse than being at school. My personal freedom is something I had worked at for so long and now it seems completely gone. I am simply not my own man any more.'

He marvelled that people had literally fought over him, one man grabbing each arm and pulling in opposite directions. It was as if he was a piece of furniture, to be sat on, a toy to be played with, or a trophy paraded around by people intent on inflating their egos.

Even well-meaning people unwittingly subjected him to further ordeals. After a full day of interviews, lunch and personal appearances if, by some remote chance, James had nothing scheduled in the evening someone would want to be hospitable, deciding that he surely wouldn't want to dine alone. The host, without telling James, would bring along a party of friends and the World Champion would be expected to perform late into the night.

James admitted it was all a wonderful ego trip but right now his ego was getting 'seriously over-fed'. Wherever he went people showered him with gifts and when he came away from yet another function where he had to be famous he wondered what it all had to do with motor racing. He didn't mind signing an autograph for a fan but there was never just one and several times he found himself facing a queue of over 500 impatient supporters waving pieces of paper which he knew he had to sign. The admiration of fans was understandable, as was all the attention from the press, but sometimes the reaction his celebrity status created with adults caused James acute distress.

'I get incredibly embarrassed when very successful men come up to me and start gushing. OK, I've done a good job in a racing car, but some people get it all out of proportion.

'I am very anxious not to let all this get to me. It is easy for me to sit back and take advantage of all this adulation but it would be very destructive.

'I don't want to abuse people. I don't want to start believing all the flattery. It can lead to bad behaviour and I could end up a very objectionable person.'

9

MASTER JAMES

1977

'JAMES HUNT IS A STEAMING TURD' proclaimed a sign which appeared in the pits and paddocks at several races during the 1977 season. The author of the condemnation might have been any number of Formula 1 people who felt that James's personal fears that he might become 'an objectionable person' were fully realized.

James felt that the pressures of being World Champion might eventually change his character for the worse, but in the opinion of some Formula 1 journalists the transformation had already taken place in 1976. Among the many awards he received after his win in Japan was the Prix Citron – the Lemon Prize – presented by the International Racing Press Association to the most uncooperative driver of the year. In the season to come James would win it again, hands down.

A week after the Japanese race the journalist Eoin Young was asked by a publisher (at James's request) to write a book with James – entitled *Against All Odds* – about his 1976 year. Young, one of the most experienced and respected Formula 1 journalists, was also close to the McLaren team, having originally come to England from his native New Zealand to be Bruce McLaren's secretary. In fact, when McLaren founded his team, Young was made one of the shareholders. But Young didn't want to write the book.

'I gave the publisher three reasons', Young recalls. '"Number one", I told him, "I think writing books is a pain in the ass. Two, it isn't worth it financially and three, I don't like James Hunt".

'At that stage the racing drivers I knew well were Bruce and Denny Hulme (another New Zealander who drove for McLaren) and people like that who were very serious about being a Grand Prix driver. And James clearly wasn't. Or he gave the impression he wasn't.

'I thought he was obnoxious – a pop star in a professional sport that perhaps still regarded itself as amateur. Anyway, I hadn't had much contact with him so I was somewhat surprised when I was invited to write the book.'

Eventually, when sufficient financial inducement was provided, Young was able to overcome his prejudices and he flew out to Spain to tackle the subject. The publisher's wish to get the book out into the market place as quickly as possible required a marathon session of hard labour from Young. In the mornings he interviewed James at his villa, then returned to his hotel, where he transcribed his tapes in the afternoons and wrote most of the night.

The job was done in a remarkable 10 days – and the book was a critical and commercial success – by the end of which time Young's opinion of James had mellowed somewhat, and he 'liked him a little bit more'.

Young's assistant, Maurice Hamilton, didn't. In 1977 Hamilton was just beginning his career as a Formula 1 journalist and one of his first tasks was to provide much of the editorial material for *The James Hunt Magazine*, which Eoin Young was commissioned to produce after his book was finished. Hamilton describes the magazine, the official publication of the James Hunt Fan Club, as a 'bi-monthly celebration of James's World Championship year and his new-found celebrity status. Naïveté led me to believe that this would be a journalistic nirvana. In fact, it was purgatory'.

At the races Hamilton would spend hours sitting outside the McLaren motorhome waiting for an audience. 'He knew why I was there and that it was in his best interests to talk to me. But the waiting went on and on and I didn't then know him well enough or have enough clout to tell him to stop pissing about. Once admitted to his inner sanctum the humiliation would intensify as Hunt, closeted with giggling sycophants, would act like an arrogant schoolboy. He behaved like a spoiled brat and I thought he was a right sod.'

One occasion in the McLaren motorhome Hamilton found particularly mortifying. Having finally been summoned inside, Hamilton was commanded to sit beside James at a large table where he was holding court, entertaining a group of camp followers with his jokes. As Hamilton switched on his tape recorder it captured James in the act of perpetrating an explosively loud histrionic effect. The rest of the crowd found the ferocity of his flatulence hilarious and fell about laughing when James was moved to say: 'Oh, dear. I'm afraid James's guts aren't very well today'.

When James was in a cooperative mood – which tended to be when he didn't have an audience to play to – Hamilton, like most journalists, found him a terrific interview. He was able to articulate his thoughts clearly, his comments would often be controversial and good copy was almost guaranteed. 'He was excellent. When I got him alone. In his hotel room, or a quiet corner of the pits, he'd be brilliant, and charming and polite. I was full of admiration for the guy as a driver – when he won at Mosport in 1976 it was one of the best races I'd ever seen – but his behaviour when I first met him was a great shock.'

This apparent contradiction – a quick and brave driver who behaved badly out of his racing car – was what most offended the critical members of the British motor racing media establishment.

Their view of the sport had been shaped by the dignified and responsible manner in which previous British drivers, like Jim Clark, Graham Hill and Jackie Stewart, had conducted themselves while holding the office of World Champion. To many, what a driver did with his driving title, how gracefully he wore the crown, mattered as much as winning it.

Though the winners in previous eras were never exposed to close media scrutiny which might have revealed any character flaws, the precedent had been set that Champions should be 'decent blokes'. Little thought was given to the possibility that the earlier highly esteemed British racing heroes, had they been subjected to as much media pressure as now prevailed, might also have reacted to it adversely and thus fallen off the pedestals on which the media placed them. No allowance was made for the concept that certain negative character traits – ruthlessness, arrogance, selfishness, non-conformism – might be conducive to the business of winning in the first place.

The theories that 'Nice guys finish last' and 'Winning isn't everything, it's the only thing' – which came from Leo Durocher and Vince Lombardi, hugely successful coaches in the American games of baseball and football, respectively – were not appreciated in motor sport. Instead, the nostalgically-minded Formula 1 media clung to the romantic ideal expressed in verse by the American sportswriter, Grantland Rice:

'When the One Great Scorer comes to write against your name
He marks, not that you won or lost, but how you played the game.'

Despite the fact that James Hunt had already won, many intolerant scribes thought he was now playing the game – about which they felt fiercely protective – very badly indeed, and they dutifully marked his many misdemeanours against his name. It was written of James that he was bringing Formula 1 racing into disrepute with his flagrantly petulant, insolent, rude and immature behaviour. His silly antics, unseemly public displays and antisocial mode of dress had no place at the pinnacle of motor sport, especially when perpetrated by the driver who now stood atop that pinnacle.

His supposed 'Golden Boy' image, though it had brought more attention to the sport than ever before, was becoming badly tarnished. He seemed positively to enjoy annoying people, and a great many in the sport were becoming bored by his aggressive arrogance. Unless he wanted to become known as the 'Mr Nasty' of motor racing he would have to mend his ways.

When the journalist Peter Windsor wrote words to this effect he received a call from the Nasty Golden Boy, which, according to Windsor, took the form of 'a bollocking. "I want a word with you", James said, sounding like an irate housemaster. "I was reading *Autocourse* (the racing annual) on the loo the other day and I was very distressed to see what you'd written about me. Your ludicrous attack was quite unjustified".'

Windsor and James 'slugged it out' verbally and later shook hands and there were no lasting grudges. Nor were there with the majority of those who disparaged him. In fact, when James retired from driving and became a media man himself he was equally intolerant of drivers whom he thought conducted themselves improperly, though very few, if any of them, managed to reach his levels of notoriety.

*   *   *

Most of the critics who found James an objectionable World Champion eventually came to hold him in the warmest regard – but only after he joined them on the other side of the fence. Then, they would deliberately seek out his company, but now they went out of their way to avoid him.

Nigel Roebuck, who began covering the Grand Prix races for *Autosport* in 1977, thought James was essentially 'a friendly bloke' and he enjoyed his 'wonderful sense of humour'. But Roebuck despaired at the apparent change that came over the World Champion, a transformation that he, and others, attributed partly to the entourage which James's new status attracted.

Roebuck dreaded having to enter the McLaren motorhome, where the 'loud and patronizing' retinue of Hunt worshippers would applaud and laugh uproariously at whatever James said or did. 'So whenever you went in there to ask him a question you'd get a facetious answer, given for the benefit of his audience. I found it all very uncomfortable and eventually I thought, "Well, that's it, I'm not going to bother any more".'

The absence of James Hunt interviews in *Autosport*, the most widely read racing magazine, became apparent to Teddy Mayer, who asked Roebuck why this was so. When Roebuck advised him of the situation, that it was nearly impossible to get James alone and that fighting through his obnoxious entourage was more trouble than it was worth, Mayer suggested that Roebuck write James a letter outlining his grievances.

'And I got this absolutely charming reply', Roebuck recalls. 'It was handwritten, from Spain, and James wrote, in effect, "Jesus Christ, if you felt this way why didn't you tell me", as if he was totally unaware of the effect he was having. And from then on we got on tolerably well.

'Even during the period when I hated being anywhere near his presence, I still always felt that he didn't really belong as a troubadour, playing the fool and entertaining those dreadful people around him. This seemed to be proved by the great bloke he eventually became, or went back to being, if you like.'

His close friends thought he was the same old James. John Richardson: 'I would say he was consistent throughout his life. But I would also say that those qualities which made him into the World Champion – his complete single-mindedness and ruthless determination – probably came more to the fore. He was always intransigent in his views and he could be very confrontational and abrasive. That's just the way he was.'

Bubbles Horsley: 'I don't think he changed at all. He always said and did what he felt like. I just think he had a bigger audience. More people were listening and he was taken more seriously. Which was probably a great mistake!'

Some journalists, who knew James from his earlier days in racing, also thought he was always the same man. Jeff Hutchinson first covered James, as a journalist and photographer, during his Formula 3 days. 'As a person I don't think James ever really changed. From start to finish you either liked him or you didn't. He could be outrageous, self-centred and pretentious. He was always the centre of attention and he enjoyed that. He was good fun, but he was one of those guys with whom it would be a bit much to have to spend two weeks with him.'

Another British journalist, Mike Doodson, first met 'Hunt the Shunt', the impoverished Formula 3 driver, when he was 'on his hands and knees in the car park at Pau in 1970. Flat broke after twice crashing his racing car he was surreptitiously siphoning petrol in order to get his rig back home. I donated a fiver to his cause and was repaid many times over in good fellowship and scoops'.

Doodson came to know him even better during the 13 years he would spend working as a lap scorer between James and Murray Walker in the BBC television broadcast booth. Doodson always thought James was a charming man – 'not just with women' – and that he could be very understanding and sympathetic.

However, he also had a ruthless streak and was so competitive that, according to Doodson, 'If you offered James Hunt a World Championship point for running over his granny, he would get in his car and do it without hesitation.

'But I always had a very comfortable and rewarding relationship with him. After he won the title in Japan and had finished with all the others in the press room he sat down with me and went through the whole story again in an extremely willing and totally unresentful sort of way.

'He knew me as a patient kind of bloke who would wait around until he was in the right mood to talk. The fact is that the demands on him were so great that you had to allow him a bit of leeway. But there was never a moment when I thought he was over the top or in any way affected by his success.'

Conversely, Alan Henry, another veteran journalist, thought that James went from 'being immensely genial company in the early 70s to becoming a bit tiresome, partly because he surrounded himself with some tiresome people.

'But it isn't fair to blame it on the hangers-on. James was a big enough boy to know how it all stacked up and how his behaviour would be judged. I think he genuinely believed that as a public figure he could be the way he wanted to be.

'After he went through that awkward stage James was one of the few people in the business that you genuinely looked forward to seeing. He actually had quite an uplifting presence. But I must say I sometimes found him a very boorish World Champion.'

* * *

Barefoot, unshaven and in his habitual scruffy jeans and T-shirt, James appeared at a press conference in a plush hotel in Buenos Aires early in January. The object of the exercise was to publicize the Argentinian Grand Prix, but the local press, in a city which prided itself on formality, concentrated less on the opening event of the 1977 Formula 1 season than on the shockingly disrespectful informality of the reigning World Champion.

And, it was noted by the media, the man in the unkempt blonde hair had blue circles of fatigue under his eyes and deep lines of strain on his forehead and around his mouth.

'The last three months have been absolute bloody hell', James complained. 'You don't have any idea what it means being World Champion. Since Japan there was hardly a single day when I did not attend at least three public functions. I just worked 14 to 20 hours a day. Wearing work. I appeared here, I appeared there. Here I picked up a cup, there an award. And what do I do with them? I don't want a lot of useless bowls cluttering up my life.'

His disregard for 'useless' hardware was similar to the lack of sentiment exhibited by Niki Lauda, back with Ferrari, now fully fit again and ready to challenge James in the coming season. Niki was notorious for giving away his trophies, many of them to the proprietor of a garage near his home in Austria, and he also had a reputation for ignoring the fans and being difficult when they approached him.

James, though he said 'Why the hell can't I be more like Niki?', disapproved of treating the public badly, and related one incident where a young fan came up to Niki in the paddock at a race and presented him with a gift. 'It was a scrapbook which he had collected together. Niki simply took the book and said, "Yes, now go". Even if the book was awful, which it certainly was, I think Niki should have taken it, given the kid a smile and some chat. I would have. The fans make us what we are.

'Still, there's a temptation, when the seventy-fourth person grabs you and gives you an earful of bullshit, to tell him, "Fuck off. Leave me alone".

'But that person's probably travelled three hundred miles and especially wanted to talk to you. You need their support and it's nice to have and it's not their fault they've caught you at a bad moment. They didn't mean any harm, you have to remember that. But sometimes it's very wearying, very tiring.

'Short of locking myself up in a room, I can't get away from it and the problem is that the nice people don't often come up and talk. It's the pushy ones who barge through and make you perform. You feel like some sort of mechanical toy. When they confront you it's like throwing the switch and you're supposed to do or say something clever.

'I can tell you, the business of being Champion is nearly as tough as trying to stay Champion on the track. It's almost a relief to get back to the simple life on the circuit but I realize that isn't the way I should be looking at it.

'Physically I reckon I'm all right for the first race, but mentally I'm not ready yet. I need more time to get my mind sorted out and concentrate absolutely on my driving.'

* * *

On the 32nd lap of the Argentinian Grand Prix the McLaren M23, bearing the number 1 in honour of the World Champion at the controls, flew off the Buenos Aires circuit, tossing up clouds of dust and weeds, then fence posts, as it ploughed out of control into the barriers.

James, starting from pole position, had taken the lead after 10 laps and held it until the accident. He was unhurt and rode back to the pits on the pillion of a motorcycle, worrying about what had felt like a mechanical failure in his car and feeling sick from the after affects of a 'disgusting' medical saline solution he had consumed to combat the high temperatures.

Before the real reason for his ignominious start to the 1977 season was discovered, a broken bolt in his McLaren's rear suspension, some journalists reported that the reigning World Champion had crashed of his own accord 'when it was patently obvious that I hadn't.

'But I wasn't prepared to say something had broken until it had been proven by the team. I'm not prepared to use it as an excuse. It's not fair to the team. I want them to find out after a proper inspection of the car and for them to say whether something broke or not. This is desperately important for the personal relationship between the team and the driver.'

As far as the team was concerned the relationship was excellent. They especially appreciated his willingness to admit a driving error instead of blaming the car, as many drivers tended to do. John Hogan recalls one occasion in qualifying when James appeared carless, strolling down the pit lane helmet in hand and puffing away on a cigarette.

'He went up to Teddy Mayer and said: "Well Wiener, it's up there in the barrier. It's fucked. You'll have to just throw it away and get me a new one". There was no bullshit from James – no excuses, total honesty and openness – and the mechanics loved this sort of thing.'

* * *

Morale was high among the 50 people now employed in McLaren Racing as they prepared to defend their Championship status. Jochen Mass was still there to back up James; indeed he was free to win races if he could. It was agreed that if James was running anywhere other than in the lead and Mass came up behind him James was to let him through to attack the frontrunners. James thought this was only fair since Mass had spent the last half of the previous season trying to help him win the Championship.

As for his plans to defend his title James thought there were areas where he could improve. He did not intend to rest on his laurels, and although he wasn't sure he could drive much faster he was going to apply the lessons he had learned in 1976 to reach his personal speed limit and stay as close to it as he could without getting into trouble.

In the past he had brushes with other cars because he was perhaps over his limit. As they matured, James noticed, Champions like Emerson Fittipaldi and Niki Lauda avoided such contretemps by backing off slightly in the interest of collecting points. But James preferred to collect his points 'without ever backing off at all'.

Nor did he approve of the 'absolute rubbish' of fiddling around unnecessarily with his car's setup. 'There are a lot of drivers who think the more they say, the more they'll impress everyone. There are some drivers who can ask for a tiny adjustment and come in with a story that will last 15 minutes about all the difference the change made to the car. All it does is confuse the team.

'I'm convinced half the battle is keeping it simple and the other half is to know what you want. I know what I want out of my car and I know when it's right and when it's wrong. A lot of drivers think they have to go madly technical on the car, but I don't.'

To James the car was not a piece of technology. 'It was simply a bat and ball', says John Hogan. 'He was just a sportsman who happened to be playing a game that required a car. He knew enough about how to make the car handle. But that was all. He didn't want to get into all the bloody little bits and pieces. He didn't want to hang around the garage. As far as he was concerned that was Alastair Caldwell's job.'

Caldwell was good at coping with his driver's only cursory interest in technical matters and also had to compensate for James's distaste for testing. 'He was dead lazy. Hated testing, thought it was definitely a waste of time. But in this case he was a waste of time because there was no doubt that testing is what got us the World Championship in the first place.'

James enjoyed his role as a test driver even less now that he'd won his Championship. He was prepared to flog the car for all it was worth at the races, but puttering around at a test session was far less satisfying 'when the alternative is to be home in Spain relaxing and playing golf on one of the few days off in the year that I get'.

To distract himself from the boredom of lengthy test sessions James resorted to familiar diversions. Before one test, at the Paul Ricard circuit in the South of France, James spent an evening in Salzburg with Niki Lauda, where, Niki reports, 'We had a helluva time, drank and smoked far too much, but he outlasted me and I went to bed far earlier than him'.

Niki flew his own plane (and would later found Lauda Air, the second largest airline in Austria) and the next morning he waited impatiently at the Salzburg airport for his friend to show up. Ferrari was also due to test at Paul Ricard and Niki prided himself in punctuality. Ten minutes after the scheduled take-off time of seven o'clock James had still not appeared, and Niki prepared to leave without him.

Five minutes later a taxi tore out onto the runway and screeched to a halt in front of Niki's Cessna. Two passengers fell out, one of them an exhausted-looking but attractive *Fräulein* in a white dress which was conspicuously covered in grass stains. Her escort, looking equally dishevelled and carrying a giant 'ghettoblaster' portable radio, embraced her warmly, then staggered aboard the waiting aircraft. James collapsed in the back of Niki's plane and slept all the way to Paul Ricard.

At the circuit Niki's Ferrari blew an engine, and while it was being repaired he sat on the pit wall watching James roar around in his McLaren. A few minutes later the circuit fell suddenly silent and Niki exclaimed: 'Shit! James is still pissed and he must have crashed',

An emergency alarm sounded and as an ambulance raced down the pit lane Niki and Teddy Mayer flagged it down and hopped in. Halfway down the long Mistral straight the McLaren was sitting alongside a cement wall and the occupants of the ambulance feared the worst. As the medical men ran over to see what could be done for the driver Niki noticed there didn't seem to be any damage to the car, and when he came closer Teddy Mayer was leaning over the slumped figure in the cockpit. 'James,' said Teddy, 'I think you'd better go back to the hotel and sleep it off'.

Niki: 'James – the silly asshole – he parked the car and fell asleep!'.

★ ★ ★

James's South American misadventures continued when an attempt at a brief holiday at a coastal resort in Brazil, where it rained steadily, ended in a bout of food poisoning which left him violently ill. After two days he rose from his sick bed and headed for Sao Paulo to recuperate at his hotel. En route, driving a car with his name on it and loaned to him by the organizers of the Brazilian Grand Prix, James was stopped by the police, who found he had no driving licence.

He was taken to the nearby police station where he explained that his licence was among the documents stolen in Italy in December and he hadn't had time to replace it. The policemen, who turned out to be more interested in autographs, posing for pictures and shaking hands with the racing hero, sent him on his way with their best wishes.

'But unfortunately', said James, 'the Brazilian press blew the whole thing into a major incident and announced that I had been arrested. It seemed to infuriate them in some way and I'm afraid I did not receive a warm welcome.

'I certainly don't expect to be loved wherever I go, but I do sometimes feel that the press make their own decisions about people and it is very difficult to change their minds.'

In the mind of the Swiss journalist Roger Benoit, James's idiosyncratic ways, strong personality and penchant for speaking his mind were a media bonanza.

'He was a real character and that made my job a lot easier. I always asked him for his opinions because, unlike Jackie Stewart, or even Niki, James was completely straight first time.

'He would not ask himself if he should say something, he would just say it. He never worried about saying the wrong thing, like some other drivers who only want you to write nice things about them. James was not a member of that club. He was no ass-licker.'

Benoit, who often played backgammon with James, remembers the lengthy game held in the São Paulo Hilton hotel before the 1977 Brazilian Grand Prix. It started on the Thursday afternoon and continued until the next morning, a few hours before the opening practice session at the Interlagos circuit.

Bernie Ecclestone, the wealthy owner of the Brabham team, was also in on the game and paid two waiters $100 each to supply the players with round-the-clock room service. After a leisurely breakfast a police escort was provided and, accompanied by wailing sirens, James was transported post-haste through the busy São Paulo traffic to the Interlagos circuit.

James's laps around the track during the first practice session were interrupted by frequent pit stops to answer urgent calls of nature. Each time, James hopped from his McLaren and ran for the nearest loo to seek relief from the lingering effects of his food poisoning, which had not been helped by his all-night backgammon binge.

By the end of the second session on the bumpy track he was cured – 'I think all the vibration must have cleared me out!' – and in final qualifying, when his breathtaking power slides around the fastest sixth gear corners were much admired, he secured pole position.

In the race he recovered from a slow start to lead for 15 laps, then had to make a pit stop to replace worn tyres. He rejoined in fourth place, and by the finish had worked his way up to second, behind Carlos Reutemann, who was now Niki Lauda's team-mate, and ahead of Niki in the other Ferrari.

James was satisfied to come away from South America with six points because 'somehow, these races have always been just a warm-up, a good place to get bonus points if you can. But it isn't until we start racing in Europe that the season starts to show its shape and it becomes apparent where team and driver strength lies'.

*　*　*

In early February James attended a gala function at the Europa Hotel in London, where over 300 members of the British racing fraternity met to honour the most successful participants in motor sports. A presentation was made to the McLaren team principals and all eight racing mechanics. In recognition of his World Championship James was awarded the Tarmac Trophy, a cheque for £2000, another for £500, a magnum of champagne and other awards.

The Tarmac Trophy presentation was made by HRH The Duke of Kent. The recipient, it was noted by the formally attired audience, was dressed for the solemn occasion in jeans, T-shirt and decrepit windbreaker.

James's acceptance speech was suitably gracious and humorous – he thanked the creators of the Tarmac Trophy for giving drivers something 'concrete' to aim for – but his disrespectful mode of dress, especially in front of the Royal presence, caused more tongue-clucking, and though HRH made no comment, others gave James a right royal dressing down.

The criticism of James extended outside the motor sport media to include people like Jackie Stewart, the previous British World Champion, the man credited with being the first businessman/racing driver and the man with whom James was most unfavourably compared in matters relating to personal conduct.

'He might have been a modern young person', says Stewart, 'who was anti-establishment, but his habit of dressing too casually, wearing inappropriate clothes even when meeting Royalty, I thought was bad form.

'Whereas the Jim Clarks, Graham Hills, the Jackie Stewarts, if you like, were always fairly well presented, James seemed to want to go over the top the other way. I certainly didn't approve of that because I was by then deeply involved with multinational corporations associated with the sport, and I was worried that James was projecting the wrong image.'

Stewart remembers being intrigued by James's bizarre start in Formula 1 but not taking him, or his team at the time, very seriously.

'I knew Lord Hesketh and often stayed at his country home at Easton Neston before James came along. Alexander's mother was a Scot, a fantastic lady who wore a patch over one eye and kept a wonderfully eccentric house.

'Alexander was himself an entertainingly eccentric man, and he still is for that matter, but I thought it was a bit speculative, to say the least, when he announced he was grooming James to be a future Champion.

'Hesketh Racing had this peculiar character named Bubbles Horsley for a team manager and they used to have a great entourage of glamorous, colourful and eccentric people around them. Then there was James, "Hunt the Shunt", public schoolboy and all that, with his sort of dilettante manner and scruffy and unkempt fashion. The whole thing seemed to be too outlandish to be a serious consideration for the future.

'As things developed it became clear that the team knew what it was doing and James had great skill as a driver. He had great natural talent. I could see that in the few times I raced against him before I retired. But he became abstract in quite a lot of ways.'

Stewart was unaware of it, but James once took his name in vain. With friends at a crowded restaurant in Surrey James was in his cups and misbehaving boisterously in a way the conservative Scot would never do. One of the restaurant patrons thought she recognized a famous racing driver and approached him for an autograph. The lady said, 'You're Jackie Stewart, aren't you. Could I please have your autograph?' James didn't want to disappoint a fan so he set down his drink, belched loudly, and scrawled Stewart's signature across the paper proffered by the pleased woman.

Early in 1977 Jackie Stewart said James Hunt would be all right 'when he grows up', a sentiment echoed then, and now, by John Watson. Though he admired and respected him on the track, and they were to have several hard-fought battles in the races to come, Watson believes that James's childishness might be 'understandable in somebody of 15 or 16, or even 18, but for a man in his late twenties was misplaced.

'Perhaps I am more conformist', Watson says, 'but if you are going to a function which is held in your honour, or a black tie occasion, you dress accordingly or you don't go. He seemed to take great pleasure in wearing jeans, like he was taking the mickey out of everyone. And I think it's wrong to deliberately antagonize, or confront people, whose standards are not necessarily yours.

'What lay behind it I don't know. For James the recognition in the press and as a celebrity was considerable. I thought that would be sufficient, but he seemed to need to make people squirm, make them feel uncomfortable in his company. He thought it terribly funny.

'He came from a very good family, had a good education and was extremely bright, so why he pursued this particular course I have no idea.'

☆ ☆ ☆

Perhaps James looked suspicious to the customs authorities at the Johannesburg airport when he arrived to prepare for the South African Grand Prix. Or maybe the South African Airways flight crew had radioed ahead to give advance warning of the arrival of the wild blond World Champion who had, albeit good naturedly, run somewhat amok on the long flight from London.

James, as usual, had arrived at the last minute for the flight and since the Economy section – where he always sat to save money – was full, as was the Business Class, he was upgraded to First Class, where the small group of paying passengers included a couple of dignified businessmen, a daughter of the De Beers family, the diamond merchants, and the pop singer Leapy Lee, who was famous for his rendition of the song 'Tie a Yellow Ribbon Round the Old Oak Tree'.

James, well-versed in the popular music idiom and having partaken freely of the excellent drinks service in the First Class cabin – 'I always make a point of relaxing when I travel!' – insisted that he and Mr Lee should serenade the startled Miss De Beers, who proved to be as reluctant an audience as Mr Lee was to tie yet another ribbon around his old oak tree. So James was left to sing on his own and did so lustily far too long into the night.

On his arrival at Jan Smuts airport James was confronted by customs officials who proceeded to give his luggage a thorough search. Though no illegal substances were found, the officials discovered in the sparse contents of his bag a publication which contravened South Africa's strict obscenity laws. They were not amused when James told them his copy of *Penthouse* magazine, with its profusion of full colour, full frontal photographs of undraped ladies was 'hardly likely to corrupt my mind'.

Nor did they believe him when he told them he 'needed it for business purposes'. Finally, when he showed them a six page article about himself and Niki Lauda, that section was torn out and handed to him while the remainder of the banned magazine was confiscated by the customs men.

'It was real police state treatment and very rude to foreigners', said James. But the country remained secure in his affections because 'the South African girls are terrific. And I'm available!'. With that he rushed off to a women's circle dinner, where he was to be the guest of honour – and the only male.

At the Kyalami circuit, during the week before the South African Grand Prix, James was testing the new and as yet unraced McLaren M26 when a brake calliper worked loose and cut a hole in a tyre. The car plunged off the circuit at an estimated 140 miles per hour, ripped through several rows of catch fencing and came to rest against an earth bank.

'It could have been very nasty', James told the wide-eyed journalists who saw his wild ride. 'I investigated the catch fencing rather more thoroughly than was comfortable, and fortunately it worked very well.

'But I must stay on the road if I'm to win the Championship twice running. That would really leave my stamp. Yet more than anything else I want to retire alive. So the sooner I achieve my goals the quicker I can retire.

'I intend to keep going full chat until the day I retire, because it makes sense. Life's too short – it certainly can be in a racing driver's career – to relax. You don't stand any less chance of getting killed if you relax. An accident which starts at 165 miles an hour is as bad as one that starts at 170.

'Once an accident has started happening, you've just about time to say 'Shit! I'm having a shunt'. You can't usually do anything about the fact that you are having an accident, though you might have time to get the car to go in backwards rather than forwards, which hopefully would be better. Basically, you just have time to get your head down and brace yourself.

'The danger aspect is the biggest cloud on my horizon, and a constant heavy thought at home. It's not something you dwell on in the emotionally charged atmosphere at a circuit.

'One has to weigh the odds, the risks involved, as well as one can and look at life and see if it's worth taking the risks for the time being. Once you have decided it's worth those risks it would be counter-productive to worry about it. In fact, worrying about it would be very bad for your driving. You might as well give it your best while you are racing, and then stop at the right time.'

There was no stopping James in qualifying for the South African Grand Prix, when for the third race in succession he secured pole position.

Though he was noted as one of the very best qualifiers, gathering all his skill and courage together for a single fast lap came at a price for James. He confided to John Hogan that: 'The only time I'm likely to kill myself is in qualifying. Because that's the only time I'm really over the top'.

James led the first seven laps of the race until Niki Lauda summoned up the extra horsepower in his Ferrari's engine and overtook the McLaren on Kyalami's long straight. A few laps later Jody Scheckter also passed James, but not without a struggle.

Scheckter, now driving for a new team fielded by the wealthy Canadian Walter Wolf, had won the opening race of the season and was especially keen to duplicate that effort in front of his home crowd, but he would have to do it without any help from James.

As the Wolf pulled alongside the McLaren on the inside of the entry to a corner the latter car refused to give way and they negotiated the bend in a fearful unison, their rear wheels banging together several times. Eventually, when he ran out of road, James had to give way.

Commenting later on the exceedingly dangerous-looking manoeuvre, James said, 'Oh it's all right if it's wheel-to-wheel. It's when you get a wheel between the others that it gets a bit dodgy'.

His McLaren M23 was now not turning into corners properly and James fell back into the clutches of Patrick Depailler's Tyrrell. What followed was reminiscent of their confrontation the previous year at Long Beach, only this time it was the McLaren that shut the door on the Tyrrell in the middle of a corner. Depailler was almost squeezed into the barrier and faced with the perilous prospect of the Tyrrell sliding sideways in front of him James thought it prudent to back off and he was relegated to fourth – where he finished.

After the South African Grand Prix James said: 'I was very pleased that Niki won the race. In my opinion he has been driving as well as ever since Canada last year and I have been expecting him to win ever since. The pleasing thing is that this will silence once and for all the critics and non-believers who were stupid enough to think he had lost his nerve'.

Sadly, Niki's triumph in South Africa was marred by tragedy.

On the 23rd lap two marshals ran across the track to quell a small fire in the Shadow, driven by Renzo Zorzi, which had pulled off to the side of the circuit at the beginning of Kyalami's long straight.

The first marshal made it safely to the other side but the second, weighed down by a heavy fire extinguisher, was hit by the second Shadow, driven by Tom Pryce, and killed instantly. But the Shadow did not stop. Travelling at 160 miles an hour down the straight it then veered into a barrier and ricocheted off it directly into the path of the Ligier of Jacques Laffite. Both cars flew off the track, through the catch fencing and into a cement wall. Laffite was only bruised, but Tom Pryce, it was discovered, had died when the fire extinguisher hit him in the face.

James had not seen the accident, though he had run over some debris (and Niki Lauda later found a piece of the Shadow's rollbar jammed under his Ferrari) but in the regular column he was now writing in *Autosport* magazine he expressed his concern for improved safety measures.

'I have been saying ever since I became a Grand Prix driver that until there are professional marshals trained to a high standard and with suitable experience there will be unnecessary deaths or injuries in motor racing. The sport should provide the facilities and money for professionally trained and experienced marshals and if has taken Tom's death to impress this upon the authorities then he will not have died in vain.'

☆ ☆ ☆

On his return to Europe James embarked on another busy round of personal appearances, in Sweden, Denmark and Finland, for Vauxhall and Marlboro, then spent several days shooting a TV commercial for Texaco.

He had a starring role in a commercial with the comedy team of Morecambe and Wise which included a telling bit of dialogue. James, dressed as a chauffeur, gave his two passengers a wild ride then asked them for a tip. Eric Morecambe: 'You want a tip? Watch out for women'.

James was also featured in print advertisements, one of which, featuring a photo with him and his mother and a can of Texaco oil, bore the caption: 'As used by Mrs Hunt and her son, Master James'. Master James – the soubriquet given him by journalists who saw him as a renegade, aristocratic public schoolboy – was now a hot commercial 'property'.

Those same characteristics which annoyed and infuriated the racing press – and which delighted the popular media – were noted by the journalist Nick Brittan as attributes which appealed to a wide audience.

In his irreverent Private Ear column in *Autosport* Brittan opined that Master James was the perfect hero for the 'Blue Jean, let-it-all hang out era. James, by design, or by accident, has captured the mood of the moment. He's flash, cocky and arrogant. He's casual and doesn't wear ties. He's also very much larger than life. And that's what makes real personalities. He's something that the youth (and lots of ladies under 40) can identify with'.

His dashing good looks, great personal charm, rich sense of humour, even his good manners when he chose to exhibit them, and above all his supreme Englishness, made him a national asset for the marketing people who sought to cash in on his celebrity. And Master James was equally commercially-minded.

In 1976 James had collected surprisingly little from his unexpected driving title (John Hogan suggests he was probably the cheapest World Champion in history): an estimated £160,000 – about £60,000 from his retainer and share of the prize money and the remainder from marketing and sponsorship fees. Under the guidance of Peter Hunt most of the money was invested in stocks and shares and commercial property. But in 1977 James and Peter calculated that his year as the reigning World Champion should generate income amounting to £600,000.

Bernie Ecclestone, the entrepreneurially-minded team owner, Formula 1 organizer and sometime business manager of drivers, had also done his sums and made an offer to the Hunt brothers. He guaranteed them $1 million (the equivalent then of £600,000) in exchange for the rights to all James's income for 1977.

James wanted to accept the offer, but Peter, the accountant, thought they could do better on their own, and his decision prevailed. James: 'I tell you it was a difficult decision to turn down a million dollars in one hit, but I'm glad that Peter eventually persuaded me'.

'I said to James,' Ecclestone recalls, 'what he should do is the best he could as far as contracts were concerned and put the money in the bank. He should get on with racing his cars and not worry about the money. He should draw out an allowance for personal expenses and he didn't need a lot because I never saw him spend any of his own! He didn't like losing anything, especially money.'

James did not deny his tendency to parsimony – though he could be generous to his friends – but his reluctance to part with money now was an investment for the future. 'In the long run money buys freedom – the right to do exactly what you like – and that's what I shall buy myself when I retire. Touch wood.'

While he was happy to take advice on his financial affairs James continued to rely on his own instincts to satisfy the bountiful romantic component of his life. He still occasionally kept company with the sultry actress Valentine Monnier and also had a brief fling with Charlene Shorto, a 19-year-old blonde Brazilian beauty whose sister, Baroness Denise Thyssen, was married to the richest man in Europe.

Meanwhile, an intermittent relationship with Jane 'Hottie' Birbeck was becoming more serious. They first met at a backgammon tournament in Marbella, where Jane was escorted by Mark McCormack, the founder of the International Management Group which managed James before Peter Hunt took over. The 24-year-old daughter of Brigadier Nigel Birbeck, who was at one time the Deputy Fortress Commander in Gibraltar, sometimes came to the races and at one of them the playful McLaren mechanics put a sign on James's steering wheel: 'Watch out and good luck – Hottie'.

James might have heeded that warning in the race, but he later fell into a trap laid by another girl who had designs on him.

Alissa Morien, a seductive blonde from Holland, arrived at the Hunt villa in Spain, ostensibly to interview the World Champion for a Dutch magazine. Sitting beside her at his swimming pool James thought it 'was slightly strange when she started to divest herself of her clothing. Of course, I forbade this! Afterwards I had dinner with her and the rest is up to your imagination'.

Very little was left to the imagination, as it developed, when Miss Morien, whose assignment was to make love to famous men and rate their performance in her magazine, carried out her duties and reported them faithfully to 200,000 readers. She wrote that at first James played hard to get: romping with his Alsatian dog Oscar, running for miles down the road with his stopwatch in hand, and talking about his many girlfriends, particularly Jane Birbeck. Then James took a bath and the interview continued with his comely interlocutor perched on the loo seat beside the tub. James told her he would get shy if she didn't avert her gaze.

But she didn't and finally, after they had dinner, she had her way with him and, she wrote: 'He put his hand on my knee and began stroking my leg. "I'd love to stroke you all over your body", he said. I told him: "I'd love that". And in bed I asked James for what he had promised.'

James joked that 'It never occurred to me that I was being a gullible idiot'. But he was pleased to have been able to help Miss Morien with her journalistic inquiries and thought she was 'Good. Very good. And I was on good form. But I will have to wait to read my official rating'.

The rating was positive: 'He was so nice. Very patient. He was very good indeed'.

None of the very many other women with whom he became intimately acquainted kissed and told so publicly, but James did have a reputation as a sensitive and highly skilled lover.

He was always attentive to his partner's needs. Indeed much of his satisfaction came from giving pleasure. The only problem, some of them confessed, was that his desire to please often out-stripped their needs. Nonetheless, whenever anyone grew weary of his constant attention there were always plenty of others willing to enjoy the pleasure of his company.

★ ★ ★

James won the Race of Champions at Brands Hatch, which, as usual, did not count for points in the driver standings, and he looked forward to beginning to defend his driving title in earnest at the next Grand Prix, in America.

His trip began on a positive note when he squeezed in a brief rendezvous in New York with Jane Birbeck, who was working there as a photographer's representative, but the rest of his US foray was a write-off.

After doing promotional work to drum up interest in the United States Grand Prix West, at Long Beach, James was 'aggravated when I had extreme difficulty extracting payment from the race promoter'.

At the start of the race his McLaren bounced off a spinning car (James claimed another car pushed him) and flew high into the air. Fortunately, it landed on its wheels and, after a pit stop to check for damage, James continued. But handling problems restricted him to a seventh place finish and he came away with no points.

'The Hunt Flying Act', as one of the other drivers put it, was repeated in practice for the Spanish Grand Prix, when James's brand new McLaren M26 was launched off the front wheel of the Brabham driven by Hans Stuck. When the German came to discuss the matter with James he found the door of the McLaren motorhome slammed in his face. In the race James's engine misfired badly and he retired after just 10 laps.

At Monaco he reverted to the old M23 model, but its engine gave up the ghost halfway through the race. On the eighth lap of the Belgian Grand Prix, now back in the new car, James 'really began to feel like an idiot'. He had gambled on starting the wet race on dry tyres, but the weather didn't cooperate and he was left floundering in seventh place.

James took full responsibility for making the wrong tyre decision in Belgium, but the tyre problems he experienced in Sweden were not his own doing. The ill-handling – James called it 'undriveable' – M26 caused excessive rubber wear, necessitating a pit stop that put him back to 12th place at the finish.

James thought he was driving even better than in the previous year, but with the 1977 season nearly half over, while Niki Lauda and Jody Scheckter were fighting it out at the top of the standings, the reigning World Champion was mired down in ninth place overall.

It made him angry that 'a lot of people are giving the team and me a hard time, suggesting that we simply can't get it together this season – that last season was a flash in the pan, et cetera. I know the only thing that will convince them that this is bullshit is for us to get a few results. All I can say until those results come is that I intend to retain my Championship.

'What people don't realize is that winning is easy. Losing is the thing that's bloody hard work!'

James, benefitting from changes to his car's steering system, actually led the first four laps of the French Grand Prix, his first time in front since the Brazilian race in January. Then he made 'a pig's breakfast of my gear selection' and fell back to third where he began to feel ill, not from the missed gear change but from a previously upset stomach.

When he slowed down to consolidate his third place the reduced concentration focused more of his attention on his 'tummy trouble' and he felt quite ill on the podium. There, he was joined by John Watson, who led all the way until his Brabham ran out of fuel on the last lap, and Mario Andretti who inherited the win in his Lotus.

James 'felt desperately sorry for poor Wattie' in France. Then, in the British Grand Prix at Silverstone, Watson's misfortune enabled James to win. He put the McLaren M26 on pole, with a time slightly quicker than Watson's Brabham, but a poor start caused by a troublesome clutch enabled Watson to get the lead, which he held for three-quarters of the race.

Sitting behind him, James waited for a mistake or a mechanical problem. The latter, in the form of a fuel pressure malfunction, put the Brabham out of commission, and James, with a comfortable lead, cruised home to his first victory of 1977.

'I would never have got past John', James admitted. 'If he had not run into that trouble he would have won the race. It was cruel luck and I really felt sorry for him but I still was very happy to see him go.'

The race winner, like everyone else at Silverstone, was greatly impressed by the performance of Gilles Villeneuve, who made a sensational Formula 1 debut in James's old McLaren M23. But for a pit stop to check what he thought was an overheating engine – the temperature gauge in the McLaren proved to be faulty – Villeneuve would surely have finished fourth.

James was especially pleased that his French Canadian 'discovery' had done so well and complimented 'his obvious talent and professional approach. I have long been a believer that you either have or don't have the ability to drive a Formula 1 car and the performance of Villeneuve fully supported this'.

The day after his British Grand Prix triumph James played in a charity cricket match at Althorp Park near Silverstone. He performed well for his side, the Duke of Gloucester's XI, against the Lord's Taverners' XI and the 3,000 spectators on hand noted that the World Drivers' Champion's 'whites' were instead a dirty T-shirt and a pair of tatty denim shorts.

Following a flying trip to Monte Carlo for a backgammon tournament James spent a few days at home in Spain, where he played host to Niki Lauda, then set out for England to attend the much-publicized launch of his new book. An airline strike meant he was five hours late and he arrived at the launch party feeling rather fractious. He was also apologetic and anxious not to spoil the party, laid on at considerable expense by the publisher (Hamlyn, who had also paid James an advance of £15,000) in a fashionable London club.

In his review of the book, *Against All Odds*, Stirling Moss was pleased to note that James talked frankly about his sex needs and 'like me when I was racing, James doesn't indulge before a race. But this monk-like attitude happily is flexible'.

Moss also expressed a tolerant understanding of James's character: 'Like all top class drivers James has his share of egotism and temperament and he admits to both'.

Of his literary effort (with Eoin Young) James explained why it was concerned only with his Championship-winning season. 'I didn't want to write an autobiography until I retired. If I wanted to write an honest book about the sport it would probably have ruined my career!'

* * *

James failed to finish in any of the next four races.

In Germany, where he was running third, part of the McLaren's exhaust system fell off and then the fuel pump broke. In Austria, after a brave qualifying lap landed him on pole, he led most of the race until his engine blew up. At Monza, on pole again after a magnificent last-minute effort, he had his 'annual attack of Italian brain fade' and spun, damaging the McLaren's steering irreparably, and he was forced to retire.

In Holland, the day before his birthday, which had been celebrated here with two consecutive wins in the previous years, James led the first four laps, then lost an argument with Mario Andretti over possession of Zandvoort's notorious Tarzan corner. Braking from over 170 miles an hour into the acute right-hand bend the McLaren kept the inside line while the Lotus pulled alongside and stayed there. They went around Tarzan with wheels dangerously interlocked, the McLaren slightly ahead and drifting to the outside of the corner and the Lotus with two wheels on the grass.

They touched, the Lotus spun, then continued, while the McLaren leaped into the air, crashed to the track and ground to a halt a few yards further on, emitting clouds of steam from a broken water pipe. A few laps later the Lotus halted near the pits with a blown engine and when its driver climbed out he was met by an unwelcoming committee of one.

James had already screamed at Colin Chapman, the Lotus team owner: 'Your driver will never win the Championship until he learns not to hit people on the track!'

James gave more of the same to Andretti (who did win the Championship, in 1978) and the American gave as much as he'd got.

'Hunt says you don't pass on the outside in Grand Prix racing – silly jerk! James Hunt, he's Champion of the world right? The problem is he thinks he's king of the god-damn world as well!'

James, who pointed out that in the previous Dutch Grand Prix he and John Watson had engaged in the same kind of battle around Tarzan for many laps with no trouble, said that Andretti's choice of a passing place, so early in the race, was absurd. 'It was his race, he had the best car and sooner or later he was going to get by me easily.'

James and Mario later 'kissed and made up' and James admired him as 'a real charger'. But he was upset that the press, no doubt eager to see him get his comeuppance, ridiculed him for saying 'We don't pass on the outside in Formula 1' and blamed him for causing the accident.

James: 'If they actually saw it, either live or on television, and still came to the conclusion that I was to blame then I have to say that they know less about motor racing than I know about writing'.

James, although his hopes to repeat as World Champion were now dashed (he was in fifth place, 47 points behind the leader Niki Lauda, with just three races remaining), had an insurmountable lead in the standings for the journalist's Prix Citron trophy awarded to the least cooperative driver.

Alastair Caldwell, who thought Andretti was in the wrong at Zandvoort, also tended to side with his driver in the media disputes. 'James was always sure of himself, but he became even cockier and a lot of people didn't like it. He was a bit of a smart-ass. No doubt about it. But he was getting frustrated by so many journalists asking him so many stupid questions. Some of the good ones knew how to ask sensible questions, but they were in the minority.

'So James got fed up and became aggressive and won the press hate prize. It was "Super Wop", Mario Andretti, who won the Prix Orange because he was a good bullshitter. He learned in America how to suck up to the press and cultivate them.

'James's problem with the press was partly the team's fault, because the atmosphere at McLaren at the time, mostly engendered by me, was like a fortress mentality. We were not sympathetic to journalists, mostly because most of them were just so asinine and you had to be asinine to talk to them. You needed a company asshole, a PR person to talk to them, and we didn't have one.

'I know it now but I didn't know it then, that without journalists motor racing is dead. But in those days I thought anybody connected with motor racing that didn't actively work in the trade was a hanger-on. A useless scab, somebody who just made their living off us, while we worked our arses off. All journalists and PR men were lesser beings. Whereas some of them wanted to be treated as greater beings, because they figured they were bloody superstars themselves!'

⋆   ⋆   ⋆

James's on-track performance in the United States Grand Prix at Watkins Glen, a circuit he loved, drew nothing but praise from the press. After securing pole position he led the wet race from the 15th lap to the finish. Near the end he slowed down to conserve a badly worn front tyre but quickly speeded up again when he was made aware of a fast-closing Mario Andretti.

'My mirrors were filthy and I couldn't see Mario coming up behind me. The first I knew of it was when I came past the pits and saw the Wiener leaping up to the height of the twenty dollar grandstand seats without paying! It was a real shock to see Mario so close but I gave it everything I could and all was well.'

By finishing fourth at Watkins Glen, Niki Lauda had clinched the 1977 driving title and at the next race, the Canadian Grand Prix at Mosport, he had a flaming row with Ferrari and left the team. Niki, who had already signed to drive with Bernie Ecclestone's Brabham team for 1978, was angry for three reasons. First of all, he was fed up with Ferrari's internal politics, indeed with all of Italy, where he had been called 'a trembling coward' for dropping out of the Japanese race the previous year, thereby helping James win the Championship. Second, Niki was furious over Ferrari's dismissal of his faithful mechanic, Ermanno Cuoghi, who was sent packing from Watkins Glen after expressing his wish to accompany Niki to Brabham.

Finally, Niki was unhappy that Gilles Villeneuve, whom Ferrari had signed when McLaren didn't exercise their option on his services, would be driving a third Ferrari at Mosport, and Niki felt the team couldn't adequately prepare cars for three drivers. When the Ferrari team manager suggested Niki had lost his motivation after clinching the Championship the Austrian stalked out of the pits and flew home to Salzburg.

For refusing to compete in the final two races Niki was widely condemned for his selfish disregard for the Formula 1 fans who wanted to see the new World Champion in action. However, one voice was raised in his support. 'More power to him', said James. 'You can only put up with so much aggro'.

In his eventful Canadian Grand Prix, James, who had just taken the lead from Mario Andretti, came up to lap his McLaren team-mate Jochen Mass at Mosport's Corner Two.

'Herman stayed on the right, but by this time I was right up his chuff, going much faster, and was forced to go on the left. Then, he suddenly moved across to the left, hit the brakes and waved me through on the right. But I was committed and could not avoid him and I hit him up the arse.

'He spun, then got going again, but I was launched onto the grass, careering through catch fencing before slamming into the concrete retaining wall, still travelling at over 100 miles an hour.

'Alastair Caldwell later described the crumpled chassis as "turning left at the dashboard". This was by far the worst accident of my Formula 1 career. I was very lucky not to have a broken leg or worse. My legs were trapped but by removing the steering wheel and wriggling out of my shoes I managed to extract myself from the remains.'

Predictably, James was incensed, and for several laps he stood by the side of the track shaking his fist at the somewhat bewildered driver of the surviving McLaren. Then, with the same fist he had used to threaten Mass James flattened a marshal who, in vain, tried to prevent him from running across the track.

Though he quickly apologized he was fined 2,750 Canadian dollars by the organizers, $2,000 for punching the marshal and $750 for crossing the track in an 'unsafe' manner. The aggrieved marshal, an American, also threatened to sue James.

It later transpired that James had misinterpreted his team-mate's hand signal and they patched up their differences. But not before Jochen Mass said: 'He thought I blocked him deliberately, which is stupid. He opens his mouth very quickly, which is unfortunate'.

'Hunt The Punch' and 'Prima Donna's Punchup' screamed the British tabloids, and the incident made headlines around the world. When Sue Hunt was asked to comment on her son's pugilistic behaviour she replied: 'He doesn't normally go around punching people. But he is certainly very quick tempered, especially when he has been driving'.

Jackie Stewart also had an opinion: 'When James wakes up I'm sure he will be trying to work out what happened and will think of the excessively high number of accidents and incidents he has been involved in. He must examine what is going on'.

James won the final race of 1977, leading the Japanese Grand Prix from start to finish, but the event at the Mount Fuji circuit was marred by tragedy when Gilles Villeneuve's Ferrari, after colliding with Ronnie Peterson's Tyrrell, flew in among a group of spectators and killed two of them.

At the end of the race James became embroiled in yet more controversy when he refused to mount the podium for the traditional victory celebrations. Instead, along with Carlos Reutemann, who finished second in his Ferrari, he dashed away from the circuit to catch a plane in Tokyo.

James had earlier informed the organizers of his need to leave promptly and asked them to provide a police escort to the airport. When the escort did not appear he ran for a waiting car, leaving behind a great deal of bad feeling, among both the insulted Japanese organizers and the angry Formula 1 fraternity.

Only Patrick Depailler, the third place finisher, was left to accept his trophy and spray the champagne from the rostrum. His team owner,

Ken Tyrrell, was furious: 'If a driver misses the victory ceremony he should be fined £10,000!', and Tyrrell vowed to have this requirement written into the rules.

And there was unanimous agreement that something had to be done about Master James Hunt, who seemed a law unto himself.

* * *

From a driving point of view, throughout the 1977 season James had acquitted himself exceedingly well, winning three races, the same number as Niki Lauda, and three times his McLaren had failed him within sight of victory. A combination of inferior equipment, bad luck and a couple of mistakes conspired to rob him of the larger share of success he undoubtedly deserved.

After five years experience in Formula 1 his driving had matured to the point that his racecraft and tactical skills were second to none. Beyond that, he was indisputably one of the very hardest chargers in the sport.

While it was generally agreed that fifth place in the Championship was not an accurate reflection of James's worth as a driver, there was also no doubt in the minds of the majority of the 180 members of the International Racing Press Association that their Prix Citron award had never before had a more deserving recipient.

Teddy Mayer tried his best to defend James, but admits he had become 'increasingly difficult to handle after he won the Championship.

'For instance, it wasn't easy to get him to sponsor functions or have him talk to the press. This meant we needed to spend a lot of time cajoling him into doing things that really should have been part of his job.

'He spoiled himself, allowed himself to do whatever he wanted to do. But he knew what he could get away with and what he couldn't and he always felt he could pull himself together when necessary.'

John Hogan, who often had to deal with the repercussions when his driver's untoward behaviour caused offence, speculates that some of the adverse press reaction to James stemmed from 'the apparent superficiality of his 1976 Championship – though he won it fair and square.

'Even Niki acknowledged that James had him beaten by Brands Hatch, but it was a common perception that James won the title by default. James resented that idea and he fought back by driving better than ever but also by being difficult to some of the press.

'Certainly James was a rule-breaker, but on the other hand there was also an element of resentment to his public school background – the old British class system at work – and that somebody could succeed at something without appearing to really try.

'The English never like people to succeed anyway. And they certainly don't like people who succeed easily. And they certainly don't like people who succeed easily who come from public schools.'

James's non-conforming ways, Hogan thinks, were not an affectation, but a natural result of his eccentricity. 'I think everybody has to take into account that he had quite a thick veneer of English eccentricity. He was in many ways like a Spitfire pilot – and I always thought he would have been a perfect Spitfire pilot – or a war hero decorated for bravery, or those people who try to ski alone to the South Pole. You'll invariably find that they're eccentrics and James was like that. It can be very charming but it can also be extremely wearing when you have to deal with it.

'He was a genuine eccentric and an extreme extrovert, a combination that was bound to make him outrageous and controversial. He wasn't putting on an act, though he could be mischievous and choose to present himself very well or very badly. It was simply the way he was.

'In fairness to him I must confess I only came to realize how eccentric he was after he retired, when he became more eccentric than ever. All the previous time I'd known him and all the time he drove for us I just thought he was really a bad boy.'

10

REALLY A BAD BOY

1978–1979

His reputation as a combination Bad Boy/Golden Boy brought James extremes of both criticism and praise, neither of which rested easily with him. Both aspects of his public image, he felt, were manufactured fantasy figures that unfairly suggested he had a split personality.

He was 'faintly amused' by 'Master James' – the unconventional, party-loving, public school playboy – but the perception of him as a dashing, daredevil *'Boy's Own Paper'* hero who could never put a foot wrong James considered to be patronizing. He thought he was only ever being his own man, though he understood how his steadfast refusal to be anything other than that, and the way he chose to react to the pressures of being a celebrity, could lead to misconceptions.

'Don't forget, I came from nowhere. I'd just won my first Grand Prix in the year before I became World Champion. So I was pitched pretty heavily in at the deep end. When I was driving everything was fine, but all the rest of it, what people expected of a World Champion, really got to me.

'It was a huge change and all I could do was operate in the only way I knew – which was not to compromise myself. I just had to get on with it, in my own odd style.'

As a public figure he was expected to conform to a strict code of behaviour which was at odds with what came naturally to him. He thought the whole point of being successful was to gain the freedom to do what he wanted and, just as he had resolved to live it up while he could in his early days as a journeyman driver, he made a conscious decision to enjoy to the hilt his time as a famous Formula 1 driver – now, not later.

But his playboy image, James felt, was not deserved. It was a legacy of his days at Hesketh Racing, when it was assumed that he fully endorsed the team's emphasis on the social side of racing. In truth, though he acquitted himself quite well in that department with the Good Lord's entourage, James disliked the 'jet-set' life. His idea of a pleasant evening was chatting with friends in front of the telly (preferably watching a sporting fixture of some kind), eating a takeaway meal, having a few beers and smoking a joint or two.

He hated and was made nervous by large gatherings where he was the focus of attention among strangers, especially the pestering 'idiot minority' who always seemed to surround him, while any worthwhile, less aggressive people were shoved into the background. He often turned up late at such functions, invariably under-dressed for the occasion, and to defend himself he sometimes had too much to drink, insulted the 'bores' and developed a reputation as being abrasive socially.

'I refused to be shoved around', he said. 'If that meant calling a spade a spade and not toadying to middle-class ego-massaging and being dressed in jeans and T-shirt, so what? I wasn't prepared to truss myself up in a monkey suit and I always thought I turned out cleanly and comfortably dressed. The whole point was that I was basically getting on with my life in my own way and I didn't really care about what anyone thought.

'Even though it made a lot of people dislike me intensely, I said to myself: "Stuff it. I'll do it my way".'

* * *

In the past James had treated his Formula 1 car as a getaway vehicle to escape from the outside pressures he so detested, but in 1978 his uncompetitive and, some thought, badly driven, McLaren M26 took him on a dispiriting journey that plunged him to 13th in the standings at the end of the season. He managed to score only eight points, six fewer than in his debut year with Hesketh in only half the number of races.

When Patrick Tambay, his inexperienced new McLaren team-mate, collected as many points as James, it lent credibility to the contention of some critics that James had lost interest. Granted, his car did not finish 10 of the 16 races, but Tambay's McLaren failed to finish only five times and six of James's retirements were due to accidents.

Some of the spins and crashes could be explained away by simple driving errors or plain bad luck, but his spate of accidents in 1978, after having had only two in all of the previous year, created suspicions in some quarters that James might sometimes even be driving while his judgement was impaired.

However, in 1978 everyone but the Lotus drivers had an excuse for not doing well. The cars, driven by Mario Andretti and Ronnie Peterson, dominated the season because of the 'ground-effect' advantage devised by the Lotus design genius and team founder, Colin Chapman. The ground-effect principle worked by creating a partial vacuum beneath the car which served to help keep it stuck to the ground, thus increasing cornering speeds dramatically. The system depended on 'skirts', strips of plastic material running along each side of the lower bodywork, which preserved the vacuum.

Speaking of the aerodynamic phenomenon James said he 'learned a lot about skirt fashion. Personally, I have always preferred mini-skirts but it looks as if I will have to change my taste. Nowadays the name of the game is to keep all the air out – and you know how air can get under mini-skirts!'.

☆ ☆ ☆

His favourite person in a mini-skirt was now Jane 'Hottie' Birbeck. 'Hottie' was actually a more dressed-up version of 'Hot Loins', a nickname given her by James's friend John Richardson when he first met her. Richardson meant it as a joking contradiction in terms, since she seemed 'like this very cool, very English, ice maiden. I was just teasing, but the name stuck and the press picked it up and ran with it'.

Indeed, the beautiful Hottie and her British Golden Boy boyfriend became media darlings, and a lot of their private life was played out as a kind of public soap opera in which they were the reluctant stars. Both were at first honest and direct with the press, but as the more intimate details of their relationship were broadcast far and wide they became less cooperative.

James usually called Jane 'The Hot One' or 'Loins', though it was six months before they were anything more than friends. His apparent lack of prurient interest when they first met created an initial impression which Jane eventually came to realize couldn't have been more wrong.

'I was sure he was gay, because he never made a move on me for so long. It was a rather bizarre courtship. We had plenty to talk about, but that's all we ever did. He liked conversation and would talk endlessly to me on the telephone. When we got together we'd have supper and talk into the small hours. There was no deep urge, particularly on his part, to make a permanent relationship, and we had our separate lives as well.'

Jane was educated at a girls' boarding school in Kent, then worked as an au pair for a while before attending a secretarial college. She was being groomed for a conventional life that would revolve around a 'good' marriage, or so her parents thought. But their adventurous and fun-loving daughter was more interested in having a career and a busy social life. It was her independent streak, besides her very obvious feminine charms, that James found attractive.

After the failure of his marriage, which he felt was largely due to the fact that he was unable to cater to Suzy's need for constant attention, James was reluctant to commit himself to a long-term relationship. He had enough trouble looking after himself without having someone else depending on him. But he found Jane's 'independence a great plus because I never have to worry about her.

'She has a strong personality, the strongest one I've ever met and the only one who could stand up to my strength, which is why we have such a good balance. I've never wanted to use or abuse women, but if you have a stronger personality you can't help but be the dominant one and the moment that happens you have no relationship. I don't want someone to live for me.'

Nor was he interested in getting married, which would force them together and threaten the relationship between two free-spirited individuals. His failed marriage made him realize what he really needed was an independent companion. And marriage, he felt, was not necessary if children should enter into the equation. The only thing that mattered was that the children should have two loving parents who could give them the affection and security they needed.

Their mutual independence meant that for some time their relationship was conducted at long distance. After working as a secretary at a London advertising agency Jane became a photographer's representative in London and then in New York, where James was only able to visit her infrequently. She quite liked her work in America and wanted to stay there, but when she informed James of this on the telephone he became 'instantly keener' and tried to persuade her to come and live with him in Spain. When Jane balked at that: 'we sort of broke up on the phone.

'At the time I didn't realize I was pregnant and when I found out I was I became terribly excited and rang him up to discuss it. When I told him I was pregnant he just assumed I would come back and there was no more discussion. He appeared in New York to pick me up and we set up home in Spain.'

After Jane had a miscarriage, the first of many, she busied herself designing and supervising improvements to the villa at San Pedro, which James had now bought. 'We got the builders in and made the house all nice, settled into a pretty good domestic routine and had lots of cats and dogs. Of course James's favourite was Oscar, a wonderful dog.'

'James's relationship with Oscar', John Richardson thinks, 'seemed far closer than any human relationship he ever had. He was completely devoted to that dog.'

It was Richardson and his wife Mary who introduced James to their veterinarian friend who supplied Oscar and continued to look after him when James took him to Spain. There, James would pay for the vet to come to stay at the villa just so he could check over his beloved Oscar.

They were inseparable companions, running together down the country roads and playing 'fetch' along the beaches of the Costa del Sol. James taught Oscar how to 'play' golf. The dog lay intently watching as James and his companions teed off, then raced off to locate each ball, exactly in the order it had been played, and patiently stood over each one until it was played again. Should a drive go astray Oscar could be counted on to find the ball and James said his ball-finding capabilities saved him a fortune.

The Aloha, the golf club to which James belonged, sent a circular to its members announcing that, henceforth, dogs would be banned from the course. However, the edict stated, the ban did not include Oscar because he was often better behaved than some of the members.

Oscar also sometimes dined out with James, and on one occasion, when James moved back to England, the large Alsatian caused eyebrows to be raised when he had a leisurely and expensive (£20 a head) lunch with James at Langan's Brasserie, the society café in Mayfair. Oscar, it was noted, was well behaved and perhaps as presentable as his unshaven master in his jeans. But the dog's appetite extended beyond such fare as Langan's house specialities of spinach soufflé, entrecôte de veau and cassis sorbet – as Bubbles Horsley found out to his despair.

Bubbles had invited James and the faithful Oscar to spend a weekend at the Horsley home in a Northamptonshire village near Silverstone. Bubbles, now out of racing, was devoting himself to country pursuits, including raising guinea pigs for his children. After dinner James let Oscar outside for a run and when he came back in James immediately recognized that 'Oscar's been wicked'.

Bubbles went outside with a torch and discovered 'my best breeding guinea pig, and my daughter's favourite, lying there quite dead. Oscar had very cleverly found a way into the cage and despatched her with ease. My daughter was far less upset about it than I was. I got quite emotional about the tragedy and sent James to bed. With Oscar.

'I think in a way Oscar was the child James never had at that stage. He was a remarkable dog, no question, but James thought a lot about animals and their requirements and was very concerned about their needs. He gave Oscar the very best treatment and also was keenly interested in the welfare of other dogs. He would look at a dog, wonder if its owner was treating it well and bringing it up properly and if the dog was getting everything out of life that it could.'

Before he came to know James better the journalist Nigel Roebuck was pleasantly surprised by an incident involving a stray dog. It was late in the evening after a Grand Prix and the teams were packing up to leave when James, while talking to Roebuck, saw the dog wandering around the paddock, shivering and obviously very hungry. Roebuck, also sensitive to the needs of an animal in distress, went with James to several of the team motorhomes where they got food and fed the dog. But that wasn't the end of it as far as James was concerned. He insisted that they should take the dog up to the race control centre.

Roebuck: 'He took the dog in there and would not leave until he was sure it would be looked after. James actually made this official sign a piece of paper saying he would take care of the dog and see that it was housed and properly cared for. I was very impressed with this. James was probably one of only a handful of people on this entire planet who would even give that sort of thing a second thought'.

John Watson, like Roebuck, saw in James's feelings for Oscar a side of the madcap racing driver that belied his reputation. 'I know people might laugh when you say these things, but in his relationship with Oscar James showed he was a very caring and loving man. When you saw James and Oscar together you knew he was capable of great tenderness.

'I like dogs and understand the man-dog relationship. I suspect that to James Oscar wasn't a dog. He was a companion. And he loved him. There was a very deep bond between James and Oscar that I only saw again in the great love and affection he had for his two sons.

'And his deeply compassionate and loving nature was something that, unfortunately, wasn't adequately conveyed to the public, who only ever heard about the sensational side of James Hunt.'

* * *

James's reasonable fourth place result in the first Grand Prix of 1978, in Argentina, was not an accurate indicator of what was to come.

More typical was his troubled Brazilian race, where he was fined $500 for driving around the track without his helmet on after a spin in qualifying. In the race his tyres wore out in just a dozen laps, then, after a pit stop to replace them, he spun into a sand trap.

He blamed his mistake on a lapse of concentration occasioned, he claimed, by being held up by slower cars and having to run at less than top speed: 'I simply lost interest and spun off'.

In South Africa he became a victim of 'Sod's Law' when his engine blew up after only five laps. A similar engine failure ended what James called the 'extremely impressive' effort of the young Italian driver Riccardo Patrese who led much of the race in an Arrows. Before long Patrese and James would become embroiled in a controversy that created an enmity between them that lasted for many years.

In South Africa James also noted that the newspaper reporters seemed much more interested in his off-circuit performances than what he did at the Kyalami track. But his relief that his 'nocturnal activities' were not discovered no doubt owed something to the fact that Jane, at home in Spain, would not receive news of his extracurricular amorous escapades. It was some time before she learned the truth.

Over the Easter weekend Jane, watched by James, competed in a celebrity saloon car race at Brands Hatch. Jane's motor racing debut – of which he said, 'I was proud of her achievement to be able to spin three times, yet remain unlapped' – was better than James had fared a few days earlier, in the International Trophy race at Silverstone. On the first lap James was one of many drivers to spin off the flooded track.

At Long Beach in California he crashed in practice and did it again, clipping a barrier and knocking a front wheel askew on only the fifth lap of the race. This left him 'utterly distraught at my own stupidity at a time when the team is making superhuman efforts to see me get back on the leader board'.

There was another non-finish in the streets of Monaco when a suddenly slowing car forced James off line and he sideswiped the guard rails. He made a pit stop for repairs then continued until a suspension component damaged in the accident gave way. Then there was a post-race punch-up in which, for once, James didn't land any blows, though Jane received one in the eye.

That night James and Jane went to the Tip-Top bar, a traditional gathering place for the Grand Prix fraternity. Among the celebrants were John Watson, some of the McLaren mechanics, several journalists and a lot of tourists. James thought the party was not unduly rowdy, though there was some loud singing and the mechanics moved a couple of potted plants out on to the street where most of the crowd was gathered.

James called what followed the Battle of the Tip-Top. 'Without any warning the Monagasque police charged down on the assembled throng, hitting out with rubber truncheons in the most disgraceful display of public brutality I have ever witnessed. If they had wished to disperse us they had only needed to ask. But to hit girls standing with their backs to them over the head and in the face is the sort of behaviour that incites riots. People were trampled underfoot, one girl was thrown bodily over a guard rail and Jane received a black eye.'

He missed the actual skirmish – he was inside getting drinks at the bar – but had to be forcibly restrained from going after the policeman who hit his girlfriend.

*   *   *

Jane was pleased with James's attempted gallantry at the Battle of the Tip-Top, but she was less happy about his lack of concern for her comfort and well-being on an earlier occasion that weekend in Monte Carlo.

'I had worn new shoes in the pits and developed some horrible blisters. We went back to our hotel and James said to get ready because we were going to go for some drinks at the Palace Hotel – at least that's what I thought he said. So I just put on a casual dress and sandals with plasters all over my feet. He was in his jeans and T-shirt and a blazer which the Marlboro people forced him into. A car came to pick us up and half way there it became clear it wasn't the Palace Hotel we were going to: it was Prince Rainier's Palace.

'We got there and it was a huge formal reception: the Palace Guard with drawn swords, the red carpet, the whole of the Monte Carlo elite inside and the women in diamond tiaras. The fact that I was arriving in totally inappropriate dress, with my feet covered in plasters, was completely lost on James. He thought I looked fine and was oblivious to what other people might think.'

Jane was angry at his apparent lack of consideration, but she soon forgave him and, in fact, his sensitivity to her feelings she found one of his most endearing qualities. She was only 24 when they got together (he was five years older) and, she realized later, something of a 'spoiled brat'.

In times of stress she would throw 'terrible tantrums', lapse into silent sulks and not speak to him for several days. But with the help of his patient understanding she was able to learn a great deal about herself and 'grow up'. She also came to understand why it seemed to others that James had not grown up. 'I learned he just didn't think like other people and they would become annoyed and think he was deliberately being provocative. People couldn't cope with it. Here is this guy who's got the world at his feet – his bare feet – who just can't fail. This most charming, likeable wonderful guy, terribly good-looking, gets all the girls he wants, and so on, and people would get jealous of him.

'He was terribly boisterous when he was feeling up. He just had the best time and was wonderfully happy, with great *joie de vivre*. It stuck in some people's gullets. He appeared to them as a spoiled upper class twit, public school background and all that. "What does he think he's doing, walking around in his bare feet?" – or whatever outraged them. It was understandable that they should think he wasn't for real. But James was absolutely for real – always.

'Even at the very height of his fame James would have a sincere conversation with anyone he enjoyed talking to. He really talked, with none of that glancing over the shoulder to see if there was someone better to talk to. There was never any hierarchy with him. It didn't matter if it was a dustman or the Queen of England, if James enjoyed their company he would stay with them.'

⋆   ⋆   ⋆

From the journalists who did not enjoy his company James was presented, belatedly, with the 1977 Prix Citron award (a disrespectful cartoon of himself) on the eve of the Belgian Grand Prix. In hopes of 'winning the hat-trick' James suggested to the assembled scribes that the Prix Citron was really an indicator of the driver who paid the least attention to them.

Very little was written about him in the Belgian race, since he was only in it for 10 seconds when his McLaren was hit from behind by Riccardo Patrese's Arrows and launched into the air and instant retirement.

On the weekend of his 'home' Grand Prix in Spain James was one of 10 drivers, and their companions, invited to the private home of King Juan Carlos for dinner. The arrangements had been made by Jackie Stewart, but when James appeared in jeans the plans were hastily changed to an informal buffet supper by the swimming pool where the King's pet cheetah roamed freely among the guests.

James was, of course, fascinated by the big cat but it seemed more interested in playing with Jane's skirt and its claws got caught in the garment. 'Soon', James noted, 'it had her skirt down around her knees. Luckily she was wearing knickers.'

In practice for the Spanish Grand Prix James was lucky to escape with only a bruised hand after he hit another car which had spun in front of him. The impact pushed a front wheel of the McLaren back to the cockpit where the black tyre marks on the windscreen were testimony to how close James came to disaster.

In the race, after a pit stop to change tyres, he finished sixth, a result that left him 'completely shattered' and with blisters on his hands because of a steering problem.

A distant eighth place in Sweden was followed by a well-deserved third in France for his first, and what would be his only, visit to the podium in 1978. In fact, they were the last points he scored in his career.

Near the end of the race he became nauseous and on the final lap he could hold it back no longer and was sick in his helmet. He lost concentration, had a quick spin but got going again and made it to the finish line.

That evening he dined with his team mate Patrick Tambay and some of the McLaren mechanics at a restaurant near the Paul Ricard circuit. As usual James was the life of the party and officially baptized Tambay as 'fastest frog' by pouring a bottle of rosé over the Frenchman's head. Tambay retaliated by dumping the contents of an ice bucket over James, giving him a cold shower that he would have preferred the next morning when he 'had a hellish hangover that was richly deserved'.

Back in Spain he toasted the opening of a new business venture: The Tropicana, a disco on the beach at Torremolinos. Along with a couple of partners James had invested £2,000 in the modest, wooden-walled, Hawaiian-style structure. The disco was the forerunner of a more ambitious nightclub in Marbella which he planned to open near the end of the summer. It would be called Oscar's, after his dog. Until the canine-inspired club was up and running James invited all his fans to come to the disco 'and don't forget your wallets!'.

☆ ☆ ☆

Instead of cavorting on Spanish beaches Teddy Mayer wanted James to do more testing, which was badly needed to develop ground-effect technology to put the McLarens on more equal footing with the frontrunning Lotuses. But it seemed to Mayer that his driver's mind was now less on his job than ever before. 'I can get James to talk about women, backgammon, tennis, golf, business, taxes, Spain, food, childhood, but I can't get him to talk to me about racing cars.'

In retrospect Alastair Caldwell thinks they could have better accommodated James's special needs. 'He needed to be competitive and if he wasn't quick he was disappointed. I think his interest in motor racing was never that great anyway. He didn't want to work at it. He wanted it to be easy. So when it became hard work he lost interest. He wanted to just turn up and be the star and when that didn't happen he was not happy.

'He tried to be professional. But he was always lazy. We should have hired a more competent test driver and got the car quicker. Then, on race day, we could have dragged James in on his leash, strapped him into the car and let him loose like a mad dog.'

James admitted his enthusiasm was waning and hinted that perhaps his racing future might be limited. 'It's difficult, when you're used to a good car and you go to a bad one, to maintain the interest and competitive edge. In testing, I find it a great struggle to slog around endlessly in a car that is so fundamentally bad that whatever you do to it doesn't change anything. And afterwards, to sit around and talk about this depressing fact for two hours is something I strenuously try to avoid.

'As far as racing goes, it's true I've got no peace of mind at the moment. I only get that from winning. I must win if I am going to stay in motor racing. I don't really like the sport and will only continue as long as I think I can win. I don't see myself racing on into the 1980s. It is too dangerous. I am not going to carry on risking my life indefinitely. There are too many other things I want to do.

'I'm still racing to win and at the moment I'm not doing it very well. But winning can come back to you at any time and when it comes you've got to be ready to capitalize on it. The important thing is not to get depressed about it. I've been through far too many bad patches in my career to let something like this get on top of me.'

*　*　*

To their great disappointment the multitude of James Hunt fans in England witnessed another example of just how far their hero had fallen off the pace. In qualifying for the British Grand Prix at Brands Hatch James's McLaren M26 was half a second slower than he managed in the M23 model two years previously. Then, he won the restarted race, though he was later disqualified, but this time he made an inglorious exit on only the eighth lap.

He was running alone in ninth place when his McLaren – unaccountably it seemed – spun through 360 degrees at very high speed, flew off the road and slammed into a barrier. When asked to explain what happened James said: 'Nothing broke. I wish I could tell you something had! The car was handling badly and I just made a mistake'.

He later talked about experiencing severe understeer in right-hand corners and massive oversteer in left-hand corners. He attributed the handling problem to tyre stagger – differing diameters on his car's rear tyres – but the spin took place between two corners, on the Cooper Straight. There were suspicions that it was the driver who had staggered because his head was in a spin from substance abuse.

James was a very heavy pot smoker, forever rolling joints and puffing away on them because, he claimed, marijuana relaxed him. But he was also now occasionally snorting cocaine and, while no one thought he would actually race while under the influence of anything but his own large quantities of adrenaline, some believed the lingering effects of his drug-taking might have impaired his judgement in the cockpit: slowing down his reaction times, perhaps even causing him to see things which weren't there.

Teddy Mayer doesn't subscribe to this theory, believing that James's high state of fitness and strict abstinence in the days before a race would have his system cleaned out by race day. But others, including John Hogan, think the Brands Hatch accident, in particular, might have been due to impaired judgement. Hogan never saw James ingesting any suspicious substance before a race, but at Brands Hatch there were rumours that James smoked a joint just before the start.

Some time later the journalist Mike Doodson confronted James with this story. 'I asked him if he really had a toke before the start of that race. And James said: "I heard those stories that I was out to lunch and I can assure you they are completely untrue". He convinced me. Maybe I was gullible.'

James, who seemed not to be in very good humour when he came to the German Grand Prix, was even less happy when he left, and his behaviour also angered many others.

In the final qualifying session he was trying to improve his eighth place on the grid when his quick lap was spoiled by the Surtees of Vittorio 'The Monza Gorilla' Brambilla. The Surtees had run low on fuel and was coasting, but James, who claimed he didn't see Brambilla raising his hand to indicate he was slowing, decided to teach him a lesson by repaying him in kind.

He gave him a 'brake test' – slowed suddenly in front of him – the

Surtees rammed the back of the McLaren and, as James put it, 'The Monza Gorilla finished up with his nose out of joint – literally!'.

Brambilla was incensed – 'You've got to be a crazy man to do that sort of thing!' – and ran down to the McLaren pit screaming abuse at James, who was still sitting in his car. Brambilla slammed his large fist down on James's head which was fortunately still covered by his helmet.

Those who felt the potentially dangerous brake test was totally unwarranted were not displeased when James was disqualified from the race after taking a short cut to the pits to change a punctured tyre.

James's Austrian Grand Prix became 'a non-event' when he spun off the wet track on the first lap after being nudged by another car.

It took several beers to drown his sorrows and on the way to the airport after the race he felt a pressing need to relieve himself. Alastair Caldwell, driving a rental car with James and Jane as his passengers, told him they couldn't stop or they would miss their plane. Caldwell pressed on, overtaking the long queues of traffic leaving the Österreichring circuit, and James's needs became increasingly desperate.

'So Hottie wound down the window, James pulled down his pants and tried to do it out the window while Hottie hung on to him. But he couldn't pee because the minute he got it out into the cold wind it shrivelled up. So there we were, tearing down the road passing all the traffic, with James exposing himself to thousands of Austrians. Eventually he pulled it in and piddled into the empty beer bottles he had in the car and these he threw out the window.'

'James was always good for a laugh', Caldwell remembers, 'and it was a shame to lose him at the end of '78.'

* * *

While James was still publicly disporting himself with the same old free-spirited high jinks the past two difficult years had taken their toll. The disappointment at becoming an also-ran after being on top of the world, the constant exposure to danger in a losing cause, the criticism of his driving, which he felt was unwarranted, and the continuing pressures of being a public figure, which ran against his essentially private nature, made him increasingly disillusioned and bitter. His face had become hardened, the worry lines had deepened and, it was noticed, his eyes darted about nervously as if he was looking for a way out.

By the end of August, after a dispiriting tenth place finish in the Dutch Grand Prix, he was seriously considering retiring from the sport at the end of the season.

Three things changed his mind: another chance to revive his flagging reputation as a driver, the opportunity to join a new team, which seemed a throw-back to the glory days of Hesketh Racing, and the financial inducement – made to him by the team owner, Walter Wolf – of $1 million.

Walter Wolf, an Austrian, emigrated to Canada in his youth, made a considerable fortune in the construction industry and oil exploration and spent money lavishly. He had homes around the world, a private jet and helicopter, a fleet of exotic cars and, beginning in 1977, his own Formula 1 team.

He hired Harvey Postlethwaite ('The Doc', who created the Hesketh 308) to design the Wolf cars, the highly respected Peter Warr as team manager and Jody Scheckter to drive. In its first year of operation Wolf Racing won three Grands Prix. When Scheckter announced he would move to Ferrari in 1979 Wolf made the offer, which James couldn't refuse.

James thought he had already made enough to live on for the rest of his life, but adding Walter Wolf's money to his nest egg would give him even greater financial security. He had an even better offer from Ferrari, but turned it down because, he said, Wolf Racing seemed to have the necessary enthusiasm and determination to give him the equipment and impetus for another chance to defy the 'so-called experts' who had accused him of not trying in his last year with McLaren when, he maintained, he was still giving his best as he always had done.

'The criticism from some people', he said, 'not only insults my intelligence but sums up their lack of it pretty comprehensively. In fact, the safest way to drive is as fast as possible. The harder I try, the better I concentrate, and the fewer driving errors I make. Obviously, the nearer the front you are, the greater the chance that a multiple accident will happen behind you.'

When he announced his move to Wolf Racing he said: 'I decided that on the professional level I had grown stale with the McLaren team. Our relationship had gone as far as it possibly could but this new team are a tremendous stimulus. I think they're going to provide me with a challenge that I so desperately want.

'I've still got it in me to be a winner. I know it's still there even after a year like this. I am convinced that once I get back into the right car the good results will come. My aim is to be World Champion in 1979 so that I can go out of this business on a high. That's the way I want to retire.'

But three races remained in 1978 and the first of them, in Italy, James called: 'a black day in the history of motor racing and one that I would like to be able to forget'.

* * *

For the start of the Italian Grand Prix at Monza James was back on the fifth row of the grid. He wrote about the terrible sequence of events which followed in his column in *Autosport*.

'We had just completed the warm-up lap and were taking up starting positions when the red light came on – even though only the front couple of lines of cars were actually stationary. The remainder of the pack held back, and when the green light came on, were still rolling. This certainly contributed to my excellent start. Riccardo Patrese (behind him in an Arrows) made what can only be described as an Italian home start and was right up alongside me – except that he was on the outside of the track that leads to the old Monza banking (which was no longer in use).

'I was slap in the middle of the pack, with Ronnie Peterson (in his Lotus) on my left. As we approached the funnel where the tracks divide, Patrese, with nowhere to go, without warning, barged over on me, pushing me into Ronnie. In the ensuing sandwich my car flew up in the air and slid sideways down the middle of the track. Behind me all hell broke loose.'

When James climbed out of his McLaren, which had been hit several times by spinning cars, he saw behind him a fireball, in the midst of which was Peterson's badly damaged Lotus. He ran back to the Lotus, where a track marshal was spraying the contents of an extinguisher into the cockpit. James stood watching for a few seconds, then dived into the inferno.

'I tried to pull Ronnie clear but found one of his legs trapped between the steering wheel and what remained of the chassis. Flames and smoke enveloped the whole car again but the marshall flattened them and, with additional assistance now on hand (Shadow driver Clay Regazzoni), we managed to wrench the steering wheel clear. I picked Ronnie up by the epaulettes of his uniform and dragged him clear of the car. I knew then that Ronnie's injuries must be pretty severe as there was virtually nothing left to the front end of the car.'

Peterson's legs were badly broken and mangled but he hadn't suffered burns and his injuries didn't seem life-threatening. Meanwhile, Vittorio Brambilla, hit by a flying wheel, lay unconscious with severe head injuries (though he made a full recovery and would race again). No one else was hurt, but ten cars had been involved in the accident and it was over two hours before the track was cleared and the race restarted.

James spent part of the interval in the motorhome of the Wolf team, talking to his old mate Harvey Postlethwaite and his team manager-to-be Peter Warr. They gave him a cup of tea and tried to calm him down. His hands shook, his face was pale, his voice was trembling with emotion and James talked about stopping racing – there and then.

But he got back into the spare McLaren, burnt out its clutch at the restart, circulated back in the pack for a few laps then retired with an ignition problem.

Mario Andretti's Lotus was in front at the finish and, though he was given a one minute penalty for jumping the start and demoted to sixth place, the single point was enough for the American to clinch the 1978 World Driving Championship.

But there was no joy in it, for he soon learned that his Lotus team-mate was dead.

Ronnie Peterson's death came as a great shock. His legs were badly mangled in the accident but the initial medical prognosis at the circuit was that he would easily recover and perhaps even be well enough to race the next season. But in hospital, after he underwent emergency operations on his legs, bone marrow entered his bloodstream, a blood clot formed and the doctors were unable to save his life.

Peterson, who left a widow Barbro and their small daughter Nina, was one of the great Formula 1 heroes and one of the best-liked. Colin Chapman of Team Lotus said, 'Ronnie wasn't cast in the popular image of a racing driver. He was a gentle, quiet man who loved his family'.

He was buried in Orebro, Sweden, the town where he was born in 1944. The pallbearers at the very sad funeral – which was attended by over 15,000 people – were Ake Strandberg, a racing mechanic and friend of Peterson, and five drivers: Niki Lauda, Jody Scheckter, John Watson, Emerson Fittipaldi and James Hunt.

James always admired Peterson as a driver and, after Niki Lauda, he was one of those James was closest to. The death of the man he'd known since his Formula 3 days disturbed him deeply. Jane Birbeck was with James in Italy and remembers his reaction. 'James was very, very shaken when he pulled Ronnie out of the car. It wasn't just a lifeless body then, there was eye contact. And when James looked into his face he said it was filled with fear. He saw that Ronnie knew he was in trouble and was terribly frightened.

'And that really, really got to James. The realities of dying hit home and he talked to me then for the first time about dying. He thought deeply about it and talked about what it would mean. One of the things he said was that he wanted everybody to have a big party if anything happened to him.'

In Italy a legal investigation into the Peterson accident was now under way, but the Grand Prix Drivers' Safety Committee – comprised of James Hunt, Niki Lauda, Emerson Fittipaldi, Jody Scheckter and Mario Andretti – had already reached a conclusion.

In their judgement the starter of the race should not have given the green light before all the cars had stopped on the grid. The drivers also decided that Riccardo Patrese was guilty of dangerous driving and, as punishment, he should be banned from competing in the next race, in America.

Patrese, in his second year of Formula 1, had a reputation for being arrogant and impetuous and on several previous occasions he had been criticized by other drivers for overly-aggressive race tactics. Patrese maintained that film of the accident would prove him innocent and of the Safety Committee he said: 'Perhaps they are trying to cover up the truth about the accident'.

The Royal Swedish Automobile Club announced that James Hunt would be awarded their prestigious Golden Shield for heroic accomplishment in rescuing Peterson from his burning car. But James was a reluctant hero. At Monza he had told journalists: 'Don't make a big hero thing out of this. I happened to be one of the first on the scene. I was dressed in a fireproof driving suit, so I didn't have to do anything brave.'

When the media persisted in glorifying his role in the rescue he lashed out: 'They spent the whole season knocking me then all of a sudden they were quite unjustifiably acclaiming me as a hero, which I found very embarrassing. When you're down, they kick you and then they kick you again. When you're up, they go right over the top'.

There was a growing perception that James was really angry with himself and that he felt extreme remorse about his involvement in the accident that claimed the life of his friend Ronnie. One version of the circumstances which triggered the accident was that when Patrese's Arrows moved over towards his McLaren James instinctively veered away from the Arrows and into the Peterson Lotus.

During his time as a Formula 1 TV commentator, when James seemed to single out Riccardo Patrese for especially harsh criticism, many people thought it was a legacy of what happened in the 1978 Italian Grand Prix. But James denied that he had a personal vendetta. He criticized Patrese when he thought he was performing below par, but he also praised him when his driving warranted it.

The French journalist Gerard 'Jabby' Crombac, who began covering Formula 1 racing in 1950, the year the sport was formally organized into the World Championship series, thought James was a 'charming bloke, wonderful sense of humour and quite good fun.

'But I find it hard to forgive him for the way he treated Patrese. James was the one to lead the crusade against Patrese, but if somebody was responsible amongst the drivers it was certainly James. It was a very difficult thing for him psychologically and perhaps he knew in his heart it was his fault and he was trying to get it out of himself by accusing someone else. The net result was that Patrese had to carry the can for a long time.'

It was three years before an Italian court absolved Patrese, and the race starter – both of whom had been charged with manslaughter – of any blame in causing the chain reaction of collisions at Monza. Photographic evidence showed that Patrese's Arrows did not hit Hunt's McLaren before Hunt's McLaren hit Peterson's Lotus. Included in the evidence presented in court was a letter from James Hunt which stated in part: 'For me, the responsibility for the accident is completely Patrese's'.

Riccardo Patrese continued in Formula 1 for many years, competing in more races than any other driver, and he eventually became a highly respected ambassador for the sport. But he suffered much anguish over the Monza incident and its aftermath and never forgave those whom he felt caused it. 'Inside myself I knew I had no reason to be unhappy because I knew I did not cause the accident. But I think what the drivers did to me on that occasion is very difficult to forgive.'

James once tried to discuss the matter but Patrese refused to speak to him. The journalist Nigel Roebuck thinks Patrese's enduring grudge bothered James.

'I always had the impression that James would actually quite like to have sat down with Riccardo and made up. Because I don't think James liked having enemies, at all. I think he would have felt a lot better for doing that. But they never got together and Riccardo remained bitter towards James to the end.'

Bernie Ecclestone, who had seen far too many drivers killed in his time, several of them his friends, later employed Patrese as a driver in his Brabham team and remained close to him throughout his career. Ecclestone also thinks that James should have cleared the air with Patrese.

'At the time James believed what he'd done was right. He thought he had to jump up and blame somebody, which wasn't really necessary because it was an accident. And it wasn't really the cause of Ronnie's death anyway. Nobody dies from a broken leg.

'If James had sat back and had a good look at it he might have said: "Maybe poor Riccardo was blamed wrongfully" – and he should have come forward with that. But I suppose once you've gone out on a limb like that and you don't come back early on, the longer it continues the more difficult it is to come back.'

* * *

When Patrese was not allowed to compete in the United States Grand Prix at Watkins Glen some in the motor racing press thought his ban by a 'kangaroo court' was disgraceful and that he was unfairly being made a scapegoat in a 'witch-hunt'. In the race, it was noted, one of the prime witch-hunters behaved rather childishly.

In final qualifying James was angry with the McLaren team for preventing him from improving his time when, he alleged, they sent him out with the wrong gear ratios. In the race, when the team noticed a front tyre wearing badly they hung out a sign inquiring if he wanted to make a pit stop. In response he gave them a rude 'Churchillian' gesture.

Eventually, while he was running in fifth place, the tyre problem forced him into the pits and while the wheel change was in progress there was an angry exchange and much fist-shaking by James, who wanted the tyre pressures to be set differently.

Alastair Caldwell pointed out that as he was shouting and screaming he was losing valuable time and positions. James, having dropped eight places, shot away in a huff, laying down two long black streaks of rubber down the pit lane and over the air jacks of another nearby pit crew. He eventually finished seventh.

The Canadian Grand Prix, at a new circuit in Montreal, marked the end of James's tenure at McLaren, though few of the 72,632 spectators noticed it. Their attention was riveted on the local hero in a Ferrari, Gilles Villeneuve – James's 'discovery' – who rewarded his enthralled fans by scoring his first Grand Prix win.

'This is the last one, good luck buddy – it's been a great three years' read the note from his mechanics on the steering wheel as James climbed into his McLaren for the last time. He did not have good luck, however. A wheel came loose, impeding his braking, and he shot off the road into a muddy field.

Not wishing to walk through the ankle deep mud James ran across the track to drier ground, just making it to safety before the arrival of an oncoming car. A marshal had tried to restrain him but, this time, James left Canada without throwing a punch.

James raced once more in 1978, making a guest appearance in an F5000 event at Winton in Australia. His entourage on the light-hearted 'Down Under' expedition included his faithful McLaren mechanic Ray 'Kojak' Grant, his friend John 'The Kid' Richardson and 'Norman' – the name now given to his brother Peter after he was mistakenly identified as Norman Hunt by a British newspaper.

James reported that the stewardesses on their Malaysian Airlines flight were of a standard unequalled by any other airline and he fell in love every time the crew changed. The bar service was equally bountiful and on arrival in Melbourne they 'fell off the plane'.

They hadn't expected a welcoming committee and James was rather disconcerted to be greeted in the airport by a host of dignitaries and a large press contingent. The arrival of the famous racing driver was televised and a TV journalist conducted a live interview which Richardson thought James carried off with great aplomb, since 'he was absolutely pissed to the eyeballs'.

When the lady posed a question James would sit looking composed and thoughtful, as if considering the full gravity and import of her query but in reality trying to keep from falling off his chair. He never faltered or slurred his words and the Australians were impressed with his articulate and knowledgeable answers.

James, studiously avoiding any further liquid refreshment in the days before the race, then impressed the crowd of 15,000 at the Winton circuit north of Melbourne with a thoroughly professional display of driving in easily winning the 30 lap event.

'The race was wonderfully short', he said, 'and it was gratifying to get a win at the end of a disastrous season.'

★ ★ ★

When James reiterated that the 1979 season would be his final one in racing, Jackie Stewart speculated on the reasons for his pending retirement and assessed his chances with the Wolf team. He didn't think they were very good.

'I think James has lost a great deal of the spirit he once had. I think he still desires success, the financial rewards. But desire is different from spirit and that, I think, has gone. James has never been shy about saying he drives for the money and possibly that's why he decided on one more season rather than retiring last year.

'You would have likened James's rise to that of someone in the pop music industry rather than in sport. It was a very sudden rise to adulation and big money. The good life. It's hopelessly intoxicating and very confusing. Your entire world is fantasy and candy floss. There's no substance to it and unless you're very careful you get carried along on this magic carpet ride.

'But there's a side to this business which I think has gotten to James: driving a racing car endlessly, testing chassis, developing tyres, sitting in searing heat for an unacceptable number of hours, presentations, cocktail parties and dinners with people you don't want to be with. I think all this has troubled James, along with the pressures on his private life.

'He wants to do things his way, but unfortunately you can't. If you're going to stay in the sport, you have to compromise – or you can do what James says he is going to do, which is to retire soon. I don't believe he thinks it's worth all the compromise and I think he's making the right decision.

'Another thing is that James has become very acutely aware of the dangers of motor racing, which is one of the main reasons I retired when I did.'

In qualifying for the 1979 Argentine Grand Prix James found the new Wolf WR7 difficult to handle – 'suffering from a drastic oversteer problem which we cannot do anything about' – and on one attempted fast lap the car's nose section flew off, narrowly missing his head as it whipped over the top of the car. In the race he circulated near the back of the pack before dropping out with an electrical problem.

In Brazil, his qualifying efforts in the ill-handling Wolf were further hampered when the gear lever came off in his hand. He pulled out of the race on only the sixth lap, complaining of violent instability under braking caused, it was discovered, by the steering rack having come loose.

During the first qualifying session for the South African Grand Prix at Kyalami the Wolf's brakes failed while James was trying to slow for a corner. He managed to stop without hitting anything, but when Jackie Stewart, working as a TV commentator, talked to him he found James 'a truly frightened man'.

'He was physically shaking', Stewart remembers, 'which is something I had not previously ever seen in a racing driver. When I walked with him down the pit lane right after the incident he was clearly considerably affected by it and was physically incapable of holding the cigarette in his hand steady. I mean it was a major shake.'

Rob Walker, formerly a successful team entrant (notably with Stirling Moss as his driver) and then working with the Wolf team as an advisor and time keeper, also vividly remembers how frightened James was.

Walker, highly respected in the sport for his wisdom and consideration for drivers, recalls how it took a small sermon about religion to persuade James to continue.

'James was by this time getting to dislike motor racing and that day in South Africa we had a great deal of trouble getting him back in the car. In fact, I did it myself, by talking to him about religion. I said that God would protect him, whatever happened, and as long as he knew that it would be all right.

'I told him he should know there was just one Mind in charge of him and that Mind was not his, but from above. And as long as he put himself in the hands of that one Mind, it would be absolutely safe. After about a quarter of an hour or so he, rather unwillingly, got back into the car.'

James finished eighth in South Africa, but in the next race, at Long Beach in California, he stopped on the first lap with a broken drive shaft. He aborted the Spanish Grand Prix after 26 laps, saying that the Wolf's brakes were so poor he decided to call it a day.

At the Zolder circuit in Belgium, a new version of the Wolf, the WR8, seemed to revitalize James and he drove aggressively and well for three-quarters of the race. Suddenly, the Wolf went off the track, hit a barrier very hard and bounced back into the middle of the road.

'I don't know what it caused it', said James, 'but I think it might have been a tyre. For some time the steering had been getting heavier and heavier.'

James's seventh appearance in the race through the streets of Monaco ended when a drive shaft broke after only four laps. He parked the Wolf beside the Tip-Top bar, climbed out of the cockpit and – on 27 May 1979 – he walked away from motor racing.

☆　☆　☆

A month earlier James had informed John Hogan of his intention to get out as quickly as he could, but asked him to keep it quiet because he hadn't yet got the first payment of his retainer from Walter Wolf. After the payment was made James decided Monaco – where his Grand Prix career began in 1973 – would be his last race. In Belgium, two weeks before Monaco, he approached the journalist Eoin Young.

Young, worried that James was angry about something he'd written, was summoned into the Wolf motorhome in the paddock at Zolder where James sat alone in the back room, nervously puffing on a cigarette.

'The atmosphere was ominously quiet. He checked that the door was closed so no one could hear, then told me he was planning to announce his retirement at Monaco and would I help him put together his tell-the-world announcement.'

Young told James he wanted no part of it because his unexpected retirement was bound to turn into a media circus. But James persisted, telling Young that after working with him on the book *Against All Odds* he felt he could trust him. Young eventually agreed to give James advice, beginning with the suggestion that Monaco was the last place in the world to make public his momentous decision because the news would be buried in the hoopla surrounding the most glamorous Grand Prix.

That evening Young met James and Jane Birbeck in their hotel room near the circuit. 'Hottie was very good and made constructive suggestions, but James seemed confused more than anything else. He was worried that it was getting more dangerous, that he was having to try harder to do worse and he couldn't see an end to it. He wanted to retire, but he didn't want to retire.'

In mulling over the pros and cons James calculated that, without racing, his normal life expectancy might be 75 years. Thus, now at the age of 31, he could look forward to 44 more years. If he continued racing for another five years it would take up just over 10 percent of the rest of his life. But also if he kept on racing, the odds, he thought, were only about even that he would be around to enjoy the rest of his life.

Unlike many drivers he made no secret of the danger factor being uppermost in his mind. His honesty was much admired and in later years he always said 'self-preservation' was the reason he stopped racing.

'I reckoned I'd had a fair crack at the whip. I'd done six seasons in Formula 1 and I thought that was enough for anybody. I didn't want to end up in a box or permanently injured. The main thing was self-preservation.'

On 8 June 1979 he announced his retirement, after a relatively short career that brought him 10 wins and a World Driver's Championship in 92 Grands Prix.

'I wanted to have a really good final year', he said. 'It wasn't a matter of thinking about the Championship or anything. I wanted a good, competitive car with which to win some races. It's become clear to me that our car will never get there – it's nobody's fault in particular, just one of those things. If you haven't got an absolutely competitive car these days, you can forget it. And quite frankly, it's not worth the risk to life and limb to continue under those circumstances.'

Writing in *Autosport*, the editor Quentin Spurring summed up James's legacy as a racing driver: 'This country owes James much for the talent which enabled him to win the World Championship in 1976, nothing for the hooligan side of his nature which made him such a disappointing World Champion.

'It has been frustrating during the last couple of seasons to see him struggling both with nervous tension and with uncompetitive cars, but we will always remember his battles with Niki Lauda, which have been among the highlights of Grand Prix racing in the seventies, and his remarkable string of victories which snatched the title three years ago.'

James contemplated his uncertain future: 'I have made plenty of money out of racing. But it's not material achievement that's so important. What matters is achieving the way of life that suits you so you're happy. I think happiness is the really important thing.

'Racing has always been a means to an end for me – the chance for me to find material freedom in life. My ultimate goal, since I was 18, was to make a happy well-balanced life for myself. And that is what I look forward to now.

'It comes as a great relief to stop racing and I look forward to just relaxing for a while. Then again, as with anything in life, the pleasures and relaxations are short-lived because they're soon replaced by a rush of other worries and problems.

'There are highs and lows and dreads and fears however you live your life, whether it's a racing driver or a clerk in an office. But I look forward to life after racing. I'm now taking the big step into a world that is unknown to me.'

11

A TROUBLED MAN

1979–1989

'It was over. I felt no sadness at all, just immense relief', James said when he walked away from the racing career that had dominated his life for 12 years. In racing, it is said, the highs are higher and the lows are lower than in any other sport, and because he put so much emotion into it James had experienced those extremes more acutely than most. While he was happy to leave behind the negative aspects of his profession, the euphoria it had given him left a void that would be hard to fill.

'The kick was in the striving to achieve. I was born competitive and it is the challenge of trying to win that has always turned me on. It could have been anything. That it was racing was purely coincidental. But that's over now and I'm not sentimental. I don't dwell on the past. My goal is to make a mellow, well-balanced life. I need and am stimulated by ambition but at the moment I'm happy marking time – just keeping busy chasing my tail.'

He was still doing promotional work for his personal sponsors, Marlboro and Texaco, and for Olympus, the camera company which sponsored the Wolf team. He also looked forward to playing more golf and lowering his handicap of 11 closer to scratch, and to raising his squash game nearer to international standard. Though he didn't think he would ever be good enough to be a champion, his sporting pursuits would give him a reason to keep up his fitness.

Now he would also have a chance to devote more time to his business interests. He had a property trading company (offices, shops and factories) in partnership with Bubbles Horsley. Oscar's, his nightclub in

Marbella, was due to open soon and, with other partners, he invested in a 14 court squash complex in Munich.

He supposed he was a millionaire, but speculated it wasn't enough to keep him in the lap of luxury and he needed to keep his money working for him. What mattered was that he had created a certain amount of wealth and he didn't 'want to blow it.

'I also realize that I need responsibility. That's why Jane and I are trying to have our baby. Then I would have a real meaning to my life. Someone to take care of. We both love children and when we have a family, if the situation is right, we will probably get married.'

His rather surprising wish to marry, given his previous distaste for it, Jane feels was based partly on him wanting to gain approval from both her parents and his own. He got along very well with the Birbecks, particularly her father, and James also knew Sue and Wallis would prefer him not to be 'living in sin'. They announced their engagement in November of 1979, though neither the potential bride nor groom was completely convinced about their impending state of matrimony.

Jane: 'We both wondered "What's this all about?". It all seemed a bit grown up and we weren't sure we were ready for it. I thought I had commitment from him and was very happy just as we were. There were moments when I thought I'd quite like to get married, but it was never a pressing issue. Anyway, my parents gave us an engagement dinner and James started planning the wedding.'

While motherhood greatly appealed to her Jane was still trying to develop a career of her own in London and she wondered if commuting back and forth from Spain was a contributing factor to her problem of having frequent miscarriages. And, like James, she was beginning to realize that life as an expatriate in Spain had its shortcomings. In fact, they found their villa life boring.

They didn't get involved in the local social scene because, James said, everyone was a bit 'weird'. The problem, he thought, was that because the Costa del Sol was a tourist mecca there was a tendency for visitors to 'freak out' during their brief holidays, and many of those in the resident British community joined in – year round. 'In the end', he said, 'they just rot.'

Not all the 'gringos' became decadent. Another tax exile, the actor Sean Connery, was one of James's frequent golf partners and they also enjoyed each other's company over dinner. But Connery's life revolved around the movie business and he was often away for lengthy periods at film locations around the world.

And, soon after his retirement from racing, James came to the conclusion that his own frequent absences from Spain were what had made it palatable as a home base.

'He really hated it down there', John Hogan believes. 'I don't think he ever enjoyed one day in Spain, especially that semi-colonial, incestuous cocktail party circuit, which he despised. I remember he came into my London office one day and we went out to lunch. It was just pissing down with rain, yet he said, "It's a horrible day, but this is the best country in the world, even when it's like this". He was very relieved to come back home.'

★ ★ ★

The factors prompting James's decision to move back to Britain – in the spring of 1980 – included the Conservative government's tax cuts in the higher income bracket and his need to have a base closer to the business action. But the main reason was: 'Quite simply, I am English.

'I always intended to come back to Britain to live. It is my home, where my family and friends are, and I prefer the English culture and way of life. There are quite a few things wrong with the country but on the credit side, in terms of freedom and law and order and general pleasantness, it's the best place in the world to live.'

To participate fully in what his native land had to offer he thought he might like to lead the life of both a country squire and a man-about-town. In West London he bought and renovated a mews house (for a total cost of £100,000) in Baron's Court, near a squash and tennis club, and in North Buckinghamshire he paid £1 million for a 590 acre estate. In addition to its many acres of arable land, Park Farm included a six-bedroom farmhouse and extensive outbuildings, a two mile stretch of coarse fishing on the Great Ouse river and the lordship of the manors of Tyringham, Filgrave, Sherington and Emberton.

The idea of running Park Farm himself appealed to James and he thought about enrolling in an agricultural course at a college in Cirencester (where Bubbles Horsley had studied estate management) to learn modern farming techniques and the business of breeding cattle. He also thought the wild animals residing on his estate should be left alone.

If vermin had to be controlled it should be done in the most humane way possible, and he strongly disapproved of blood sports. The very thought of fox-hunting he found 'horrible', and he vowed not to allow it on his property. His 'Hunt Saboteur' philosophy put James at odds with his prospective father-in-law, Brigadier Nigel Birbeck, who was secretary of the Bicester and Warden Hill Hunt, part of which was not far from Park Farm.

James liked horses but didn't enjoy riding them and he wasn't about to 'leap onto one of them and lead an exclusively country life'. He hoped to commute between the farm, the house in London and the villa at San Pedro. There also remained the painful task of putting Oscar into quarantine for six months before the dog could become a British resident.

While the residential arrangements were proceeding apace, there were complications in the pending matter of the new Mr and Mrs James Hunt, beginning with the fact that Mr Hunt was still legally married to Mrs Richard Burton because Suzy's 'quickie' divorce from James, obtained in Haiti, was not recognized in Britain. A proper divorce, on the grounds of more than two years' separation, was soon arranged, but now, in a reversal of form from his first wedding, James was faced with a reluctant bride.

Jane had taken advantage of an opportunity to resume her career as a photographers' representative and opened Domino, an agency in London. She didn't particularly like the work and it wasn't long before she accepted an offer from her friend Mark McCormack (whom she was with when she first met James) to work in the London office of his International Management Group empire.

'Mark created an opening for me at IMG at about the same time as James had planned the wedding. And I said to James I'd rather have the wedding later because I'd just been given this job. And that was it really. It was finished. We never talked about marriage again. It was just sort of quietly ignored. We missed our moment.'

* * *

'Pig ignorant!' was what James thought of Jean Pierre Jarier's deliberate blocking of John Watson during the 1979 British Grand Prix. It was a typical Hunt opinion, typically expressed, only this time it was heard by several million TV viewers, since it was delivered while he was a guest commentator on the BBC coverage of the race.

The BBC was impressed with James's communications potential and offered him a contract to work on their television coverage of the 1980 Grand Prix races. He accepted, even though, 'I know that I will be working my backside off to pay the taxman – but I'd sooner do that than sit here getting frustrated'.

Part of his frustration was because he could have been racing again himself, instead of talking about those who did. For the 1980 season his old team, Marlboro McLaren, offered him £1.4 million to make a comeback, but he turned it down, though he hinted that he might more seriously consider returning if the sport was somehow made safer.

Formula 1 racing was suffering from his absence, and from Niki Lauda's. At the 1979 Canadian Grand Prix, four months after James left the sport, Niki followed him, saying his 'heart was not in it any more'and he retired to concentrate on building up his airline.

Thanks largely to the Lauda and Hunt rivalry in 1976 Formula 1 had built up a tremendous public following, but now, to the chagrin of the sponsors and those in the business of selling the sport as entertainment, there was a distinct shortage of superstars. This of course greatly increased the market value of colourful former World Champions.

For the 1982 season Bernie Ecclestone, owner of the Brabham team, tried to lure James back by offering him £2.6 million for 16 races worth of work. James gave it serious thought, then rejected it, saying: 'I have decided to carry on living the easy life. There is no point in risking your neck for money you don't need. You can't spend a fortune if you're dead'.

David Hunt thought the danger factor was one reason James refused to contribute financially to his racing career. After he left school James's youngest brother worked as a mechanic, a painter and decorator, a milkman and door-to-door pedlar of magazines to generate funds to go racing. He eventually progressed as far as Formula 3000 before giving up on the sport, mainly because of lack of funds.

'James was a funny kettle of fish', David thought, but he understood why he wouldn't give him any money. 'It's not because he doesn't want me to race, but if he encouraged me in that way and I got killed, he would feel responsible.'

But James also felt anyone who wanted to go racing should have to work as hard as he had, including any son of his own. 'I would discourage him because if he was going to be any good he would do it in spite of anything I said, and if I managed to put him off he wouldn't have been any good anyway. The first thing you need is massive motivation from within. You'll never be any good at anything unless you have that.'

* * *

In 1980 James very nearly did accept a one-off opportunity to race, in the United States West Grand Prix at Long Beach. The McLaren team's new young driver Alain Prost (who eventually scored the most wins in Formula 1 history) injured his wrist, and John Hogan invited James to fill the vacancy. James, only half joking, asked for $1 million for the weekend. Marlboro responded with less than half that, but the negotiations ended when James hurt his knee while skiing.

James thought the Long Beach circuit would be safe enough for a single outing, but in that race his old rival, Clay Regazzoni, crashed into a concrete wall and received injuries that left him permanently paralysed from the waist down.

Ten years later, when he was in financial trouble and Formula 1 racing had become much safer, James again considered a comeback. A few months earlier he had tested a Williams car at the Paul Ricard circuit, ostensibly to see what the modern cars were like, but also with a view to testing himself. He was several seconds off the pace, but still felt he could work himself back into racing shape.

He tried to persuade John Hogan to endorse his comeback, presenting him with bank statements to prove how broke he was. In return, Hogan wrote James a long letter which said, in essence, 'Forget it. You're absolutely mad!'.

While Hogan in this case thought James's sagging fortunes had overpowered his reason he appreciated how astute he was in evaluating the capabilities of other drivers, beginning with Niki Lauda. In 1981 Niki approached Hogan about making a comeback. Lauda Air had run short of money and Niki wanted to return to his old profession to bolster his airline's dwindling resources. No retired driver had ever made a successful return to Formula 1 and Hogan had misgivings that Niki was up to it.

'So I went to James and asked his opinion. He said, "Look, if you're a good tennis player or a good golf player you always hit the ball in the same way. The most important thing is do you want to do it? And Niki being Niki, if he says that he wants to race it's because he wants to do it. Because that's the sort of animal he is". So on the strength of that I said, "Right, let's have Niki back".'

Hogan's investment – and James's assessment – paid off handsomely for Marlboro McLaren. In the next four seasons Niki won eight Grands Prix and the 1984 World Championship (his third) before finally hanging up his helmet for good a year later.

Impressed with James's foresight and insight John Hogan hired him as an adviser and tutor to young, up-and-coming Marlboro-sponsored drivers (James also privately tutored the Swedish driver Thomas Kaiser), instructing them not only in driving technique but in tactics and the mental approach to racing.

He proved to be an excellent teacher and took a keen personal interest in his pupils, often inviting them to his home. One of his most successful graduates was the Finnish driver Mika Häkkinen, who went on to race for the Marlboro McLaren team. Hakkinen talked to James not only about motor racing 'but about life in general. James was a person who went through lots of different things in his racing career and his life. He had his own style and he always lived flat out. I liked him a lot and he was a very great help to me'.

John Hogan: 'James was the only driver I've ever seen who had the vaguest idea about what it actually takes to be a racing driver. Others, like Niki, could say so and so might be good. But they couldn't tell you why. James's big strength was that he could articulate the game. More than anyone James had that ability to articulate and communicate, That's why he was such an outstanding TV commentator'.

Jonathan Martin, who became head of BBC television sport, created the BBC's *Grand Prix* format in the late 1970s and was producing the program when James was still racing. As a driver to be interviewed Martin found him to be charismatic, very opinionated and clearly able to communicate his opinions, though he could sometimes be brusque. He always spoke his mind and did so with a natural broadcaster's voice: deep and authoritative, well modulated and toned. These qualities would be ideal for a TV commentator, and Martin hired James, though he had some reservations.

'One of my concerns was whether James would play around with it for a while or actually settle down and do it properly. The problem in those early days was convincing him of all the disciplines that were required. I had to nudge him from time to time and say, "We need to be sure that you're putting a bit more homework into it". He sometimes tested the people around him in the broadcast team and it was frustrating for those who had different ways of working.'

One of James's most disconcerting habits was showing up in the broadcast booth at the last minute. Martin thinks he did it deliberately. 'He was a guy that lived on adrenaline and the thing about broadcasting that really attracted him, apart from enjoying talking about the sport he'd lived with, was that it does have its pressures. I think he loved the tightrope nature of live broadcasting, slipping into the commentary box just before the start of a race, when the mouth goes dry and the palms start to get wet and it's pressure time.

'The irony of his partnership with Murray Walker was that on the air James was the audience's navigator. If you can imagine the two of them in a car, Murray – the hyperbolic enthusiast – was doing the driving, keeping it strictly on the road, while James was discussing the tactics and strategy around the course in his laid back way – lying back, as it were – quite often literally!'.

Murray Walker's earliest memories of his broadcasting partner-to-be were typified by what he had seen while doing the television commentary of the Crystal Palace Formula 3 race where another driver was felled by a blow from Hunt The Shunt. 'James Hunt was, in my eyes the archetypical, loud-mouthed, totally irresponsible, Hooray Henry. It was a matter of enormous surprise to me that this rather erratic, emotional and violent Formula 3 driver actually did well in Formula 1 racing. It exploded all my theories and beliefs about what ought to happen!

'When Jonathan Martin told me there were going to be two *Grand Prix* commentators and the other one was going to be James Hunt my immediate reaction was a mixture of concern and irritation. I wondered if the BBC was trying to ease me out of my job. I had been doing it alone, quite happily, for two years and I didn't want somebody else horning in on the act. Particularly some bloody Grand Prix driver who knew nothing about commentating, and particularly James Hunt.'

Murray Walker certainly knew what he was talking about when it came to motor sport, having been 'born into it' in 1923. His father Graham was a successful motorcycle racer, winning the European Championship in 1928, and when he retired he became the motorcycle racing commentator for BBC radio. Murray, who was given a motorcycle of his own at the age of 14, competed regularly and won a gold medal in a six-day international motorcycle trial in 1949. In the same year he did his first BBC radio commentary, filling in for his father at a hill climb in Worcestershire.

Murray went to Sandhurst, served in the Royal Scots Greys during the invasion of Normandy, finished the war as a Captain and then had a highly successful career in advertising, helping build up a small London-based agency into a thriving enterprise with 54 offices around the world.

But motor sport commentating remained his passion. After taking over from his father as the BBC voice of motorcycle racing, he began covering various forms of car racing on radio, then television. He was delighted when BBC TV began extensive coverage of Formula 1 racing in 1978, and worked very hard at it.

'I was doing my best to do a professional, authoritative and informative job and now here I was lumbered with this irresponsible bloke James Hunt, who seemed totally lacking in application. My low opinion of him was confirmed when he joined us.'

Murray prided himself in being a 'team' player, travelling to the races with the BBC producer, engineer and cameraman, staying with them at the same hotels and spending hours doing research and planning strategy in the three days leading up to a Grand Prix. But James always made his own travel arrangements and his whereabouts were often a mystery; indeed there were doubts on many occasions that he would show up at all.

Murray: 'In fact, it became something of a joke: "Has anybody seen James?". His modus operandi was to arrive in the commentary box – appearing for the first time that weekend – five minutes before the start of the race, if that. And as soon as the chequered flag appeared – as though he'd got a trigger-operated spring up his ass and he pressed some secret control – he was immediately vertical, shot out of the box and was gone'.

'Right then Murray. Who's on pole?', was a typical greeting James gave when he sauntered into the commentary booth. Murray, having laboriously compiled reference notes on all the drivers and cars, was infuriated at James's lack of preparation and refused to enlighten him. 'My attitude was that I had sweated blood to produce these itemized details which I can refer to at a moment's notice and I'm damned if I'm going to let this lazy interloper benefit from all my hard work.'

Murray had got his first taste of what he was in for when, as a dress rehearsal for their Grand Prix partnership, they covered a Formula 5000 race at Silverstone in the spring of 1980. James's very limited contributions were made from the floor of the commentary booth, where he lay watching a TV monitor with his leg, injured in a skiing accident, in a plaster cast. When the rather boring race was over Murray passed him the microphone for a final comment and he replied, 'What a load of rubbish!'.

James's 'laid back' approach was in stark contrast to Murray's constant mobility while he was commentating. He remained standing throughout the race, moving around, jumping up and down, pointing at the TV monitor and sounding, as Clive James (the writer and television personality) put it, 'as if his trousers were on fire'.

They shared a single microphone, to avoid speaking over each other, but Murray found that James, when he first came, 'sat there like a sullen lump and didn't actually say anything unless I physically put my hand on his shoulder and asked him what he thought. He very seldom took the initiative to speak, perhaps because he thought, 'This bugger talks too bloody much anyway!'.

The journalist Mike Doodson, who sat between them in the BBC commentary booth for 13 years, keeping a lap chart of the race and acting as their spotter, remembers how James, at first, was sometimes even unsure of the names of certain drivers. For several races he referred to the Austrian driver Gerhard Berger as 'Helmut' or 'Jochen'. Another source of concern, Doodson recalls, was James's tendency to drink on the job in the early days. 'This of course really got up Murray's nose, because there's no cleaner living, harder working, more conscientious man than Murray Walker.'

For his first Grand Prix commentary, at Monaco in 1980, James arrived in the booth in the nick of time, clad in a dirty white T-shirt and shorts, shoeless and with his leg still encased in plaster. He planted the injured limb in Murray's lap and proceeded to consume two bottles of rosé during the broadcast.

'Like a spare prick at a wedding', was the way James described how uncomfortable he felt returning to the Grand Prix scene as a commentator. 'What really compounded it and made it particularly unpleasant was that people, especially the general public, were still treating me like a driver. This was specifically one of the things I was trying to get away from. So there I was, walking back into the fire, having just got out of the frying pan.'

To help douse the flames he drank and socialized during lengthy pre-race lunches at his old 'hibernation point', the Marlboro motorhome. He was bored by the atmosphere in the rest of the paddock and seldom visited the pits. 'The only reason I ever walked up and down the pit lane when I was a driver was to look at the crumpet. But now, with the modern pass system, there aren't any women around and you have to go outside. Pity, that.'

John Watson, who also became a Grand Prix commentator after he retired from driving, identifies with the 'spare prick at a wedding' syndrome. 'The first time I walked into the paddock after I stopped driving I thought I was a leper. Formula 1 is like a little clique, a private club, and there is an elitism about wearing a driving suit or a team uniform or becoming part of the media contingent. Until you're identified and accepted as a member of this society you feel very uncomfortable, like a useless hanger-on.'

Mike Doodson points out another aspect of the plight of a former driver who is forced to play a secondary role when they return to the scene of their former glories. 'When top sportsmen in any field have to stop what they have done so well they are made acutely aware of the fact that they're over the hill and going down the other side fast. It must be pretty difficult in motor racing to come back and see other people doing the thing you did so supremely well.

'I think in James's case his difficulty in adjusting was nothing more complicated than the fact that he had been on the other side of the fence. And to come to our side of the fence was a big let-down. In income. In prestige. In everything.'

James also had trouble adapting to the role of a businessman, and his farming plans fizzled out. After selling off some of his Park Farm acreage he sold the remainder of the estate for slightly more than the £1 million he paid for it. He sold his share in the Munich squash club and, because he no longer lived in Spain, he eventually severed his connections with Oscar's, the nightclub.

The novelty of being a retired racing driver soon wore off. James began to experience withdrawal symptoms and he became increasingly restless. 'Nothing to do made me very frustrated. It's not easy for a man of my energetic disposition to sit around twiddling my thumbs.'

Unfortunately, one of the first ways he chose to channel his energies – skiing, which he had always avoided during his driving years – resulted in a crippling injury – much worse than any he had while racing – that left him with even more time on his hands and great pain which he found difficult to endure.

In March of 1980, just before he was due to end his tedious tax exile, James went on a skiing holiday at Verbier in Switzerland. He was a guest of a Marlboro-sponsored team of acrobatic skiers called the 'Marlboro Hot Dog Ski Team'. After enjoying 'a major lunch' with the team, James joined them on the slopes and promptly 'fell over and did myself a major mischief'.

The injury, detached ligaments in his left knee, was at first not painful because he was still under the influence of his lunchtime 'anaesthetic', but it soon became 'torture'. He was unprepared for the 'agonizing' pain following the operation in which a team of doctors knitted his knee ligaments back together. He lay immobilized in hospital for several weeks and spent two and a half months with his leg in a full-length plaster cast. When the cast was removed his leg wouldn't bend beyond 90 degrees and he endured seven months of 'excruciating' physiotherapy to get his leg back into proper working order.

In his haste to get back to running, golfing and playing squash and tennis, he rushed the rehabilitation process, tried to do too much too soon and had to go back into the hospital for yet another operation. The re-injury, which occurred when he was with Jane at their Spanish villa, was a shattering experience.

He went for a week without sleep, tossing and turning all night and crawling from one end of the bed to the other in a futile attempt to find relief. During the day he stared blankly at the television set, but that distraction was also unsuccessful. He tried pain-relieving prescriptions and sleeping potions – 'every conceivable drug' – but none of them worked and he thought 'I would go out of my head.

'Poor Jane. My brain became so addled with pain I couldn't talk to her. But as much as she wanted to help there wasn't much she could do. An ordeal of pain is something very personal. It has to be seen through alone.'

Jane thinks the crisis of his skiing accident was a turning point in his life, sending James, and their relationship, into a downward spiral. The enforced immobility meant he couldn't work off his frustrations physically, and the insomnia that afflicted him for the rest of his life set in. He started going on drinking binges and smoking dope more heavily and he withdrew into himself.

They communicated easily about every conceivable subject (including the female reproductive system, which he studied to try to help Jane conceive), but James had difficulty letting himself go to the point of discussing his innermost feelings. It was not in his nature to ask for help to overcome a personal problem. His self-reliance was so highly developed that he had never learned how to confide in others or to really 'need' anyone.

Jane became greatly distressed by his suffering and at her inability to help him. In her frustration she turned to his ways of escape and also began drinking and smoking more than she should have. James, she thought, could have straightened himself out – though he was always 'potentially dodgy on booze' – but she worried about her own 'addictive personality' and their increasingly 'debauched life. I felt he was just pulling me down.

'I remember I didn't go to see him in the hospital as often as I should have. I was terribly selfish. When he needed me I really wasn't there for him because I was trying so hard to straighten myself out. We were still very close – there were moments when we were incredibly close – but I just thought that something went out of our relationship after that.'

At the end of August 1980, Jane threw a surprise birthday party for James – he was 33 – at their London mews house, but their domestic situation was far from blissful. Jane had another miscarriage and 'At Christmas-time', she said, 'we couldn't have been more depressed. The whole of 1980 was a wretched year'.

Their next year was worse, and before it was over they had gone their separate ways.

Some of their friends think Jane and James might have stayed together if they had been able to have a child, but she thinks it would only have prolonged their inevitable parting. As his leg injury healed James became more distant and Jane began to sense he was looking for a way out. She was by now well aware of his roving eye, the factor that ultimately caused them to end their relationship, but she was unprepared for the despair he felt over his *bête noir*.

One evening she returned to their London home to find James in tears. He was tormented by feelings of guilt caused by his lust for other women. He confessed the full extent of his unfaithfulness, that it was unfair to her and that for her sake they couldn't remain a couple. It wasn't that he was bored with her, but that his desire for other women was insatiable and uncontrollable. He held Jane in his arms and they both wept.

'It was a pretty horrible time and I think I fell apart for a few days. But there was no acrimony and we were both very loving towards each other. We planned how to help each other through the transition. It was very bittersweet.'

James insisted that they visit her parents to break the news gently to them, and he decided to bring in Bubbles Horsley to act as a mediator to make a financial settlement with Jane. The three of them sat around a table with a bottle of wine. 'We thought it was going to take hours, but it was all over in five minutes. It was very amicable. James gave me the house in London and it was agreed he would give me an allowance for three months. Then, at the end of the meeting, he suddenly decided he was going to make the allowance for six months.'

Later, James also invested in 'Bodys', an exercise club Jane opened in Chelsea, and while she was setting it up they had a brief reconciliation. 'James came around to the house one night and said he wanted to get back together again. But even when he was saying it I think he knew, we both knew, that it wouldn't work. But he moved back in, for about six weeks, and then one night he just didn't come back.'

They had a fight over that, but soon patched up their differences and remained friends and confidantes. James asked Jane's advice about the large house he eventually bought in Wimbledon and about the woman who would share it with him as his wife and become the mother of his children.

⋆ ⋆ ⋆

Sarah Lomax, then 24, met James in September of 1982, while she was on a Spanish holiday with some girlfriends who immediately recognized the famous racing driver. Sarah knew nothing about motor racing but was flattered when James paid more attention to her than any of the others at the beach party they attended.

When she came back to England she was surprised when James called her up and invited her out, and they dated frequently that winter. She was even more impressed when she went to America, where she worked for an interior decorating firm in Washington DC, and James flew over to spend weekends with her.

'I was smitten, totally smitten, by James. I couldn't believe he was interested in me. I remember somebody said "He's a celebrity and he'll soon drop you". But he appeared to be incredibly keen. He wrote me wonderful letters and I wrote him back and he kept them. Then he showed them to me with all the spelling corrections!'.

In Washington Sarah had a seven mile trip to work each day, involving three bus routes, and James told her he would give her a present to solve her transportation problems. Given his automotive background Sarah looked forward to travelling in style. Her heart sank when James gave her a bicycle and helmet.

On his third visit to Washington she accepted James's invitation to come and live with him at his home in Wimbledon. They were married on 17 December 1983, in a registry office at Marlborough, Wiltshire. James showed up several minutes late and the proceedings were further delayed while his brother Peter dashed out to a local shop to buy him a tie.

Sarah grew up in an old rectory in a pretty Wiltshire village and seemed to have an idyllic country childhood. Her father Ian Lomax was a master of foxhounds and captain of the county cricket club and her mother, Rosemary, rode point-to-point and trained race horses. Sarah, when she was 14, was devastated by their unexpected divorce.

The Lomax's adventurous daughter – 'I actually quite liked scaring myself' – rode racehorses when her young girlfriends were still on ponies. She was not a particularly good student at boarding school in Great Malvern and achieved success in a bookkeeping course at secretarial college by stealing a look at the exam paper beforehand. She was a debutante for a month, ran off to Corfu for a while, and worked in pubs here and there. But it was all innocent fun and she was a country girl at heart.

'All I wanted to do when I was a kid to get married and look after my man. And this is what James thought he wanted, the normality of a family home. I was well organized and practical. He loved the home I kept. He loved my cooking. I think he couldn't believe his luck when he met me: a country girl who could keep a great home. I think James thought I could give him security and stability.

'But he was also a non-conformist. So he wanted to party. I could party with him. I could be outrageous. We were both certainly outrageous. We were total soul-mates. I was in love with him. We laughed and we had a really wonderful time. And James said he married a wild, drug-taking sex maniac.'

They called each other 'Beast'. For them, it was a term of passionate endearment, but some of their friends thought that one of the beasts should be less wild, to be able to look after the other.

Their noisy parties at the rambling, five bedroom 1930s home on the edge of Wimbledon Common often went on until dawn. The extensive renovations and additions at the house included in the spacious garden a large jacuzzi, where it was not unknown for naked bathers to spill out of the pool and cavort on the lawn.

When visitors arrived at the Hunt home they were greeted by Winston, a rather eccentric Jamaican man who called James 'Boss'. They met when Winston, then a taxi driver, was ferrying James to an appointment for which he was late. When James urged him to speed up Winston was apprehended by the traffic police and lost his driving licence. James felt responsible and hired him to work as a gardener, chauffeur, chef and general factotum, and he became a fixture in the household.

Winston came to the house each weekday, and when there were no pressing tasks to be performed – which was often the case – he would take what James – never a stern taskmaster – called 'Jamaican PT', which meant he was asleep upstairs. Winston was fiercely loyal to his 'Boss' and guarded his privacy zealously. On the numerous occasions when sensation-seeking journalists would arrive unannounced Winston would bar the door.

While James was no longer performing on the world stage his private life was still of great interest to the popular press. Frequent newspaper stories kept readers up to date with the latest developments in the increasingly eccentric Hunt household and the menagerie therein.

Besides Oscar, his faithful Alsatian, James had Humbert, an African Grey parrot that had been in the Hunt family for many years. Like Oscar, Humbert loved James and would dance on his perch in the living room whenever his master appeared. But he was less warmly disposed to others and had a rather rude vocabulary, characteristics which, according to the tabloids, nipped a promising stage career in the bud.

It was reported that after successfully auditioning for a role in a Christmas production of *Treasure Island* at the Mermaid theatre Humbert disgraced himself in rehearsals. Instead of squawking the required lines 'Pieces of eight! Pieces of eight!', Humbert shrieked 'Shut up! Shut up!', and other language deemed unsuitable for a family audience. Finally, after biting a piece out of the ear of the actor playing Long John Silver and repeatedly soiling his costume, Humbert was judged to be temperamentally unsuited for the role and was sacked and returned home in disgrace.

Out in the garden James had a golf net where he practised his swing. Unable to run, or play as much squash or tennis after his knee injury, he had taken up golf on almost a daily basis and, as was his wont, became fanatical about it. 'In fact', says Bubbles Horsley, 'he used to bore one rigid, ringing you up and telling you how he played the third hole at Sunningdale Golf Club, even though you knew nothing about that course. But he was enjoying himself then, having retired in one piece and with the money to spend on his freedom.'

In the new games room at his home James had installed a tournament-sized table for his other new passion: snooker. He played with his friends and neighbours for hours, often for money. 'He played a wicked game', his friend Chris Marshall recalls, 'and it used to go on until the early hours of the morning. We drank wine or whatever was available. By the end we'd be playing for double or nothing and it used to be absolutely hilarious.

'But you had to be careful going around to his house because you knew the evening was going to be a humdinger and the next day was going to be a complete write-off. His life was fairly wild and I got the feeling that maybe James was a little bit lost.'

★ ★ ★

Lost on Murray Walker were the reasons for his BBC commentating partner's apparent lack of interest in his work. James still showed nothing like the dedication he lavished on his golf and snooker hobbies – or his partying.

It was after a particularly wild birthday party that James missed his only Grand Prix, in Belgium. He was in the neighbourhood, he said – in a phone call to the BBC crew at the circuit, 20 minutes before the end of the race – but had become stricken by food poisoning after over-indulging in some rich Belgian pâté the previous evening. Presumably then, the disbelievers said, the two young ladies seen entering his hotel room that night were nurses.

There were other near misses at several races – when he forgot to set his alarm clock, missed the channel ferry, was the victim of a delayed flight, and so on – and Murray Walker found his colleague's irresponsibility exasperating. 'My attitude was that I was extremely lucky to be in the situation where literally millions of people worldwide were depending on me – depending on us – to inform them entertainingly and excitingly about the thing that was dearest to their hearts. And I deeply resented the fact that this chap was not putting his all into it.

'I don't want to give the impression that we couldn't stand the sight of each other. James always had enormous charm. There was no animosity. We always got on. But what I didn't do in the beginning was respect him.'

One of the things that most maddened Murray, when James eventually did begin to make a greater contribution to the commentary, was his penchant for 'rubbishing' certain drivers. Murray thinks it was partly due to his naturally provocative nature – he loved to wind people up – and partly because James thought it was his role to be the outspoken expert.

But Murray, and many others, often felt his pointed criticisms were over-stated – and repeatedly over-stated – and quite often unfair. It was also frequently a case of the pot calling the kettle black. Murray remembers thinking of reminding James that some of the things he did in his driving career were no better, and sometimes much worse, than anything done by the drivers he chose to disparage in his commentary.

Murray only had to mention a name on James's 'hate' list, hand him the microphone and 'he would immediately launch into a searing attack on the laziness, inadequacies, character defects, or whatever, and he would go on and bloody on about his point of view'.

Among his favourite targets were veteran drivers he thought weren't trying hard enough. Of the Brazilian driver Nelson Piquet he said, 'The problem with Piquet is that he's never grown up. He's only racing for the money to keep his 45 metre yacht afloat. What I can't understand is why he doesn't drive faster just out of self-respect'.

Piquet was one of the few drivers to challenge James about his TV comments: 'And that', said James, 'was just Piquet being childish about my calling him childish. One would expect it from him'.

In James's view, Alessandro Nannini lacked brainpower behind the wheel; Mauricio Gugelmin was slow in all the lesser formulae, even slower in Formula 1 and had no reason to be there; René Arnoux was a menace to other drivers, Andrea de Cesaris was an embarrassment to himself, his team and the sport; Alain Prost's motivation was suspect; Nigel Mansell (the next English World Champion after James) made silly mistakes, defamed the office of World Champion by not staying in

Formula 1 to defend his title; and so on.

Many thought he went overboard with his criticism of Riccardo Patrese, the driver involved with James in the Ronnie Peterson accident. James would go on about how slow Patrese was, how badly he was driving, how many accidents he was having and that he should be pensioned off to make way for new talent.

When asked to defend his opinions James would go to elaborate lengths to prove he was right. In the case of Patrese he spent hours poring over race reports and lap times, performing mathematical calculations which showed that Patrese was 0.94 seconds slower than his team-mate in one season, then 1.14 seconds slower the next year.

On television, to avoid having James go off on such tangents, and getting into an argument with him, Murray would try to obliquely gloss over his more controversial statements. But it irritated him that people might think him a 'wimp' for not standing up to James.

In the case of Patrese, Murray would get a form of revenge and help tip the balance of power by throwing in such lines as, 'Well, meanwhile, on lap 54, Riccardo Patrese – who has won six Grands Prix, scored eight pole positions and finished second and third in the World Championship – has moved up to fourth place'.

James didn't think he was being unduly controversial, though he agreed his thoughts were strongly delivered. 'I simply describe things as I see them. If someone makes a cockup, then I say it's a cockup, rather than watering it down.

'It's as if I'm sitting at home with my mates, watching the Grand Prix on the telly. All I'm doing is colouring it in for them because I can see things they might not pick up.'

Regarding his 'mate' on the BBC, James was quick to defend Murray when he was criticized by viewers, mostly for getting drivers mixed up and for becoming overly excited during a race. 'Look, it's bloody difficult to get it right. I certainly get confused from time to time. It's not easy. Why people insist on criticizing him I don't know. The trouble is all Murray ever hears in this country is criticism. He's a tremendous enthusiast and he does a hell of a lot for the image of the sport.'

James, like most of the Formula 1 media corps, tended to praise drivers he liked personally, even though he had himself been a victim of this kind of selective discrimination, which sometimes paid more due to character than performance. He preferred drivers with a sense of humour and a positive attitude, like the ever-smiling Johnny Herbert and the happy-go-lucky Gerhard Berger. Stefano Modena (whom he tutored for Marlboro) James thought 'an absolutely charming guy', though Modena never fulfilled his promise as a driver.

But James could change his mind about a driver, as he did with Ayrton Senna. When the hugely talented Brazilian first came to Formula 1, James, like many others, roundly criticized him for preventing another driver from joining his team. James was 'horrified and disgusted, to put it mildly'. He thought Senna had 'a strange personality'. In one race Senna 'broke every rule of safety and common sense'. In another he 'did a spectacularly stupid thing'.

But on another occasion James in his commentary blamed Senna for causing an accident, then reviewed the incident at home on tape and decided the blame had been misplaced. 'So I sought out Senna when I got to the next race, told him I had wronged him and that I would not only apologize to him personally but also put the record straight on the air, which I did.'

Senna, who became one of the greatest Formula 1 drivers before he was killed in 1994, was disliked by many of the journalists, and consequently the fans, because of his perceived arrogance and ruthlessness. A deeply sensitive man, Senna shut himself off from most of the press, but in James he found a kindred spirit and he came to rely on him for advice and support. At one stage of his career, when Senna was disillusioned and thinking of retiring, James helped convince him to stay in Formula 1.

'I considered James a friend. I always had a tremendously good time with him. He was good to talk to and wouldn't give you any rubbish. He would always tell you the truth – his truth. I respected his opinions and sometimes he would convince me I was wrong. I would accept it, but I could also convince him that perhaps he didn't do justice to me and he would accept that too. That was his great strength.

'James was a very special man, by his own character and personality. He was always capable of embarrassing somebody. But I liked him the way he was.'

☆   ☆   ☆

James embarrassed a lot of people shortly after he became a father for the first time. On 12 September 1985, Sarah gave birth to Tom, prematurely, at St Theresa's hospital in Wimbledon.

'I am jolly pleased with him', said James of his 5½ pound son. 'I didn't mind a boy or a girl but Sarah is very pleased at having a boy. But it's a daunting prospect. I have lived 37 years without responsibility.'

He committed an act of considerable irresponsibility a few weeks later, on a British Airways flight to the Australian Grand Prix. As an airline official put it: 'Mr Hunt had problems controlling his bodily functions during the flight'. James, after consuming as much free beer as he felt it would take to make the long journey tolerable, slumped back in his seat and soon dozed off. Inevitably, he felt an urgent call of nature and, sleepily, he arose and wandered off down the aisle in search of a toilet. But they were all engaged and James, unable to contain himself, sought relief against the curtain separating the First and Club Class sections of the Boeing 747.

In his 'Hunt For Relief', as the tabloid press reported it, he splashed the television personality Esther Rantzen and her little daughter. Ms Rantzen later denied she 'saw, heard or felt anything', but the 'drunken shame of the speed ace', his 'Going on the Boeing', created a flood of negative publicity. A steady stream of reporters appeared on his doorstep when James returned home and Winston had to do double duty fending them off.

James's excuse for the airborne incident was that he was sleepwalking, which he tended to do, especially when he was drunk. His friends thought that, besides taking on too much beer during the flight, he might also have had a tab of acid or a dose of 'Night Nurse', his preferred sleeping potion.

Some friends thought the incident was funny, but Bubbles Horsley (godparent to Tom Hunt) was not amused. In their relationship there always remained an element of team manager and driver, or schoolmaster and schoolboy, and James tended to behave himself in Bubbles' company.

'I thought that business on the aeroplane was very sad', Bubbles remembers. 'He made the rather half-hearted excuse about sleepwalking, but I said, "Well you were sleepwalking because you were behaving like an asshole. And you know you do that and you shouldn't have done it on the aeroplane. So don't go making half-baked excuses. If you want to go and piss in the cupboards at home, that's another matter".

'And James took my point. He was contrite and said, "You're absolutely right". I think he was drinking more and going on benders then because the marriage was going wrong.'

* * *

During her confinement in hospital before she had Tom, Sarah was full of apprehension about the pain of childbirth and whether she would be able to love her baby. She was also extremely upset by rumours that her wayward husband was seeing other women.

To calm her fears, James, despite the disapproval of the nuns at St Theresa's, brought an elaborate music system into the hospital ward. During his visits to his wife's bedside, until the nuns took it away from him, he also made use of the gas which had been provided to soothe Sarah's discomfort. 'And when I asked James about whether I could love my baby he said, "Don't worry Beast. God is a great designer and you will love that little thing when it was born". And he was so right.

'By the time the nine months had gone by and I'd gone through the process of giving birth I was half-way changed to this new person. But James wasn't changed, and that's when things started to go wrong.

'He would be partying and I would be panicking, worrying about getting up to breastfeed at four in the morning. I would say we can't party but he would say, "Don't be silly Beast. Of course we can". But I couldn't do it. I just wanted to look after my babies.'

Little Tom was 22 months old when his brother, Freddie Alexander (Alexander Hesketh, then Government Whip in the House of Lords, was a godparent), was born at Mount Alvernia hospital in Guildford.

In that autumn of 1987 James celebrated his 40th birthday in grand style, presiding over a lavish gathering at the Wimbledon house, where the guests included his parents, several of his brothers and sisters, many friends and assorted celebrities. It was a fancy dress party on the theme of 'Bird or Beast', and the exuberant host pranced around in a kilt, under which he wore nothing but a three-foot-long salami sausage. His costume, James explained, was a representation of the famous racehorse Northern Dancer, now retired and put out to stud. Envious of that position James said that in another life he would like to have been a stud and receive $1 million each time he covered a mare.

Late the next day, when he arose and discovered that Oscar had consumed half the sausage, James said, 'It's just as well I wasn't still wearing it!'.

At the birthday party Sarah was dressed as a budgerigar, wearing a feathery wig and beak, in honour of the hobby which James, having dabbled in it as a schoolboy, had now taken up in earnest.

A large (26 x 12 foot) aviary, fully fitted and insulated and equipped with 30 wire breeding cages, was built in the garden, and there, after starting with about 30 budgies, James began breeding top-quality exhibition birds. His exotic stock, which eventually reached 150 birds (some of them worth several thousand pounds), included sky blue and green Normals, brown-winged Cinammons, Opalines and Spangles.

'I like them because they are decorative and make a cheerful sound', he said. But he was also very serious about showing his budgies and soon the aviary was adorned with prize-winning rosettes and trophies collected from exhibitions around the country.

To bring his birds to the shows he acquired a 1957 Austin A35 van for the bargain price of £900. His other transport was a venerable 6.9 litre Mercedes saloon, which he treated as utilitarian vehicle for ferrying passengers around. But he had great affection for his little van – 'It really is a jolly good car and I'm very attached to it' – not only because it gave 35 miles to the gallon of petrol but because its limited performance meant he could 'chuck it about and drive it right on the limit without breaking the law'.

He did break the law on one of his budgerigar expeditions, to Doncaster in South Yorkshire, though his offence wasn't a traffic infraction. One of his birds won top prize at a show. and James, in his jeans, decided to go out on the town and celebrate. When the doorman at a nightclub informed James that he was not suitably attired there was a scuffle and some hot coffee was thrown in the doorman's face.

Two policemen witnessed the incident and charged James with assault and drunkenness and carted him off to jail. He was released after two hours and bailed to appear in court. But the charges were later dropped and James returned to the club and apologized to the doorman.

At home James became increasingly introverted, uncommunicative and reclusive. He gave up golf and spent more and more of his time in the aviary tending his budgies. While the parties continued he would often leave the guests to Sarah and closet himself in the aviary for hours on end.

It became obvious that James was very troubled, but only Sarah and his closest friends knew the full extent of the anguish and despair James suffered during his bouts with what he called his 'Dippers'.

'Black Dog' was the term Winston Churchill used for the recurring depressions which afflicted him throughout his life. Bubbles Horsley thinks James was 'born with a black dog on his shoulder. His racing pushed the dog away far enough so that it was no longer visible. But underneath that wonderful *joie de vivre*, the laughter and enjoying life, he was given to black moods. He was fearful of them and maybe it was that fear that drove him on. Perhaps without it he would never have been World Champion.

'And I think after the initial "honeymoon" of retirement from racing the black dog came and sat on his shoulder and wouldn't go away. So he became more fearful and sought distraction in various ways, through sex and drink and drugs and rock and roll, as it were.'

Bubbles and other friends tried to help James but couldn't. James thought he could work it out himself. But eventually he sought professional help and after one visit to a psychiatrist James told a friend that the psychiatrist said he was 'a bit of a cold fish'.

Other male friends noted that James shied away from physical contact: he never liked shaking hands, and if he fell while skiing he would flinch when they tried to help him up. James was more open with his women friends, but even they were unable to penetrate the barriers he now placed around his feelings.

Jane Birbeck heard about his trouble and invited him out to lunch to see if she could help. She was shocked by his appearance. 'He looked like death warmed over, wearing the dirtiest jeans you've ever seen and I swear his teeth hadn't been cleaned for a week. His tension was so tangible. He was just rigid with depression. It was overwhelming.'

At home Sarah watched her husband's condition worsen and desperately sought to help him. She thought his depressions might partly be due to a chemical imbalance that James was born with, a theory that James explored himself. Then, too, to keep his 'dippers' at bay he consumed too much alcohol and marijuana, both of which can temporarily bring relief but over the long term can have depressive effects.

Like others, Sarah felt that another reason for his 'dippers' might have been because he cut off his emotions early in his life and never learned how to open up to people, or to need them. He was essentially a lonely man and his inability to form close relationships made him despair. His depressions further deadened his feelings, and when he was unable to respond emotionally to marriage and children he grew progressively more despondent.

Sarah: 'He was at war with himself. His depressions became intolerable and towards the end he stopped trying to fight them coming on because he knew they would take over for two days or a week. His face would go black and he would take to his bed and stay there, even on Christmas Day. He'd gone to bed two days beforehand and we had Christmas stockings for the boys. I said "Come on Beast, the boys are waiting". And he said, "Beast, I can't do it". And he was crying.

'And it was killing me. I wanted to take his pain, to ease his suffering. I would say "Look, we've got everything. We've got the boys. We've got the house. I'm still your Beast and when the kids get older I can party again with you". And he would say, "Beast, I know you're trying to help. But you can't". And it was killing us both. It just broke our hearts.'

Seeing her husband in such torment and being unable to help him made Sarah depressed. She began drinking heavily and losing weight. They saw psychiatrists and marriage counsellors together. But nothing worked.

In October of 1988 Sarah and James decided to separate, but they continued to live under the same roof for the sake of the children, and they hoped that over time their marriage might be saved. James even thought about dividing their home into two separate sections, but Sarah didn't want it and James preferred that the boys didn't see him when he was in a dipper. However, he insisted on being near his 'little men'. When they were infants James was less attentive, but as they grew older and developed personalities he came to love them deeply and became a proud and doting father.

He bought a house (for £350,000) just around the corner where Sarah and the boys lived for 18 months. James moved them in, and on the first night, when they were settled in, he came back with a large bouquet of flowers and wept.

12

A THOROUGHLY DECENT MAN

1989–1993

When they separated, Sarah and James said it was the saddest time of their lives. For Sarah, who had only ever wanted a husband, children and a home of her own, the prospect of a failed marriage was as devastating as it was for James, who had desperately hoped that a happy marriage and fatherhood would bring him the peace and contentment he longed for.

When they married Sarah described herself as '24 going on four', but the responsibilities of motherhood made her more mature and responsible. When James wouldn't change – or couldn't change – their relationship, which had from the beginning been one of 'love–hate', rapidly deteriorated and they had little in common other than the boys – whom James visited regularly, playing with them and reading them stories – and a shared remorse over their marriage breakdown.

In November 1989, eleven months after they separated, James and Sarah were divorced on the grounds of his adultery. The divorce was James's idea; Sarah hadn't wanted it. She felt wronged and she fought 'like a cornered animal'. James fought back and there was a bitter, lengthy and costly court battle over custody rights and the financial settlement.

They were both 'torn apart' by the proceedings, which went on for several months, but James seemed to suffer most. He was made despondent by all the acrimony and humiliation surrounding the court case, including a threat that he might only be entitled to see his children when there was another adult present.

He reached rock bottom, mentally and physically, and the dippers – and the benders to make them tolerable – threatened to take over his life.

★ ★ ★

The friend most exposed to James's deteriorating condition was Mike Dennett, who was staying with him at the Wimbledon house. Dennett grew up in the same area of Surrey as James, but only came to know him well after James retired from racing. Like him, he suffered from depressions, and when Dennett, then a creative director in an advertising agency, became too troubled to work James invited him to move in, and he was a house guest on an off for several years.

'When James was very depressed he was driving everybody away, and I was just about the only one who could cope with it because I understood what was going on. Our depressions rarely coincided, but when they did the house was dead still. I was at one end and he was at the other.

'When James felt a dipper coming on he would go on two- or three-day benders, mostly drinking vodka. He would just keep going and going, which was always a bit terrifying, and after these deep, dark, blank days he would suffer real self-loathing. He could forget his trouble with drink, but it always came back.

'For many years trying to get rid of his depression was his major concern, which is why he got the budgerigars. He thought it would be such a huge amount of effort that it would distract him and they became an obsession rather than a hobby. He would sit in the aviary for hours, but he would come back still in the grip of gloom. And for a long time he was so down it was very hard to even converse with him.

'But James was a fighter. He didn't wait for things to happen, he made them happen and he decided to do something about it. He treated himself, like a doctor, cutting out one thing after another to see what might be making him depressed. He would stop drinking, smoking cigarettes, smoking dope, taking acid. He liked the odd acid trip, but he never bought LSD or cocaine and had no craving for them. He might take them if they were offered, but hard drugs were not his style.

'He tried different treatments – acupuncture, Chinese herbal medicine – and looked into every possible theory. He went to different healers, therapists, psychologists, psychiatrists, psychoanalysts, the lot, to try and find the root of his depression. And in the end he cracked it.'

His friends began to notice a change in James during the divorce case. The longer the proceedings dragged on the more determined he became to fight back. He assembled comprehensive files containing reams of documents and hand-written letters. He focused all his attention on the

273

case (and would later even consider writing a book about it), examining it from every conceivable angle, the way he did when he was consumed by racing. While the whole business was very painful for him, all the effort he put into it seemed to help concentrate his mind, and to clear it.

He also benefited from having to respond to the challenge of attending to his dwindling financial resources. As Sarah puts it, he was a victim of the 'three Ls: love, lawyers and Lloyd's'. Besides the many thousands of pounds the divorce case cost him in legal fees, James, a Lloyd's Name, also lost money in some of the most troubled syndicates, an estimated £60,000 in 1989 and as much as £120,000 the next year.

It was also erroneously reported that he lost money when the £2 million James Hunt Racing Centre collapsed soon after it opened, at Milton Keynes in 1990. In truth, James only lent his name to the venture, which was intended to bring the pleasures of single seater racing to businessmen and everyday motorists, and was paid handsomely for it. (When his estate was finally evaluated it amounted to £1,232,942, with £376,895 remaining after the debts were paid off.)

But he was feeling the pinch, and eventually sued the firm of solicitors who handled the divorce case, claiming they had given inadequate advice. To pay for the cost of the lawsuit he obtained Legal Aid and to help confirm his impoverished status he put his Mercedes up on bricks in front of his house because, he said, he couldn't afford to insure it. He used the Austin van to take the boys on outings and to look after his budgies, but his regular form of transport became an old upright bicycle.

There was another reason for cycling around Wimbledon every day and into London on frequent excursions. He had resolved to become fit again, and pedalled vigorously wherever he went. He began to become more diet-conscious and to eat healthy foods. He also consumed information, in books and magazines, on overcoming addictions, and sought more professional help.

He knew he should stop smoking cigarettes and reduce his marijuana consumption, and he told some friends he thought he might be an alcoholic. He worried that his need for women was another form of addiction and feared he might contract AIDS and infect someone else.

John Hogan: 'So he stopped it all. Straightened himself out by absolute willpower. The strength of character of the man enabled him to get out of it. He cut out the cigarettes, the dope and drugs, the booze and the womanizing and his sense of priorities became more well-balanced'.

* * *

James became serious about strengthening his position in the media side of Formula 1 racing. He took on an internationally syndicated newspaper column (in Britain it appeared successively in the *Independent*, the *Daily Mail* and the *Daily Telegraph*) and spent many hours gathering information for it. Working with a journalist he applied himself conscientiously to making sure that every word was written to his satisfaction. He developed a network of contacts among the drivers and within the teams and delighted in revealing scoops in his column. His writing also featured the same trenchant style and wit, and the controversial points of view, which characterized his BBC commentating.

Influenced by his own experiences with the media he tended to be tolerant of those who displayed post-race anger. After one such occasion involving Ayrton Senna, James wrote, 'This episode illustrates how vulnerable drivers are when interviewed too soon after the heat of battle, before their passions have cooled and they have time to consider their remarks. Of course the media takes advantage of this, exploiting it for the news value, and in the process making or breaking personalities'.

While Senna was one of his favourites, James was often critical of Alain Prost: 'When a driver of Senna's type comes along, then adds brainpower to his natural brilliance, it's bad news for everybody else. Certainly it's been bad news for Prost who has handled Senna's growing dominance over him extremely badly and this has been of great detriment to his driving. It began when they became team mates at McLaren where Prost saw Senna was going to outqualify him and quite clearly began to sulk about it.... Sadly, the pressure from Senna has brought out the worst in the most successful Grand Prix driver of all time and the sport is the poorer for it'.

Sometimes a driver he criticized would take him to task, and if he could be persuaded that he was wrong James would apologize. But he continued to enjoy the response his column provoked. 'In my day we had our share of on and off track feuding but now the big money in the sport has thickened the plot which, among other things, has placed today's drivers under much more media pressure – and I'm one of those applying it! Though I certainly sympathise with them, it's fascinating to see how they handle it.'

He tried to be fair in his comments about drivers and would, when he felt the occasion warranted it, even praise his favourite target, Riccardo Patrese. After one race he wrote, 'Patrese provided the only real entertainment in the race. He certainly had a real go at everyone he encountered, including his Williams team mate Nigel Mansell whose presence undoubtedly helped inspire Patrese's increased aggression'.

This was followed in another column by: 'To save himself further embarrassment, to make way for younger drivers and, most of all, to avoid exposing himself to further dangers, surely it's time Riccardo Patrese seriously considers retirement'.

When the racing was unexciting James found entertainment in the off-track goings-on, but his main concern was always for the sport. 'All the acrimony and aggravation we had during the past season made Grand Prix racing more interesting for me than if everything was going smoothly. But I think we've had enough of it and everyone should get down to some good, hard, pure racing.'

His criticism sometimes ran to the events themselves. 'Monaco is a silly event, not a proper Grand Prix at all.... It is really just an exhibition in which the unfortunate drivers are asked to perform and it still exists only for the benefit of the sponsors who want to show off in the "glamorous" atmosphere and for the people who want to preserve the "image" of Formula 1. They should have a parade instead. Then all the cars could tour around like the "jetset" poseurs who are thicker on the ground at Monaco than anywhere else in the world'.

If a circuit didn't measure up to his standards he called a spade a spade. 'As expected, the traffic was extremely heavy on the Magny-Cours circuit because of its badly flawed design. The Mickey Mouse configuration, while testing and demanding and quite hard work for the drivers, makes it nearly impossible to overtake. Transferring the French race here from the perfectly adequate Paul Ricard track was done to massage political egos. It may serve that purpose well but it fails miserably as a suitable Grand Prix venue.'

Of a very wet Australian Grand Prix he wrote: 'For the drivers to even compete required more lunacy than courage. It was only due to good fortune that there were no serious injuries. As a race, this was a farce that had very little to do with motor sport'.

James felt it was his duty to condemn the politics to which Formula 1 is prone. 'The Michael Schumacher affair, his being poached by the Benetton team from Jordan, I find quite deplorable. It has much more to do with big business, vested interests and pure greed than motor racing. Particularly distasteful to me is the horse trading, the tearing up of contracts and generally amoral behaviour which saw decisions being made with scant regard given to the welfare of the drivers involved.'

He tended to be attracted to the more colourful personalities in Formula 1. Of the Jordan team leader he wrote: 'Eddie Jordan understands motor racing and he understands drivers, which makes him a very rare beast among Formula 1 team managers!'.

James always looked for humour and enjoyed writing about drivers who approached their profession the way he had. 'Gerhard Berger is that sort of chap, true testimony to the fact that you can be a proper professional racing driver and still smile and laugh. It is really quite ridiculous, all those frowning faces you see wandering around the paddock.'

In his new-found enthusiasm for the sport James came to the Grand Prix races earlier and stayed longer, but he still appeared in the unconventional dress which made him especially conspicuous among the immaculately uniformed personnel at his favourite hangout in the paddock, the Marlboro McLaren motorhome. The team leader Ron Dennis (who took over from Teddy Mayer and once said he would never hire anyone with dirty fingernails), welcomed James as he was and enjoyed his company.

'I think most people would see James as quite a straightforward individual. But I think he was really quite complex. He had this strange mix of analytic probing sophistication about him which at the same time was blended with an apparent cavalier attitude to the social graces normally found in achievers of his level. That never changed but James changed his own life. He decided, I think, to not conform but to attack life without any escapisms built into it.

'He decided to make a clean, fresh approach, but that did not extend into all areas. He still had no time for airs and graces and his disregard for convention included his lack of desire to wear shoes through to a total distaste for ties, freshly pressed shirts and jackets.'

One of the McLaren team's sponsors and suppliers, Shell International Petroleum, hired James to work in a public relations role and also sponsored a version of his racing column. Mike Branigan of Shell remembers how James made a grand entrance at the company's London headquarters.

'There he was in the lobby of the Shell Centre, in his pair of shorts and plimsolls and we were going to have lunch in the senior executives' private dining room. When I asked him if he had found a place to park his car he showed me this bloody old bicycle parked behind the security desk. The security people loved him, the World Champion on his bike, and he chatted happily to them all and completely charmed the waitresses in the dining room.'

'James at an airport after a Grand Prix in white shorts and T-shirt and brown business shoes with no socks was really quite an odd sight', says

Peter Collins, director of Team Lotus, and one of those in Formula 1 who most appreciated James's understanding of the sport. He often advised Collins and his drivers on tactics and strategy, which helped Team Lotus in the races.

'I found that James had a far, far greater insight into the technical aspects of motor racing than anybody I've ever come across. He had a vision for understanding a race, being able to read how it would go, and he could very quickly identify the weaknesses in other competitors and where that could be used to advantage. He was very good at understanding the driver's point of view from the cockpit and one of the things he taught me was that as a team strategist you need to think as though you're the man in the car with the helmet on.

'He was an inspiration to us and one of the most disciplined and business-like people you could meet when he was doing something for you. He would apply himself, he would think it through and he would give you an honest assessment of something, even if it wasn't necessarily what you wanted to hear. I thought he was one of the most genuine and honest people that I dealt with in motor racing and came to regard him as a very sincere friend.'

Collins was delighted when James sometimes brought his boys Tom and Freddie to the races. Those who had never seen James's tender side were surprised at the affection and attention he gave his 'darlings', Tom and Freddie.

'Doc' was how James referred to Professor Sydney Watkins, a neurosurgeon at London hospital and the man in charge of driver safety at the Grand Prix events. A gentle and kind man who also enjoys a good time, Watkins admired those same qualities in James and they developed a friendship. Several times James and the boys were invited up to the Watkins home in Scotland for weekends.

'They were great fun. The boys were real handfuls to look after but he was awfully good with them and he really fathered and mothered them extremely well. He was always up early in the morning cooking their breakfast and then the four of us would go off salmon fishing. James would fish properly and I would fool around fishing with the youngsters. And then in the evening we used to settle down and he would tell them stories.

'James was a child of the 60s and he didn't grow up in a way. He was still a boy at heart and I found that charming. But he was a very clever, sensitive and perceptive person. I didn't know him well during his decadent stage, but he took control of himself and at one time wasn't drinking at all. And then he was able to get back on it in a controlled sort of way and we enjoyed a few drinks together.'

Niki Lauda, who was now attending the races as an adviser to the Ferrari team, was surprised and impressed by his old friend's transformation.

'James had a bad time, no question. When he retired he had nothing to do so he enjoyed himself too much. But he got himself out of the shit completely. Didn't smoke. Didn't drink. I think one day he just woke and said: "Shit. I can't go on like this". He realized this is not the way he wanted to go on so he was completely clean and clear. This strength was unbelievable for me.'

The reformed James Hunt won over his former detractors in the Formula 1 media fraternity, among them the journalist Nigel Roebuck, who now found him 'urbane, charming, lucid, kind. I came to hold him in great affection, as well as respect. I always thought he had a natural dignity and that he was a very honourable man.

'He changed the way he felt about the sport. James said to me: "I enjoy going to Grands Prix because I love racing now. I never really liked it when I was driving".

'He told me he stopped drinking because "the tail was wagging the dog". Then on one occasion, on a flight back from the Australian Grand Prix, he had a few drinks and I asked him if he was off the wagon. James said, "No, I've allowed myself to have a bit of fun". And when I asked him if he really could stop it he said, "Yes. I really can".'

Maurice Hamilton, the journalist who had felt humiliated by James the 'Prix Citron Champion' Hunt now found him 'just a lovely bloke'. Instead of going to strenuous lengths to avoid him, Hamilton now sought out his company at the races and at home he welcomed his telephone calls. Hamilton became one of those James would call up for lengthy chats about the latest Formula 1 gossip.

'My office is at the back of the house just behind the kitchen. My wife would be working there and she would know when James was on the phone because there would be gales of laughter coming from my office. And she used to say, "You're just like two silly schoolboys". And I suppose we were, really.'

The new James Hunt also won over Eoin Young, the reluctant co-author of the *Against All Odds* book. Young was one of those startled and amused when James appeared for a memorial service for Denny Hulme (the New Zealand World Champion who died of a heart attack) riding his bicycle and carrying a knapsack on his back. Outside the church in Chelsea James dismounted, produced a rather rumpled black suit from the knapsack and proceeded to change into it, unconcerned at the stares of passers-by.

Young regularly hosted luncheon gatherings of racing people at a pub in a village in Surrey and invited James to attend one of them. James, neither drinking nor smoking, was the life of the party. 'He was so good. He was a completely different guy. He sat across the table from Ken Tyrrell (the Formula 1 team owner) and they had a wonderful slagging match. Ken had been stung by some of James's references to his drivers on TV and he said, "James, sometimes you should keep your mouth shut". James shot back, "Unfortunately, Ken, the BBC pays me to keep it open!".'

His BBC cohort Murray Walker was struck by the changes in James. He first became aware of just how different he had become when they were having dinner before a Grand Prix. When Murray asked him what he would like to drink James said orange juice. But for the meal, Murray said, what about the wine? James said he had stopped drinking wine and everything else because, 'I think I've had my share'.

Murray: 'James changed physically and he changed mentally. Before he had been dour, sleepy-eyed and flaccid, but he now became lean, ruddy-faced and, most significantly, bright-eyed. Before you felt he wasn't with you, or was seeing you through a veil. All of a sudden, he was very much there.

'At the same time he became, to me, an altogether different, enormously likeable chap whom I greatly respected. A much more charming and jolly chap who actually began to communicate with me, whereas before we had been talking to each other through millions of people by means of television, but not really communicating. James was now positively demanding the microphone and making significant and interesting contributions to the whole presentation and we were now producing, in my opinion, an incomparably better product.'

Mark Wilkin, who became the producer of the BBC *Grand Prix* programmes, notes that James, in the old days, 'led a charmed life at the BBC and was given more licence because he was so good. It wasn't until he approached it in a more professional manner in later years that we realized he could be even better'.

When James became more keen about his job Wilkin remembers how a brief power struggle was settled between the two commentators in the broadcast booth. 'Both James and Murray came to me, quite separately, and said, "I've been thinking over the last few races that I haven't been getting my share and I think you should do something about it. Because it's not fair. I'm not talking as much as he is". I said I understood and agreed with them both and that I would fix it. So I did absolutely nothing and both of them came to me after the next race and said, "That was much better. Well done. Whatever you said worked".'

Murray Walker: 'Now as for the reasons for the new James Hunt, I'm no psychologist, but my analysis is this. One: James suddenly had a driving need to earn money. Two: the driving need existed because he had two things that mattered enormously to him: his sons. Three: he had "reformed" because I suspect he knew or had been told his health was at risk if he didn't knock off the drink and other things. And four: possibly more important than anything else, he had a good woman behind him'.

* * *

Helen Dyson was working as a waitress in Hamburger Heaven, a restaurant in Wimbledon where James often went, at first only to eat but increasingly, as it developed, just to see her. He later told her he consumed far more hamburgers than he ever wanted just so that he could be served by the young blonde beauty with the dazzling smile and cheerful personality. But he was uncharacteristically hesitant in making advances to her, perhaps because she was 18 years his junior.

Helen worked at the restaurant on weekends to help pay for her studies at Middlesex Polytechnic, where she obtained a degree in fine arts, specializing in fabric design. With her parents, Molly and Mark Dyson, a chartered accountant, Helen lived just across Wimbledon Common from James's home, though she was unaware of that and knew nothing about him when, early in the winter of 1989, he first asked her out on a date.

'If I had known who he was I might not have had the courage to say yes. I thought he was some charming village man and that it was sweet of him to ask me out. It was on a Saturday and I was in a very jolly mood and so we went out to dinner. It was bit awkward at first and the conversation was stilted but I really began to fancy him and became completely infatuated.'

But when Helen, a Catholic, found out James had been married twice she worried about what her parents might think. Revelations about his decadent past 'horrified' her, especially his reputation for womanizing. She didn't want to be just 'his latest bimbo' and wind up discarded and hurt and she became more hesitant about continuing to see him. But he persisted in pursuing her.

James at first kept their blossoming relationship secret from his friends, other than Mike Dennett, who saw the dramatic effect Helen had on him. 'Very quickly it all became very special to James. Helen came around to the house more and more often and he just seemed to light up in her company. But he also seemed less sure of himself.'

James became confused when the initial physical attraction between them took on an emotional component he had never experienced before. Eventually, they fell head over heels in love, but while Helen more easily surrendered to being swept off her feet James was distinctly unsteady on his.

'James told me he had never been in love and thought that, as a person, he was incapable of it. What happened between us was absolutely magical, something I had never dreamed of either. And when I eventually moved in with him things went from great to simply wonderful and just got better and better. He made me the happiest person in the world.'

But it was two and a half years before Helen agreed to share his home. At first she resisted because it might mean a loss of independence and interfere with the career she hoped to establish as an artist. That obstacle was removed when James became interested in her work and encouraged it. He helped get her commissions to paint murals in private homes and in his own home he created for her a spacious artist's studio in the gallery above his snooker room.

Influenced by Helen's distaste for his previously decadent lifestyle James began to mend his ways, but there remained the 'wall' he had built up around his emotions, and it was his difficulty in breaking down this barrier that most delayed their living together. In the end it was his profound need for Helen that provided the catalyst for James to straighten himself out and, gradually, it was his developing love for her that helped drive away the demons that caused his dippers.

Though his depressions did not disappear overnight – in fact some of his worst came when he worried that Helen might leave him – James now began the process of critical self-examination which led to the self-understanding that became his salvation. Much of his soul-searching was conducted in a series of letters to Helen.

The letters, which began shortly after they met and continued after Helen moved in with him when he was away at the races, were written in James's bold and deliberate schoolboyish scrawl. But the content of his letters was at first anything but confident. He wrote about 'the growing turmoil' in his mind over the difficulty he was having in surrendering himself to his new-found emotions. But he was desperate for

'...the peace and strength you imbue in me when I lie next to you and hold you.

'Inside me there is a warm heart that increases to glow in your presence. But it's struggling to get through the insulation in me. This layer was constructed solidly early in my life but it's one I now understand and have started to deal with. I think the process is similar to giving up drink. I knew at least two years before that I should give it up, but it was a slow process of adjusting the psyche. You can't just jump from A to B. You have to wander about probing the undergrowth.

My heart aches to see you,
James'

He later wrote of his intention to embark on a two to three-year rebuilding programme

'...for my life and my spirit. I want to work at building a proper, healthy, committed, loving relationship with you. I really think this is the arrival of the missing motivation in my life for which I've waited so long. I want to put this declaration of the new me on record, for you to hold me to it and also for me to hold myself to it. To that end I've been presumptuous enough to pray and ask God to witness my sincerity.

With more love than I ever thought I had,
James'

By May 1992 James was able to declare the depth of his feelings for her and wrote to Helen:

'My darling YOU ARE THE LOVE OF MY LIFE. At last I'm beginning to feel able to allow you to love me, which will in turn free me to love you properly. If I lean on you and you support me we can grow strong together and achieve a deeply bonded interdependence and love. In being helped I will hope to break down my wall and start to share my life. This is my last chance. I HAVE to make it work. I WANT to make it work. Also I believe I CAN make it work.'

A year later, after attending his parents' 50th wedding anniversary, James wrote about how that experience was a pivotal point in his emotional breakthrough.

'...I went to the parents' 50th in a totally negative frame of mind, feeling very much an outsider and wanting the floor to swallow me up. As the day went on, although I remained "outside", I could see and feel lots of generous, undemanding love around me. Something changed for me there with my family. Everyone was exuding love and I saw the wonder of it and want to be part of it, but firstly with you.

'I realise now that the feeling of not being loved as a child made me close up to any incoming love projected onto me. I do see that I cannot live on without love. You brought it home to me when you pointed out how well I'm doing with the boys. Well I have had to work at that and I've got better at it and I have to do it with you. You are the girl of my dreams. Without you I have no future. I want to make you happy and continue to do so until I die.

All my love for the love of my life,
James'

*　*　*

His close friends agree that Helen was the major turning point in James's life, but she thinks his love for Tom and Freddie was also a major factor in helping him change. Helen was often there when James had the boys for weekends, and she saw how his increasing devotion to them helped develop his self-esteem.

'In the beginning he felt guilty for abandoning his children after he split up with Sarah. It bothered him that he wasn't loving them enough and it made him think he was an awful person. Then, when he let himself go and opened up to them, it really helped all his relationships. He let that barrier down and learned to like himself. You can't love other people if you don't love yourself.

'And he began to face himself and to understand himself. Before he was always dashing about and used his "busyness" as a way of avoiding things. It was as if he was not really there. But once he decided I was the girl for him and that he wouldn't be looking for anyone else he began to really focus on his problems and he began to deal with them. All his morals and values completely changed.'

James confessed to Helen that he was unable to be faithful to anyone in the past because sex was for him just another addiction and he needed women to get his highs. He disliked social gatherings and only had parties or went to them to pick up women. Helen was willing to forgive and forget what went on before, but told him she wouldn't tolerate it in their relationship and he agreed to be faithful to her.

When 'Helenus' or 'H', as James called her, stopped smoking with the help of a book about how to break nicotine addiction she gave it to him and he began to cut down his 40 cigarette a day habit. He stopped completely when she told him his smoking might tempt her to begin again. She also convinced him to reduce his dope consumption to more reasonable levels, and, as he became happier in her company, it was no longer necessary for him to use alcohol as a means of escape from his dippers.

When Helen suggested his budgies were taking up too much of his time and she tired of having to look after them when he was away on race weekends he sold his collection. When she got a mountain bike James put his Mercedes up on blocks and took up cycling in earnest. However, Helen's influence did not extend to changing the way he dressed.

'He cycled everywhere in his scruffy gear. Snooker, like cycling, became an obsession after he got rid of the budgies and he used to cycle off to play at the RAC in London with his cue and his suit in a knapsack. Outside the Club he would have to change, standing in Pall Mall in his underpants.'

His cycling expeditions – which he tended to treat like races – were followed by a bracing ritual involving a quick hot shower and then total immersion, which he timed with a stopwatch, in a tub of ice-cold water kept expressly for that purpose. He lay shivering in the tub for precise intervals varying from 30 seconds to one minute because he had read that such a practice would strengthen the immune system and libido.

When it came to his personal ablutions James did not believe in using soap or deodorant because, he maintained, the body cleans itself naturally and people should smell like people. (Before he stopped playing the field he also said that boys who smelled like boys attracted more girls.)

For internal cleansing James, following the advice of a Chinese herbalist 'guru', indulged in what he called 'hocus pocus', brewing up separate concoctions of bark and herbs for his spleen and Helen's complexion.

Each morning, to get rid of toxins and strengthen his throat, James drank a potion comprised of crushed ginger, lemon juice, honey and hot water. Then he would prepare orange juice and coffee for Helen and bring them to her in bed.

Winston sometimes cooked for them, but most evenings James and Helen prepared their meals together (he insisted on fish and chips once a week) and sat down to eat with the resident pets, often in front of the television set in the living room. Oscar, much to James's distress, had passed away and was replaced by his grandson Jackson and Muffy, a terrier which had belonged to Sarah.

At meal-times Humbert the parrot sat on James's shoulder, scolding the dogs – 'Naughty dog! Bad dog!' – and uttering such exclamations as 'You can tickle my ass with a feather!', or 'I'm a neurotic bird!'. The menagerie was sometimes joined by a robin which James had tamed to come in from the garden.

James and Helen hardly ever left the house and began to plan their future. At first they thought about moving, to make a fresh start in another home, but as their life together became more and more idyllic they decided to stay where they were. The outside of the house was redecorated and they planned, when his financial situation improved, to renovate the interior. One of the rooms, they decided, would be made over into a nursery for children of their own.

☆ ☆ ☆

James's belief that family relationships were crucial to his future happiness owed much to what had transpired during his parents' golden wedding anniversary celebration. Besides mentioning it in his letter to Helen he also wrote a letter to Sue and Wallis, saying how lovely it had been to see them and all the family so happy together, how pleased he was for them and how he had found it an uplifting experience.

Sue Hunt thought it 'extraordinary how just that one day, a few hours really, made such a change in James. When he arrived with Tom and Freddie he seemed a bit downish. He wasn't sparky. Then he talked with people and we had a little thanksgiving service in the drawing room, conducted by a very good friend who's a clergyman. He said a few prayers, Sally read a passage from the bible and Wallis' sister played the piano for a couple of rousing hymns and that was that. And when James left he seemed much happier'.

A few weeks after this, when James was looking after Tom and Freddie during a school break, he invited his parents to come up to Wimbledon to have lunch and spend the afternoon with their grandchildren. After lunch the six of them went over to Wimbledon Common and fed the geese and Sue and Wallis had never seen James so happy. That evening James asked Sue and Wallis to bring Tom and Freddie back to Sarah. The Hunts hadn't seen their former daughter-in-law since the divorce and James thought they should end their estrangement. The reunion was successful and Sarah felt part of the family again.

James also made peace with Sarah, who was now living with the boys in a charming cottage in a village in West Sussex. They began talking regularly on the telephone. 'Extraordinary things happened. I became "Beast" again on the phone. When we were fighting it was always

"Sarah". He sent me all the nasty letters from the divorce case and asked me to burn them. When I became depressed I used to phone him up and he would listen and always support me in my emotions, because he understood me. We were still soul-mates.

'He told me how happy he was with Helen and I was delighted for him. There was no more acrimony between us. He had come to peace with himself at last and began to organize all his relationships. I think he had a premonition.'

★   ★   ★

In the second week of June 1993, Helen went on a trip to the Greek island of Lesbos with her girlfriend Christina, who was also planning to become pregnant. It would be a final 'little girls' holiday' for them both and, though it was Helen's first trip away without him, James enthusiastically endorsed it and stayed up all night helping Helen pack for her early morning departure.

James invited Mike Dennett to stay with him while Helen was away and it was also his weekend to have Tom and Freddie. On Friday night, after he said their prayers with the boys and put them to bed, James and Mike played snooker until the early hours of Saturday morning. Then they watched a rugby game between the British Lions and New Zealand.

That night James and Mike went to a small party which Chris and Suzie Jones had organized for the people they had known since their teens. His old mates were struck by how much younger James looked, how contented he seemed and how relaxed he was, though he had nothing to drink.

On Sunday James cycled the six miles into London to the BBC Television Centre, where he and Murray Walker did the commentary for the Canadian Grand Prix in Montreal. When he returned home Sarah came to pick up the boys and James invited her in for tea and they had a warm and enjoyable conversation.

Mike Dennett: 'I can't remember James being so happy as he was that whole weekend. He was in such a good mood. Just radiating charisma and when he turned it on he was such an irresistible character that he made everybody else happy'.

On Monday evening, after he finished working on his newspaper column for the Canadian race, James telephoned Helen at her hotel in Greece. When she heard what James had to say Helen shrieked with joy. 'He proposed to me and I accepted. It was the last time I ever spoke to him'.

Following his telephone call to Helen, James's spirits rose even higher as he resumed his marathon snooker match with Mike Dennett. But after they took time out for a meal of spaghetti James complained of pains in his upper body. Mike suggested it might be just indigestion from wolfing down his food.

'We played for about another hour and then he said, "Well, I feel really shitty". He sat down, sort of huffing and puffing, and then he phoned a "medical-ish" friend to speak to him about it. James said, "I just feel sort of strange all over. And my arms feel strange". He chatted and joked away on the phone and then he said, "Even as I'm talking to you it's going away. Now it's gone".

'This was about 12:30 or 1 o'clock in the morning and I said to James: "Look, we've had a bit of a go this weekend. We're all knackered so let's go to bed". So I went upstairs to the room I was staying in, right over the kitchen. And he always made a great performance about going to bed. His coffee had to be made in a certain way, and so on. So I heard him making coffee and that was it.

'In the morning I got up very late. About 10:30. When he had not come down to breakfast I went up to wake him. Found him lying there on the floor. By the side of his bed. He was in his dressing gown but he hadn't even got into bed. The dogs Jackson and Muffy were with him. I called an ambulance but it was too late. And then I started calling out to people. It was awful. Just awful.'

* * *

It was Mike Dennett's sorrowful task to break the devastating news of James's death, from a massive heart attack in the early hours of 15 June 1993, to his family, friends and associates. His passing, at the age of 45, was an enormous shock and everyone reeled in disbelief that the man who had consumed life with such vitality and had survived so much could so suddenly be no more.

James's intimates were especially concerned for his two little boys and for the woman with whom James planned to share the rest of his life, but it took some time to track Helen down in Greece. When Mike finally reached her by telephone, and broke the awful news, she went into deep shock. She endlessly packed and repacked her suitcase while she waited for a private jet, sent by Ron Dennis of the McLaren team, to bring her back to England. When she arrived home at Wimbledon, Helen collapsed into the arms of James's brother Peter, who carried her inside the house and closed the door.

At their cottage in West Sussex, Sarah struggled with her own grief and with the difficult task of explaining to the boys that their father, who had laughed and played with them just a couple of days ago, was gone forever. She sat Tom, now seven, and Freddie, five, in her lap in the garden and told them their 'Dadda' had died and gone to heaven.

The boys cried for a while, but then they remembered something James had taught them: that God is everywhere and that everyone's spirit is part of God. Sarah remembers that little Tom said: 'Well his spirit will still be with us', and she, too, felt James's spirit was with her and helped comfort her during the trying times that lay ahead.

Sarah said she loved James when she met him, she loved him when they fought and divorced, she loved him when he died and she would love him forever. She also had the boys to remember him by and Sarah felt 'terribly sorry for Helen' who was left with only her memories of James.

But after her initial shock wore off, Helen's thoughts of James and his love for her were a source of great inspiration and strength. Losing him meant nothing in her life could ever be so bad again, but her feelings of him remaining beside her, thinking about her and watching over her, were so acute as to make his presence almost tangible.

Knowing that James had found serenity gave to Helen a sense of peace and comfort that she wanted to share with others. 'It will be a great comfort to all his friends to know that James was happier than he had ever been just before he died. He was famous for living life to the full, but I knew a much quieter man. He was a wonderful father to his sons and he was my best friend. He is and always will be the love of my life.'

✩ ✩ ✩

On 21 June a private funeral, attended by the family and close friends, about 30 people in all, was held at St Mary's Church in Wimbledon, where Tom and Freddie Hunt had been baptized. Before the service began Sarah and the boys placed a bouquet of foxgloves wrapped in the boys' christening blanket on the coffin, inside of which Helen had earlier put the lead of James's beloved dog, Oscar.

The short service included a lone trumpeter playing a voluntary and lively hymns intended to lift the spirits of the mourners. Wallis Hunt read a lesson and finished by saying that James wouldn't have wanted everyone to be mooching around with long faces. He would want them to cheer up.

From the many letters of condolence sent to the family Wallis read a couple of humorous extracts, including the anecdote about James putting the family deck chair in his racing Mini. The other, from an elderly lady who was David Hunt's godmother, said, 'Formula 1 racing will never be the same for me now that James is gone. But what fun they must be having in heaven'.

The pallbearers – Wallis, Peter, Tim and David Hunt, Mike Dennett and Bubbles Horsley – carried the coffin out of the church and the cortège drove the two miles to Putney Vale Crematorium, where James's body was cremated.

Most of the mourners returned to Peter Hunt's home, where they opened a 1922 claret, bottled in the year of Wallis's birth and given to him by James eleven years earlier as a present for his 60th birthday. Reminiscences of James were exchanged and plans were discussed to hold a memorial service in celebration of his life.

Tributes to James and messages of support for his family and friends poured in from around the world. The press, which had sometimes not treated him with such respect, was full of praise for James and what he had accomplished in his brief lifetime. His passing, reflecting the prevailing public opinion, was treated as a tragic loss of a great British hero who had a tremendous following, and James was widely mourned by more people than he could ever have imagined.

Some of the most moving and perceptive tributes came from those who had been most closely associated with James. Tony Dron, his friend from their days together as Formula Ford racers, wept when he heard the sad news, and later said: 'James Hunt was a naturally great man'.

His Formula 3 team-mate Brendan McInerney thought an old proverb could be applied to the way James lived his life. 'It goes something like this: "When you are born, you cry and everybody else laughs. Try to live your life so that when you die you laugh and everybody else cries". And I think that sums up James very well.'

Lord Hesketh was 'absolutely shattered' when James died and rued the fact that 'so few sporting figures in this country today combine, as James did, steely determination with delightful insouciance. He was truly outstanding and represented the archetypal British sportsman. He not only drove for me but was a great friend. Goodbye Superstar. You will never be forgotten'.

James's old rival Niki Lauda was 'just devastated by the news of his death. From my point of view James was an incredible personality because you could see him with people on the street, talking low-key, maybe, and you could even put him at the table with the Queen of England. He would always know how to behave. For me he was the most charismatic personality who's ever been in Formula 1'.

Innes Ireland, the retired driver and president of the British Racing

Drivers' Club, was one of the last free spirits in the sport before James came along, and appreciated that quality in him. 'Often verging on the outrageous his sometimes wild behaviour hid the fact that he was a warm, friendly person of deep understanding and intelligence. More recently the depth of his caring nature became obvious with the love and consideration he showed for his two sons. Always something of a rebel he appeared to take some delight in standing – not always gently – on the toes of the establishment. I must say I thought he went a bit over the top on one or two occasions. Somehow, with his acute sense of humour, he always managed to get away with it.'

The journalist David Tremayne began following the Golden Boy of British motor racing when he was a schoolboy, and then befriended him when James became a member of the media. Tremayne spoke for all his colleagues when he said 'He was articulate and amusing, the sort of person you didn't have to agree with to like. I liked most about him his unending cheerfulness, his lack of pomp and the engaging dignity with which he conducted his life. "Keep charging and keep having fun", he would say, but it will be a while before we can recall those words without great sadness.'

Murray Walker, who sat beside James for the last time during their BBC broadcast just before he died, was badly shaken by the loss of the colleague he had come to regard as his friend: 'I am completely overwhelmed. I know that all over the world millions and millions of people who have been watching Grand Prix racing over the years and enjoying everything he had to say are going to feel very much the poorer as a result of the fact that he's no longer there to say it. I know I feel that an enormous hole has opened in my life. I'll miss him terribly'.

Bubbles Horsley considered James to be his 'best friend, by miles' and was devastated by his passing. He took some comfort in knowing he had turned his life around and was especially thankful for the relationship, though cruelly short, James had had with the boys. Bubbles noted how James as a father was finally able to really understand and communicate with Tom and Freddie and could comfort them with just a few words when they were troubled.

'That was one of his great strengths. And his ability to communicate was why he was so good on television. But people who are brilliant at solving other people's problems often struggle with their own. And, like everybody, there was a plus and minus column to James. But I think his pluses far outweighed the minuses. At the end of the day I think you'd have to say he was a thoroughly decent man.'

EPILOGUE

A Celebration of the Life of James Hunt was held on 29 September 1993, at St James's Church in Piccadilly. The memorial service, attended by over 600 people, was conducted by the Reverend Andrew Studdert-Kennedy, curate of St Mary's Church, Wimbledon. Music was provided by a trumpeter, two organists, two soloists and the Wellington College Choir.

Readings were given by Wallis and Sue Hunt from the book of Ecclesiastes, Chapter III and James's sister Sally Jones, who read Hilaire Belloc's poem 'Jim' (which James and his brothers and sisters enjoyed as children and he often read to Tom and Freddie). Innes Ireland (who died a few months later from cancer), the president of the British Racing Drivers' Club, read Rudyard Kipling's poem 'If' and Helen Dyson read Psalm LXXXIV.

Peter Hunt extended the Welcome.

'On behalf of James's family, it is my great pleasure to welcome you to this celebration of James's life. We would, of course, all much rather not have to be here. But it is wonderful to see a full church and so many old friends.

'Several things I know for sure. Firstly, James would have loved to have been here with all his friends. He'll be absolutely livid he's missing all the fun! Secondly, that we're having lots of his favourite music. Lots of trumpet, lots of noise and lots of singing. We know he liked the hymns because he had two of them at his first marriage service and three of them at his second. Thirdly, that he would have wanted everybody to enjoy the music and sing as loudly as possible.

'Now a lot of you are aware that he left me instructions in his will to organise a party for his friends after he died. That party is being held this evening, and I hope James would approve. One of my hardest jobs has been trying to decide who to invite. James had so many friends, it has simply not been possible to invite all of you. Please accept my apologies if you think you should have been on the guest list.

'Anyway, the point is that the message to me and to all of James's family is that we should enjoy ourselves today. We all have very happy memories of him and our aim today is to share those memories with his friends and see lots of laughter and smiling faces.

'I should like to thank all of you very much for coming to this service and for all your wonderful letters, tributes and messages of support over the last few months. You have all been fantastic. I should particularly like to express my sincere thanks to Mike Dennett for all his invaluable help, both to Helen and me, immediately after James died, to Ron Dennis, for his thoughtfulness and generosity and to Roger Carey and his assistant Patricia for all their help, support and enthusiasm in the organisation of today's service. My thanks also to everybody taking part in the service and for those who have helped make it possible.

'I am now going to hand over to my parents, Sue and Wallis. The last time the family got together before James died was to celebrate their 50th wedding anniversary in April this year. It was a wonderfully happy day for all of us and their many friends. Since then, we have been dealt a terrible blow, but with your help we are getting through it. Let's try and make today as happy and memorable as we possibly can for James's family and friends.'

Nigel Davison, Director of Music and Master in charge of Running at Wellington College (1963–67) prefaced the Second Reading.

'James was one of the most remarkable teenagers I have met in a long career of teaching. He was very single-minded and always seemed to know exactly what he wanted to achieve. He also had a very clear view of how to achieve it, which sometimes conflicted strongly with conventional wisdom. He must have been quite a trial to some of the more narrow-minded school masters.

'I don't think he was too interested in team games, preferring what he saw as more individual sports: squash, tennis, racquets and cross-country running. He represented Wellington College at all of them.

'I couldn't repress a smile when I re-read the other day what I'd written for the 1965 *Wellington Yearbook*, about the year's cross-country running. "With one notable, if successful, exception, the team threw themselves wholeheartedly into the rigorous training program." The notable exception was, of course, James. He had quickly decided that team training was not for him. It probably wasn't rigorous enough. He thought he knew best how to train himself and events proved him right. For he either won or came first equal in every race of that year that I can recall, including a particularly gruesome and arduous inter-house match, whose finish involved wading through a large lake.

'James was also a talented and enthusiastic trumpeter. If he had decided to make himself an instrumental virtuoso, he might well have become the James Galway of the trumpet. As it was, trumpet playing was for him a rare form of relaxation and we spent many enjoyable half hours working away at the Trumpet Voluntary, which you didn't hear this afternoon, incidentally, or the Haydn trumpet concerto, or in his final term, the finale of a Mozart concerto which he thought would be fun to play an octave higher than Mozart had ever intended.

'James was full of original ideas. I well recall playing the organ for his wedding to Sarah. He had planned the music in great detail. I had to bring with me a trumpeter and a soprano, so there could be lots of trumpet tunes, lots of descants to the hymns and, using all three of us, Handel's "Let the Bright Seraphim" during the signing of the register. Who but James could have chosen for a November wedding the hymn "O Come All Ye Faithful?"

'I have only happy memories and am grateful for the way he once brightened my life.'

Stirling Moss, the former racing driver, prefaced the next Reading.

'Well, as we have heard, James was truly unique. He was a man of immense personality and charm. A total non-conformist who was a curious mix of wit, intelligence and unparalleled stubbornness. Someone who stood firmly behind his actions and beliefs. Right or wrong, he certainly provided food for thought and fuel for debate. Whatever else he may have been, James was not boring. Never.

'He was definitely no saint, either. Particularly for one of my generation, his behaviour could be quite appalling. I've been with him on occasions when it was difficult to admit I even knew him – let alone that he was a friend of mine. But somehow, because it was James, one could overlook it.

'The contribution he made to our sport, through his television and his writing, was enormous. He brought to televised motor racing a dimension that had not previously existed. His explanations and pithy comments, often controversial, brought to the general public an interest and understanding that raised the level of Formula 1 far above that of being merely a spectacle. He turned moderately interested viewers into well-informed enthusiasts. He brought in thousands of extra followers and fans to our sport.

'Now I never raced against James. In fact, I had to wait until later in his life before getting to know him as a friend. Over the years, he was a man that I grew to know, to like, to trust and respect. A man whose opinions and friendship I valued greatly. Like all of you here today, I miss him.'

The next Reading was prefaced by Lord Hesketh.

'When Peter honoured me by asking me to introduce this preface, I was told that I could only speak for 90 seconds. I reminded Peter of the last time that he gave me an instruction, which was asking for James's retainer. And I recited to him at that time the two Belloc poems – or telegraphic poems – which came from a boy at Prep School, which said:

No mun,
No fun,
Your son.

To which I replied:

Too bad,
So sad,
Your dad.

'I first met James 21 years ago in the paddock, if you can call it that – it was a sort of a mucky meadow in Belgium – at Chimay. I'd arrived there from Monaco, and Bubbles had resigned as chief driver for Hesketh Racing and become team manager by his own appointment. We had no driver and James had no car.

'Twelve months later, we lifted him exhausted from a car which had finished and broken down on the last lap at Monaco and we were classified ninth. Twelve months later, he won his first Formula 1 race at Silverstone and the *Daily Express* International trophy. Twelve months later, he won his first Grand Prix. And twelve months later, he was World Champion.

'It was an honour for me, in my life, to be able to call him a friend. But he was much more than that. He represented something very, very English. He was the combination of the Corinthian casual and the anarchist. Hesketh Racing gave him very little. He gave a great deal to us. What we gave him was because we were also anarchists. We didn't get embarrassed when he kept flying off while in the lead while educating himself in the craft of driving. What he gave to Hesketh

Racing was the difference between being in the record book at the back of the *Autosport* Annual Review under Did Not Qualify: DNQ, DNQ and DNQ.

'I know that in many ways his career was dogged by criticism which had nothing to do with his ability. And the judgement on James's career will improve as the years go by and the turnout today, I believe, reveals his real quality. I know that the people who care about racing, the fans who are, after all, the lifeblood of the sport, are the people who held him in the highest regard. And it is in his passing, in the obituaries that were written, that something of his real, international all-time ability can be seen.

'I know this. That when his two boys, Freddie and Tom, by whom he put so much, grow to be men, there will be by then, middle-aged and older, men and women – hopefully wiser, certainly greyer – and they will come up to those two boys who will then be men, and they will see them and they will talk to them and they will touch them.

'And of the memory that I will always hold – of that spring day in 1974 when James overtook Ronnie Peterson with two wheels on the grass at Woodcote, a corner that no longer exists, and now sadly, the driver who no longer exists – they will speak to those boys who will then be men, and they will say possibly with misty eyes: "We were there".'

Murray Walker delivered the Address.

'We're here today to remember and to honour James as a very special person, who in different ways has been part of the life of each and every one of us. To his family, he was a loving son, brother, father. To the motor racing world of which he was such an outstanding part, he was a great competitor, a forceful teammate, a determined and gifted rival. And to millions of Formula 1 fans all over the world, from Adelaide to Andover, who listened to the calm, authoritative and witty television commentaries he gave, his was the voice that made sense out of an involved and complicated sport. And to me, he was a respected and admired colleague, whose wit and wisdom added immeasurably to our joint efforts to communicate the sport that meant so much to both of us.

'But to everyone, James was a charismatic personality whose untimely departure has made our world a duller place. In today's world, most of us stand out like grey against black. Conforming to the general standard, unable or unwilling to do their own thing, make their own mark, be their own man. Which is something that you most certainly could not say about James.

'Quite apart from his talents, his success, his commanding presence and his natural dignity, he was an immensely likeable, warm, different kind of human being. One who made wherever he was a livelier and more stimulating and enjoyable place to be. Because James didn't think like other people. He didn't act like other people. He refused to conform to the rules that govern most of us. And he had the presence and the charm to get away with it.

'I bet almost everybody here could tell a personal story about something that James did or said. And they'd tell it with affection and warmth, to emphasise that he was no ordinary person.

'The first commentary I ever did with him was on a Formula 5000 race at Silverstone. When James, with his leg in plaster, lay on the floor, looking up at the monitor, at an extremely boring and uneventful race. When I handed him the microphone to sum it up, he simply said: 'What a load of rubbish!', and handed it back to me.

'But later, at Monaco, for his very first Grand Prix commentary, wearing no shoes, a T-shirt, shorts that had certainly seen better days, and clutching a bottle of rosé, he planted his plaster cast in my lap and sailed into the comments that were to endear him to his vast following for 13 years.

'Now our gathering here is to celebrate James's life rather than mourn his death – much as we all do so. And I'm jolly sure that that's what he'd like. You don't need me to tell you about his twin careers. About his *Boy's Own Paper* leap from virtual obscurity to World Champion in an incredibly short time. About how he became the nation's sporting hero and the focal point of their obsessive interest – which was something he hated, incidentally. About how he retired from Grand Prix racing far too soon, dispirited by his lack of success in an uncompetitive car, when there isn't a shadow of doubt that his talent could have made him World Champion again, and again. About how he effortlessly changed gear into a new role, as the BBC's voice of authority in Formula 1.

'James raced in an era where it was possible both to succeed and enjoy yourself. And he did both to the full. And then he matured, to pass on his experience and his knowledge to his successors, and an enormous audience, by means of that commanding voice, presence and his natural authority.

'His sudden death, totally unexpected, and tragic for one so young and seemingly so fit, touched the nation like few other things in my experience. It's a theory of mine that television communicates people to the viewer like they really are. And it certainly did in James's case. I have had dozens and dozens of truly moving letters telling me that the writers felt they'd lost a real and valued personal friend, whose warmth and humour had enriched their lives, and whose experience, knowledge and outspokenness had kindled and developed their interest in Grand Prix racing.

'Now if my theory is correct, it's not difficult to see why. They saw James as a character, which he certainly was. They saw him as his own man, which he most certainly was. They saw him as a having a bright, breezy, lively personality, which he did. And they loved his irreverence and his provocative comments. Because James, anywhere and everywhere, was never reluctant to speak his mind. An incredibly clear-thinking and analytical mind, which may sometimes have produced words his targets didn't like – I didn't like some of them – but which he was always ready to defend to their faces with logic and eloquence that usually won them over.

'"I'm just off to have it out with so-and-so about last week", he'd say. And then you'd see him calmly justify his case in the paddock, when most people would have laid low and hoped that it would go away. But then he would always apologise if he felt he'd been wrong. Apropos of which, I have never known a public figure of his magnitude, of his very considerable magnitude, who was as unaffected by his success and as self-effacing as James was.

'Letter after letter told me how the writer had met him somewhere and been overwhelmed by the fact that he found the time to stop and just chat like any other enthusiast. You know, the paying public on the other side of the track get next-to-no direct contact with their heroes, these days. But they got the consideration they deserved from James.

'"One of the reasons I retired, Murray", he told me, "was that I just couldn't stand being a human honey pot wherever I went. Restaurants, pubs, out on the street. Everyone wanting a part of me. No privacy. No way could I lead a normal life." Hardly surprising when practically everything he did created national headlines at the height of his racing fame. But James was essentially a private man, and he didn't really like the ceaseless adulation.

'When his racing career was over, he was glad to get away from it, go about his new life – forever accompanied by his beloved Oscar – become a truly loving father, and do something which must have seemed totally out of character to most people: successfully breed and show budgerigars.

'So, a paragon of humanity? Nothing to criticise? No weak points? Well of course there were, and thank heavens too. None of us is perfect. There are people here who could write a book about James Hunt's escapades. And an immensely readable bestseller it would be, too. And when the adrenaline was running high, he could be a fearsome chap. I've seen him fell a rival competitor who angered him. I've seen him do the same to a marshal who incurred his wrath. I bet Teddy Mayer hasn't forgotten the roasting he got at the end of his Japanese Grand Prix whilst he was vainly trying to tell a furious James, who thought he'd failed, that he had in fact clinched the World Championship. And I certainly won't forget the tongue lashing that an unfortunate technician got in Australia when a communication failure made James look silly.

'But, that same adrenaline surge gave him the selfless courage to rescue Ronnie Peterson from his blazing Lotus at Monza. Bravery can take many forms, but surely none greater than voluntarily plunging into fire to save your fellow man.

'James could charm the birds out of the trees, but sadly he wasn't spared hard times in recent years. Personal and financial problems had made things very tough indeed for him. But you'd never have known it. He was unfailingly cheerful and remained the kind, courteous and helpful English gentleman he had always been. And he industriously knuckled down to getting out of the trouble he was in.

'In his job as racing consultant, he passed on his hard-won knowledge and expertise to a new generation of drivers. Ask his friend and mentor, John Hogan. Ask Johnny Herbert. Ask Mika Häkkinen.

'In his job as a TV commentator, he was a friend and talented contributor to his colleagues. Ask Jonathan Martin, the BBC's head of sport. Ask Mark Wilkin, the producer of Grand Prix. Ask me.

'And in his new job as a journalist, he was a very welcome and lively addition to the press room. One who had shown the same dedicated determination to succeed as he had at the last three Grands Prix of 1976, where quite outstanding drives against the odds won him his World Championship.

'On Sunday, June the 13th, James cycled from his home in Wimbledon to the television centre at Shepherd's Bush, gave his customary, authoritative commentary on the Canadian Grand Prix, did his column and cycled home again, seemingly his usual self. Little more than 24 hours later, to stunned disbelief, he was no longer with us. Even now, it seems hardly conceivable that we're no longer going to enjoy his ebullient presence and it hasn't, somehow, all been a ghastly dream.

'They say the gods take those they love early. In which case, we can only console ourselves with the knowledge that 45 years of James's life contained at least as much as 90 of anybody else's.

'His loved ones, motor racing, his countless friends and all those who admired him from afar are infinitely the poorer for his passing. May he rest in peace.'

* * *

That night the final party that James had asked that his friends be invited to (and for which he provided £5,000 in his will) lasted into the small hours of the following morning. Everyone agreed that, as with the memorial service in celebration of his life, James would be absolutely livid he missed all the fun.

JAMES HUNT
CAREER RECORD

EARLY RACING

1967 SPECIAL SALOON CARS (MINI)

8 October: Brands Hatch	*Retired*
Two other unsuccessful races	

1968 FORMULA FORD (RUSSELL-ALEXIS, MERLYN MkII)

2 September: Mallory Park	*Second*
9 September: Lydden Hill	*First*
30 September: Brands Hatch	*Sixth*
7 October: Snetterton	*Seventh*
14 October: Mallory Park	*Accident*
26 October: Oulton Park	*Accident*
18 November: Brands Hatch	*Fourth*
25 November: Brands Hatch	*Third*
27 December: Brands Hatch	*Sixth*
29 December: Mallory Park	*Fifth*

1969 FORMULA FORD (MERLYN MkIIA)

24 February: Brands Hatch	*Third*
10 March: Mallory Park	*Fifth*
16 March: Brands Hatch	*Fifth*
24 March: Snetterton	*Accident*

8 April: Zandvoort (Holland)	*Third*
14 April: Aspern (Austria)	*Second*
21 April: Brands Hatch	*Seventh*
5 May: Lydden Hill	*First*
12 May: Mondello Park	*Fourth*
26 May: Snetterton	*Accident*

1969 FORMULA 3 (BRABHAM BT21, MARCH 693)

11 August: Mallory Park	*Seventh*
17 August: Brands Hatch	*Third*
24 August: Brands Hatch	*Fourth*
8 September: Brands Hatch	*First*
14 September: Brands Hatch	*Sixth*
14 September: Brands Hatch	*First*
18 September: Crystal Palace	*Eighth*
21 September: Brands Hatch	*Second*
28 September: Cadwell Park	*Fourth*
11 October: Mallory Park	*Fourth*
19 October: Brands Hatch	*Tenth*
26 October: Brands Hatch	*Third*

1970 FORMULA 3 (LOTUS 59)

26 April: Silverstone	*Fourth*
3 May: Magny-Cours (France)	*Fourth*
9 May: Monaco	*Accident*
17 May: Österreichring (Austria)	*Second*
25 May: Oulton Park	*Second*
31 May: Chimay (Belgium)	*Second*
6 June: Silverstone	*Sixth*
14 June: Hameenlinna (Finland)	*Third*
28 June: Rouen (France)	*First*
11 July: Croft	*Ninth*
17 July: Brands Hatch	*Third*
19 July: Cadwell Park	*Third*
9 August: Karlskoga (Sweden)	*Accident*
16 August: Knutstorp (Sweden)	*Second*
6 September: Zolder (Belgium)	*First*
13 September: Cadwell Park	*Third*

3 October: Crystal Palace	*Accident*
18 October: Brands Hatch	*Second*

1971 FORMULA 3 (MARCH 713M)

28 March: Montlhery (France)	*First*
3 April: Brands Hatch	*Accident*
12 April: Nürburgring (Germany)	*First*
17 April: Barcelona (Spain)	*Accident*
25 April: Pau (France)	*Accident*
2 May: Brands Hatch	*Third*
8 May: Silverstone	*Accident*
16 May: Zandvoort (Holland)	*Accident*
18 June: Crystal Palace	*First*
20 June: Brands Hatch	*Retired*
3 July: Paul Ricard (France)	*Third*
10 July: Croft	*Second*
1 August: Thruxton	*Second*
7 August: Crystal Palace	*Accident*
15 August: Brands Hatch	*First*
29 August: Thruxton	*Eighth*
10 September: Crystal Palace	*Sixth*
3 October: Snetterton	*Accident*
16 October: Thruxton	*Second*
24 October: Brands Hatch	*Disqualified*
31 October: Brands Hatch	*Fourth*

1971 FORMULA TWO (MARCH 712)

30 August: Brands Hatch	*Twelfth*

1972 FORMULA 3 (MARCH 723, MARCH 713M, DASTLE MK9)

5 March: Brands Hatch	*Fourth*
19 March: Brands Hatch	*Fifth*
26 March: Snetterton	*Eighth*
31 March: Oulton Park	*Accident*
3 April: Mallory Park	*Third*
16 April: Silverstone	*Seventh*
23 April: Silverstone	*Accident*
13 May: Monaco	*Accident*

| 21 May: Chimay (Belgium) | *Fifth* |
| 11 June: Silverstone | *Accident* |

1972 FORMULA 2 (MARCH 712M)

28 August: Brands Hatch	*Fifth*
3 September: Salzburgring (Austria)	*Retired*
16 September: Oulton Park	*Third*
24 September: Albi (France)	*Fifth*
1 October: Hockenheim (Germany)	*Eighth*
29 October: Interlagos (Brazil)	*Fifth*
12 November: Interlagos (Brazil)	*Fourth*

1973 FORMULA 2 (SURTEES TS15)

| 9 April: Hockenheim (Germany) | *Retired* |
| 23 April: Thruxton | *Tenth* |

The above are a selection of his most notable results. Some dates to 1973 are approximate.

GRAND PRIX RACING

1973 FORMULA 1 (MARCH 731, SURTEES TS9B)

18 March: Race of Champions (Brands Hatch)*	*Third*
3 June: Monaco GP	*Ninth*
1 July: French GP (Paul Ricard)	*Sixth*
14 July: British GP (Silverstone)	*Fourth*
29 July: Dutch GP (Zandvoort)	*Third*
19 August: Austrian GP (Österreichring)	*Retired*
9 September: Italian GP (Monza)	*Practice Accident*
23 September: Canadian GP (Mosport)	*Seventh*
7 October: United States (Watkins Glen)	*Second*

1973 WORLD CHAMPIONSHIP STANDINGS

1. Jackie Stewart	71
2. Emerson Fittipaldi	55
3. Ronnie Peterson	52
8. James Hunt	14

1974 FORMULA 1 (MARCH 731, HESKETH 308)

17 March: Race of Champions (Brands Hatch)*	*Retired*
7 April: International Trophy (Silverstone)*	*First*
13 January: Argentine GP (Buenos Aires)	*Accident*
27 January: Brazilian GP (Interlagos)	*Ninth*
30 March: South African GP (Kyalami)	*Retired*
28 April: Spanish GP (Jarama)	*Tenth*
12 May: Belgian GP (Nivelles)	*Retired*
26 May: Monaco GP	*Retired*
9 June: Swedish GP (Anderstorp)	*Third*
23 June: Dutch GP (Zandvoort)	*Accident*
7 July: French GP (Dijon-Prenois)	*Accident*
20 July: British GP (Brands Hatch)	*Accident*
4 August: German GP (Nürburgring)	*Retired*
18 August: Austrian GP (Österreichring)	*Third*
8 September: Italian GP (Monza)	*Retired*
22 September: Canadian GP (Mosport)	*Fourth*
6 October: United States GP (Watkins Glen)	*Third*

1974 WORLD CHAMPIONSHIP STANDINGS

1. Emerson Fittipaldi	55
2. Clay Regazzoni	52
3. Jody Scheckter	45
8. James Hunt	15

1975 FORMULA 1 (HESKETH 308)

12 April: International Trophy (Silverstone)*	*Retired*
24 August: Swiss GP (Dijon-Prenois)*	*Eighth*
12 January: Argentine GP (Buenos Aires)	*Second*
26 January: Brazilian GP (Interlagos)	*Sixth*
1 March: South African GP (Kyalami)	*Retired*
27 April: Spanish GP (Montjuic Park)	*Accident*
11 May: Monaco GP	*Accident*
25 May: Belgian GP (Zolder)	*Retired*
8 June: Swedish GP (Anderstorp)	*Retired*
22 June: Dutch GP (Zandvoort)	*First*
6 July: French GP (Paul Ricard)	*Second*
19 July: British GP (Silverstone)	*Fourth*
3 August: German GP (Nürburgring)	*Retired*

17 August: Austrian GP (Österreichring)	*Second*
7 September: Italian GP (Monza)	*Fifth*
5 October: United States GP (Watkins Glen)	*Fourth*

1975 WORLD CHAMPIONSHIP STANDINGS

1. Niki Lauda	64.5
2. Emerson Fittipaldi	45
3. Carlos Reutemann	37
4. James Hunt	33

1976 FORMULA 1 (MCLAREN MP23)

14 March: Race of Champions (Brands Hatch)*	*First*
11 April: International Trophy (Silverstone)*	*First*
25 January: Brazilian GP (Interlagos)	*Retired*
6 March: South African GP (Kyalami)	*Second*
28 March: US West GP (Long Beach)	*Accident*
2 May: Spanish GP (Jarama)	*First*
16 May: Belgian GP (Zolder)	*Retired*
30 May: Monaco GP	*Retired*
13 June: Swedish GP (Anderstorp)	*Fifth*
4 July: French GP (Paul Ricard)	*First*
18 July: British GP (Brands Hatch)	*Disqualified*
1 August: German GP (Nürburgring)	*First*
15 August: Austrian GP (Österreichring)	*Fourth*
29 August: Dutch GP (Zandvoort)	*First*
12 September: Italian GP (Monza)	*Retired*
3 October: Canadian GP (Mosport)	*First*
10 October: US East GP (Watkins Glen)	*First*
24 October: Japanese GP (Mount Fuji)	*Third*

1976 WORLD CHAMPIONSHIP STANDINGS

1. James Hunt	69
2. Niki Lauda	68
3. Jody Scheckter	49

1977 FORMULA 1 (MCLAREN MP23, MCLAREN MP26)

20 March: Race of Champions (Brands Hatch)*	*First*
9 January: Argentine GP (Buenos Aires)	*Retired*
23 January: Brazilian GP (Interlagos)	*Second*

5 March: South African GP (Kyalami)	*Fourth*
3 April: US West GP (Long Beach)	*Seventh*
8 May: Spanish GP (Jarama)	*Retired*
22 May: Monaco GP	*Retired*
5 June: Belgian GP (Zolder)	*Seventh*
19 June: Swedish GP (Anderstorp)	*Twelfth*
3 July: French GP (Dijon-Prenois)	*Third*
16 July: British GP (Silverstone)	*First*
31 July: German GP (Hockenheim)	*Retired*
14 August: Austrian GP (Österreichring)	*Retired*
28 August: Dutch GP (Zandvoort)	*Accident*
11 September: Italian GP (Monza)	*Retired*
2 October: US East GP (Watkins Glen)	*First*
9 October: Canadian GP (Mosport)	*Accident*
23 October: Japanese Gp (Mount Fuji)	*First*

1977 WORLD CHAMPIONSHIP STANDINGS

1. Niki Lauda	72
2. Jody Scheckter	55
3. Mario Andretti	47
5. James Hunt	40

1978 FORMULA 1 (McLAREN MP26)

19 March: International Trophy (Silverstone)*	*Accident*
15 January: Argentine GP (Buenos Aires)	*Fourth*
29 January: Brazilian GP (Jacarepagua)	*Accident*
4 March: South African GP (Kyalami)	*Retired*
2 April: US West GP (Long Beach)	*Accident*
7 May: Monaco GP	*Retired*
21 May: Belgian GP (Zolder)	*Accident*
4 June: Spanish GP (Jarama)	*Sixth*
17 June: Swedish GP (Anderstorp)	*Eighth*
2 July: French GP (Paul Ricard)	*Third*
16 July: British GP (Brands Hatch)	*Accident*
30 July: German GP (Hockenheim)	*Disqualified*
13 August: Austrian GP (Österreichring)	*Accident*
27 August: Dutch GP (Zandvoort)	*Tenth*
10 September: Italian GP (Monza)	*Retired*
1 October: US West GP (Watkins Glen)	*Seventh*
8 October: Canadian GP (Montreal)	*Accident*

1978 WORLD CHAMPIONSHIP STANDINGS

1. Mario Andretti	64
2. Ronnie Peterson	51
3. Carlos Reutemann	48
13. James Hunt	8

1978 F5000 (ELFIN MR8)

12 November: Rose City 10,000 (Winton)	*First*
(Australian F5000 series)	

1979 FORMULA 1 (WOLF WR7)

21 January: Argentine GP (Buenos Aires)	*Retired*
4 February: Brazilian GP (Interlagos)	*Retired*
3 March: South African GP (Kyalami)	*Eighth*
8 April: US West GP (Long Beach)	*Retired*
29 April: Spanish GP (Jarama)	*Retired*
13 May: Belgian GP (Zolder)	*Accident*
27 May: Monaco GP	*Retired*

1979 WORLD CHAMPIONSHIP STANDINGS

1. Jody Scheckter	51
2. Gilles Villeneuve	47
3. Alan Jones	40

* Non championship event

INDEX

PUBLISHERS

ACKNOWLEDGEMENTS

The publishers would like to thank the following for supplying photographs for this book:

Autosport p 2 (top right)
Belgrave Press Bureau p 3 (top left)
Diana Burnett pp 7 (top), 8
A B Cole p 5 (bottom)
Colorsport p 14 (top)
Dutch Motor Racing p 4 (top left)
Helen Dyson p 15 (top)
Express Newspapers p 15 (centre right)
J W F Gleave p 2 (bottom left and right)
Sue and Wallis Hunt pp 1, 15 (bottom)
International Press Agency pp 3 (top right), 7 (bottom right), 9
Phipps Photographic pp 2 (top left), 4 (bottom), 6 (top left and centre), 10 (bottom right), 11 (top and bottom right), 13 (top)
Press Association pp 10 (top), 14 (bottom left)
Professional Sport p 16
Rex Features front cover, pp 11 (bottom left), 15 (centre left)
Nigel Snowdon pp 4 (top right), 5 (top), 6 (top right), 7 (bottom left)
Sporting Pictures back cover
Sports Consultants International pp 12, 13 (centre)
Bryn Williams pp 10 (bottom left), 13 (bottom), 14 (bottom right)

We would also like to thank Ian Kingston, Sandra Cowell and Anne McCarthy for their work on this project.